STAGING GHANA

Ethnomusicology
Multimedia

Ethnomusicology Multimedia (EM) is a collaborative publishing program, developed with funding from the Andrew W. Mellon Foundation, to identify and publish first books in ethnomusicology, accompanied by supplemental audiovisual materials online at www .ethnomultimedia.org.

A collaboration of the presses at Indiana and Temple universities, EM is an innovative, entrepreneurial, and cooperative effort to expand publishing opportunities for emerging scholars in ethnomusicology and to increase audience reach by using common resources available to the presses through support from the Andrew W. Mellon Foundation. Each press acquires and develops EM books according to its own profile and editorial criteria.

EM's most innovative features are its web-based components, which include a password-protected Annotation Management System (AMS) where authors can upload peer-reviewed audio, video, and static image content for editing and annotation and key the selections to corresponding references in their texts; a public site for viewing the web content, www.ethnomultimedia.org, with links to publishers' websites for information about the accompanying books; and the Avalon Media System, which hosts video and audio content for the website. The AMS and website were designed and built by the Institute for Digital Arts and Humanities at Indiana University. Avalon was designed and built by the libraries at Indiana University and North-western University with support from the Institute of Museum and Library Services. The Indiana University Libraries hosts the website, and the Indiana University Archives of Traditional Music (ATM) pro-vides archiving and preservation services for the EM online content.

STAGING GHANA

Artistry and Nationalism
in State Dance Ensembles

Paul Schauert

INDIANA UNIVERSITY PRESS

Bloomington & Indianapolis

This book is a publication of

INDIANA UNIVERSITY PRESS
Office of Scholarly Publishing
Herman B Wells Library 350
1320 East 10th Street
Bloomington, Indiana 47405 USA

iupress.indiana.edu

Manufactured in the
United States of America

Library of Congress
Cataloging-in-Publication Data

Schauert, Paul W., author.
  Staging Ghana : artistry and nationalism in state dance ensembles / Paul
Schauert.
  pages cm. – (Ethnomusicology
multimedia)
  Includes bibliographical references
and index.
  ISBN 978-0-253-01732-1 (cl : alk. paper)
– ISBN 978-0-253-01742-0 (pb : alk.
paper) – ISBN 978-0-253-01749-9 (eb)
1. Folk dancing – Ghana. 2. Ghana Dance
Ensemble. 3. Dance companies – Ghana.
4. Nationalism and the arts – Ghana.
5. Ghana – Cultural policy. I. Title.
  GV1713.G4 S33 2015
  793.3'19667 – dc23

2015016736

1 2 3 4 5   20 19 18 17 16 15

For

PROFESSOR NKETIA

Contents

Preface

WITH A *LUNA,* "TALKING DRUM," UNDER MY ARM, I STOOD ON A
large auditorium stage, surveying a sea of primary school children and
their teachers who were awaiting a performance of "African culture." It
was the spring of 2002, and I was poised to lead the University of North
Texas (UNT) African Drumming and Dance Ensemble for the first time
without my mentor – Ewe master drummer Gideon Foli Alorwoyie. I
was anxious but not about the execution of the performance itself, for I
had participated in this group for nearly four years, meticulously learning supporting and lead drum parts to various dances, and was confident in my abilities to perform its small repertoire. Draped in kente
cloth, as I readied the students of the ensemble, memories of my first
trip to Ghana the previous summer flashed across my mind. Thunderous
echoes of *brekete* drums accompanied images of twirling spirit mediums
in *gorovodu* possession ceremonies. Filling my consciousness too were
drummers and dancers performing at all-night wake-keepings, children
playing clapping games, and fishermen singing over polyrhythmic bell
patterns as they pulled in their nets. I began to recall the many disparities
I had noticed between staged dance performances of the UNT ensemble
and their counterparts in Ghana.

These differences invited a host of questions about the representation of Africa and African dance on stage, in the West, and in an academic setting. Such questions brought me back to the performance at
hand, begging further inquiries. Who were we to represent this music
and dance? We were a group of mostly white, middle-class American
students, most of whom had never been to Africa. Like David Locke

had wondered decades earlier while performing Ghanaian music and dance, I contemplated whether my (racial) identity would "undermine my legitimacy as a teacher [musician]" (2004, 170). Nevertheless, we were in a position to "perform Africa" (Ebron 2002) for an audience of impressionable minds. Despite my momentary existential anxiety, the performance was well received. The audience was not critical but had only praise for our abilities. As I led subsequent performances, however, the questions regarding representation and my role in this ensemble only intensified and multiplied.

With these concerns in mind, I entered graduate school with the intention of studying the stage performance and representation of Ghanaian music and dance. Through discussions with Gideon, I learned that he had participated in a type of staging of traditions in his home country as a member of the Ghana Dance Ensemble (GDE) – a state-sponsored national music and dance company. The choreography he had learned in the GDE informed his staging of dances in the UNT ensemble. Subsequently, I began to recognize that many of the most prominent African drumming and dance ensembles in the United States and Europe are led by former members of this ensemble or individuals who have been significantly influenced by it. I knew that if I hoped to find answers to some of my questions about the representation of Ghanaian music/dance, the GDE would be a good place to look.

This ensemble became the driving force that propelled my career. I began to search for information about its history, including discussions of the ways it constructed its choreography and represented the cultural forms of Ghana. Additionally, I began to examine the literature on state/ folkloric music and dance as well as nationalism and the postcolonial African state; I also continued to explore phenomenology, which encouraged focus on the lived experience of individual participants and a privileging of their perspectives. Informed by this theoretical paradigm, I noticed that while the literature on state/folkloric performance was valuable in many respects, it was primarily concerned, as I first was, with issues regarding the representation of symbolic forms (such as authenticity and divisions between sacred and secular); consequently, it often inadequately interrogated the lives of the performers within such groups.

Following a phenomenological approach, when I returned to Ghana in 2004, I attempted to bracket, or suspend, my previous assumptions about the staging of African culture. My only explicit intention was to understand the lived experiences of participants in this nation's dance ensemble, focusing on issues that were salient to their daily existence. But first I had to address more fundamental and pragmatic problems: locating the ensemble and gaining access to its staff. After finishing my first language class in Twi at the University of Ghana (Legon), I walked down the main boulevard that bisected campus, eventually stopping at the School of Performing Arts. As I approached, looking to find the ensemble's location, I heard a voice call my name. "Who knows me here?" I wondered. It was Wisdom Agbedanu, a dancer whom Gideon had brought to UNT numerous times to participate in the annual African festival. After we exchanged a warm greeting, I asked where I could find the Ghana Dance Ensemble. As his eyes motioned to the large white edifice he was leaning against, he replied, "Here, this is where we rehearse." This was the first I had learned of his participation in this ensemble, and I was surprised and grateful that I had an entrée into my field research. Immediately, I began observing rehearsals and meeting the members of the ensemble, cultivating relationships that would allow for a close understanding of not only the representation of cultural forms but also the experiences of participants in these national ensembles.

On subsequent research trips – summer of 2005 and 2006, six months in 2007 (February to August), and a short follow-up in 2012 – my ethnographic work with this group intensified. Additionally, in 2005 I began to work with members of the National Dance Company (NDC), an offshoot of the GDE, located across town at Ghana's National Theatre in central Accra. Dividing my time between these two ensembles, I conducted formal interviews, received private drumming and dance instruction, observed rehearsals, took a copious amount of field notes, and accompanied the ensembles on various public performances, video recording as many as possible. With the aid of my research assistant, Apetsi Amenumey, an Ewe drummer and former member of the GDE, I additionally located and interviewed former members of the ensemble in and around Accra. Recognizing their close association with the GDE, I also observed numerous amateur culture groups in and outside of the city. While most of my time was spent in the capital, I often traveled to various locations within Ghana to witness and participate in a wide range of music and dance in community, or idiomatic, cultural contexts such as funerals, weddings, outdoorings (child-naming ceremonies), and the like. This participant-observation was supplemented by archival materials from the National Archives of Ghana as well as from a collection of files in the GDE office at Legon.

In many ways, however, my fieldwork for this project actually began as soon as I entered college and began studying with Gideon, participating in the staging of Ghanaian culture on a daily basis. Through this association, I met, performed with, and interviewed many of the former members of the GDE who had relocated to the United States and Europe. In graduate school I spent a considerable amount of time performing and talking with Kwesi Brown, who was a member of the Abibigromma drama troupe at Legon, which has close associations with the GDE. Over the last several years, I have performed and conversed extensively with Bernard Woma, former member of Ghana's national dance ensembles. Since my undergraduate days, I have witnessed and participated in countless stagings of Ghanaian/African culture on both sides of the Atlantic, which have all informed the present project. Like so many Ghanaian and foreign performers of this nation's music and dance, I continue to have reservations regarding the representation of African culture on stage; however, like many of these individuals, I am most concerned with the ways in which this music and dance contribute to a meaningful and satisfying existence.

Acknowledgments

MY JOURNEY INTO THE WORLD OF GHANAIAN MUSIC AND DANCE was initiated when I studied with the exceptional Ewe master drummer Gideon Foli Alorwoyie. I am forever grateful for his patience and continual willingness to share portions of his vast knowledge with me. As Gideon taught me to hear music with new sensibilities, I was also introduced to new ways of conceptualizing music in general through the discipline of ethnomusicology. I was fortunate to have Steven Friedson as my guide into this field of study. Through his study abroad program in Ghana, I became convinced, as I watched dancers twirl in spirit possession ceremonies in a tiny village in Eweland, that ethnomusicology would become my career path. He helped me tremendously in those formative years and has continued to encourage my intellectual development.

Particularly, he recommended that I study at Indiana University. At IU, I had the great pleasure of interacting with a diverse range of faculty who shaped my scholarly work and academic career. I am indebted to Ruth Stone for her continual guidance, sound advice, and generous support over the course of my career. Additionally, in my first semester of graduate course work, I had the pleasure of taking a class taught by Daniel Reed. With his interest in West African music and performance, he quickly became a mentor. I am thankful for the music we have made together, the projects we have worked on, and his unwavering support for my intellectual pursuits. I would also like to thank a number of other IU faculty who have had a positive impact on my work, including Marissa Moorman, Beverly Stoeltje, and Samuel Obeng, who provided constructive feedback on this project.

While at IU, my fieldwork was supported by several generous Foreign Language Area Studies grants through its African Studies Program and the U.S. Department of Education, as well as by a Project on African Expressive Traditions grant from the university. Thanks also go to my Twi professor, Seth Ofori, at IU and to other language teachers at the University of Ghana – Paul Agbedor, Kofi Agyekum, and Kofi Saah. I would also like to thank my home department of folklore and ethnomusicology for several graduate assistantships that kept me afloat over the course of my graduate career while enhancing my professional skills.

I would like to give a special acknowledgment to several other non-IU scholars who have contributed greatly to my intellectual development. After meeting her in the course of fieldwork in Ghana, I became fast friends with Jill Flanders-Crosby. Our conversations regarding dance, authenticity, Ghana, and a range of other topics have contributed immensely to the shape of this ethnography. I particularly appreciate her for taking the time to read early drafts of this book and for providing insightful feedback along with enthusiastic encouragement. I also thank her colleague Brian Jeffery for inviting me to participate in his choreographic "journey" and allowing me to use his time with the GDE as a case study. Thanks also go to Kelly Askew, who provided insightful feedback on portions of this work presented at the Society of Ethnomusicology annual meeting in 2010. And, for our conversations on contemporary dance, I am grateful to K. Natasha Foreman.

Across the Atlantic, there are a number of individuals in Ghana to whom I am forever indebted. Most notably, Professor Kwabena Nketia provided consistent mentoring and encouragement for this project. His insights into the GDE, which he founded, were vital to this ethnography. I am grateful for his generosity, openness, and willingness to share his intellectual brilliance. I hope that this ethnography does justice to his hard work over the years with the dance ensemble. I would also like to give praises to my research assistant, Apetsi Amenumey. He provided immeasurable insight into the dance ensembles, led me to past members, helped with interviews, and took care of many everyday tasks while I lived in Accra. This research truly could not have happened without his help. I will forever be trying to repay him for his efforts. I am grateful for our friendship and for all the laughter it has provided throughout these many years. This work equally would not have been possible had it not been for the generosity of Ben Ayettey, director of the GDE at Legon. I am eternally grateful to him for allowing me to accompany the ensemble on public performances and for giving me access to daily rehearsals. He also provided deep insight into the history of the group and the choreographic process. I would also like to especially point out several staff of the GDE at Legon who made this work both possible and enjoyable: (Uncle) Willie Diku, Jennies Darko, Zachariah "Baba" Abdellah, Wisdom Agbedanu, and Mercy Ayettey. A special thanks goes to David Amoo and Grace Djabatey at the National Theatre. Thanks also go to former directors of the ensembles: Francis Nii-Yartey, E. A. Duodu, and Oh! Nii Kwei Sowah. Overwhelming gratitude is due to the drummers and dancers in the GDE and the NDC (listed in the interviews section of the bibliography) who took time to sit with me and share their experiences. I am proud to call them collaborators and friends. And a special acknowledgment goes to David "Baby" Quaye for his assistance with copyright permissions and valuable insight into the GDE's history.

Thanks are due to the staff at the National Archives of Ghana, in particular to Bright and Killian. I would similarly like to acknowledge the support of the staff of the International Centre of African Music and Dance at the University of Ghana. I thank Dr. John Collins for his encouragement and guidance while in Ghana. And to Gavin Webb, who seems to know everyone in Ghana, I value your tremendous insight into Accra and the country in general, including, of course, its music. Likewise, there are numerous other teachers and friends who made my field research rich and unforgettable: S. K. Kakraba, Dela Botri, Francis, Mr. Johnson, Seth Gati, and Gasco Ablordey.

Throughout my studies at IU, I was fortunate to develop close friendships with a number of fellow students who made my graduate school experience memorable and enjoyable. I would particularly like to thank Anthony Guest-Scott, Colleen Haas, and Aditi Deo for their comments on early drafts of this work and for their close friendships over the years. Nate Plageman, a friend and classmate, deserves special thanks for introducing me to Apetsi and for his feedback on late drafts of this manuscript. Other colleagues who have particularly influenced my work and provided support throughout my time at IU include Cullen Strawn, Ed

Wolf, Austin Okigbo, Mark Miyake, Ramon Bannister, Clara Henderson, Kwesi Brown, Sheasby Matiure, Fred Pratt, Bernard Woma, and Angela Scharfenberger. Although I did not know him well as a graduate student, another IU alumni, Alex Perullo, became a friend and ally in this project in 2012; I am particularly grateful for his knowledge and help with issues concerning copyright in Africa and Ghana.

Several people were vital to the completion of this project at IU Press. I would like to express my gratitude to Dee Mortensen, Sarah Jacobi, Mollie Ables, Julie Bush, and Nancy Lightfoot for their assistance in bringing this book to print and assisting with online media. I give special thanks to my parents for their support. Language fails to capture the enormity of their generosity and love. Last, and certainly not least, it is with a full heart and infinite gratitude that I acknowledge my partner, Jennifer Hart. Her love and support throughout the past several years have contributed immeasurably to this work as well as to the quality of my life in general. Her insights into the history and people of Ghana and Africa have undoubtedly strengthened this book. I could never write words worthy of the praise she deserves.

Ethnomusicology Multimedia
Series Preface

GUIDE TO ONLINE MEDIA EXAMPLES

Each of the audio, video, or still image media examples listed below is associated with specific passages in this book, and each example has been assigned a unique Persistent Uniform Resource Locator, or PURL. The PURL identifies a specific audio, video, or still image media example on the Ethnomusicology Multimedia website, www.ethnomultimedia. org. Within the text of the book, a PURL number in parentheses functions like a citation and immediately follows the text to which it refers, e.g. (PURL 3.1). The numbers following the word PURL relate to the chapter in which the media example is found, and the number of PURLS contained in that chapter. For example, PURL 3.1 refers to the first media example found in chapter 3; PURL 3.2 refers to the second media example found in chapter 3, and so on.

To access all media associated with this book, readers must first create a free account by going to the Ethnomusicology Multimedia Project website www.ethnomultimedia.org and clicking the Sign In link. Readers will be required to read and electronically sign an End Users License Agreement (EULA) the first time they access a media example on the website. After logging in to the site there are two ways to access and play back audio, video, or still image media examples. In the Search field enter the name of the author to be taken to a webpage with information about the book and the author as well as a playlist of all media examples associated with the book. To access a specific media example, in the Search field enter the six digit PURL identifier of the example (the six digits located at the end of the full PURL address below). The reader will be taken to the web page containing that media example as well as a playlist of all the other media examples related to the book. Readers of the electronic edition of this book will simply click on the PURL address for each media example; once they have logged in to www.ethnomulti-media.org, this live link will take them directly to the media example on the Ethnomusicology Multimedia website.

LIST OF PURLS

CHAPTER 1

PURL 1.1 Performance: *The Map* at the National Theatre of Ghana, 2007
http://purl.dlib.indiana.edu/iudl/em/Schauert/910307
PURL 1.2 Performance: *Akan Ceremonial Dance Suite*
http://purl.dlib.indiana.edu/iudl/em/Schauert/910308
PURL 1.3 Performance: Togo *atsia*
http://purl.dlib.indiana.edu/iudl/em/Schauert/910309
PURL 1.4 Performances: State dinners with Chinese and Beninese delegations
http://purl.dlib.indiana.edu/iudl/em/Schauert/910310

CHAPTER 2

PURL 2.1 Performance: *Adowa*
http://purl.dlib.indiana.edu/iudl/em/Schauert/910311
PURL 2.2 Performance: *Agbadza*
http://purl.dlib.indiana.edu/iudl/em/Schauert/910312
PURL 2.3 Performance: *Bamaaya*
http://purl.dlib.indiana.edu/iudl/em/Schauert/910313
PURL 2.4 Program with Opoku's handwritten notes
http://purl.dlib.indiana.edu/iudl/em/Schauert/910314
PURL 2.5 Performance: *Kete*
http://purl.dlib.indiana.edu/iudl/em/Schauert/910315

PURL 2.6 Performance: *Beating the Retreat,* Independence Square, 2007
http://purl.dlib.indiana.edu/iudl/em/Schauert/910316
PURL 2.7 Performance: *Damba/takai*
http://purl.dlib.indiana.edu/iudl/em/Schauert/910317
PURL 2.8 Performance: *Agbekor*
http://purl.dlib.indiana.edu/iudl/em/Schauert/910318
PURL 2.9 Performance: *Fontomfrom*
http://purl.dlib.indiana.edu/iudl/em/Schauert/910319
PURL 2.10 Performance: *Bewaa*
http://purl.dlib.indiana.edu/iudl/em/Schauert/910320
PURL 2.11 Performance: *Dagomba Dance Suite*
http://purl.dlib.indiana.edu/iudl/em/Schauert/910321
PURL 2.12 Program with choreographers' names
http://purl.dlib.indiana.edu/iudl/em/Schauert/910322
PURL 2.13 Performance: Drummers carrying drums at funeral
http://purl.dlib.indiana.edu/iudl/em/Schauert/910323

CHAPTER 3

PURL 3.1 Performance: *Drill,* dance hall at Legon, 2007
http://purl.dlib.indiana.edu/iudl/em/Schauert/910324

CHAPTER 4

PURL 4.1 Performance: At the GBC studios in 2012 for the Mills
memorial performing *atenteben, adenkum, kete, and fontomfrom*
http://purl.dlib.indiana.edu/iudl/em/Schauert/910325
PURL 4.2 Performance: *Beating the Retreat,* part 2
http://purl.dlib.indiana.edu/iudl/em/Schauert/910326

CHAPTER 5

PURL 5.1 Performance: *Lamentation for Freedom Fighters,* GDE/NDC,
dance hall at Legon, 2007
http://purl.dlib.indiana.edu/iudl/em/Schauert/910327

CHAPTER 6

PURL 6.1 Performance: Introductory contemporary African dance choreography, 2007
http://purl.dlib.indiana.edu/iudl/em/Schauert/910328
PURL 6.2 Performance: *Journey* excerpt, 2007
http://purl.dlib.indiana.edu/iudl/em/Schauert/910329
PURL 6.3 Performance: *Journey,* full performance, 2007
http://purl.dlib.indiana.edu/iudl/em/Schauert/910330

STAGING GHANA

[The nation] is in principle two things at once:
a collection of individuals and a collective individual.

LOUIS DUMONT, 1970

Introduction

Managing Nationalism, Crossing Crocodiles,
and Staging Ethnography

ON JUNE 18, 1989, TWENTY MEMBERS OF THE GHANA DANCE
Ensemble (GDE), the country's state-sponsored national company, left
Accra for a tour of Canada.[1] Invited by the National Council of Ghana-
ian-Canadians and the Ghanaian-Canadian Association of Calgary, the
ensemble participated in a celebration of Canada Day. The performance
aimed at strengthening bonds between Ghanaians in the diaspora as it
sought to expose foreign audiences to a variety of African dance traditions. To this end, led by artistic director Francis Nii-Yartey, the ensemble performed a set of dances that were emblematic of various ethnic
groups in Ghana; these included a suite of Akan royal dances followed
by the Ewe *atsia,* Akan *sikyi,* Ga *kpanlogo,* and two original trans-ethnic
choreographies – one by the ensemble's first artistic director, Mawere
Opoku, and the other by Nii-Yartey himself.[2] Given this varied repertoire of dances, the ensemble embodied the Ghanaian state's rhetoric
of "unity in diversity." Its performance also recalled the notions of African Personality and Pan-Africanism put forth by Ghana's first president, Kwame Nkrumah, for which the troupe was originally designed
to propagate.

During this performance, as Canadians commemorated their nationhood, Ghanaians similarly proclaimed their patriotism and, implicitly, their allegiance to their country. Yet, following the "remarkable" and
"high-spirited"[3] display of national culture, six young members of the
GDE illicitly "ran away" and did not return to Ghana. Though it was
not the first time ensemble members had done this, it was a significant
number for one trip, and it changed the policies of the GDE.[4] Since its

founding in the early 1960s, the ensemble has embarked on numerous international tours. Occasionally performers have used this opportunity to "seek for greener pastures."[5] Consequently, this troupe has developed a reputation in Ghana as an escape route or "long-term immigration strategy."[6] One former GDE member explained, "That is all they do over there. They join the ensemble just to go abroad and stay to make money" (Asante 2005). While many join the group primarily to pursue and develop interests in music and dance, never attempting to run away, ironically some Ghanaian dancers and drummers have used this national/state ensemble to desert their nation-state. Many artists have emigrated via the ensemble, both legally and illegally, using its high visibility and status to forge international careers.

Stories that glorify these activities of former members become narratives of achievement; these accounts solidify the reputation of the ensemble as a viable path to individual enrichment, which includes the accumulation of wealth and status as well as artistic and personal development. Ensemble members regularly share heroic tales of past GDE members who have built reputable careers, predominantly in the United States and Europe (often Britain). Such narratives are not a recent product of neoliberalism's elevation of the individual or of particular periods of economic decline in Ghana but have been a consistent part of the ensemble since its inception. Buoyed by the visibility and prestige associated with Ghana's national ensemble, founding members have parlayed this connection into cosmopolitan careers. During fieldwork, I would often hear the legends of founding members such as Abraham Adzenyah (Wesleyan University), Alfred Ladzekpo (Columbia; CalArts), C. K. Ladzekpo (University of California, Berkeley), Kobla Ladzekpo (UCLA; Zadonu African Dance Company), Freeman Donkor (Wesleyan University), Kakraba Lobi,[7] and Mustapha Tettey Addy. Tales of my teacher Gideon Alorwoyie, who joined the GDE for a brief period in the late 1960s, highlighted his status as a professor in the United States, which he achieved many decades later.[8] George Dzikunu's name was often mentioned along with the London-based Adzido Ensemble, which he founded and directed. More recently, the life histories of renowned performers based in America – Bernard Woma, Habib Chester Iddrisu, Emmanuel Eku, Adjei Abankwah, and Francis Kofi – have become inspirational tales for young GDE members. These biographical narratives of travel, fame, and accumulation are held up as models for individual success. While certainly such tales, and the actions they portray, speak to the economic situation in Ghana, the perception of the West as a "land of opportunity," and general global inequities, these narratives point to broader concerns that frame this ethnography.

Such practices raise important questions about participants' engagement with nationalism, the nation, and the state. How heavily are individuals invested in the national project of which they are, at least ostensibly, a part? What other ways might ensemble members strategically *use* these national institutions to pursue personal ends, both abroad and domestically? How do participants balance or reconcile their individual objectives with those of the nation and the state? Furthermore, does participation in these national groups actually increase patriotism and allegiance to the nation, as they were designed to do? Or does the experience in an ensemble perhaps diminish such feelings? Or might theatre, as Jay Straker (2009) suggests in his work with the national dance company in Guinea, represent a "double-life" in which an ensemble's disciplinary practices simultaneously produce loyalty and resentment? Finally, have the motivations and practices of ensemble members changed over time?

Addressing such questions, this book explores how artists in Ghana's state dance ensembles "manage" nationalism. As in Nigeria (Klein 2007), "managing" is a common expression in Ghana, and the term has particular salience for members of its national troupes. When conducting field research, I typically began my workday by walking into the dance hall at the University of Ghana. Exchanging greetings with GDE members, I often asked in pidgin, "How be?" A common response was, "Managing, oh," frequently followed by, "I dey run things proper." As I heard these phrases repeatedly, often juxtaposed, I began to understand "managing" not only as a way to denote the capacity to get by but also as an expression of personal agency; participants often employ it to articulate a sense of control over the situation at hand – the ability to "run things" by navigating economic, political, and social challenges, turning the social order to their advantage. Similar to Ghanaian market traders,[9] hiplife artists,[10] and bar women,[11] members of the GDE characterize such activities as "hustling," working hard at a chosen profession, harnessing available resources to pursue individual conceptions of success. Many in the ensembles articulated success as "self-improvement," a term that referred to the development of their artistic talents and the accumulation of wealth and social status. Inspired by the narratives of achievement of past ensemble members, artists I worked with saw Ghana's state troupes as viable domains in which to "improve" themselves as they hustled and managed to pursue personal enrichment.

Fundamentally, such managing, especially within the context of nationalism, involves a particular negotiation of the dialectic between individuality and collectivity. As drummers and dancers engage in the process of staging culture and their nation, they are pushed into a unified entity; yet, as this study illustrates, they do not lose sight of their individuality and individual ambitions and aspirations. For, while the nation is a collective individual, it is nevertheless made up of a collection of individuals, each with their own interests and identities (see Dumont 1970). Ghanaians, and particularly the Akan, have been keenly aware of this fundamental component of nationalism, as evidenced by the following adinkra symbol and proverb: *Funtumfunafu, denkyemmfunafu, won afuru bomu nso wodidi a na worefom efiri se aduane ne de ye di no mene twitwi mu* (Two-headed crocodiles fight over food that goes to a common stomach, because each relishes the food in its throat) (see fig. 1). Recalling a myriad of commonplace African metaphors that link politics to the belly and the act of eating (or chopping) (see Bayart [1989] 2009), this proverb/symbol marks an idiomatic "African" expression and understanding of the basic dialectic between collective and individual objectives, which is inherent to nationalism as individuals balance self-interests with those of the state and nation. Such activity requires adaptability, which is also captured within this symbol. Because crocodiles live in water but breathe air, they symbolize adaptability for Akans and Ghanaians.[12] Hence, the crossing crocodiles articulate the fundamental social processes of managing nationalism by denoting the abilities of individuals to adjust to challenging economic, political, and social circumstances to pursue both personal and collective interests. Within this study, this symbol provides a metaphorical framework for interrogating the ways in which artists stage their nation and state while seeking self-improvement.

0.1. Akan adinkra symbol, *Funtumfunafu, denkyemmfunafu.*

With this fundamental dynamic between collective and individual agendas as a framework for this study, I investigate how artists manage the institutions, rhetorics, practices, and logics of nationalism, transforming them to suit their needs. Exploring the politics of managing in Ghana's national dance troupes, this discussion demonstrates that participants in such organizations are more than mere instruments of the state; they are also virtuosic managers of the surrounding political machinery, using it to their benefit. Analyzing such practices, this study augments anthropologist Henrik Vigh's theory of social navigation, which attends to "the way in which agents seek to draw and actualise their life trajectories in order to increase their social possibilities and life chances in a shifting and volatile social environment" (2006, 11). Like his study of urban youth in Guinea-Bissau, this ethnography is concerned with the "construction and realization of social being" and the processes of "social becoming" (11). Yet, while Vigh's work interrogates how young people navigated a terrain of war, this study examines how people of various ages manage national/state domains through the performing arts.

As I conducted research, it became increasingly clear that while many members of these troupes participated in the state project of propagating nationalism and claimed to believe in its ideologies, the artists were often more concerned with quotidian matters, devising strategies to exploit the resources at their disposal. Recognizing the value of these everyday lived experiences, this book, while it interrogates the performance of the nation (in Africa),[13] moves beyond analyses of nation building to explore how individuals employ state/national resources to accomplish objectives outside the purview of the nation and the state. And, while this study investigates the process of staging the nation, including the folklorization of traditions, it transcends such well-worn scholarly terrain, which often concentrates on issues of authenticity and representation; instead, this study focuses more keenly on how such discourses are deployed for personal ends.

Examining such practices, this ethnography both recalls and augments the scholarly discussion on "instrumental nationalism."[14] This discourse has shown how political elites "invented,"[15] institutionalized, and mobilized the cultural resources of the masses to legitimize their power while propagating an array of other state objectives, the primary one being to build a sovereign and unified nation. However, this paradigmatic lens has largely fallen out of favor because it advances a "top-down," or "statist," approach to nationalism, which marginalizes "ground-up" processes – those enacted by the nation (the masses, nonelites).[16] While certainly both directional streams of power are at work, discourse in the last few decades has turned toward the latter in an attempt to highlight the agency of the citizenry. Building on Africanist scholarship that has explored the instrumentalization of disorder,[17] religion,[18] and wage labor,[19] I employ the phrase "managing nationalism" to avoid both the intellectual baggage associated with "instrumental nationalism" and the overly reductive and functionalist mode of analysis that an instrumentalist paradigm can invite.[20] Informed by phenomenology, the instrumental qualities of "managing" are formulated as lived experience. Such an approach highlights the ways in which participants engage in meaningful acts, strategically harnessing the resources at hand not only to accomplish objectives but also to construct satisfying lives. My analysis thus attends to the construction of meaning itself, accounting for a multitude of emergent possibilities, actions, and outcomes that constitute the everyday experiences of participants. This formulation of instrumentality is informed by participants' own definitions of "self-improvement," which include not only their aspirations for the accumulation of wealth and status but also for increased feelings of well-being.

In this way, managing nationalism – conceived as social, cultural, and political processes of instrumentality – is an iteration of the "politics of the belly" (Bayart [1989] 2009), whereby Africans use their political, often governmental, positions to accumulate wealth and status. This accumulation, particularly in West Africa, is often expressed in terms of eating, or "chopping," and thus the belly is a potent metaphor for uses and abuses of (political) power; for instance, in Ghana, those who engage in such practices are said to be "eating from their desks" as they attempt to become "big men."[21] While Bayart acknowledges that "all actors – rich and poor" (235) engage in the politics of the belly, like the discourse of instrumental nationalism, much of his work and that which it inspired has focused on the practices of political elites. By concentrating on musicians and dancers, who often do not have elite status, this ethnography offers further development of Bayart's thesis; placing it within the framework of the performing arts, I explore how the politics of the belly operates within such domains. While I agree with Bayart that the strategies adopted by the masses are similar to those employed by elites (237), the goals, perceptions, and consequences of such actions vary widely. Whereas elites often use their government positions for opulent accumulation and securing their own political power, non-elite artists are more often concerned with survival and creative development. Furthermore, while the politics of the belly practiced by elites is often considered a form of corruption involving large-scale, explicitly illicit activities such as embezzlement of public funds, bribery, fraud, and voter intimidation,[22] that which is practiced by non-elites, particularly by those in the GDE, does not typically entail the transgression of state (or international) criminal law. Nevertheless, the consequences for this chopping by non-elites can be serious.

As it investigates these instrumental aspects of national culture, this study highlights how nationalism becomes a resource for the construction and performance of the individual self. Similar to anthropologist

Saba Mahmood, who has written on the construction of the self in Egypt through practices of religious piety, I show how nationalism acts "as a means of being and becoming a certain type of person" (2005, 215). To accomplish this personal transformation, performers employ various "tactics," as described by Michel de Certeau, that "draw unexpected results from [their] situation" (1984, 30). These tactics are an art – an art of being-in-between. Through their clever "artistry," members of Ghana's dance ensembles maneuver between self-interests and state interests; they carefully calculate and calibrate their activities to maintain their positions as state employees and nationals while simultaneously furthering their individual creative development, expressing democratic dissent, and enacting global citizenship. Using this tactical artistry, nationalism becomes what Michel Foucault calls a "technology of the self," which, as he states, "permits individuals to effect . . . operations on their own bodies and souls, thoughts, conduct, and way of being, so as to transform themselves in order to attain a certain state of happiness" (1988, 18). "By placing Foucault's ideas in dialogue with de Certeau's," as ethnomusicologist Jeff Packman has noted, "tactics emerge as quotidian moments when a subject does not deny self, and acts instead to take care of himself or herself" (2011, 416). Within a nationalist framework, these moments of self-awareness and self-care become somewhat subversive; that is, although individuals are ostensibly pressed into a nationalist unitary identity while simultaneously employed to act on behalf of the nation and state, participants do not jettison their *individual* goals and quest for self-fulfillment. It will become evident that by engaging in tactical maneuvers, members of the GDE and NDC artfully manipulate and "dance in between" the political structures and strictures of nationalism, the state, and capitalism in unexpected ways in their pursuit of self-improvement.

Operationalizing the concept of the self, this ethnography moves beyond mere identity politics; while also taking these into account, I seek to avoid some of the pitfalls of identity as a theoretical framework. Like Fredrick Cooper (2005), I often find identity as an analytical category "too ambiguous" to be useful; identity can also be overly limiting as an analytical lens, often not taking into account the total being of a person as it encourages focus on labels placed on individuals by external and internal means. While there is an extensive scholarly discourse on the self, I employ it here to refer to the entirety of a person's being, including his or her subjective experiences, identities, ideas, ambitions, ontologies, abilities, and values. As such, employing the analytic category of the self allows my inquiries to account for the multiple ways in which musicians and dancers pursue "self-improvement," for the local understandings of this concept transcend mere identity politics to include social navigations, which augment artists' existential possibilities and competencies while transforming their ways of being-in-the-world.

With this analytical focus, this ethnography demonstrates that nationalism is a somewhat unique tool for constructing the self, because it highlights specific social dynamics and encourages certain forms of reflexivity. While the self is always rendered in relation to others of all types, nationalism particularly invites a contemplation of the self in relation to the complex of ethnicity, the state, and other nations. When confronted with nationalism, individuals ask: What does it mean to be part of a nation, to be a citizen with a particular government? How is my nation and national identity similar to, and different from, other nations and nationals?

Examining such reflective acts invites a consideration of the broader social dynamics and contexts in which the politics of managing nationalism take place. Sociologists and anthropologists have offered a myriad of models and metaphors in their attempts to give materiality to the often intangible concepts of society, culture, and power. For instance, Max Weber's "iron cage,"[23] Pierre Bourdieu's "field,"[24] and more recently Vigh's "terrain" have all been used to lend substance to social dynamics. Many scholars have found Lila Abu-Lughod's (1990) metaphor of "webs" of power to be constructive in analyzing the politics of culture and social interaction. However, this comparison often emphasizes power's binding effects; thus, I employ the term "matrix." Recalling its Greek origins as pertaining to a biological enclosure or womb, a political matrix thus denotes the organic, malleable, and evolving attributes of power as it re/produces reality. As a biological term, this concept emphasizes that power is often negotiated through the body, which is crucial to a discussion of dance and music performance. Conceived in this way, a matrix also highlights that individuals are born through, and of, existing power relations and that it is only within such structures of power that the possibilities for agency are rendered. That is, as Saba Mahmood notes in summarizing Foucault, "the subject . . . does not precede power relations" (2005, 17). Overall, a political matrix defines a known realm of possibilities and limits, which one can replicate or deviate from in each performative iteration.[25] Augmenting the symbolism of the Akan, as multitudes of crocodiles cross – or, as individuals interact – they form an interlocking, yet flexible, biopolitical latticework. Throughout this text, I show how artists manage this political and social matrix (of crocodiles), consequently transforming it and themselves through a plethora of mutually constitutive cultural processes.

To understand the particular matrix in which members of Ghana's national dance ensembles operate, I have parsed it into the following dynamics: (1) negotiations of individual identities, such as those associated with family, gender, class, profession, ethnicity, nation, and international domains; (2) the internal disciplinary apparatus of the ensembles, which often includes institutional regulations of the university; (3) the relationship between the GDE, its splinter group (the National Dance Company), and other similar cultural ensembles; (4) the dialectic between the international community, the nation, and the individual; (5) the ensembles' relationship to local power brokers such as chiefs and elders; and (6) the dynamic between the national ensembles, participants, and the postcolonial state, including the impulse for creative self-expression within an overwhelmingly collectivizing official ideology. While compartmentalized in this way, it must be noted that such spheres overlap and interact. Like Sherry Ortner (1995) and Lisa Gilman (2009), I recognize that each individual is uniquely situated within this political configuration. That is, each GDE performer operates within a personal matrix, which consists of an individual's "personality, needs, abilities, desires, and multiple social relationships, all of which can inform each decision that [a person] makes" (Gilman 2009, 170). This personal matrix is mapped onto, and adapted to, the larger political order.

Managing the matrix of Ghana's state dance ensembles involves being and becoming simultaneously more local, national, and cosmopolitan. As paradoxical as this may first appear, scholars have come to understand local/global and national/cosmopolitan dynamics not as oppositional but rather as mutually constitutive.[26] Although there are numerous works that have explored such relationships,[27] studies of African popular music (Askew 2002; Turino 2000; White 2002) have been particularly productive in this regard and have deeply informed my work. Following ethnomusicologist Thomas Turino's study of Zimbabwean popular music, I recognize nationalism as an inherently cosmopolitan phenomenon – widely diffuse around the world but somewhat distinct in each locale (2000, 7). That is, on the one hand, nations must resemble other nations by incorporating widely recognizable institutions (schools, courts, laws, governments, and so on) and symbols (flags, anthems, and the like) to be recognized as such; simultaneously, nations must remain distinct from other nations to ensure they do not disappear in the vast sea of the international community. In short, managing nationalism necessarily includes a negotiation of cosmopolitanism and localism.

Both nationalism and cosmopolitanism require a "strategic integration" (Askew 2003) of local and foreign cultural resources whereby the "global" is "domesticated" (Diouf 2000) – manipulated and "deeply embodied" (Turino 2000). Thus, while exploring the managing of nationalism, I illustrate how cosmopolitanism is "discrepant" (Clifford 1992), "vernacular" (Bhabha 1996), and "rooted" (White 2002) as culture that is widely diffuse around the world becomes imbued with provincial and personal sensibilities, rendering it meaningful for Ghanaians. Cosmopolitan, as a qualifier, then becomes a term to denote both individuals who engage in this local/national/global complex, whether elite or non-elite, and cultural forms and processes that are deeply informed by such a tripartite relationship. Throughout, I employ this conceptualization to explore cosmopolitan identities, aesthetics, power, and creativity. For instance, cosmopolitan modes of power are markers of authority and status that are widely recognized around the world – academic credentials, copyright, monetary wealth, government officialdom, and military discipline – but are integrated into local cultural practices. Similarly, cosmopolitan aesthetics are those that are informed by foreign (mostly Western) practices but are rendered with idiomatic sensibilities in Ghana. And cosmopolitan creativity denotes processes of artistic construction that are a hybrid of local and foreign methodologies, which often include international collaborations.

Through such processes, this study shows how the local, national, and cosmopolitan are subjectively embodied and instrumentalized in the pursuit of individual self-making and self-improvement. For individuals, this entails a managing of various ways of being and becoming local, national, and cosmopolitan. Such activity, as James Ferguson (1999) has noted in his work on the Zambian Copperbelt, requires performative "competencies" in numerous "cultural styles," which are modes of practical social action (98, 221) that differentiate one from another. These various styles, or performative capacities, are "cultivated" through a long and arduous process, and the fluidity with which individuals may slip between them belies the hard work and training involved in the acquisition of such competencies. As this study will illustrate, participation in Ghana's state dance ensembles is one way in which individuals acquire, perform, and manage a set of local, national, and cosmopolitan competencies and styles, enacting them in certain contexts at particular moments as they attempt to further their ambitions for personal enrichment.

In sum, this ethnography explores how members of Ghana's state dance ensembles use tactical artistry to manage nationalism. Inspired by narratives of achievement, artists harness the rhetoric, institutions, logics, and practices of nationalism to pursue self-improvement while balancing such personal interests with more collective goals of the nation and the state. Along the way, participants acquire a plethora of competencies, artistic and otherwise, allowing them to navigate a local/national/cosmopolitan matrix by strategically employing various cultural styles. As individuals reflect on such experiences, nationalism is rendered an implement for the construction of the self as artists are transformed by their experiences within these groups.

CULTURAL NATIONALISM AND FOLKLORIC DANCE

As African states gained their independence, most by the early 1960s, these burgeoning nations employed culture to construct and project a new way of being-in-the-world. Several African countries extensively employed music and dance to propagate political ideology by establishing national dance ensembles. Although many such troupes were formed throughout the continent at various moments,[28] two cases in particular informed Nkrumah's politico-cultural thought and acted in some degree as models for the GDE. In Senegal, Léopold Sédar Senghor created the National Ballet du Senegal to lend performative power to his philosophy of Négritude, which used a variety of artistic forms – from poetry to sculpture – to assert an African presence in the world. Since its founding in 1960, this company has worked to build Senegalese solidarity while strengthening diasporic connections in both political and social domains (see Castaldi 2006). That same year, Guinean president Sékou Touré similarly adopted the previously established and world-renowned Les Ballets Africains as the national dance company in Guinea, using it to promote a Marxist-socialist political revolution after independence (see J. Cohen 2011; Straker 2009).

In Ghana, Kwame Nkrumah, like his contemporaries and political cohorts, launched a host of cultural programs that set out to strengthen the bonds between nationals and Africans in general (see Botwe-Asamoah 2005). The Ghana Dance Ensemble, for instance, initiated by Nkrumah in 1962, has been an overtly nationalist project; housed at the University of Ghana, the ensemble became the "nucleus" of his National Theatre Movement, which was an artistic extension of his political philosophies (ibid.; July 1987). Namely, Nkrumah employed the GDE to propagate his interpretations of African Personality and Pan-Africanism, which attempted to unify diverse African peoples and raise their "dignity" by promoting African-centered approaches for achieving continental and diasporic solidarity as well as economic prosperity for Africans across the globe (Nkrumah 1963, 174–75). While many African national dance ensembles have been disbanded over the past several decades, the GDE, along with its splinter group, the National Dance Company (of Ghana), founded in 1992, have remained. Given this longevity, the GDE, like the state dance companies of Senegal and Guinea, has become one of the seminal models for other similar institutions in Africa and elsewhere.

Focusing on Ghana's state dance ensembles, this ethnography nuances the interdisciplinary discourse on cultural nationalism – "the use of art and other cultural practices to maintain national sentiment" (Turino 2000, 14). Culture has occupied a central place in the studies of nationalism at least since the seminal work of Benedict Anderson ([1983] 1989) and Ernest Gellner (1983). While Anderson's attention to "print-capitalism" shifted the study of nationalism from its products to the processes of construction itself (Askew 2002, 9), his model inadequately explained the solidification of nationalism in areas of the world with low levels of literacy. Addressing such inadequacies, recent research across several disciplines (notably, ethnomusicology, folklore, history, and anthropology) has highlighted the integral roles that music and dance have played in "imagining" and performing the nation, both within Africa[29] and elsewhere.[30]

Within such discourse, music and dance have emerged as powerful social forces of nation building, providing the connective tissue between the nation and the state as they link ideology to social action. Generally, these works show that while states use music and dance as a way to perform their power, galvanize and move the citizenry to political action, promote ideology, and represent the nation, artists conversely often reinterpret the rhetoric and institutions of nationalism to produce multiple expressions of nationalism. This multiplicity of nationalisms interacts in various countries in ways that often conflict, including a particular disarticulation between state and nation (the people). Given this, I heed Askew's call for a shift in the conceptualization of nations from "imag*ined* communities" – a phrase that invites finality, uniformity, and essentialism – to "national imaginaries: the multiple and often contradictory layers and fragments of ideology that underlie continually shifting conceptions of any given nation" (2002, 273). By using a phenomenological lens, which attempts to account for a plethora of perspectives on a given phenomenon, this study underscores the protean nature of nationalism as it investigates the various ways in which this social phenomenon is experienced and expressed in Ghana's state dance ensembles.

By recognizing a myriad of contestations, imaginings (Askew 2002), and fragmentations (Chatterjee 1993), scholars have made important interventions, showing how both elites and non-elites participate in performing the nation into existence. Literature that analyzes the performance of nationalism through music and dance, however, has been primarily concerned with how these artistic expressions have been deployed for the purposes of nation building and achieving group objectives. Augmenting discussions of nation building, this study predominantly interrogates the processes by which non-elites strategically use national/state resources to pursue personal economic, political, social, and artistic objectives. In other words, rather than focus on the construction of the nation through music and dance, this ethnography is primarily concerned with how these artistic forms participate in the construction of the self as non-elites work to re/imagine their individual identities while seeking personal enrichment in multiple ways. Interrogating the ways in which individuals manage nationalism, I alternatively explore how *individuals* instrumentally mediate and exploit the institutions of the state for their own purposes, which often lie outside of the explicit aims of nationalism. In this way, this study reinforces the notion that "most of what is happening in the African political realm is of an 'informal' and personalized nature" (Chabal and Daloz 1999, 1) and brings such insights into the domain of artistic performance.

Within literature that analyzes the performance of nationalism, state dance ensembles occupy a growing portion of this discourse (see Castaldi 2006; Edmondson 2007; Hagedorn 2001; Kaschl 2003; Shay 2002; Schramm 2000; Sörgel 2007; Turino 2000). Despite the existence of such dance ensembles since at least the late nineteenth century, this literature has only recently rescued them from their academic reputation as insignificant "fakelore."[31] That is, given that culture in such troupes is typically folkloricized – commodified and altered for the purposes of achieving wider commercial appeal, financial profit, and an increased visibility – "scholars have avoided the study of state folk dance because it has largely been seen as merely imitation, an artificial adulterated version of the original . . . [which has] no real impact on the culture in which it is a part" (Gore and Koutsouba 1992, 30). For example, Robert Nicholls has avoided the study of the national/staged/folkloric performance of dance because he claims that "each stage [performance] represents a loss of authenticity, a loss of aesthetic quality, and a corresponding loss of historical significance and cultural relevance" (1996, 53). Such attitudes about folkloric performance rely on (outmoded) objective notions of authenticity that romanticize "folk" and rural culture. Citing such attitudes, Anthony Shay has remarked that researchers "have produced little material in English about the choreographic creations of the various state [folk] dance ensembles, preventing an analytical comparison" (2002, 15).[32]

Only within the last few decades has work such as Eric Hobsbawm and Terrance Ranger's *Invention of Tradition* (1983) been more fully embraced by dance and music scholars, encouraging a closer attention to folkloric culture. Because such scholarship has shown that folk culture is "invented," just as folkloric culture is, researchers have shifted their studies from seeking "pure," "authentic" culture to attempting to understand the constructive processes by which culture reflects and affects individuals in a variety of spaces.[33] Thus, the performance of music and dance in a national/stage context becomes a potent study object because it has profound impact on the social processes involved in constructing both a nation and the lives of individuals. In other words, the recent scholarship on state dance ensembles has proven them to be legitimate and powerful sites of social action and change wherein national, ethnic, and global (cosmopolitan) identities are reshaped and the various goals of individuals and groups are achieved. Following the general discourse on the performance of nationalism, the specific literature on state music/dance troupes has, however, largely focused on the ways in which such groups have participated in nation building. That is, such ensembles are primarily analyzed as instruments of the state, which are employed to cement government legitimacy and propagate nationalist ideologies.

To do so, states seize culture from local community and ritual contexts, subsequently modifying and essentializing music/dance to suit new cosmopolitan, folkloric, and national domains. This migration and transformation of cultural forms has invited a particular scholarly fascination with issues of authenticity and sacred/secular boundaries within these nationalist performance spheres. This general focus on the re/presentation of symbolic forms, while productive in many ways, has nevertheless precluded a more detailed investigation into the lived experiences of participants in such groups. While not denying the importance of authenticity and sacred/secular boundaries to participants, this study, by focusing on the quotidian concerns and actions of individual performers, goes beyond analyzing state dance ensembles as mere cultural tools to construct a nation; that is, it not only interrogates state dance ensembles as instruments of nation building but examines them as implements of personal expression, creativity, ambition, social mobility, and achievement. In other words, while analyzing how individuals participate in the construction and maintenance of nationhood, this study conversely emphasizes the processes by which the collectivity of nationalism informs transformations of self.

POSTCOLONIAL NATIONALISM IN AFRICA AND GHANA

While contributing to the discourse on the performance of nationalism, and particularly to that by state dance troupes, this ethnography also augments scholarship on postcolonial nationalism in Africa. Focusing on the Ghana Dance Ensemble, which began in 1962 (five years after Ghana's independence), this book goes beyond much of the literature on nationalism in Africa[34] and Ghana in particular,[35] which has largely concentrated on the periods leading to and directly after independence (1950s and 1960s). Given the temporal focus of this previous discourse, it is unsurprising that it has analyzed African nationalism predominantly as an anticolonial movement, emphasizing its role in galvanizing the masses to remove imperial rule. While I do not deny that nationalism in Africa *was* a movement pitted against European powers in the charge to attain self-rule, this book demonstrates that it has taken on new dimensions over the last several decades as the events of African liberation have become increasingly distant. That is, while there remain some continuities in nationalism's function and expression, these have been re-formed to meet the demands of the contemporary moment.

Exploring this, I ask: What happens to nationalism, and its performance, after independence is established? How do nationalism (in Africa) and its artistic expressions remain relevant when they are not necessarily defined in opposition to colonial rule? And how might postcolonial nationalism draw, and deviate, from this social and political movement in the colonial period? In this way, I follow recent scholarship that examines the performance of nationalism in Africa well after the independence period (see Askew 2002; Castaldi 2006; Moorman 2008, 165–89; Turino 2000, 311–54) to investigate culture's "new functions" (Turino 2000, 321) in this context.

Consequently, this study shows that nationalism is a continually evolving cultural phenomenon, which remains relevant in postcolonial African nations as it is adapted to the needs of its governments and citizens. While Ghana's state-sponsored dance troupes have continued to perpetuate the trans/nationalist ideals of Nkrumah, they have reimagined and augmented them to meet contemporary needs, reshaping the nation and nationalism in the process. As the articulation of nationalism changes over time, the intensity of it is similarly dynamic, waxing and waning with shifts in governments. That is, while certain Ghanaian regimes have concentrated more efforts on nation building, working to create broad political and social momentum, other more reactionary governments have placed more emphasis on patriotism, stirring national pride in Ghana's citizens to sustain the status quo. Namely, as will become evident over the course of this text, while Nkrumah expended much effort in various nation-building projects, many of these were abandoned after he was deposed in a 1966 coup. The subsequent quick succession of governments, primarily led by military dictators, through the end of the 1970s paid little attention to building the nation and the promotion of national culture. While the GDE remained intact and underwent a change in leadership, its practices and policies stayed remarkably consistent; yet, as I will show, certain choreographers used the ensemble to express their dissatisfaction with the social, political, and economic troubles plaguing the country during this period and thus offered a more critical expression of nationalism. In the midst of economic crisis, President J. J. Rawlings renewed nation-building efforts beginning in the 1980s, reviving Nkrumahism and, with it, reinvigorating cultural nationalism in an attempt to restore Ghana to economic and political stability. Despite borrowing heavily from Nkrumah, cultural nationalism was articulated quite differently under Rawlings, particularly within Ghana's state dance troupes. Subsequently, in the twenty-first century, J. A. Kufuor's government marginalized the arts. His increasingly neoliberal, or "business," approach to governance significantly impacted the shape and intensity of cultural nationalism while encouraging clandestine performances of political dissent among those in the national ensembles. Elaborating on these historical and political shifts and on the ways in which they have been articulated through artistic performance, this ethnography clearly attests to the dynamism of postcolonial African/Ghanaian (cultural) nationalism.

STAGING ETHNOGRAPHY: REPRESENTATION
AND A PHENOMENOLOGY OF NATIONALISM

Ethnography is staged. Like the enactment of national culture, ethnography requires a process of staging. Whether engaged in to produce a text or a choreographic work, "staging" involves an inevitable confluence of performance, power, and representation. That is, as many studies have shown (see, for example, Askew 2002; J. Fabian 1990; Erlmann 1996), while power must be performed in order to be effective,[36] performance inevitably involves negotiations of power; performance, whether implicitly or explicitly, always represents someone, something, and/or some idea; and representation assumes a performance within some kind of political field. Staging thus becomes a way to articulate this tripartite configuration, or nexus, in which both participants and researcher are situated.

When the staging of African culture is observed, parallels between such processes and the construction of ethnography become evident, which has informed my own "choreographing" of this text as well as my reflexive understanding of it. Like the artistic directors of the GDE who stage various dances, ethnographers must carefully negotiate this politics of representation as they assume the authority to "act on behalf of someone else" (Bottomley 1987, 1). As choreographers reconfigure cultural traditions for the national stage, they act on behalf of various ethnic groups, the nation, and the state. In many cases, choreographers attempt to capture the "essence" of particular dance forms while altering them to suit new performance domains. Similarly, authors are responsible for representing others' words and actions, seeking to portray and analyze social experience; this inevitably includes a process of translation or textualization – rendering social action into text. Like artistic directors who transform and compress the traditions of their nation, ethnographers must distill a large body of data, making important decisions regarding what to include and exclude from the final product. This constructive process, in both cases, invites a collapsing of time – a reordering of history. While ethnographers generally seek to avoid a reification of an ethnographic present, artists often intend to depict a nostalgic "choreographic time,"[37] in which they project a "past without history"[38] that essentializes as it romanticizes for political purpose. This reordering is executed in both cases for an intended audience, rendering each as a performative act in its own right (see Bauman [1977] 1984). Last, choreographers and ethnographers imbue their works with their own sensibilities and subjectivities (see Clifford and Marcus 1986).

More precisely, ethnography is intersubjectively constructed, or staged, as it requires a social interaction and collaboration between the researcher and the researched. Such a dialectic is unavoidably political, with the author typically having the upper hand. Rather than reify the authority of the ethnographer, my extensive inclusion of participants' own words is an attempt to "decenter" this authority (D. Reed 2003, 10). I recognize, however, that "attempting to do away with scholarly author- ity would be denial; ethnographers assume a certain authority, without which this type of work would not be possible" (ibid.; cf. D. Reed 1993, 83) and that ultimately it is the author of the ethnography who "holds the editorial and publishing keys" (Van Maanen 1988, 137; cf. Tyler 1986). Nevertheless, throughout this study I attempt to privilege the expres- sions of participants, creating a *polyphony of voices,* which invites a poly- phonic authority (see Clifford 1983). Such an approach addresses a con- cern I share with Susan A. Reed, who notes that "the voices, the agency, and the stories of subaltern performers are often completely absent from national dance histories" (2010, 14). Highlighting a plethora of individual voices brings the multiple subjectivities, or interpretations, of national- ism into focus. Weaving together a diverse patchwork of voices to create ethnography, I seek to reflect the intersubjective, and often contentious, social processes that construct both nationalism and the individual ex- periences thereof.

Foregrounding the multiple perspectives/voices of participants is not merely a move to counter the authority of the ethnographer and mirror social interaction but also a reflection of my understanding of the relationship between theory and data. Spurred by the so-called reflex- ive turn in anthropological research, scholars began to more acutely question the relationships between subject and object, researcher and

informant; they also became more attuned to how the dynamics between data and theory related to the authority of the ethnographer and
the representational style of ethnography. Like John C. McCall's "heuristic" approach to ethnography, I follow a group of scholars who "treat
indigenous models as theories rather than as data" (McCall 2000, 10;
A. Apter 1992; Feld 1982; Jackson 1982, 1989; Stoller 1989, 1997; E. Turner
1992). I agree with McCall's assertion that "the indigenous understandings of the world that we gain knowledge of through field research do
not merely provide data for analysis. They can, and must, be mobilized
as a source for theoretical insights" (2000, 12). This does not necessarily
preclude the use of academic theories, or my own ability to offer theoretical insights, but attempts to position so-called informants on equal
footing with social scientists, transforming them into collaborators. It is
important to recognize these collaborators as thinking individuals with
theories of their own about culture and the ways in which the world
works. My intention is to illuminate these "indigenous" theories, highlighting the ways in which they inform social action – particularly the
negotiation of power in the course of managing nationalism.

Whether referring to an ethnography or choreography, "staging," in
the progressive tense, highlights the *processual* attributes of such works.
To explore such attributes, performance theory has proven productive.
While there are a plethora of articulations, interpretations, and applications of performance theory (Bauman [1977] 1984; Drewal 1992;
V. Turner 1969, 1982; Schechner 1977, 1981; Schieffelin 1998), all such
theorists take performance events as the focal point, recognizing these
events as emergent and actively crafted, relying on a process of production (see Bauman and Ritch 1994; Stoeltje and Bauman 1988). Therefore,
it is not only the public display of culture (that is, music and dance) that
is important but also rehearsals and any other "behind-the-scenes" activities that may contribute to these performances. Attention to these production processes within my own work has revealed a number of ways
in which the social negotiation of power, on- and offstage, has informed
the staging of nationalism in Ghana.

Yet, when discussing the disadvantages of this theoretical paradigm,
Charles Briggs has noted that "the focus on performance events has
proven to have its own limitations: it is conducive to reification of con-

text" (1988, 12). This reification often leads to a neglect of other aspects of performance. In other words, while this paradigm has encouraged a focus on the interaction between performers and audiences within given events, it has not provided a model in which to explore aspects of participants' experience and social interaction that may lie outside a direct connection with the events themselves. Moreover, although more recent applications of performance theory have offered a corrective (Askew 2002; Berger 1999), this paradigm often invites an emphasis on the analysts' point of view, consequently marginalizing participants' voices. Because this study is primarily concerned with the perspectives and experiences of participants, both within performance events and beyond them, I augment my theoretical model to include adaptations of phenomenology.

Like other ethnomusicologists (Berger 1999; Friedson 1996; Rice 1994; Stone 1982; Titon 1997), I was encouraged by phenomenology to more closely examine not only the processual aspects of performance but also the lived experiences of it, including the meanings that are constructed by it. Guided by these notions, I deliberately chose not to focus on performance events or particular genres of performance but rather entered the field with the conscious intention only of understanding the experiences of participants in Ghana's national dance ensembles. Phenomenology has also encouraged my interest in the ways in which the perception of cultural objects informs experience. Throughout this ethnography, I show the intimate relationship between the staging of cultural forms and the social interaction surrounding such practices. That is, I am not solely concerned with representation for its own sake but only as it is relevant to the experience of participants.

Overall, this paradigm has invited a close engagement with *participants themselves* and their perspectives. By identifying and suspending one's own assumptions, through the application of epoché, one quickly recognizes that all knowledge held by individuals is partial – both subjective and incomplete. Moreover, I follow anthropologist Michael Jackson, who encourages "the suspension of inquiry into . . . objective truth of particular customs, beliefs, or worldviews in order to explore them as modalities or moments of experience, to trace out their implications and *uses*" (1996, 10; emphasis mine). Thus, this study does not search for an ethereal essence of cultural practices or engage in a fruitless quest for an "authentic" culture but is concerned only with the ways in which individuals deploy cultural discourses and resources to understand their "uses" and the "implications" of such action.

Phenomenology has also urged a close attention to emotions in studying the lived experience because they reveal a way of being-in-the-world that other modes of consciousness cannot.[39] Moreover, emotions are not just expressions of experience but are ways of understanding being because, rather than clouding judgment, they fundamentally inform reason, rationality, and thus the formation of the self.[40] Emotions are particularly crucial to the study of nationalism because this social phenomenon is rendered meaningful through intense, passionate, and intimate engagement with the state and its ideologies as individuals reconcile these with deeply held beliefs about ethnicity and kinship.[41] Tapping into this "primordial" domain of experience, governments attempt to create an emotional bond with their citizens; music and dance have been vital in attempts to achieve a level of "cultural intimacy" (Herzfeld 1997) between the nation and the state. While I examine how the state attempts to accomplish this emotional intimacy with the nation, I focus on the ways in which individual artists manage their emotional expressions; this relies on an understanding of emotions and their articulations as socially constructed and guided by what Arlie Hochschild calls "emotion rules" (1983) – social conventions for the appropriate display of emotion in a given cultural context. Therefore, while throughout my discussion I attempt to pay close attention to the emotional displays (gestures, facial expression, timbre of voice, and so on) of participants as they engage in performance events and tell me their stories of nationalism, I am aware that *"the expression of emotional experience may differ greatly from the experience itself"* (Schauert 2007a, 153).

Emotions and, thus, being-in-the-world are experienced through the intermediary of the body (Merleau-Ponty 1962, 137). Consequently, as Thomas Csordas has argued, within this ethnography "the body is not [merely] an object of study in relation to culture but is . . . considered as the subject of culture, [and] . . . as the existential ground of culture" (1990, 5). This becomes readily apparent when studying dance but is equally important when examining the performance of music because this activity requires intricate and elaborate bodily movement of its own.[42] In all, studying the performance, and managing, of the nation through music and dance offers fertile ground for exploring the relationships between nationalism, the body, and embodiment.

To examine this intersection I develop the concept of corporeal ontology – bodily ways of being-in-the-world. In constructing this analytical concept, I take cues from various phenomenologists who have recognized the body's centrality in lived experience and theorized about its role in the creation of meaning. Most notably, Norman Denzin's notion of the "lived body" (2007) has contributed to my understanding of bodies and embodiment in Ghana's dance ensembles. Denzin describes this concept as a combination of three previous notions of the body. First, the lived body is partially founded on Maurice Merleau-Ponty's concept of "body-for-the-person" (1962), which, in short, is a consciousness and understanding (physical and emotional) of one's own body. Second, the lived body is simultaneously a "body-for-others" (Sartre 1969) because it is known by others as an object. Third, the notion of a lived body is also a product of William James's "psychic body" ([1890] 2007), which elucidates the ways in which individuals come to understand the world through a combination of bodily sensations and cognitive processes. In all, the lived body is a "repertoire of choreographed actions, movements, and feelings" (Denzin 2007, 110; cf. Merleau-Ponty 1968, 256). The lived body is thus a corporeal ontology that both is choreographed by the social world and contributes to the lived reality of others.

With this notion, I recognize that individuals come to understand and *feel* nationalism in their bodies. As performers take the stage, their bodies become bodies-for-others – objects in the world – that are representational. This objectification affects the experiencing of one's own body, or body-for-the-person, as private bodies – or personal understandings of the body – are shaped by public displays of the body. But, as dance scholar Sabine Sörgel notes, while dance theatre presents the "more passive conveyance of representational stage image," it is also an "actively empowering activity of embodied self-knowledge" (2007, 15). Given this, I explore the ways in which the ideologies and practices of nationalism shape the self. This occurs through a process of embodiment, whereby individuals unintentionally and *intentionally*[43] internalize external sensory experiences through self-reflexive acts that, in turn, produce bodily ways of being-in-the-world and bodily ways of self-knowledge. This embodiment can be deeply engrained – not easily forgotten – forming a lasting part of an individual's understanding of the world and of himself or herself. For instance, the training that performers receive in the GDE often profoundly informs the ways in which these individuals move in the world, or their kinesthetic ontology. Embodiment can also be superficial and temporary as the ideologies of nationalism are grafted onto performers' bodies but are not fully embraced and are quickly forgotten by participants.

Highlighting these dynamics of embodiment, this study reaffirms the role of individual agency, illustrating that while participants embody/represent nationalism – displaying it onstage through bodily action – they often make strategic choices about the degree to which they internalize its ideologies and practices. In short, embodiment is often instrumental as artists use their bodies to manage nationalism. By participating in Ghana's state dance ensembles, performers acquire a set of bodily competencies, or bodily styles, which become a repertoire of self-improvement used to pursue self-interests. In this way, as Saba Mahmood has stated, "bodily behavior does not simply stand in a relationship of meaning to self and society, but it also endows the self with certain kinds of capacities that provide the substance from which the world is acted upon" (2005, 27). Within this study, nationalism is rendered as a set of embodied practices and modes of experience that contribute *to various degrees* to the staging of the nation, the development of corporeal ontology, the construction of the self, and the foundations for meaningful lives. As such, not only is the body semiotically analyzed as a site upon which national identity is inscribed, nor is the body merely seen as a metaphor for the nation deployed as a rhetorical strategy to create "cultural intimacy" between it and the state; rather, this ethnography explores how the ideologies and practices of nationalism profoundly inform bodily lived experiences, which transform the individual self and its abilities to manage a matrix of possibilities.

With a keen attention to the body from an ethnomusicological stance, this ethnography integrates music and dance to reflect participants' ontologies. While acknowledging the inextricable connection between music and dance, studies of African performance often privilege one over the other. This practice seems to counter the "constellation of the arts" (Stone 2007) that typifies much of African performance practices. In general, despite numerous works in the anthropology of dance (for example, Hanna 1979; Royce 1977; D. Williams 1997b) and the considerable growth of interest in the anthropology of the body (Lock 1993), Susan A. Reed rightly points out that "the study of moving bodies remains on the periphery" (1998, 504). For instance, African dance scholarship (see Welsh-Ashanti 1996) remains relatively small when compared to African music studies (see Agawu 2003; Nketia 1998),[44] despite the unparalleled ability of dance to express the "deepest emotions" of individuals (Gbeho 1952). In Ghanaian studies, for instance, while there is a vast literature on its music (see Schauert 2005), authors often marginalize or neglect to explore its corresponding dances. This study seeks to integrate these forms of expression and, in turn, connect them to nationalism. Furthermore, by adopting a phenomenological framework, my work bridges the gap between scholars who have used this theoretical approach, on the one hand, to emphasize the experience of dancing bodies (Fraleigh 1987; Sheets-Johnstone 1966) and, on the other, to primarily examine musical experience (Berger 1999; Friedson 1996; Rice 1994; Stone 1982).

Last, phenomenology has informed my approach to history. Given the nature of nationalism as a movement of large groups of people, it is not surprising that many scholars have analyzed nationalism in sweeping historical strokes that, while accounting for mass social actions, infrequently explore how artists embody and experience this sociocultural phenomenon as uniquely situated individuals. While I underscore the importance of the historical context of Ghana's dance ensembles, I do not focus my study on the historical processes that have shaped the development of nationalism in Ghana vis-à-vis the GDE; rather, I attempt to understand how history has shaped the experience of individuals in the recent past. This view of history is again informed by phenomenology, which, as Michael Jackson states, "is less concerned with establishing what actually happened in the past than in exploring the past as a mode of present experience" (1996, 38).[45] Thus, while I recognize that participants have crafted their interpretations of historical events in relation to their contemporary lifeworlds, the exploration of memories becomes a critical tool for understanding personal experiences of nationalism.

In all, engaged in the process of staging ethnography, I have attempted to produce a phenomenology of nationalism and its performance. As such, I have sought to represent others' lives with as much richness as possible, paying close attention to their emotions, their bodily ways of being-in-the-world, and their processes of embodiment. Throughout this discussion, I emphasize participants' perspectives as well as foreground their own theoretical contributions, seeking to represent the polyphony of voices/subjectivities that contributes to the managing of nationalism in Ghana. In this way, I follow Paulla Ebron (2002) and others (Drewal 1992; J. Fabian 1990) by taking an "agency-centered" approach to my research, recognizing that nationalism is a deeply individualized process as participants give nationalism "the impress of their own personality" (Sapir 1934, 412). In sum, by coupling particular phenomenological principles with select theories of performance and power, my analysis seeks to capture the individual negotiations of nationalism, including how participants navigate a cosmopolitan political matrix to achieve individual and collective ends, which may or may not be nationalistic.

MUSICAL/DANCE LANDSCAPE OF ACCRA (AND GHANA)

It is crucial to understand the GDE and the experiences of its members as situated within the broader musical and dance landscape of Ghana because this ensemble draws on such a wide variety of cultural traditions in its attempts to represent the nation's diversity. While a detailed exploration of Ghanaian music and dance is beyond the scope of this book, fortunately it has been among the most studied of any in Africa.[46] A cursory overview here, furthermore, could not do justice to the richness of these performance traditions. Nevertheless, this ethnography considers the GDE in relation to a broader matrix of these traditions. Along with its national context, the GDE must also be viewed within its immediate urban domain. Since its inception in the early 1960s, the dance ensemble has been based at the University of Ghana in Legon, a suburb of the capital, Accra. As will become clear, the ensemble's attachment to the university and its location near Accra have had a significant impact on its development and that of its members.

Founded at the end of the sixteenth century by Ga people who migrated south to this coastal area after several conflicts with the Akwamus, Accra eventually became a collection and consolidation of three Ga townships that came together by the beginning of the eighteenth century. By this time, Europeans had established themselves in the area; the Portuguese, French, Dutch, and British had all built forts in the city by the end of the seventeenth century. Acting as a quintessential "middleman" state (Parker 2000, xviii), Accra increasingly became a center for West African and transatlantic trade, attracting a wide variety of individuals looking for economic and social opportunity. By the nineteenth century, the British had established themselves as the most dominant European power in this region; in 1877, at the end of the second Anglo-Asante War, Accra became the headquarters of the British colony known as the Gold Coast. Soon after, an influx of British migrants flooded the city as more infrastructure was built, including, most notably, the Accra-Kumasi railway in 1908, which facilitated extraction of the colony's cocoa and gold resources. Spurred by an economic boom in these and other exports, people from across the colony and West Africa increasingly came to the city to take advantage of various wage-labor employment and educational opportunities. The 1939 earthquake that struck the city did not diminish this growth but encouraged a rise in residential construction. World War II brought even greater numbers of African migrants to Accra because it served as the headquarters for the allied West African Military Operations. The period from the end of the war through independence saw a major expansion of the city, its population, and its infrastructure as new roads, theatres, banks, schools, cinemas, stores, and residential areas were constructed.

When liberation from British rule came in 1957, Accra became the capital of sub-Saharan Africa's first independent state. Following independence, Accra experienced the "biggest impetus to [its] growth and development . . . when an urban-biased development strategy was vigorously pursued by the [Nkrumah] government" (Yankson and Bertrand 2012, 33). Despite the economic decline of the 1970s, it has been growing steadily, from a few hundred thousand in the late colonial period to over two million today. In all, given the dynamic and diverse scope of its denizens, Accra is a "precocious exemplar" (Parker 2000, xxviii) of transformative power, acting as a crucible not only of social, economic, and political change but of personal transformation as well. Thus, it must be noted that while this discussion primarily demonstrates the transformative experiences brought about through participation in the GDE, such experiences are additionally informed by everyday urban life. That is, while most members of the GDE maintain deep connections with social networks in various regions of the country, much of their time is spent in and around the vibrant cosmopolitan city of Accra as they attend school and churches while going to markets, (chop) bars, clubs, movies, and theatres.

Accra has been at the heart of nationalism in Ghana. It has been a political and intellectual center for Ghana, hosting the nation's most well known universities and schools along with houses of parliament, other government headquarters, national museums, stadiums, theatres, and archives. Moreover, given the influx of people from every region of Ghana, it is a microcosm of the nation because its pluralism mirrors that of the country writ large. These migrants, of course, have brought along their various cultural traditions. As such, Accra is a reflection of the rich diversity of Ghanaian music and dance forms that eventually have become incorporated and codified into a repertoire of national culture.

Along with school[47] and church programs, a primary way in which this diversity has been performed within Accra is through funeral events. On any given weekend in Accra there are dozens of funerals, which typically last three days, including a Friday night wake-keeping, Saturday funeral, and Sunday burial. I would often attend such events with dance ensemble members in and near Accra, as they were frequently hired to perform at these occasions. The cultural content of these funeral performances depends primarily on the ethnic identity of the deceased, although in more recent years, due in part to the efforts of the GDE, such events feature music and dance that transcends ethnic and international boundaries. Given that Accra remains at its core a Ga town, many funerals include Ga social/recreational dances such as *gome,* kpanlogo, and *fumefume.* While gome was initially developed in the nineteenth century as Ga people adopted influences from Congolese fishermen and Caribbean migrants, the latter two were developed in the 1950s and 1970s respectively as a response to highlife. *Adowa* is also frequently performed at many of these events. Although it was originally an Asante funeral music, it, and its emblematic *atumpan,* large twin "talking" drums, have been widely adopted, particularly by the Ga and Ewe. Originally reserved for the Asante royal court, the towering *fontomfrom* drums and colorful red and black *kete* drum ensemble similarly have been widely adopted and can be heard in Accra, particularly for funerals of prominent persons of various ethnic backgrounds. Likewise, Ewe music and dance such as *agbadza, gota,* atsia, *agbekor, gahu,* and *boboobo* are occasionally performed by non-Ewe in Accra. When attending funerals for Dagbamba people from the Northern Region, I would typically witness the large barrel-shaped *gungong* drums and smaller cylindrical *luna* drums in performances of *bamaaya, damba,* and *takai;* although these dances were initially reserved for particular festival, religious, ritual, and occupational occasions, in Accra they have become somewhat decontextualized and generalized as markers of Dagbamba identity more broadly. The buzzing tonality of the wooden *gyil* (xylophone) resonated at funerals for deceased hailing from the Upper West Region, which includes groups such as the Lobi, Sissala, and Dagara. In all, these music/dance practices make up the core of the GDE's "traditional" repertoire but have often been significantly altered from their community-based iterations. Additionally, funeral events, in recent years, have increasingly featured recorded popular music as well, often played simultaneously with the acoustic music described above.

Although "traditional" music and dance have continued to exist within Ghana (and Accra), they have been increasingly overshadowed by highlife, gospel, and other popular forms of expression. Since at least the 1920s, the jazz-infused West African music known as highlife has come to dominate the musical landscape of Accra, first through big bands performing in elite clubs and later by small jazz-style combos such as E. T. Mensah and the Tempos, who performed for an increasingly diverse audience in the 1950s.[48] While the popularity of highlife was harnessed by Nkrumah and his Convention People's Party to rally political support, it has not been a prominent part of the GDE. Similarly, when highlife music was driven into the churches due to the curfew that

Rawlings imposed in the 1980s and gospel music began to gain wide recognition in Ghana, the GDE largely did not incorporate it into their repertoire. Since the 1980s, reggae and Afro-pop have come to dominate the
soundscape of Ghana. Subsequently, in the 1990s, hiplife, a combination
of older highlife styles and American hip-hop, became the prevailing
force in Ghanaian musical culture.[49] Yet such music and its accompanying dances have infrequently filtered into the repertoire of the GDE;
only occasionally is recorded Afro-pop used as background for "contemporary" choreographies, which Francis Nii-Yartey began to develop in
the mid-1990s to break away from preexisting forms. Given its focus on
"traditional" forms of music and dance, the GDE offers a particular lens
to view the nation. Consequently, while some criticize the ensemble as a
museum with an outdated collection of cultural relics, others point to it
as an important repository and promotional outlet for Ghana's cultural
heritage. The following chapters will highlight the politics of these perceptions and the ways in which they are managed.

THE PROGRAM

The subsequent six chapters and conclusion are largely organized –
staged – thematically, although chronology informs my decision to begin with the ideological foundations of the GDE in order to provide a
broad historical orientation. Moreover, chronology often informs the
arrangement within chapters. Each chapter highlights particular configurations of the cosmopolitan political matrix that participants manage and instrumentalize. The themes used to choreograph this narrative
grew organically as I took note of the issues, relationships, and political
dynamics that were most salient for members of the GDE.

The first chapter situates the initiation of the Ghana Dance Ensemble within a historical context of Ghana's independence, African
independence, and colonialism. Because the ensemble was explicitly
part of Kwame Nkrumah's cultural nationalist project, I lay out the ideological basis for his philosophies of nationalism – Pan-Africanism and
African Personality – and illustrate how these ideas have shaped the development of the company. This includes exploring how Pan-Africanism
and African Personality are staged and embodied by both the ensemble

writ large and individual performers as they go "beyond ethnicity" and "beyond Ghana," transcending social and geographical boundaries in the pursuit of trans/national unity. I contend, however, that unity, while emphasizing the universal, is nevertheless embodied subjectively as individuals choose to adopt certain tenets of nationalism that suit their own needs, allowing them to capitalize on their trans/national identities. This focus on subjective embodiment and expediency builds a foundation for exploring the personal and instrumental aspects of nationalism as well as the transformation of the self.

A fundamental challenge of staging culture is to maintain the essence of various dance forms while adapting them to simultaneously resonate with local and foreign audiences. Chapter 2 conceptualizes this phenomenon as "sensational staging," a process whereby dances are altered to appeal to the senses of cosmopolitan aesthetics. Given this reimagining of symbolic forms, studies of such processes inevitably invite examinations of authenticity. While scholars have long criticized folkloric/state dance ensembles for their supposed inauthentic representations of cultural forms, this chapter follows more productive work that has instead concentrated on the authentication of culture. Such a focus moves the discussion from one that searches for elusive essences to one that attempts to understand the politics of representation. By interrogating who represents national culture and why, I analyze authenticity as a discursive strategy, exploring its poetics and instrumentalization. The rhetoric of authenticity is shown to be a vital part of self-making as this discourse serves to create and maintain both personal status as well as the surrounding structures of power. Authenticity emerges here as dynamic and relational, shifting as individuals compare the repertoire of the GDE to other local representations of culture in community and stage contexts. Ultimately, this chapter evinces that individuals choose to adopt, or believe in, certain fluid configurations of authenticity, creating "felt groundings" that reify their sense of self as well as their political and social positions.

While staging the "essence" of Ghana's dances, artists manage a rigorous system of discipline. As this system attempts to mold the actions and character of individuals, it transforms them into "soldiers of culture." After detailing the mechanisms of this disciplinary machinery, chapter 3 explores the ways in which these "soldiers" mediate this political gauntlet, using their clever "artistry" to avoid reprimand and even voice dissent as they mock the very structures of power that produce their stagings of the nation. Offering a clear illustration of managing nationalism, this chapter examines how artists take advantage of the ensembles' "alternative education." Ensemble members not only learn a variety of dance traditions but hone their language and social skills, "study abroad," and develop business sensibilities, becoming entrepreneurs as they transform aesthetic into economic value (see Shipley 2013). As such, this chapter argues that the dance ensembles offer alternative routes to power, allowing individuals to bypass traditional forms of authority (parents, elders, chiefs, and so on) to accumulate wealth, access education, achieve personal aspirations (such as marriage; see Allman 1996), and command respect (see Miescher 2005).

Subsequently, my discussion moves beyond the internal power dynamics of the ensembles to explore a similarly power-laden interaction between these groups and the Ghanaian government. While I explore the state's attempts to appropriate the nation's culture to perform and legitimize its authority, as with previous chapters the focus remains on the members of the ensembles. Offering a diachronic narrative of the relationship between particular postcolonial regimes from Nkrumah, Rawlings, and Kufuor through Atta Mills, chapter 4 provides an anthropology of the state – a view of the state from below – by illustrating how individual citizens come to comprehend the state and their relationship to it through music and dance performance. Employing the well-known practice of African indirect communication as an analytical lens, this chapter examines the ways in which artists "speak to the wind" as they devise clandestine strategies to express dissatisfaction, dissent, disapproval, and discontent with the state of their nation. As such, this discussion reveals how performers mediate their precarious positions as both citizens and government employees within an ostensibly democratic society. Examining the state in this way further emphasizes the subjective construction of nationalism and the agency of participants as it illustrates how artists reconfigure nationalistic rhetoric and institutions to express their personal interpretations of a state, which often marginalizes them and inadequately provides for their needs.

Similarly exploring the choices of individuals as they deploy rhetorical strategies, chapter 5 examines how the bifurcation of the GDE in 1992 invited negotiations of power and narratives of differentiation. Namely, I explore the contentious debates leading to this split that began in the 1980s as plans were devised to build a new theatre in the capital. These debates highlight the dancing politics of the ensembles vis-à-vis notions of tradition, authenticity, and (artistic) development. When a law was finally ratified in 1991 that encouraged the ensemble to move to the newly built National Theatre, approximately half the artists left, eventually becoming known as the National Dance Company (NDC), while the other half fought to retain their name and remained at the University of Ghana (Legon) campus, where the ensemble had been based since 1962. (Throughout this ethnography I will use the acronym GDE in regard to the Ghana Dance Ensemble either before the split or when referring to topics that pertain to both groups. If I am discussing the GDE at the university after the split, it will be obvious from the context or "[Legon]" will appear after the acronym GDE.) While members of the Legon group claim that they are "the originals" because they maintain the "traditional" repertoire, those in the theatre ensemble contend that they are "moving forward" by pointing to their concentration on African contemporary dance. This chapter unpacks the meanings, functions, and performance of these two narrative phrases, tracking their participation in the concurrent construction of self and nation.

Similarly concerned with expressions of the self, chapter 6 examines the ability of performers to enact their creativity within a national framework. Confronted with a national institution that is predicated on the ideology of resemblance – unity and uniformity – this chapter explores how artists articulate their individuality within a domain that ostensibly invites conformity. This discussion thus illustrates the roles of performers in constructing national culture, including the ways in which their individual creative efforts give the ideologies of nationalism (including African Personality and Pan-Africanism) the "impress of their own personalities" (Sapir 1934, 412). Personal creativity, I suggest, is encouraged most noticeably within the genre of repertoire known as African contemporary dance, where cosmopolitanism becomes an engine for artistic and self-expression as well as for articulations of the nation. Creativity, here, emerges as a form of social capital – a currency that is valued and traded in the quest to make a name for oneself. While nationalism seeks to reify a unitary identity, ironically, by standing out, artists increase their chances of securing limited travel opportunities and garnering inter/national recognition.

Ultimately, this ethnography is propelled by the themes of transformation and instrumentality. While this study explores the artistic alteration of music and dance required by the staging of nationalism, it primarily investigates the transformation of the individuals who carry out such political action. Participants in Ghana's dance ensembles become a dancing cadre of citizens yet remain grounded in ethnic identities while strategically embodying new national personas. Participants also implicitly become biographers, cartographers, and archivists as they perpetuate the legacies of Nkrumah and Opoku as well as preserve the nation's traditions, reimagining history and geography in the process. Becoming soldiers, these individuals navigate disciplinary machinery, emerging as entrepreneurs that build cosmopolitan careers. And, while acting as employees of the state, these performers take on the roles of political critics and satirists, indirectly reproaching their government under its direct gaze. Within this multilayered complex of personalities and personas, participants in Ghana's state ensembles remain, most importantly, artists. Through their training they not only become virtuosos of music and dance but also masters of managing the political and social order, seizing the opportunities and resources at hand to mold this matrix to their advantage. Thus, this study illustrates that as individuals – elites and non-elites alike – perform and reform nationalism, they carefully craft ways in which to exploit it for personal ends. Nationalism and the dance ensembles that promote it, consequently, are more than mere political implements of the state; they are rendered technologies for constructing the self.

I am depending upon the millions of the country, and the chiefs and people, to help me to reshape the destiny of this country. . . . We are prepared to pick it up and make it a nation that will be respected by every nation in the world. . . . We have awakened. We will not sleep anymore. Today, from now on, there is a new African in the world!

KWAME NKRUMAH,
March 6, 1957

ONE

Beyond Ethnicity, beyond Ghana

Staging and Embodying African Personality

THE MAP

As the guitar on a recording by Senegalese Afro-pop star Youssou N'Dour sounded a cheerful melody, six female dancers, one by one, skipped onto the stage of the National Theatre of Ghana. Clad in the red, gold, green, and black of the Ghanaian flag, they swung their large calabashes as they moved to their positions in a semicircle at the back of the stage. They began a refrain of unison movements, collecting imaginary water as they moved their calabashes with ease. They continued this playful sequence as a male dancer entered from stage left, performing a series of elegant gestures and acrobatic rolls. Two more dancers quickly followed, all dressed in costumes that streamed with the colorful symbolism of the Ghanaian flag. They paused as two more dancers entered from backstage, performing, in unison, a series of fluid gestures, spins, and stretches. The audience, comprising Ghana's president J. A. Kufuor, a host of government officials, and an assortment of local teachers and schoolchildren, all watched quietly as the five male dancers came together. They began a complex series of contemporary dance movements in close proximity, blurring the boundaries between them. Three dancers exited the stage, leaving a pair of dancers to perform a short duet as the female dancers continued their refrain. The duet included a combination of counterpoint and unison, leaps and lifts. After mirroring each other's movements, one leapt into the other's arms. They displayed their strength as they balanced in a statuesque form. The female dancers, still gesturing with their colorful calabashes, moved forward and consolidated behind the male figures. The male dancers triumphantly stretched out their arms as the dancers continued to close in, forming a mass of moving bodies as the audience applauded.

Suddenly the female dancers scattered offstage, and a new song played on the speakers. "Africa oh!" the chorus sang, while performers quickly scurried to their positions for the second movement of this dance suite. The dancers formed groups of four, three males fronted by a female. Moving in rhythmic harmony, they made their way forward while gesturing and turning. After a few movements and brief pauses, the male dancers broke away to form a tight mass in the center of the stage. Looking left, looking right, leaping, rolling, and bending forward and back all in unison, they embodied social solidarity. Subsequently, they quickly ran offstage, and the audience applauded.

A moment later, two females came to the back of center stage. The curtain behind them slowly opened to reveal a giant three-dimensional map of Ghana with a framework outlining the various regions of the country. As the map became recognizable to the audience members, they cheered. Several male dancers then dutifully walked in a line onto the stage, each carrying a large, colorful cardboard object that resembled a particular region of the country/map. They paraded the regions of Ghana around the stage before bringing their pieces to the map. One by one, the dancers inserted the pieces into the appropriate positions. As the map was filling in, applause started to build, and as the final piece was hoisted into place, the audience let out whistles, thunderous claps, and yells of joy and approval. The dancers, male and female, then united in front of the map, bobbing to the musical refrain "Africa, Africa, Africa, eh!" Fanning out across the stage, they danced, combining movements from the various Ghanaian regions that were represented in the multicolored map behind them. In unison, a pair of dancers leapt into the arms of their respective partners and posed for the final time as the singer let out a climactic "Africa!" (PURL 1.1).

This choreography was an original artistic work performed ceremoniously by the Ghana Dance Ensemble during the nation's Golden Jubilee anniversary. On April 11, 2007, the Ministry of Education, Science, and Sports (MOESS) launched "Education Reform 2007." To give cultural expression to this political action, the MOESS called upon the national dance company to perform a piece that would "unify the country around education reform."[1] As I watched the performance I was reminded that, as education must be reformed and updated to suit the present, so too must nationalism be reshaped to resonate with contemporary times. This particular educational reform aligned Ghana's public schools with the grade level system of the United States. As such, while departing from the previous British model, Ghana maintained connections to the West. The dance, however, reaffirmed Ghana's national identity and connection with Africa. State officials and organizers of this event were exploiting the power of music and dance to "integrate the affective and identity-forming potentials of both icons and indices in special ways" that often are "central resource[s] in events and propaganda aimed at creating social unity, participation, and purpose" (Turino 1999, 236). The icons and indices of each region of the map could also be associated with particular ethnic or language groups within Ghana. Thus, as the "geo-ethnic" pieces of the map came together and the dancers moved in rhythmic unison amid the Afro-pop musical chants of "Africa," the ensemble signified both Ghanaian and transnational unity; the performance produced an emotional outburst from the crowd of Ghanaians, indicating that these individuals were perhaps simultaneously appreciating the achievements of their nation and continent.

Five decades after Ghana's independence, this ensemble continued to reinforce national and transnational solidarity, staging unity by propagating Kwame Nkrumah's notions of African Personality and Pan-Africanism. Exploring the emergence, institutionalization, performance, and embodiment of these ideological principles, this chapter not only provides a historical and analytical foundation for this ethnography but also moves into more recent times as it reveals components of the cosmopolitan political matrix that have continued to impact the representation of culture and the lived experiences of participants within Ghana's state dance ensembles. Focusing on the ways in which these performers go "beyond ethnicity" and "beyond Ghana," it illustrates the individual managing of ethnic, national, and Pan-African identities as artists use the practices and logics of nationalism to construct senses of self and pursue self-improvement.

NKRUMAH, AFRICAN PERSONALITY,
AND CULTURAL LIBERATION

As a young man growing up in the Western Region of the Gold Coast, Kwame Nkrumah excelled at scholastics, and in 1926, at the age of seventeen, he entered the Achimota Training College, located near Accra. It was through his studies at Achimota, over the course of four years, that Nkrumah developed a deep passion for the ideas of cultural nationalism, Pan-Africanism, political national movements, and the liberation of the Gold Coast (Botwe-Asamoah 2005, 3). Notably, it was at Achimota, where he was exposed to a variety of performing arts from several ethnic groups in the Gold Coast, including plays and dancing from Ga, Ewe, Asante, and various northern groups, that the seeds were planted for his later refinement of Ghanaian cultural nationalism. Cultural programming was a significant part of the curriculum at Achimota, because while it aimed to produce African elites who were Western in their intellectual orientation, it encouraged its students to retain links to "tribal life, custom, rule, and law" (Achimota College 1932, 14), which colonial officials predicted would better facilitate indirect rule. This hybrid of Western and African ideas and cultural practices was carried through to Nkrumah's later interpretation and implementation of African Personality.

While at Achimota, Nkrumah was primarily mentored by one of its founders, Dr. Kwagyir Aggrey, who encouraged his students to study well the lessons of the past in order to overcome colonial rule in Africa. Emulating other Pan-African pioneers he had learned about through Aggrey, such as Marcus Garvey and W. E. B. Du Bois (S. Taylor 1994, 87), Nkrumah took his professor's advice and studied in the United States and Britain. At Lincoln University in the United States, Nkrumah received bachelor of arts degrees in theology, economics, and sociology. Later he obtained a master of science degree in education and a master of arts degree in philosophy at the University of Pennsylvania.

Subsequently, Nkrumah left for Britain, where his excellence in education granted him an appointment on the organizational committee of the Fifth Pan-African Congress meeting held in October 1945. At this conference, Nkrumah stated, "A definite plan of action was agreed upon" with the "fundamental purpose of ... national independence leading to African unity" (1963, 135). Realizing this ideal became the primary aim for the remainder of Nkrumah's life as he joined other African leaders in an attempt to elevate Africa to a position of an influential world power. Nkrumah proclaimed that "a Union of African States will raise the dignity of Africa and strengthen its impact on world affairs. It will make possible the full expression of the African Personality" (ibid., 174–75).[2]

Emerging from his interpretation of African Personality, Nkrumah viewed the attainment of national independence as the first measure toward the restitution of African humanity. By way of numerous political maneuvers (see B. Davidson 1989) enacted through his Convention People's Party, Nkrumah led Ghana to its official independence on March 6, 1957. At midnight on this date, Nkrumah gave the most notable speech of his life. That evening, he told the thousands of Ghanaians assembled at Independence Square in Accra, "We are going to demonstrate to the world, to other nations, that we are prepared to lay down our own foundation – our own African identity.... We are going to create our own African Personality" (1957).[3]

Attempting to put these words into action while president of the newly created nation of Ghana, Nkrumah's cultural policies were guided by his philosophical notions of African Personality:

> African personality is merely a term expressing cultural and social bonds which unite Africans and peoples of African descent. It is a concept of the African nation, and is not associated with a particular state, language, religion, political system or color of the skin. For those who project it, it expresses identification not only with an African historical past, but with the struggle of the African people in the African Revolution to liberate and unify the continent and to build a just society. (1973, 205)

In other words, African Personality simultaneously encompassed many forms of nationalism and transnationalism as it created communities based on culture, territory, ideology, and language. In particular, Nkrumah's concepts position him as a "cultural nationalist," because his philosophies imply that the essence of a nation is its distinct culture. This conception stems from the Herderian idea that "humanity is endowed with a creative force which endows all things with individuality – nations are organic beings, living personalities" (Hutchinson

1987, 12) – and in Nkrumah's formulation, African personalities. Like many of his contemporaries (most notably, Léopold Sédar Senghor), Nkrumah subscribed to the notion that nations and national identity could be constructed and should be built on a foundation of cultural practices.

As Robert July argues, African Personality is also a form of *cultural liberation* of Africa from the West that attempts to reassert and interject African modes of expression, aesthetics, ethics, philosophy, and art into the world (1987; cf. Botwe-Asamoah 2005). Although Ghana had achieved political independence in 1957, it had a long road to travel in order to reach the ambitions of African Personality. Namely, as Kwame Botwe-Asamoah remarks, African Personality acknowledged that "a level of solidarity [and] the mere sovereignty of a nation did not ensure a cultural independence," and it was not faithful "unless it was rooted in African people's historical and cultural experiences" (2005, 71). Hence, before exporting African Personality to the world, Nkrumah had to first decolonize the culture of his nation by utilizing African-centered approaches to policy formation.

Achieving this cultural independence, Nkrumah knew, was essential to the political and economic independence of Ghana and the rest of the continent. As July notes, however, there had to first be an "intellectual decolonization" before traditional African values could be revived and then allowed to adapt to the environment of modernity (1987, 19). Nkrumah ascribed to the notion that indigenous elements may provide the "firmest foundation for building economically healthy, politically autonomous, and physically secure African societies" (ibid., x). Yet, as July shows, Western cultural practices were so "deeply imbedded" in African life that the leaders of independence movements could not reject them entirely; neither did African leaders naively appeal to a romanticized African past. Rather, in many instances they combined Western and African practices to reinvent traditions to suit Africa's interpretations of modernity (ibid., x). Despite concerns that "[Africa may be] degenerating into a collection of client states and economic satellites guided by an adulterant version of Western civilization ill adapted to the African environment" (ibid., x), the methodology of merging Western and African practices continued to be Nkrumah's approach to the cultural liberation of Ghana and, in turn, to his policies directed at the arts throughout his presidency.

In short, revealing nationalism's cosmopolitan character, the global and the local coalesced to shape this cultural phenomenon in Ghana. The ideas of nation-state and colonial rule, which were imposed on Africans, had to be countered, in part, on their own (Western) terms, but also in ways that resonated with local Africans. The mobilization of indigenous cultural forms, Nkrumah asserted, was the most productive way to consolidate and galvanize African populations to create a distinct and viable *African* nationalism. Yet Western practices and ideas were not wholly discarded but reconfigured in African-centered ways. African Personality and Pan-Africanism were the expressions of such a form of nationalism. As part of Nkrumah's National Theatre Movement, which sought to institutionalize the cultural arts of Ghana, the GDE became a central platform for the realization and dissemination of these nationalistic ideologies. The following section briefly outlines the struggles of Nkrumah and others as they mediated colonialism and its remnants to create a space for African Personality and the GDE to flourish in Ghana.

INSTITUTING THE ARTS AND THE
NATIONAL THEATRE MOVEMENT

Nkrumah was a cultural nationalist and as such recognized the importance of the arts in building a strong unified nation. He attempted to harness this artistic power by creating various institutional bodies, which he anticipated would ensure that the arts were directed according to his philosophical principles. There were signs of a movement toward institutionalization and incorporating the arts into a national agenda starting in the mid-1950s. For instance, as Nkrumah became the leader of government business in 1951, an indigenous arts organization – the Asante Arts Council – was established by Dr. Yaw Kyeremateng (Botwe-Asamoah 2005, 181); it set out to preserve traditional culture that many Ghanaians perceived was "suffering from foreign adulteration and possible annihilation" (Okyerema 1995, 5). This institution was later subsumed by the Kumasi Municipal Council in 1954 to promote the artistic aspirations of the Asante nation.

Informed by the model of this institution, the following year Nkrumah directed the Ministry of Education, which in turn contracted the
British Council, to set up a body that would investigate the possibility
of forming a national theatre movement. The council's recommendation
was that another agency be created to promote the arts. In June 1955, the
Arts Council of the Gold Coast was officially established to promote African cultural activities. Phillip Gbeho was the council's first chairman;
he was chosen for his accomplishments as an Ewe master drummer,
a published author (see 1951a, 1951b, 1952, 1954), and a promoter of the
traditional culture of the Gold Coast. Under his leadership, Ghanaian
poet/dramatist Efua Sutherland and others worked within this institution to initiate the National Theatre Movement in Ghana. During the
pre-independence period, however, it is difficult to find evidence of its
activity.

Before independence, the Arts Council of the Gold Coast was attached financially to the British Arts Council (part of the British Council), which inhibited its ability to promote an indigenous agenda. Shortly
after independence, however, the council blossomed when it was reconfigured as the Arts Council of Ghana. Nkrumah charged the council
with increasing the scope of the National Theatre Movement, and as
Kwabena Nketia, one of its founding members, remarked, "[It] gave
birth to many new performing arts groups across the country" and was
"fast stimulating" a new awareness of theatre based on indigenous traditions (qtd. in Botwe-Asamoah 2005, 160). This agency's purpose was
to "emphasize the underlying unity of the nation and the equal importance of the contributions which can be made by her people in every
region."[4] Hence, the goals of this organization were directly in line with
Nkrumah's objectives of African Personality and Pan-Africanism. To
ensure that this organization would carry out Nkrumah's political ideas,
he made himself president of the Arts Council in December 1958. Working with key members of that council, Nkrumah established in every
region a myriad of performing groups, including drama, dance, music,
choral, and orchestral ensembles (see Botwe-Asamoah 2005, 163–65),
which performed in numerous state-sponsored festivals (ibid., 166–67).
Although the Arts Council had made great strides in promoting and
disseminating indigenous art forms, Nkrumah was not wholly satisfied

with its accomplishments. Thus, he proposed that the council become subsumed under a new body – the Institute of Arts and Culture, which was created in 1962. This act, Nkrumah stated, would "give more effective direction" to cultural arts in Ghana ([1963] 1992, 15). In short, a wide variety of art and cultural organizations, including the Arts Council, the National Museum, the Library Board, the National Archives, and the National Cultural Center in Kumasi, were consolidated to ensure a more unified execution of Nkrumah's agendas (Botwe-Asamoah 2005, 171–75).

While the aforementioned institutional bodies were important sites in disseminating Nkrumah's political agenda, he was not unaware of the enormous power of education. Nkrumah saw his educational policy as the "centerpiece of his cultural policy and aim of the development of African personality" (Hagan 1991, 5). Therefore, to ensure that schools (primary through college) were in line with his vision of nationalism, Nkrumah's government, in 1951, assumed full responsibility for educational policy. In particular, Nkrumah continually emphasized the role of higher education, asserting the need for change at the University of Ghana. The university, in Nkrumah's view, was a double-edged sword that could be both an effective tool to focus the national sentiments of students and a "breeding ground for unpatriotic and anti-government elements" (Haizel 1991, 70). Hence, Nkrumah instituted policies that would encourage the former, making the university into a site where Africans of all nationalities could be reeducated in an African-centered and socialist manner in order to produce freedom fighters and liberators of colonial oppression. After all, it was in college at Achimota that Nkrumah's national ideals were first generated. In short, Nkrumah anticipated that the university under his leadership would be a place to impart African Personality; he wanted it to "relate its activities to the needs and the interests of the nation, and the well-being of the people" (ibid., 71). However, before Nkrumah's presidency, the University of the Gold Coast, as it was then known, was headed by an Englishman who had an opposing view of education.

When this university was established in 1949, with a mere ninety students, David Blame was its director. Blame had immigrated to the Gold Coast with a degree in classics from Cambridge. Relishing the civilizations of Greek antiquity, he asserted the authority of Western culture and implemented a curriculum at the university that centered on the "great Western traditions" (July 1987, 162). Consequently, during his tenure, there were few African professors and only marginal attention was given to teaching Africans about Africa. The sociology department, however, was headed by a Ghanaian, Kofi Busia, and offered opportunities for Ghanaians to excel at the university. For instance, in 1952 a promising young scholar named Kwabena Nketia, who had previously studied with the revered Ephraim Amu,[5] was appointed as a research fellow in sociology. Nketia was charged with the task of collecting and analyzing a variety of African languages, music, dance, and folklore. Despite Nketia's ambition and enthusiasm for African culture, overall the university remained largely European in character. It was evident to many Ghanaians that the university needed a larger African presence in order to develop in culturally relevant ways. Reflecting on the university situation pre-Nkrumah, Nketia has remarked, "The creation of modern African states requires both cultural and material development. If we wait for these things to develop on their own we run the risk of haphazard growth and aimless drift; the evident need therefore is for some form of institutional organization that will provide national integration through the artistic and other programs designed to encourage cultural interaction . . . in a national program for the arts" (qtd. in July 1987, 185). Several political hurdles would have to be overcome, however, before Nketia's call for a national arts program could be realized.

The first obstacle fell shortly after independence, when Blame left the university, allowing an African voice to emerge at the school. Namely, Kofi Busia had proposed the idea of an Institute of African Studies (IAS) to be located at the newly renamed University of Ghana (Legon)[6] and convened several conferences throughout 1960 to develop a prospectus for the program. After two years of discussion and planning, the committee's secretary, Thomas Hodgkin, presented a proposal to Nkrumah, and upon its acceptance Hodgkin became the first director of the IAS in 1962. At the inauguration of the institute, Nkrumah asserted:

> One essential function of the institute must surely be to study the history, culture and institutions, language and arts of Ghana and of Africa in new African-centered ways – in entire freedom from the propositions and presuppositions

of the colonial epoch. . . . By the work of this institute, we must re-assess and assert the glories and achievements of our African past and inspire our generation,
and succeeding generations, with a vision of a better future. (1963, 14)

In short, Nkrumah viewed the IAS as an ideal place to foster African Personality. Within this institute, Nkrumah identified the School of Music,
Dance, and Drama as the "nucleus of the National Theatre Movement"
(1963, 32). This was supported by Nketia's notion that "a national theatre
movement must be backed by a training institution such as an academy
or school of music. . . . Such a school could be a centre for building up the
artistic fragments, in which ethnic groups specialize, into larger wholes
for wider audiences" (1964, 92). At long last, the National Theatre Movement, initiated by the Arts Council in the mid-1950s, had a focal point
and a space in which to prosper.

In his speech inaugurating the IAS, Nkrumah stressed the importance of linking theatre to society writ large. According to Botwe-
Asamoah, "Nkrumah saw theatre as an intellectual forum whereby the
vital values in African heritage and African personality could be exam-
ined and recovered to influence the socio-economic aspirations of the
new Africa" (2005, 11). Thus, he wanted the drama studio to be located
off campus so it could receive feedback from the community and reach
out to the populace. "In this way," Nkrumah asserted, "the institute can
serve the needs of the people by helping develop new forms of dance and
drama, of music and creative writing that are at the same time closely
related to our Ghanaian traditions and express the ideas and aspirations
of our people" ([1963] 1992, 15). In other words, through the IAS, most notably by engaging in music, dance, and drama, individuals were molded
by faculty into a community of Ghanaian citizens. As Robert July and
Peter Benson note, the faculty of the IAS "developed community stability and pride. They evoked understanding among peoples seeking
to give birth to new and viable nations" (1982, 76). Based at the IAS, the
GDE became the emblematic expression of the National Theatre Movement and the philosophical/political objectives of Nkrumah's African
Personality. As shall become clear, the decision to locate the GDE at the
university has had an enduring impact, including on the development
of a group of individuals who would be responsible for spreading African
Personality domestically and abroad.

A DANCING CADRE

Nkrumah was highly influential in forming the initial ideological objectives of the IAS and, in turn, the GDE. Although the IAS was initially directed by Thomas Hodgkin, he was under the direct authority of Nkrumah, who had appointed himself chancellor of the entire University of Ghana in 1961. This position allowed Nkrumah to hire faculty who were likely to further his politico-cultural policies. Kwabena Nketia was chosen by Nkrumah to head the newly established School of Music, Dance, and Drama. This same year, the IAS received a subvention from the Ministry of Culture to found a national dance company (GDE), with Nketia as its first administrative director. Nketia was appointed not only for his knowledge of various African cultures and Western credentials but also because he shared many of Nkrumah's views concerning the role of art to further African Personality. Nketia, according to July, "recognized the importance of cultural awareness in generating a desire for independence" (1987, 181). Additionally, Nketia's conception of African Personality was similar to Nkrumah's. In an interview, Nketia stated,

> The concept of African Personality was meant to be at once liberating and creative, bringing into focus *African alternatives to Western values* and *institutions* that had been imposed upon subject peoples by colonialism. It was important to combat the claim to the universality of Western culture ... [and] to put forward an African alternative that would assert a valid African civilization, both at home and abroad. (qtd. in July and Benson 1982, 71; emphasis mine)

Like Nkrumah, Nketia asserted the need to create an African-centered approach to revitalizing indigenous traditions in order to overcome racism and colonial oppression.

Yet, recognizing that nationalism paradoxically relies on cosmopolitanism as it is threatened by it (Turino 2000, 15), Nketia and Nkrumah argued that these idiomatic cultural displays had to simultaneously resonate with international audiences. In short, both men were keenly aware of the need for Ghana to resemble other nations to gain credibility as such. Regarding the time of the dance ensemble's formation, Nketia stated:

> We had a special relationship with London University.... But Nkrumah wanted an independent university. At the time, the University [of Ghana] was starting

from scratch [1961], and we had to build on a tradition too. It was good to have [a relationship with] London University, which was a well-established university. In 1961, the University [of Ghana] became independent, but we still kept some of the mechanisms for ensuring standards. [In] those days it was important visibly to have certain standards that the academic world approved of, and for others to know they were also being maintained here. (2005)

In short, the University of Ghana, through adopting European standards of education, was aligning itself with the Western world and the international community.

In addition to this outward visibility, Nketia also attempted to ensure social stability within Ghana through means that resonated with local communities. In general, Nketia shared Nkrumah's desire to institute practices that would influence a large group of individuals, stating, "It is certainly my hope that in the creative arts there will be interaction between the narrow circle of intellectuals and the community at large, so that the gap between past and present, between the traditional and the contemporary can be bridged, creating social solidarity and national unity" (1959, 2). The arts were viewed by Nketia as a part of the postcolonial shift of nationalism from an elite-driven movement to one that attempted to include the masses.[7] Consequently, Nketia recognized the vital role that regional practices would have to play to create this broad movement, remarking that "it is only then that we can restore, through the media now available to us, the *African* concept of the arts as a form of community experience" (2; emphasis mine). This traditional "community experience" ascribed to past "African" societies, however, was becoming reconfigured to serve contemporary nationalistic agendas such as unifying his country's populace in order to create a Ghanaian community. Namely, his aim as the director of the IAS was to train students so that they could eventually teach in a national school system, forging a new community of citizens, or cadre, which would propagate African Personality within Ghana and abroad. Therefore, one of Nketia's most important tasks as the director of the IAS was to hire faculty to carry out these objectives.

Nketia chose Mawere Opoku as the GDE's first artistic director. Nketia did so for four primary reasons: Opoku's knowledge of indigenous traditions, his elite education in Ghana, his Western training, and his nationalistic ideologies. Opoku was brought to Legon in 1962 in part for his exceptional abilities in the traditional arts of Ghana. There were Asante chiefs on both sides of Opoku's family, ensuring that Opoku had received special training in traditional lore and etiquette. As a result, Opoku was especially sensitive to indigenous cultural aesthetics expressed in terms of linguistic symbolism and religious or communal ceremonies. This included, particularly, dance, which occupied such a central position in African social and cultural life (July 1987, 97). Additionally, like Nkrumah, Opoku had received an elite education at Achimota College, which included "tribal drumming" as part of the colonial curriculum. In the early 1930s, as he witnessed and participated in a multiethnic array of music, dance, and drama on occasions such as Founders' Day and "African night" (Coe 2005, 60), his nationalistic approach to the performing arts was cultivated. Moreover, Opoku was tapped by Nketia and Nkrumah to lead the GDE because of his familiarity with Western culture; such knowledge, they surmised, would ensure that this ensemble would resonate with international audiences as well as local. Like many others in the Ghanaian intelligentsia, Opoku had studied in Britain and the United States. Opoku had gone to New York to work with the renowned dancer/choreographer Martha Graham in order to gain a greater understanding of theatrics, body movement, and staging. He also traveled to London to study with leading dance instructors. Illustrating his nationalistic agenda, according to July, "when Opoku was still in London, he and other Ghanaians had looked forward to the day when they could form a traveling team that would visit the country's regions, not to play soccer matches but to exhibit *the nation's* dances" (1987, 98; emphasis mine).

Upon his return to Africa, Opoku was eager to promote indigenous Ghanaian culture, which would further his previous work in this regard. During the 1950s, Opoku gained a reputation as an excellent organizer and performer of indigenous Ghanaian art forms through his leadership of a dance troupe at the Asante Cultural Centre, a civic enterprise founded by his cousin Alex Kyerematen. This group primarily staged Asante dances for Akan dignitaries, but on special occasions they performed dances of other ethnic groups, which foreshadowed Opoku's nationalistic leanings. On weekends this ensemble frequently traveled to Legon to teach dance forms from many Ghanaian regions. While at the university, Nketia became familiar with Opoku's excellent work, and when Nkrumah asked for someone to organize music and dance performances for the Independence Day celebration in 1958, Nketia recommended Opoku. It was because of this performance, Opoku remarked, that Nkrumah got the idea to form a national group in order to further the "cultural emancipation of Ghana and Africa" (Adinku 1994, 6).

Subsequently, when the National Dance Company (later, GDE)[8] was officially established at the University of Ghana in October 1962, Mawere Opoku became its first artistic director. The president welcomed this suggestion because Opoku, like Nkrumah, had both national and Pan-African agendas. Opoku's approach to the dance company was to "unify the country through the dance forms, thereby underscoring Nkrumah's drive for a unified nation and a unitary government" (Opoku qtd. in Botwe-Asamoah 2005, 200). Supporting this position, Opoku remarked that "traditionally, the artist and citizen were one" and that "in African societies the artist has always had the civic duty of political commentary . . . [or] public mouthpiece" (qtd. in July 1987, 230). Opoku also aligned with Nkrumah's cultural thought, stating that African Personality meant, in part, refuting the lies told about the past by European scholars (Opoku 1976).

In all, Opoku, Nketia, Nkrumah, and the members of the GDE fused Western influence and training with local sensibilities to form a type of cosmopolitan "dancing cadre" that became a vital way to assert African Personality within Ghana and abroad. Achieving the full expression of African Personality, however, was a process that "entailed hard work."[9] One of the most important and difficult tasks within this process was to unify individuals of various ethnic groups.

BEYOND ETHNICITY

Like most African nations, Ghana has borders stemming from its colonial past, which arbitrarily lump together numerous ethno-linguistic groups. The largest of these groups is the Akan, who account for nearly half of this country, with the Ewe, Ga, Dagbamba, Guan, Frafra, and other minorities making up the remainder of the nation.[10] In 1960, two years before the GDE's founding, the Ghana Statistical Service attempted to account for its nation's diversity; based on population data from that year, it produced a map (map 1.1) that sought to establish a "multicriteria classification," taking into account factors such as language and "geographic affinity" (1964, xi). This task proved difficult, however, because as Carola Lentz and Paul Nugent point out, "on the ground the census became thoroughly entangled in the ambiguities of territorial as against ethnic names" (2000, 10). While its solid lines belie the interethnic cultural exchanges that have occurred over centuries and its antiquated nomenclature reflects a bygone era, the map nevertheless illustrates that a sense of ethnicity did exist in postcolonial Ghana. Despite its flaws, this map, furthermore, attests to the complexity of this ethnic identity within Ghana, alluding to the challenge that Nkrumah, Nketia, Opoku, and the dance ensemble faced in their attempt to create a unified nation.

Although Ghanaians were unified in their quest for liberation from colonial rule, political fissures within this new nation continued to persist. Generally, in the wake of Ghana's independence, as Victor Ametewee states, "political party rivalry became linked up with the ethnic background of the leaders" (2007, 33). Such "ethnic" or "tribalistic" assertions threatened the political stability and solidarity that Nkrumah sought. Writing about the early days of postcolonial Ghana, David Apter notes that "by the summer of 1957 bitterly anti-Nkrumah groups could be found everywhere" (1963, 328). These political organizations often coalesced along ethnic and regional lines. Gaining their strength during the run-up to independence, the most well-known of these oppositional groups were the Asante National Liberation Movement (NLM) (Allman 1993), the Togoland Congress (mostly Ewe) (Austin 1964), the Northern People's Party, the Anlo (Ewe) Youth Organization, and the Ga Shifimo Kpee (ibid.). As Ben Abdallah (former chairman of Ghana's Commission on Culture) recalled, the NLM was "practicing terrorism – explosions – of the Flagstaff House [Nkrumah's office and residence], trying to kill Nkrumah" (2007). To combat this separatist activity, Nkrumah strategically appropriated the cultural (royal) symbols of the nation, attempting to seize power from local chiefs and elders, undercutting their authority in the process (Coe 2005; Lentz 2008; Rathbone 2000).

Map 1.1. Map based on the 1960 population census of Ghana, Special Report E. This dense image alludes to the complexity of ethnic boundaries within this nation.

Most notably, Nkrumah viewed the public display of the performing arts, and particularly "drumming and dancing," "as the best able to legitimate [state] power" (Coe 2005, 54) and unify a diverse population. That is, while there were many disputes between Nkrumah's Convention People's Party, the NLM, and other anti-Nkrumahist groups, "these disturbances invariably vanished in the dance arena" (July 1987, 100). Nkrumah and the staff of the national dance ensemble recognized this unique ability of music and dance to transcend political and social classes, reunite ancestors with the living, and cut across ethnic boundaries. In phenomenological terms, the national ensemble was tapping into the "tuning in" (Schutz [1964] 1971) phenomenon that can occur through the performance of music and dance as performers partially share each other's experiential flux of inner time. In this way, as Martin Stokes notes, these arts "can provide a powerful affective experience in which social identity is literally 'embodied'" (1994, 12). The following discussion explores the processes by which members of the Akan, Ewe, Dagbamba, Ga, and other ethnic groups have embodied the social and national identity of being "Ghanaian" through music and dance performance.

To implement their national agenda, Nketia and Opoku, after some debate, decided to recruit specialists from several regions to teach a range of dances to young students with various ethnic backgrounds. Nketia and Opoku predicted that individuals would become familiar with the traditions of their Ghanaian and African neighbors, resulting in the solidification of unity among diverse groups through shared cultural experiences. When asked about this recruitment process, Nketia remarked, "We were trying to go beyond ethnicity.... We are all involved in things that cut across ethnicity, and that cutting across ethnicity is the national thing" (2005).

In going "beyond ethnicity," the GDE directors attempted to display the diversity of the nation rather than solely use the politically and demographically dominant culture group (that is, the Akan) to represent the nation – a practice that has been common in many national dance companies (Castaldi 2006; Shay 2002). Francesca Castaldi (2006), for example, describes the "Wolofization" of national music and dance generally in Senegal as the majority Wolof ethnic group dominates the country's national culture. Particularly, there has also been a "Mandification" of Dakar's ballets because these companies "tend to privilege exclusively the Mande dance complex" (154). One could easily imagine an "Akanization" of dance repertoire within the GDE because this ethnicity comprises nearly half of the entire population of Ghana. While Akan dances are prominent in the ensemble in various ways, other minority ethnic groups (most notably, the Ewe and Dagbamba) have actually dominated the dance repertoire, both in number of pieces included and the frequency with which they are performed. Despite placing emphasis on certain ethnic groups at various times, the ethnic diversity of the GDE staff has encouraged an overall diversity of the ensemble's repertoire. According to William Adinku (2000, 132), a member of the ensemble since its inception, there were staff from Ga, Asante, Ewe, and Dagbani language groups who each taught and performed their respective traditions. In this way, author Kwame Botwe-Asamoah states, "the repertoire of the GDE and its performance represented the highest expression of African Personality that Nkrumah envisioned" (2005, 208).

However, the representation of particular ethnic groups by the GDE has been uneven over time, which raises questions regarding the ensemble's management of ethnicity and the motivations of its staff. A book published on the GDE in the mid-1960s attests to the efforts made by its staff to represent diversity. It states that the ensemble's repertoire consisted of twenty-three Ghanaian dances – six Asante (Akan), nine Ewe, five Dagbamba/Hausa, one Lobi, one Nzema, and one Ga (Opoku 1968, 25–26). While there are many ethnic groups that are not represented at all within the GDE's repertoire, the ones that are included roughly mirror the demographic of the country writ large with one glaring exception: the Ewe, which make up about 13 percent of the population, are reflected in about 40 percent of the repertoire. An examination of forty-six programs between 1965 and 1975 (when Opoku was the artistic director) reveals a similar dominance in the actual performance of Ewe dances at various events in Ghana.

Nevertheless, within this set of programs, the Akan emerge as a dominant force in the early performances of the GDE. The *Akan Ceremonial Dance,*[11] choreographed by Opoku (an Akan/Asante), appeared first on all but five (of forty-six) programs. Moreover, as Isaac Hirt-Manheimer has keenly observed, in early programs for the GDE, other ethnic groups' dances were often described in relation to Akan dances or with Akan terminology. For instance, a medley of northern dances titled *Dance Suite for Donno and Brekete* uses Akan names for two Dagbamba drums. Similarly, in an early program, Hirt-Manheimer notes that the Ewe *agbekor* is described in terms of Akan dances, as the description reads, "They [agbekor] are essentially soldiers' dances like the Asonko dance of the Twi [Akan] people," while *kundum,* an Ahanta dance, is linked to the Akan *asafo,* and the Ewe *gahu* is linked to *sikyi* (2004, 57–58). It is important to note, however, that these programs were rarely circulated to audiences and thus had limited impact on the representation of ethnicity. Therefore, while Opoku's personal identification

with the Akan undoubtedly influenced his construction of GDE performances and, in turn, the representation of ethnicity by this ensemble,
I maintain that the examples of "Akanization" cited above are minor
in relation to the actual performance of the repertoire. The dominance
of the Ewe – both in total number of pieces included in the ensemble's
repertoire and in the frequency with which these dances were performed – seems to weaken an argument for the Akanization of the GDE.

As the dance ensemble progressed, its staff conducted further research and brought more dance repertoire into the company. In the early
1970s, five "new" pieces appeared on the GDE programs – the Ewe *borborbor,* the Akan *atenteben,* the Dagbamba *bamaaya,* the Dagara *bawa,*
and the Frafra *bima.* The newly added dances were performed with more
frequency, giving an increased prominence to northern ethnic groups
(such as the Dagbamba, Dagara, and Frafra). Furthermore, in 1976 Francis Nii-Yartey assumed the role of artistic director and choreographed
a piece from the north called *nagla* from the Paga ethnic minority. By
examining programs from the 1970s and 1980s, it is clear that throughout
Nii-Yartey's tenure as director, the northern dances of the Dagbamba,
Frafra, and others gained prominence, paralleling the consistent prevalence of Ewe dances. The Ewe and northern dances each were performed
twice as frequently as Akan dances during this period. Although too few
programs were found from the 1990s and early 2000s to make any assessment of the GDE's performances of this period, the patterns of performance I witnessed from 2005 to 2012 showed a continuing trend of privileging both Ewe and northern dances.

When I asked Nketia about this disproportionate representation,
he claimed that the directors were not concerned with numbers and
"were just thinking of things that would be interesting in terms of the
spectacle and in terms of the *artistic* combination" (2005). Corroborating
such notions, numerous directors stated that the frequency with which
particular dances are performed is largely based upon audience reaction, and high-energy spectacles seem to connect more strongly with
audiences (both Ghanaian and abroad). This ideology became clear as I
witnessed numerous events. The vigorous, fast-paced dances of minority
groups such as the Dagbamba and Ewe were performed more often than
the slow, stately dances of the Akan.

Hence the cosmopolitan aesthetics of dramatic spectacle, which serve to spread nationalism's ideologies to a diverse range of audiences, have consequently shaped the representation of the ethnic diversity within Ghana. In this way, whether intentional or not, the GDE acts as a way in which minority ethnic groups counter the political dominance of the Akan and assert their influence in constructing their nation. While it cannot compensate for the political and economic (allocation of resources) marginalization of the various northern (see Botchway 2004) and Ewe (see Nugent 2000) ethnic groups within Ghana, these groups do attain some degree of notoriety and status through the representation of music and dance by the GDE. In all, despite the emphasis on spectacle rather than on a deep concern for representing the ethnicity of Ghana equitably, GDE directors have consistently included a wide range of dances in their repertoires; thus, throughout its existence, the ensemble has reflected the ethnic pluralism of the nation, the state's slogan of "unity in diversity," and the ideology of African Personality.

The repertoire's diversity did not necessarily ensure that performers would actually adopt these varied cultural practices, appreciate this pluralism, or unite across ethnic lines. When asked about how diversity was approached in the early days of the ensemble, Nketia stated that "the object [of the GDE] was to ensure that whatever constitutes the national heritage is shared and that you had a model of what we thought the nation could profit from in terms of making use of what all the culture groups had to offer in a national context" (2005). According to Patience Kwakwa, an original member of the GDE, the "sharing of culture" did, in fact, guide the procedures of the ensemble:

> Opoku had this thing. If you come from [a certain] area, Opoku would not allow you to do that dance. You would do a dance from other areas.... The whole idea was to unite the people in Ghana. And if you could perform somebody else's dance, it was already an element of familiarity that is being expressed. So you get closer to the people when you can do their dance. It's just like speaking a language. So what's the point of coming in with what you have and sticking with that? So he forced us to learn dances from other ethnic groups. (2006)

Because she said she was "forced" to learn dances outside her own ethnic group, I asked her how it made her "feel" to learn others' dances. She replied, "Oh, it was a very good feeling, because wherever you go, people take you as one of their own. And therefore they are cordial and they co-operate with what you do." Several interviewees remarked that learning a variety of ethnic dances made them feel "more proud of Ghana" and "more Ghanaian" as a result because, as Grace Djabatey commented, "you can fit in anywhere at all" (2006).

Another dancer's comments highlight Opoku's encouragement of ethnic boundary crossing. When I asked Abubakari Salifu Merigah, a self-identified Dagbamba from the Northern Region, about learning Akan dances, he remarked,

> Some people, they ask: Where is this guy from? He's a northerner, and he can dance [Akan dances] like that, eh! Because of Professor Opoku, people say that I don't express myself like a northerner, but I express myself like an Asante [Akan]. And he [Opoku] is very happy, and nice, and smiles very big. Opoku made himself very open and willing to teach you. They can see the will coming, so they like it. It's because of the company; without the company I would not have been able to jump inside the dances like that. . . . It empowered me to do any dance I would meet on my way. (2006)

Merigah was not the only GDE performer to experience the empowering effects of embodying national unity. More broadly, referring to the time soon after Ghana's independence, Nketia recalled, "In terms of our concept of a national culture we were beginning to integrate. . . . We had Dagomba [*sic*] drummers playing Asante dances, and Ewe playing Akan, and so forth . . . so Gideon [a regional specialist employed by the GDE], an Ewe drummer, became an expert *adowa* [Akan dance] drummer" (2005). By convincingly performing the traditions of neighboring ethnic groups, Merigah and others embodied national unity and often felt empowered by their ability to identify with these groups. Overall, Opoku was largely successful at putting his ambitions for a unified Ghanaian nation into practice, encouraging performers to "go beyond ethnicity."

Although the musicians and dancers were quick to adopt cultural diversity, audiences required more time to accept the shift to a national culture. Regarding the early days of the dance ensemble, Nketia noted:

> Right at the beginning of independence the ethnicity was very strong, even though we were bringing things from various places. People would identify with a particular group, and as soon as they come and begin to dance they are shout-

ing and so forth. And then a couple of years later we were getting used to the things from various places, so that you find when the *agbadza* [an Ewe] dance comes on, the Asante, all of them are clapping. So you are beginning to appreciate the differences, which become part of the composite. (2005)

In short, music and dance played a vital role in the creation of a national consciousness. As Ghana entered a new phase of its political and cultural history following independence, its citizens began to embrace the ethnic diversity of their nation through these cultural forms.

Following the brief period where "ethnicity was very strong" in Ghana, both audiences and performers crossed ethnic boundaries with increased fluidity. During the formative years of the G DE, members performed in local communities, seeking and often receiving approval for their interpretations of cultural forms. As Nketia narrated, "We [the G DE] went to Christian village, which was close by [to Accra] and had an Ewe community. Our dancers danced [Ewe dances] with them ... and they [the villagers] would make comments. They liked it, and point[ed] to the ones they liked best. Sometimes the dancers were not even Ewe" (2005). I have collected a plethora of examples in which dancers were attributed the ethnic identity of the dance they were performing despite self-identification with a different ethnic group. For example, a senior Ewe dancer in the ensemble, Wisdom Agbedanu, stated that after a G DE performance of the northern Dagbamba dance called bamaaya, an audience member came up to him and greeted him in Dagbani. The audience member, who was from the Northern Region, was shocked to learn that Wisdom was an Ewe and rewarded the dancer with 10,000 cedis (about one U.S. dollar) and a handshake (2005). Similarly, Nketia remarked that when Gideon Alorwoyie (see Davis 1994), an Ewe master drummer employed by the G DE, played Asante dances for an Akan community, the "teacher of this [Akan] tradition" preferred Gideon's drumming to that found in the local community (2005). Furthermore, many dance ensemble members stated that they enjoy performing dances from other ethnic groups and identified with those groups as much as or more than with the groups with which they regularly affiliated. Many of these individuals have also stated that they have never received criticism for their performances of others' traditions and to the contrary have received noticeable praise. In all, these performers have convinced audiences of their artistic ability to embody multiple ethnic identities. As such, they have provided a tangible illustration of the national integration that Nkrumah envisioned.

Subjective Unity

Although dancers and drummers performed a variety of dances – ostensibly going beyond ethnicity – several performers' comments remind us that identity is always multilayered. Adopting a new national identity does not necessarily eradicate the strong ties individuals may have with a particular ethnic affiliation. "Ethnicity does not preclude national identity," Jean Allman has remarked in reference to Peter Osei-Kwame's work (1980), "but in fact provides a basic building block for it" (1993, 7). Ethnic and national identities can coexist.[12] Yet their juxtaposition may create individual struggles to reconcile the two.

A vivid example of this identity negotiation is offered by Mustapha Tettey Addy. When I asked him about ethnic tension in the early days of the GDE, he replied, "I remember one time I beat one guy. He was calling me a Ga, and I said, 'Don't call me that; I am a Ghanaian.' And he kept calling me that. He was older than me, but the way I beat him, he got shocked [laughing]" (2007). His comments indicate that identity formation within the GDE not only was an internal struggle but could entail an external physical confrontation in some instances. Subsequently, he acknowledged that it was partially the experience in this state ensemble that inspired him to create original drum and dance compositions that, while rooted in Ga traditions, incorporated those from other ethnic groups in Ghana and Africa. As such, Addy and his artistry embody and perpetuate Nkrumah's ideological legacy of "unity in diversity" while reaffirming the subjectivity of this process.

More recently, although national identity has become increasingly accepted in Ghana, participants continue to struggle to reconcile it with their ethnic heritage. One young male Ga dancer from Accra stated,

> [The] dance ensemble has ... really changed my life, because at first I always think about my ethnic background. I always do what the Gas do. I don't respect anybody's tradition. When I came to the dance ensemble I always fight with them and say our festival is the best. Our festival is richer than everyone else's

festival. But when I got to know about other people's festivals, I said, "Oh, so there are [other] festivals like that." Because, when I came to the dance ensemble, I only knew about my own festival, and I was not the type to go out.... Now I think everybody is one. I respect other traditions now as a whole. I respect each and everyone's ideas. I feel like I am a part of all Ghana. (Agyette 2007)

Although the dance ensemble had helped this individual to adopt and appreciate a national identity, his later comments illustrate that his ethnic affiliation remained strong. "When I first joined the ensemble," he continued, "I always came early to come learn my own hometown dances first – to learn *kpanlogo,* to learn *gome,* to learn *kpatsa.* Because it would be a shame if someone asked me my ethnic group, and I say, 'I am a Ga,' and then they say, 'Do something from your area' and you can't. So I just thought it would be wise to learn my traditional dance first." Many other past and present GDE members' remarks also pointed to the strong ethnic affiliation that remained as they adopted a national identity. For instance, when I asked a former female member of the GDE if she felt differently when she performed other Ghanaian dances outside her self-proclaimed Ga heritage, she stated, "I feel mine more than other Ghana dances" (Abua 2007). Similarly, one Ewe ex-member stated, "Because I am an Ewe I need to feel mine. I feel all, but let me say I feel Ewe's [dances] more than the different tribes" (Mensah 2007).

Overall, musicians and dancers have noted that participation in the GDE has been a transformative experience. Yet, while ensemble members have frequently crossed ethnic boundaries by performing a mosaic of Ghanaian dances, nearly all noted that they were strongly linked to particular dances that were associated with their own self-identified ethnicity. In short, while Ghanaians strive to form a collective identity, they remain a collection of individuals (see Dumont 1970). National unity or unification, in other words, although embodied through similar processes by members of the GDE, is experienced subjectively as each uniquely situated individual negotiates and creates his or her own identity through music and dance. That is, while national unity is predicated on the adoption of a collective identity and identification with others, it is paradoxically *subjectively embodied* as it is reconciled with a participant's unique set of memories, identities, and ontologies – including bodily ways of being-in-the-world. Consequently, the meanings and manifestations of ideologies such as African Personality, Pan-African-ism, and others employed in the pursuit of uniting Africans/Ghanaians are individualized as they are brought into contact with the conscious-ness and bodies of particular participants. Thus, ethnicity (and national identity) is not merely a "mode of consciousness" (Comaroff and Coma-roff 1992, 54) that encompasses a "subjective belief in a common descent" (Weber 1968, 389) but is better understood as a *practice* of embodiment, often employed strategically here as a way to manage nationalism.

COMPETING UTOPIAS: CHOREOGRAPHING UNITY AND COMPARTMENTALIZING ETHNICITY

As people have moved throughout West Africa over centuries, there has been an abundance of cultural contact and exchange through trade, conflict, intermarriage, and travel. Such fluidity defies the imagined, or invented, notion of a circumscribed "tribe" or "ethnicity" in Africa that was largely imposed, or at least encouraged, by colonial rule and early anthropological studies.[13] Within Ghana, the fluidity of social boundar-ies is evidenced in the ways in which locals have adopted and merged nu-merous cultural traditions from their neighbors, including borrowings of language,[14] foodways, folklore,[15] music, and dance. However, within the GDE, even as artists go beyond their own ethnic identities, the troupe as a whole has predominantly staged ethnicity in a compartmentalized fashion. Dances are classified and presented as belonging to only one ethnic group. In prefaces to written programs and in live announce-ments, each dance is attributed to a particular ethnic group – for ex-ample, the Ewe agbadza, the Akan *kete,* and so on. This representational practice conceals, for example, that there are Ewe and Ga versions of the Asante *fontomfrom* and kete, or that the Asante and Ewe have a long tradition of borrowing musical instruments, rhythms, and dance from northern groups such as the Dagbamba. While the ethnic affiliations of dances presented by the GDE are often based on the dominant group that performs these traditions, such staging practices serve to reduce the complexities and cross-pollination of these dance/music traditions. Such practices appear to undermine one of the major goals of the ensem-ble – unification across ethnic lines – as they obfuscate the long contact between diverse communities and reify outmoded notions of bounded (African) "tribal" groups.

The performance practices of the GDE have, since its inception, overwhelmingly reaffirmed such compartmentalization. As one dancer explained, "Opoku was a traditional man" (Atsikpa 2006a) who was often conservative in his approach to working with cultural forms, despite ironically creating new ways of representing Ghanaian music and dance on the theatrical stage, which required innovative modification to these traditions (see chapter 2). Opoku's conservative side was reflected in his position regarding the ethnic mixing of various dance forms. An interview with one of the original members of the ensemble, who is also well known for his recordings of Ghanaian musical fusions,[16] reveals this position. Mustapha Tettey Addy first began to experiment with "polyethnic" musical arrangements while in the GDE. When I asked about this creative endeavor, he explained, "I started making my own music. I took pieces from Akan music and Ewe music and put them together. [Opoku] didn't like it. He told the boys, 'Don't dance like Mustapha is teaching you'" (Addy 2007). And when I asked about the responses from others, he added, "Everybody loved it, except Opoku. All my friends liked it. Even Prof. [Nketia] liked it." Did Addy's re-arrangements (as he calls them) not reflect the spirit of pluralistic national unity that the ensemble sought to propagate? It seemed contradictory that a dance ensemble that stood for tradition as well as creativity (Nketia [1967] 1993, 14) while working to build trans-ethnic solidarity would condemn this type of expression.

As several state ensemble members told me, however, Opoku did not approve of mixing the various ethnic styles into one piece. E. A. Duodu, an original member of the GDE who eventually became its artistic director for several years in the 1990s, in particular remarked, "Opoku didn't like to combine. Like you are dancing adowa [Asante] and in the middle of it you do agbadza [Ewe]. He hated it" (2007). Opoku kept dances separated by ethnicity to display and retain their distinctiveness. Unity was therefore merely choreographed through the performance of several different ethnic dances on a single program and not through their direct interaction. Even when Opoku choreographed pieces that combined a number of dances, they were all from the same area. For example, his

Akan Ceremonial Dance Suite (PURL 1.2) comprised only the Asante kete and fontomfrom, the *Anlo Dance Medley* was a combination of only Ewe pieces, and his *Lamentation for Freedom Fighters,* while highly respected as an innovative creative dance-drama,[17] did not overtly cross ethnic lines, using only the Ewe *husago* and *atsia.*

Such action by Opoku set a precedent that has largely endured, as the GDE's "traditional" repertoire continues to be staged as distinct ethnic dances. Consequently, like the lines on the 1960 census map, the GDE acts as a normalizing mechanism of the state, which seeks to "obliterate the fuzziness of communities" (Chatterjee 1993, 227) as it creates and performs an idealistic cartography of ethnicity. Ironically, in this way the state seems to undermine its push for an overall unitary identity, downplaying the history of interethnic exchange that has taken place in Ghana and Africa. Within the GDE, as Homi Bhabha states, "the separation of totalized cultures . . . live unsullied by the intertextuality of their historical locations, safe in a Utopianism of a mythic memory of a unique cultural identity" (1994, 34). Through the dance ensemble the Ghanaian postcolonial state "domesticates diversity" (Edmondson 2007, 50), placing a yoke on culture, and cultural diversity, asserting its control over the complex pluralism of the nation. As such, diversity is disempowered – rendered docile and nonthreatening and even transformed into an obedient element of the nation to be harnessed and mobilized as needed. Moreover, by creating an imaginary compartmentalization of ethnic traditions while celebrating their connectedness, the state is able to highlight its accomplishments as a unifying political force, diminishing the cultural work of its citizens. In short, by exaggerating ethnic difference, the state renders unification, for which it often claims credit, a more profound achievement.

Despite the GDE's perpetuation of rigid ethnic boundaries within its "traditional" repertoire, within other segments of its catalog, artistic directors have increasingly created single choreographic works that combine dances from multiple ethnic groups. In 1976, Francis Nii-Yartey became the GDE's artistic director who brought about some significant changes in regard to the staging of ethnicity. While his early dance-drama *The Lost Warrior* followed Opoku's lead by using only Ewe dances, Nii-Yartey soon began to experiment more freely, incorporating a diverse mix of ethnic styles into one piece. It is important to note that this type of artistic ethnic integration occurred only within a genre referred to as "contemporary African dance" or "creative dance." As he explained, "I just loved everything. I pull from everything, and that's the way I work. I use what I call compatibilities. If I take this and that, I don't know how I do it, but I always find a way to bridge the two of them" (2006). Nii-Yartey's contemporary work has become renowned throughout Ghana and the world for its innovative combination of local and global elements. Yet debate has continued over the appropriateness of combining various ethnic traditions into one piece. Some choreographers have refused to create ethnic hybrids, claiming it adulterates these traditions, while others freely use their artistic license to re/arrange a diverse cross-section of influences into one expressive statement.

The current director of the GDE (at Legon), Benjamin Obido Ayettey, is one of the latter types. In the summer of 2005, while observing a rehearsal one afternoon, I saw a dance performed that I could not recognize as a "traditional" form. The piece began with the Ewe drums as three male dancers came from stage right, performing the agbekor movements; they abruptly stopped. The fontomfrom drums of the Akan quickly answered the Ewe performance with a series of drum language praises as the Akan dancers imitated a chief dancing for a few moments, and then they soon halted. The Ewe drums then resumed, and the two ensembles continued in this call-and-response manner for another few minutes, creating a drama of tension between the two groups. The drummers and dancers were playing and moving in such a way as to try to outdo one another. They were in effect creating a rhythmic/dancing battle scene. Then to my astonishment, the two ensembles began to play simultaneously. The overlapping Akan and Ewe rhythms were extremely complex, yet they did not sound chaotic. The piece was structured in such a way so that the pulses were aligned, creating a harmony of rhythm. However, the dancers did not share this unity and continued to dance their respective dances in a confrontational way, becoming increasingly aggressive toward one another and drawing ever nearer to the other side. Eventually the opposing sides collided in dance, knocking each other down, and the music abruptly ended. With dramatic flair, the fallen dancers then slowly came to their feet. They acted worn and tired but nonetheless as though they were going to fight – this time, however, without the use of dance movement. Just as they were about to contact one another, a woman carrying a bundle of straw stepped in from off-stage and separated the two groups. Coming to the front of the stage, she took a single piece of straw and broke it in half. Then she put the bundle together again and gave it to a male Akan dancer. She motioned for him to try to break the bundle. He tried, kneeling down and giving it his all, but he could not break the collection of straw. An Ewe dancer then attempted the same feat and also failed. The two groups of male dancers acted as though they were pondering the significance of this exercise. They eventually came to the realization that because the straw was together, it retained its strength. The Akan and Ewe drums then began to play simultaneously as the dancers taught each other their respective dances, and they all danced in harmony with one another.

The obvious lesson of strength in unity dramatized by this creative choreography illustrated an Akan proverb/folktale, which uses the metaphor of the bundle of straw to teach tolerance. Ayettey's "contemporary" choreography, consequently, was intended, he said, "to bring politicians together . . . or to bring anybody together" (2005). The dance reinforced the notion that various, seemingly distinct "ethnic" groups in Ghana should go "beyond" their ethnicity in the spirit of unity, creating national and international solidarity. Thus, Ayettey called the dance simply *Peace and Unity* and publicly debuted the piece in 2007 during Ghana's celebration marking fifty years of independence.

Regarding the GDE's creative/contemporary dance-drama repertoire, while some Ghanaians still maintain that dance styles from differing ethnic areas should not be directly combined onstage, this view appears to be increasingly in the minority, as Nii-Yartey, Ayettey, and other contemporary Ghanaian choreographers have readily fused ethnic styles into singular artistic works. While ethnic tensions may still exist in Ghana, these choreographic works offer a powerful utopian imagery of national unity intended to inspire distinct groups to put aside their differences in the spirit of mutual cooperation. Within the GDE's contemporary repertoire, the growing integration of various ethnic traditions into singular choreographies not only reflects the subjectivities and politics that have informed the representation of culture in Ghana but also points to a notion that Ghanaians have accepted the pluralism of their nation with increasing ease.

When one views the ensemble's repertoire as a whole, a paradoxical image of the nation emerges. On the one hand, the GDE's "traditional" repertoire has continued to reify ethnic boundedness, countering the cultural fluidity that exists outside the ensemble. Conversely, within the troupe's "creative," "dance-drama," and contemporary African dances, choreographers have exploited their artistic license to create works that depict idealized visions of trans-ethnic unity. Hence, the GDE juxtaposes competing utopias: a "traditional" image of circumscribed ethnicity along with a "contemporary" utopia of unproblematic ethnic integration. Both utopias serve the state's interests because they appear detached from social, political, and historical context. Through dramatic spectacle, the state attempts to "bury history in culture" (Debord 1995, 137). The GDE's dancing utopias conceal ethnic antagonisms, including the ongoing marginalization of northern groups, chieftaincy disputes, armed civil conflict, and the ways in which ethnic rivalry has translated into political party differences (see Tonah 2007).

The GDE's staging of diversity, furthermore, reflects the utopia that is democracy. Although various ethnic groups are represented to differing degrees, such emphasis is often minimized by the overall impression that the GDE is an emblem of the nation as a whole. This effect creates a utopian spectacle of dancing democracy – a depiction of a nation rejoicing in the perfected realization of equal voice and opportunity for all. Compounding such idealism by highlighting the culture of "the people," the dance ensemble simultaneously projects the notion of democratic rule – the power of citizens over the state.

BEYOND GHANA: PERFORMING PAN-AFRICANISM

As Ghana celebrated its freedom from colonial rule on March 6, 1957, Kwame Nkrumah declared, "Our independence is meaningless unless it is linked up with the total liberation of Africa." His statement alludes to his strong advocacy for Pan-Africanism throughout his political career. Kwame Nkrumah certainly did not invent the concept of Pan-Africanism; the seeds of this movement, which sought to unite diverse

African populations across the globe, had been planted long before his birth (see Esedebe 1982). Nevertheless, he was a powerful figure in the post–World War II era. Nkrumah, a "passionate pan-Africanist" (Maillu 2007), organized and attended a number of Pan-African conferences, continually advocating for the union of African states (see Nkrumah 1963). As an initiative of Nkrumah, the GDE has consistently performed Pan-Africanism. However, the ways individuals have interpreted and woven these ideas into the fabric of their own identities has varied. While emphasizing this subjective embodiment of nationalism, the following discussion marks a contribution to the discourse on Pan-Africanism. That is, although scholarship abounds on the topic of Pan-Africanism as a political movement, and even on Kwame Nkrumah's particular brand of it (see S. Asante 2007; Maillu 2007), it is less common to find a discussion of the ways in which this ideology has been artistically put into practice and embodied.[18]

As the "nucleus" of the National Theatre Movement in Ghana, the GDE was an artistic extension and expression of Nkrumah's Pan-African ideals. Speaking about his experience in this ensemble during Nkrumah's presidency, Duodu remembered, "In those days, 'this ethnic group is superior to that.' Nkrumah tried to kill that kind of tribalism and nepotism. And, whether you are Nigerian or Malian, you are the same people. And the dance ensemble projected this" (2007). One of the ways the ensemble "projected" this sentiment was by incorporating a number of pieces from outside Ghana. A book about the GDE published in the 1960s, for instance, lists a Nigerian dance called *ijaw,* while the *Dahomey Dance Suite I* and *Dahomey Dance Variations* listed therein are both based on cultural material from this ancient kingdom, presently known as Benin. Additionally, I have found pictures from the 1960s of the dance ensemble performing Togo atsia (which was still performed regularly during my fieldwork) (PURL 1.3). This, however, was the extent of the GDE's "Pan-African" repertoire at the time. Furthermore, after examining the same set of the ensemble's programs listed above (1965–80s), it was clear that while the Dahomean dances were performed with relative frequency, the ijaw was a rare sight in Ghana. Nketia explained this limitation by stating that "there were always problems, because when you do it you need the music and then you need the musicians.

And there is a limit to the budget" (2005). In other words, pragmatic obstacles prevented the ensemble from being more Pan-African.

Over the years, the company's inclusion of African dances outside Ghana has grown only slightly, but the Pan-African spirit of the ensemble has not necessarily diminished. Since the 1990s, Nii-Yartey has collaborated with a number of choreographers from the African diaspora. For instance, Nii-Yartey co-choreographed the piece *Images of Conflict* with Germaine Acogny from Benin/Senegal. Additionally, a piece titled *Musu* was co-created with Monty Thomson from the U.S. Virgin Islands. This piece draws on the experiences of African slavery and has undoubtedly resonated with individuals throughout the diaspora as it has been performed on numerous international tours. Additionally, many of Nii-Yartey's choreographies have incorporated dance styles and music from the African community writ large (for example, *Solma, Sal-Yeda*). Moreover, both Nii-Yartey and Ayettey often use Afro-pop music (for example, Baba Maal, Youssou N'Dour, and so on) from various African countries as accompaniment for their "contemporary" pieces, as evidenced in *The Map* choreography discussed at the beginning of this chapter.

More recently, the GDE (at Legon) had learned the *dumba* from a Senegalese dancer brought to the university in 2005. Within this dance piece, the *djembe* drum, which has West African roots but is not of Ghanaian origin (see Charry 1996), is used. According to participants, the ensemble adopted the djembe sometime in the late 1980s or early 1990s. Since this time, the GDE has increasingly incorporated it into its contemporary choreographies and occasionally has even used it in place of the local kpanlogo (Ga) drums within its "traditional" repertoire. Because this drum has become ubiquitous throughout Africa and the world over the last few decades, it acts as a powerful Pan-African symbol, connecting Ghana to its neighbors in West Africa and the diaspora. Yet the presentation of particular African dance styles from outside Ghana, performed as individual choreographic works within themselves (for example, ijaw, Togo atsia), remains limited. Similar to Nketia's remarks above, Ayettey stated that "the repertoire would probably include more dances from outside Ghana, if the funding was available to bring in specialists to teach at the university or travel outside the country to conduct research more often" (2005). In all, while choreographers have found nu-

merous creative ways to transcend national boundaries and include the
African diaspora, the pragmatic financial situation of the GDE remains
a significant obstacle to achieving an even greater expression of Pan-
Africanism within the ensemble.

Despite the limited scope of its repertoire, the GDE, through its
touring, has reached nearly every corner of the continent and the globe,
performing Pan-Africanism and creating bonds between diasporic populations. In July 1964 Nkrumah commissioned the ensemble to represent Ghana at Malawi's independence celebration, which was its first
performance abroad (Adinku 2000, 133). The following year, Nkrumah,
a leader who adopted many socialist ideas, sent the ensemble on a three-
month tour of Eastern Europe, including Czechoslovakia, East Germany, Hungary, the USSR, and Poland, as part of his "Moscow-oriented
foreign policy" (133). The ensemble later represented Ghana at the first
World Festival of Negro Arts in Dakar in April 1966. Although the GDE's
own written documentation from the late 1960s through the 1980s is
scarce, I was assured by Nii-Yartey and others that the ensemble had
toured "all the corners of Africa and all over the world" (Nii-Yartey
2006).

Beginning at least as early as 1970, the *Spectator,* a weekly newspaper
published in Accra, periodically reported the travels of the GDE. From a
thorough search of these periodicals, coupled with a list of tours printed
in a performance program from the early 1990s, I discovered several
of the international tours on which the ensemble had embarked.[19] In
all, there seems to be a conspicuously small number of African tours
throughout this period (1968–2007), with only two tours of Nigeria, one
of Zimbabwe, and one of Malawi among the more than forty tours sur-
veyed. An overwhelming majority of international touring has been to
the United States and Europe. While this data points to political tensions
within Africa and global economic imbalances, these figures also reveal
that the GDE's performance of Pan-Africanism, in this way, ironically
neglects Africa itself. Nevertheless, the GDE's performances abroad have
undoubtedly reaffirmed and strengthened bonds with diasporic African
populations within Europe, America, and Asia.

The GDE's direct interaction with other African nations seems to
overwhelmingly occur domestically through its performance in Ghana

for visiting dignitaries from neighboring nations. For example, the *Ghana Daily Times* reported that after Major General Yakubu Gowon (the Nigerian head of the federal government and commander-in-chief of the armed forces at the time) had witnessed and participated in a ninety-minute performance of the GDE he remarked, "As far as I am concerned [there] is excellent relation between Nigeria and Ghana" (June 3, 1968). Throughout the history of the GDE, the ensemble has regularly performed for visiting African dignitaries and heads of state. During my field research I accompanied the ensemble on several state dinner performances for African delegations (such as Benin and Togo) (PURL 1.4). Moreover, there were several instances in which the ensemble performed at conferences in Accra of the African Union (AU) – a political body that is a direct outgrowth of Nkrumah's Pan-African ideology.[20] Overall, the dance ensemble has continued to welcome and impress dignitaries with its powerful performances, reaffirming social bonds and aiding in the formation of new alliances between African states.

As the GDE performs Pan-Africanism, artists interpret and embody this ideology as individuals, reconciling these ideological notions of identity with those already held. Given this, to what degree do various performers adopt Pan-Africanism? How strongly do they feel Pan-Africanism in their bodies? When I asked a group of dancers about how it felt to perform other African dances outside Ghana, one remarked, "I am from Ghana, first; I have to remember that, and do my tradition" (Agyari 2007). Another agreed and said, "I just learn mine. I just do mine. I learn Nigerian dance too, but I *feel* Ghana dances more than other African dances" (Abua 2007). Other dancers present nodded in agreement. Generally, many performers I interviewed told me that they preferred Ghanaian dances to those of other African nations. Many noted that, although Guinean dances were extremely popular with ensemble members, they did not necessarily feel "more Pan-African" merely because they performed a few dances from another African country. For individuals, going beyond Ghana often appeared more difficult than transcending ethnic boundaries.

Such comments reveal the subjective nature of embodying African Personality and Pan-Africanism. When I asked the current artistic director how the dance ensemble balances national and transnational identities through performance, his remarks revealed his own emphasis on nationality over a Pan-African identity. While Ben Ayettey stated, "We try to present African unity, not Ghanaian unity; it's African culture that we are portraying," he conceded that "normally when we go outside we don't perform dances from a different [African] country, because we've got to be proud of our country. Other countries sell their material, so we should also sell our material. Because others believe theirs is the best I also believe that mine is the best" (2005). Ayettey affirmed his desire to assert his national identity rather than to explicitly project Pan-Africanism. His assertion, moreover, is responsive, which reminds us that (national) identity and patriotism are relational. Confronted with a social world that is given to him, he sees national pride in others and counters it with his own.

In all, when national and transnational identities are juxtaposed, patriotism emerges as a salient bedrock for the formation of the individual sense of self. While the GDE helps to forge bonds between Africans across the diaspora, the Pan-African repertoire is somewhat limited, and the focus of the ensemble has largely been on the dances of Ghana. As evidenced by performers' comments, national identity has remained stronger in most cases than does a connection with Africa or its diaspora. Much like when people graft new national identities onto ethnic ones, as individuals adopt transnational/pan-African identities, they remain deeply grounded in those already internalized. As a former GDE member told me, "I love Ghana. There's peace and freedom here. It's good to travel to different places to experience different countries, but I like Ghana. It's nice to come home" (Mensah 2007).

EMBODIMENT AND CHAMELEONISM

"Nkrumah never dies" was a popular slogan among his supporters following a series of failed assassination attempts on his life in the early 1960s. His critics claimed that such a declaration encouraged Nkrumah's growing megalomania and autocratic ambitions while reifying the president's reputation as the immortal savior of the nation among his supporters who regularly compared their leader to biblical figures such as Christ and Moses. Deflecting such hyperbolic notions, defenders of this slogan claimed that it was meant to denote only that the ideas and work of Nkrumah would live on, after his mortal end (see Ahlman 2011, 224–27). Affirming this slogan, the GDE since its inception has attempted to propagate Kwame Nkrumah's notion of African Personality, performing nationalism and Pan-Africanism. Attesting to the continued relevance of these ideologies more than forty years after the ensemble's founding, a GDE artist explained in 2006, "African Personality still has a stand, and that stand is our culture, and our culture is our identity. We need to keep our identity. We need to keep our culture. We need to preserve it so that it will become our weapon to fight" (Merigah). For over five decades, the GDE has worked to fulfill its political duty to stage the state's rhetoric of "unity in diversity," encouraging its members and audiences to go beyond their ethnicity and beyond Ghana. As such, Nkrumah's legacy has been immortalized.

Nkrumah's presidency set a precedent for the ways in which ethnicity has been staged by Ghana's national dance ensembles. Successive Ghanaian regimes have done little to shape the groups' general policies and practices in this regard. While the state has encouraged the staff of the ensembles to equitably incorporate the plurality of the nation, aesthetic and pragmatic concerns have often taken precedence within the troupes, resulting in warped refractions of the national citizenry. Artistic utopias of national unity have coexisted alongside outmoded notions of circumscribed ethnicity. Thus, the GDE has acted as both a dynamic mirror and a map – a projected image that reflects the nation's ethnic diversity as it simultaneously invents it, distorts it, reifies it, and reforms it. Thus, through a dancing cadre, the state in/directly domesticates ethnic diversity, enacting a conventional form of instrumental nationalism as it uses the culture of its citizens to promote its ideological agendas.

While the ensemble has sought to promulgate African Personality along with the collectivism it often encourages, this process has ironically been informed by the idiomatic personalities of individuals. That is, performing and embodying nationalism requires an interaction of subjectivities – an intersubjective social process – as artists negotiate the political dynamics between self, nation, and state. Employed by the state to represent its ideologies and the nation writ large, artists in the GDE must reconcile such demands with their own preexisting memories and (corporeal) ontologies, continually negotiating and re/constructing a cohesive sense of self. Therefore, embodying nationalism is somewhat unique for each person; however, it typically involves an expansion of the self as individuals adopt and attempt to mediate multiple senses of self. Thus, members of the GDE are not merely performers of music and dance but are *artists* in that they are "people who can negotiate the inner tensions of these multiple selves and *manage* their antagonistic drives more or less successfully" (Scherzinger 2007, 93; emphasis mine). Managing multiple senses of self, GDE artists often remain *grounded* in those that are older (longer held). When national identity is adopted, ethnic ties often remain strong, and similarly, when a transnational identity such as "African" is adopted, national identity does not disappear but is reaffirmed. Yet the degree to which each artist feels this "groundedness" is mediated by his or her own experiences. It seems paradoxical, then, that the ideology of unity, while generally emphasizing human commonalities and universals, is embodied subjectively.

As nationalism becomes a basis for the construction of self, members of Ghana's state dance ensembles harness its logics and ideologies in personally expedient ways. When performers go beyond ethnicity and beyond Ghana, they enact their "postcolonial subjectivity" wherein a multiplicity of (ethnic) identities are strategically deployed and performed "instrumentally" (Shipley 2003, 130; cf. Mbembe 1992). That is, artists engage in a type of "chameleonism,"[21] in which their ethnic and national identities are often performed in ways that blend into one another and the immediate context. Such "blending in" allows these individuals to capitalize on their talents in both domestic and foreign markets. As one drummer remarked, "Now that I have been trained in all these dances, I can get more work. People, especially foreigners, like to see different dances, not just your home one. The people in the village, they only know their tradition, but me, I know all, so people will hire me more. It is because the audiences don't know that I am Ewe when I play Akan or Dagbamba dances" (A. Amenumey 2007). Ensemble members often remarked that their ability to perform a plethora of Ghanaian and African dance repertoires made them more sought-after as national and international artists. Through their participation in the GDE, provincial drummers and dancers deliberately transform themselves into "Ghana-ian" and "African" cultural experts, learning to strategically embody ethnic identities outside their own or concealing their ethnic affiliations altogether when it is deemed necessary. For instance, Bernard Woma, a former ensemble member from the Upper West region, remarked, "When I am representing Ghana, I don't put on my Dagara traditional hat; I leave it at home so people just see me as Ghanaian" (2013). In a globalized economy, artists like Woma have a distinct advantage over musicians and dancers in local villages/towns. Ensemble performers are often able to appeal to cosmopolitan expectations for variety, while provincial performers are less desirable in such contexts because they are usually able to perform only the traditions into which they are born.

With such a chameleon capacity, ethnicity can be understood not only as a mode of consciousness but also as a "cultural style," that is, "a kind of skilled social action you do with your body" (Ferguson 1999, 98). As GDE artists learn various "ethnic" dances, they gain a performative competency to not merely "wear" (98) another's identity but to inter-nalize it to a convincing degree. Thus, the adoption of another's ethnic tradition is not merely mimicry but is rendered a powerful source of in-dividual agency. While acquiring the ability to embody multiple ethnic styles, GDE performers additionally learn to deploy them in ways that suit their needs. In all, chameleonism serves as a type of tactical artistry for managing nationalism whereby artists strategically enact various cultural styles in their pursuit of personal ambitions.

TWO

Dancing Essences

*Sensational Staging and the Cosmopolitan
Politics of Authentication*

THE ESSENCE OF NATIONALISM

On the evening of November 11, 1967, during the official inauguration, or outdooring,[1] of the Ghana Dance Ensemble, Professor Kwabena Nketia addressed a crowd at the Institute of African Studies on the campus of the University of Ghana, Legon. Toward the conclusion of his speech he stated:

> We have approached our task as a creative experiment. We have tried not only to learn and teach the dances as they are done in the villages, but also face the problem of presentation in the new context of the theatre, to work out a form of presentation which highlights and clarifies the *essential* forms of the dances without destroying their basic movements and styles, their emotional, spiritual and cultural values or their vitality and vigor. In this respect, we have tried to use as our yardstick the comments and criticisms of experts in our villages and towns who helped us all along to spot and crystallize the *essential* qualities that are looked for in our dances. ([1967] 1993, 13; emphasis mine)

Nketia's remarks alluded to the ensemble's modern quest, or "longing" (Bendix 1997), for authenticity and to the challenges associated with it.[2] The GDE's staff sought to give performative expression to an "objectively definable *essence* or core of customs and beliefs" (Linnekin 1991, 446; cf. Handler 1986; Handler and Linnekin 1984), upon which the nation and the state could rest their legitimacy. Like Johann Herder, who argued that the "authentic spirit [read essence] of a people" was to be found in "the folk's natural poetry," Kwame Nkrumah (and other such cultural nationalists)[3] mobilized and modified cultural forms of the masses/non-elites (or folk) to reflect the essence of his nation. In this way, Nkrumah and the GDE used a type of "strategic essentialism" to create an "aura of uniformity" (Gaard 2001, 17), which reinforced the unifying ideologies of African Personality and Pan-Africanism.

Because nationalism is a cosmopolitan phenomenon of modernity, the ensemble's dances had to appeal not only to provincial experts but also to the global community. Particularly, the GDE needed to create cultural forms that would highlight local traditions in order to carve out an identity for Ghana that was both unique and recognizable to its citizens while developing new artistic forms that resonated with international audiences and the aesthetics of the theatre. To mediate these modern/traditional, global/local, "village"/stage dialectics, Ghana, like other nations, relied on the concept of modernist reformism, which "refers to projects based on the idea that a 'new culture' . . . should be forged as a synthesis of the 'best' or 'most valuable' aspects of local 'traditional' culture and 'the best' of foreign 'modern' lifeways and technologies" (Turino 2000, 16). Nations employ this modernist reformism to persuade individuals to believe in the nation; particularly, states rely on its *cosmopolitan aesthetic* practices that encourage the production of "spectacularized" forms of culture, which appeal to the senses and sensibilities of domestic and foreign audiences.[4] This particular process of aesthetic transformation is what I call *sensational staging.*

Exploring this concept, this chapter demonstrates that in order to convince Ghanaians and others of the cosmopolitan ideologies of African Personality and Pan-Africanism, Nkrumah and the GDE relied on such aesthetic ideals and practices. Nkrumah often appropriated a wide variety of cultural symbols to disempower local leaders as well as to legitimize the nation and his own leadership (see chapter 4). As part of this political strategy, the GDE attempted to identify and use the "best" or "most valuable" features of "traditional" culture to represent the essential core of "the people," which would consequently serve as the basis for a viable, "authentic," and distinct nation. These political ideologies, however, also acknowledged that despite its detrimental effects, Western culture, nevertheless, had a profound impact on Africa and thus could not be entirely dismissed. Moreover, if Ghana was to be recognized as a "modern," "civilized" nation in the eyes of the contemporary global community, local traditions needed to be reformed to meet such expectations. The first section of this chapter will examine the ways in which the GDE "preserved" the "essential core" of various cultural forms as it sensationally staged dances to appeal to the aesthetic demands of cosmopolitan audiences.

As the essences of cultural forms were derived and manipulated to suit these expectations, the "best" and "most valuable" portions were selected and spectacularized, inevitably leaving out significant pieces of these forms while altering and exaggerating others. Both performers and audiences, consequently, experienced commodified, essentialized, dramatized, nationalized, staged cultural forms that resembled those found in local communities but were not quite familiar. Thus, dances were subjected to a rigorous process of verification by both Ghanaians and foreigners as the authenticity of these "new" forms often came into question. As such, while social scientists often distrust discourses of essentialism, it is paradoxically precisely because of such essentialist discourses embedded within modernist reformism that authenticity emerges as a salient issue of debate for locals (and scholars).[5]

To explore this debate, rather than adopt an outmoded objectivist approach to authenticity, which claims that authenticity is inherent in cultural objects, I follow constructivists (see Handler 2002; Hobsbawm and Ranger 1983) who locate authenticity in social discourse. More specifically, I build on Clifford Geertz's statement that "it is the copying that originates," (1986, 380), which, as Barbara Kirshenblatt-Gimblett notes, "shifts the focus away from authenticity and toward the problem of *authentication*" (1988, 62; emphasis mine). Such a perspective moves the analytical lens from the cultural products and instead raises questions about the sociopolitical process of authenticating, highlighting the individuals who engage in such practices. Particularly, as Kirshenblatt-Gimblett continues, "How do some representations become authoritative? Who needs authenticity and why? How has authenticity been used?" (62). Or, how is the discourse of authenticity *managed* for political and personal ends? And how is this discourse further linked to the construction of satisfying and meaningful lives? Such questions align my study with those who ask, "Who has the power to represent whom and to determine which representation is authentic?" (Kirshenblatt-Gimblett and Bruner 1992, 304).[6] Exploring these questions reveals that power within the GDE is an idiomatic combination of local and global markers and practices of authority and status, which I refer to as *cosmopolitan modes of power*. In short, this chapter illustrates how cosmopolitan aesthetics inform a sensational staging that is, in turn, upheld, or authenticated, by these cosmopolitan modes of power.

Yet this discussion goes beyond the political discourse surrounding the authentication of cultural forms to explore how such interaction relates to the modern existential quest for a "felt authentic grounding" (see Lindholm 2002). Modernity has produced a debate of the authenticity not only of culture but of our own lives – our existence. Lionel Trilling states, "That the word [authenticity] has become part of the moral slang of our day points to the peculiar nature of our fallen condition, our anxiety over the credibility of existence and of individual existences" (1972, 93). This existential anxiety has been linked directly to the modern practices of mass production, consumption, and media as well as to the modern intellectual emphasis on the social construction of reality (see Berger and Luckmann 1966; Berman [1982] 1988) and the increasingly pervasive presence of simulacra and simulation (Baudrillard 1994). When all that was once thought solid "melts into air,"[7] it is not surprising that individuals may feel anxious about the authenticity of their own existence.

The final section of this chapter explores how individuals mediate this anxiety and create meaningful lives within the "constructedness" of their lifeworlds. I build on the work of Mattijs van de Port, who has recently asked, "For what is beyond the constructedness of things?" (2004, 8). Per his intellectual query, this chapter illustrates "how . . . people manufacture and maintain a sense of authentic grounding . . . [and] describes and analyzes . . . the techniques and the resources that people have at their disposal to *believe,* in the sense of taking things as true" (10). Thus, rather than compartmentalize questions about authenticity into those concerned with experience and those regarding the authenticity of an object (see Handler 2002), I merge the two, suggesting that the perceived authenticity of cultural objects informs a sense of authenticity that people *feel*. Broadly, I ask: How do individuals find authentic grounding when confronted with explicit artistic constructions of culture? Or, how is authenticity *managed* as part of self-making within a national institution? What tactics are used, and how?

STAGING ESSENCE: THE SENSATIONAL TRANSFORMATION
OF "TRADITIONAL" GHANAIAN DANCE

Members and staff of the GDE generally identify three categories of
dances that make up the ensemble's repertoire. These are (1) "dance-
dramas," which liberally use foreign and theatrical elements to construct
a narrative through music and movement; (2) "creative"/"contemporary"[8] dances, which combine dance and music from a variety of local
and global (often Western) influences to develop dances in new artistic directions; and (3) "traditional" dances, which are overtly based on
preexisting dance forms. The two former types – "dance-dramas" and
"creative" – do not use names already in practice in local communities
as their titles. Thus, dances in these two categories often avoid derision,
because they make no implications that they faithfully represent the culture of local communities. These two dance types will be discussed more
fully in subsequent chapters. The GDE's "traditional" dance repertoire,
however, is of particular interest here because it explicitly references local practices by using preexisting material and names. As such, the GDE's
"traditional" repertoire implicitly claims to preserve the "essence" of a
dance, inviting debate regarding its authenticity.[9] Before moving to a
examination of how these "traditional" dances have been received – both
lauded and criticized – by local and international audiences, it is important to understand how they were transformed in order to appreciate the
subsequent discussion of the assessments made by various individuals.

 "Traditional" dances found in local communities, author Krista Fabian notes, "have to suit the needs of modern contexts to survive in urban and international markets" (1996, 15). With the modernist reformism
brought about through nationalism, traditional dances, in other words,
have to undergo various degrees of transformation in order to resonate
with the sensibilities of both local and global audiences – that is, "cosmopolitan aesthetics" (Turino 2000, 16). This typically results in abridged
dances, which overemphasize emotionally charged dramatic features
such as sexual gestures, crying, excitement, and aggression. Moreover,
with certain dances, stage presentations deemphasize the religious aspects, shifting the performance's intention from spiritual efficacy to

secular entertainment (see Thram 1999). Often movements are also emboldened – subtle gestures are made more pronounced in order to be perceived on a large stage, which is often far from a non-participatory audience that is frequently unfamiliar with the idiosyncrasies of local dances. These audiences, furthermore, may have certain stereotyped images and expectations for the performance, which choreographers regularly play into. The challenge for the artistic director becomes how to "preserve the essence" of these dances while simultaneously developing them for new artistic expression (Adinku 2000, 131). In all, this section illustrates how choreographers of the GDE have managed to preserve the essence of various dance forms while spectacularizing and sensationalizing them to appeal to diverse audiences.

When I asked Patience Kwakwa, a founding member of the GDE, about the general choreographic process of Mawere Opoku, she stated,

> He just wanted to see how best he could present the dances on stage. You see, some movements you can just do anyhow, when you are at a festival or a gathering or whatever. But once you take it to the stage you have to think of the artistic content of what you are doing. And so he was always conscious of what would be *artistically pleasing*. And you know he was a painter and a sculptor. So lines made a very real impression on him. . . . Opoku looked for movements that were very exciting, which would catch the eye of the audience. So he had to select. He selected the most exciting ones. (2006)

Opoku was formally trained as a visual artist, was well known for his sketches of dancers, and even taught art classes at the Kwame Nkrumah University of Science and Technology. He also studied staging and choreography in the United States and Britain. Therefore, he choreographed dances with his artistically developed eye, using his knowledge of line, shape, and form. With the GDE and the stage as his canvas, Opoku "painted" artful spectacles of Ghana's dances. Yet, as a person born into a royal Akan family and thus steeped in the formal traditions of the Asante, he was also keenly aware that dances had to retain certain features – their "essence" – to remain relevant and recognizable to local audiences. In all, Opoku staged dances with a cosmopolitan eye, merging sensibilities drawn from a wide palette of provincial and foreign sources.

"Basic" Rhythms and Movements and Time Compression

As Opoku transformed local cultural forms through his artistic cosmopolitan eye, he attempted to ensure that the essences of these dances
remained intact within his choreographies. Former GDE director E. A.
Duodu explained:

> The traditional movements are there; Opoku did not necessarily choreograph
> them but rearranged them. It's merely a reorganizing, because *adowa* is adowa.
> [Basic movements] should be there to recognize it as adowa. So [choreogra-
> phers] will maintain certain elements. . . . The basic movements are there. It is
> the basic movements that will identify the dance – the essence of the dances.
> What distinguishes adowa from *agbadza*? It's the basic movement of the hand
> that distinguishes adowa from agbadza. (2007) (PURL 2.1 and PURL 2.2)

Similarly, when I asked about the essence of the *bamaaya* dance, Kofi
Gademeh – a former member of the GDE and local choreographer/leader
of a culture group – told me, "You don't choreograph bamaaya and take
the shaking of the waist out. Still you have to shake the waist. If you go
to the north and you don't shake the waist, they will slap you" (2005)
(PURL 2.3). Underscoring this point, a senior member of the National
Dance Company remarked, "We can change the movements small, and
it's okay. You have a style for agbadza and you have to do something that
agrees with agbadza. If you do this, [demonstrates standard agbadza
movements] is fine, but if you start doing this [demonstrates a very common *kpanlogo* movement] it [does] not agree with agbadza" (Atsikpa
2006a). Opoku and his staff were aware of the appropriate (basic) movements and music for each dance they staged, carefully conserving them
to preserve the dance's integrity and essence. Yet Opoku often chose
only the most "exciting" movements – those that he deemed to be the
most visually appealing; his decisions in this regard significantly contributed to the sensationalization of his staged versions.

While identifying the basic elements of various "traditional" dances
was part of a strategy to preserve their essence, dances were simultaneously significantly abridged to meet one of the temporal expectations
of post/modernity – "time compression." As described by David Harvey
(1989), time compression is a byproduct of modern capitalist production
and informs contemporary social existence. As the pace of the social

world has seemingly hastened with the advent of various technological advances in manufacturing, communication, and transportation, cultural forms and aesthetics have been re-imagined to meet these new expectations of modernity (see Urban 2001). Duodu commented on this time compression during an interview with Katharina Schramm, stating, "What we did was to take the nice movements. . . . We selected and condensed it, made it compact, aesthetically excellent, acceptable. So that within five minutes you can see all the essentials, the best that [the dance] can offer" (qtd. in Schramm 2000, 39). Illustrating Opoku's awareness of time restraints, I discovered several GDE programs in which he had marked the duration of each dance choreography (PURL 2.4). David Amoo, director of the NDC since 2007, further explained that

> [in] *kete* [Akan royal dance] they can perform one movement for about fifteen minutes. Sometimes [in the village] you see some of the movements are similar, so why should you do this? It's repetition. See, we [NDC] can sum up all these movements in about fifteen minutes. So ours is more interesting than that of the traditional setup, because they relax, they don't have a time limit. They know the whole day is for them to dance. So maybe they [in the village] can do more movements, improvisations, and variations. (2006) (PURL 2.5)

In many cases, the repetition of movements is seen as "boring" and is thus discarded to create a compact spectacle comprising only the dance's "best" qualities; that is, dances are staged with modernist reformist principles to simultaneously highlight the dance's essence and excite the senses within a limited temporal frame.

Time compression was taken to an extreme on March 7, 2007 (one day after the celebration of Ghana's Independence Day) as the dance ensemble participated in *Beating the Retreat*. This ceremony dates to the sixteenth century and was "originally used in order to recall patrolling units to their castle."[10] As explained in the event program, "These days, most Armed Forces of the commonwealth perform some ceremonial form of the retreat . . . used as a . . . test for new band members." After welcoming the Duke of Kent and President J. A. Kufuor, the sparse crowd at Independence Square, weary from the previous day's celebrations, watched as Ghana's military band paraded around the infield performing a series of exercises while sounding their brass and percussion instruments. When the band concluded, after about twenty minutes, a voice boomed over the loudspeakers, "We will now be treated to some cultural performances by the Ghana Dance Ensemble." As three female and three male performers danced their way into the large open square, the announcer said, addressing the president and the duke, "Your Excellencies, the first dance is called *agbekor* and is from the Volta region." The dancers performed the "turning"[11] refrain as the brass band played an instrumental arrangement of an agbekor vocal melody. After a brief sampling of this dance, which lasted no more than two minutes, these dancers made their way offstage as another group of GDE performers started a new dance – "the *kundum* from the Western Region," the announcer told the crowd. Several dances followed in this fashion – adowa, *gome,* and finally bamaaya – each announced with its corresponding region and lasting only for approximately two minutes. The ensemble adhered to a strict timetable because several other performances were scheduled that day (PURL 2.6).

While embodying the principles of modernist reformism and sensational staging, *Beating the Retreat* dramatically collapsed time and space as it demonstrated the importance of identifying the "basic" movements and musical aspects of a dance in order to meet the temporal demands of post/modernity. On a day that celebrated Ghana's national unity, the desire to showcase "all the cultures" of the nation seemed an apt ideal. In practice, due to the restraints of the postmodern context, this representation occurred in a concise manner, resulting in "hyper"-compressed, highly essentialized versions of dances. In a type of performative synecdoche, one or two movements stood for an entire dance, an ethnicity, and a region or even several regions. For instance, the waist shaking of the bamaaya, a Dagbamba dance, represented the several northern regions of Ghana that day, since no other northern dances were included on the program. In this way, "a certain repertory of markers was sufficient to function emblematically, reinforcing the spectators' sense that they were somehow gaining access to the essence of a culture or nation" (Arkin and Smith 1997, 35–36).

Witnessing such an array of dances in one performance, moreover, is a spectacular sight to behold as it jars the senses and keeps audiences engaged with quick changes of pace, costume, and scenery. In all, this strategic essentializing, or compression, contributes to the production of an "authentic" sensational staging of culture, appealing to the senses in order to convince individuals that they are experiencing the most important features of a larger "imagined community" (see Anderson [1983] 1989). By engaging in these "authentic" performances and sensational experiences, Ghanaians are encouraged to transcend various social (and cultural, that is, ethnic) boundaries and to embody a *feeling* of connectedness to the nation as a whole. This embodied *sense* of community goes beyond mere imagining and in turn acts as one way in which individuals mediate the anxiety of modern existence.

Bigger, Faster, Louder!

Appealing to cosmopolitan sensibilities, Opoku and other GDE artistic directors have attempted to reform Ghana's dances to render them more "exciting." This objective has translated into the aesthetics of bigger, faster, and louder. To make dances "bigger," Opoku often enlarged or emboldened movements of dances. As dances moved from smaller community settings to stages in ballrooms, auditoriums, and stadiums, the audiences became physically farther away from the performers, making it necessary to enlarge movements. Opoku and other GDE choreographers consequently had to learn how to adapt Ghana's dances to these large spaces. Duodu, who as artistic director rearranged some of the ensemble's repertoire in the 1990s, explained, "I took Togo *atsia* [Ewe dance] and used seven people. Before, the company performed only Opoku's version with only three dancers. I realized that with three people dancing in a big auditorium, you don't see much" (2007). Not only were movements made "bigger," but the dances as a whole often increased in size by the addition of performers in order to fill large spaces, which resulted in a multiplication of action onstage. As one dancer summarized, "You see, when you have big movements and lots of dancers on stage, it makes the [dances] more interesting, more exciting. You see that sometimes ours are even more exciting than the ones they have in the village" (Akowian 2006). Ensemble directors implicitly have understood larger movements as more visually appealing to diverse contemporary audiences and have bombarded them with intensified spectacular imagery reminiscent of large-scale Broadway, Hollywood, or Bollywood productions, all of which have influenced the ensembles' choreographers.[12]

Incorporating a cosmopolitan auditory aesthetic, "excitement" is also often equated with increased tempos. Zachariah Abdellah, a griot from northern Ghana, commented on the GDE's version of a dance of his home area: "When the ensemble performs *damba sochandi*, they don't start with the slow procession – with the sochandi. They start with the damba proper, which is faster, and they play it too fast. The dance should be cool [slow and relaxed]" (2005)[13] (PURL 2.7).

Similarly recognizing the GDE's hastening of tempos, Apetsi Amenumey, a former master drummer of this state troupe, offered a vivid example of how performing in the ensemble affected his ability to perform in village settings:

> Apetsi: Everything is changing, changing. If you go to Bukom [Ga traditional area] and see the real kpanlogo there, they will sing the Ga songs, and they will say that we [the dance ensemble] are playing it too fast. I remember one time my group is performing at a funeral, and I hear this group, with some of the old fishermen. They are singing the songs. So I stop what I am doing and go listen to them. I understand the songs because I speak Ga, but some of the songs I hadn't heard before. I wanted to play with them, but I can't because my hand will be moving too fast and people will say, "Oh *chale*" [sighs].
>
> Paul: But couldn't you just slow your speed down?
>
> Apetsi: I can, but I can't sustain it. Because I have been playing the fast one in the ensemble [GDE], that is what my hand is used to. I remember one time some people hired my amateur culture group to come and play agbadza, and this old man comes and tells me I am playing too fast. But the music is already going, so I don't know how to bring it down. So I had to stop the music. The old ones were saying, "Do you want to break our waist or something?" It's because I am playing the [dance ensemble] way. We've been playing fast agbekor and all these things we put inside. So I use the same feeling to play for them [the "old ones"]. I forget that it's not my culture group I am performing for, and I am playing for so many different people to dance [not just young people as in the culture group]. So we come back and we play a slower way; we [the culture group] don't really feel it, but they [the "old ones"] like it more. (2006)

Like Amenumey, many in the GDE have *embodied* the new cosmopolitan aesthetic of speed, playing faster tempos both in and outside of the ensemble.

The final part of this tripartite aesthetic framework is volume, or musical dynamics. Almost daily during my fieldwork one of the senior drummers in the ensemble, who often refused to participate in rehearsals, mentioned to me that the master drummer was playing too loudly. He repeatedly told me, "You see, you should be able to hear the supporting drums, the bell, and the rattle. Everything should be clear. But the drummers here cover all that. They play too loud" (Zigah 2007). Amenumey corroborated these remarks: "The dancers [in the GDE] like when I play, because if it's 45 [referring to volume], I play 45; I don't play 65. Sometimes [the current master drummer] plays too loud, and I have to tell him to come down. I say, because of your muscles, you have to learn to control yourself. Sometimes Opoku will say, 'Hey, you are making noise!' So it came to some point that [this master drummer] was playing level" (2006).

Yet the ability to play loudly can be an advantage. Master drummers in the GDE often have to play with extreme volume so that the dancers can hear their cues in large spaces such as auditoriums and stadiums. The challenge for individual artists is to manage their bodies (muscles) in order to perform appropriately to meet the various aesthetic demands of each context.

Dramatizing Dance

To present Ghana's dances in a more "interesting and exciting" manner, Opoku and subsequent GDE choreographers often added dramatic elements to their "basic" movements and music. When I asked one former ensemble dancer about how Opoku transformed traditional dance, he recalled the director's rearrangement of an Akan social dance known as *sikyi*. He explained that "the real sikyi dance is not a story. They [in the village] do not put it in a story form. It's just something small, to entertain, like kpanlogo [Ga social dance]. The three of us can get together and just start playing. For sikyi, people will be playing and one dancer will come for a solo. It's like a solo dance; let's take it like that. But Opoku has turned it into a drama – a dance-drama. It talks about love" (Azadekor 2007). "So they don't do the drama in the Asante region?" I asked. "They don't know anything like that!" he exclaimed. "That time [sikyi] was very deep in the village, and they don't even know what is theatre work" (ibid.). Sikyi began in the 1920s and flourished in the

1950s – around Ghana's independence movement. It was a flirtatious social dance performed by Asante youth, but in the Asante region it was performed in an ad hoc fashion, with male participants inviting females to dance according to their own desires. It has a few "basic" movements that can be performed in any sequence according to the will of the participants and does not include an explicit story line. Witnessing this dance in his hometown, Opoku became particularly fond of it and decided to add an explicit narrative, which illustrated the courtship of male and female dancers. As a former member of the G D E explained, Opoku considered his dramatized version of sikyi to be his "baby" and one of his "artistic masterpieces" (Quaye 2007a).

Other dances were also altered to emphasize, or "overemphasize," their dramatic elements. According to C. K. Ladzekpo, one of the initial master drummers of the G D E, Opoku significantly altered the Ewe dance named agbekor. Ladzekpo explained that Opoku modified the dance to emphasize the theme of war (see Hirt-Manheimer 2004, 82). In a particular section of the dance, Opoku altered a formation so that dancers who formerly all faced the drummers instead faced each other to appear as though they were fighting one another. As Ladzekpo recalled, "I can . . . still remember how Opoku was yelling 'attack, attack!' He wanted it to be forceful, but that was his creation" (qtd. in ibid.). While agbekor is associated with battle, the dance primarily tells the story of Ewe migration. It does not include movements that portray direct confrontation between dancers (see Locke 1978). Furthermore, Opoku's removal of the slow, somber, a cappella *hatsiatsia* section of the agbekor dance also served to increase the choreography's emphasis on war and dramatic spectacle (PURL 2.8). While presumably rendering the dance more appealing to cosmopolitans, this emphasis on war reinforces long-held negative stereotypes of Africans as overly aggressive and violent, essentializing Ghanaians and undermining the goals of African Personality to combat such colonial-era generalizations.

It was not only Opoku who dramatized Ghana's dances. Subsequent directors have also made similar modifications. The G D E's performance of a northern dance called *nagla*,[14] choreographed/rearranged by Francis Nii-Yartey in the 1970s, illustrates the dramatization of dances and recalls earlier points about artistic cosmopolitan aesthetics. I asked a former N D C dancer who worked closely with Nii-Yartey if this director had "changed even the traditional dances." The dancer replied,

> Yeah. He used to. I got to know because I asked him so many questions. I learned that he was the one who researched nagla. So I went to him, because I traveled to [the north] to see nagla for myself. So, when I came back, I asked him [Nii-Yartey], "Why is it that [the N D C] nagla is different from what I saw?" [Nii-Yartey] told me that "I research it and I choreograph it. It shouldn't have to be like the real one. Because the real one bores. If you watch it you can even sleep." But this [dance ensemble] one, he had to change it so it would be more stronger than how it is. . . . You see, the real one, they dance in a circle. It's one-way rhythm; the rhythm is *binti bop, bintibop bitibi bop*. It's just something . . . you no like it, but Nii-Yartey changed it, put fast one in it. You start from the slow and then move to the fast. So he put all those things inside. . . . In the north they do only the men, strong men. But over here, he put women inside, and *he made it like a story*. Because if you watch it now . . . you see the man will dance and invite the woman. It's like a love story. But the real one is not like that. (Azadekor 2007)

In the north, the dance is performed in a circle with only men, but Nii-Yartey choreographed the dancers into two lines – one male, one female – and dramatized the themes of love and courtship. In all, artistic directors of the GDE have regularly and intentionally added dramatic features to the "real" dances in local communities; such practices intend to keep the attention of non-participatory audiences by playing into cosmopolitan stereotypes and enacting narratives that increase their effectiveness and persuasiveness as sensational spectacles of nationalism.

Musical Mixing and De-emphasizing Religious Ritual

For both pragmatic and artistic purposes, directors of the GDE have mixed musical genres that are distinct in community contexts. Comments by Sulley Imorro – a dancer brought from the Northern Region to Legon for his renowned abilities as a Dagbamba performer – point to such musical hybrids. When discussing the GDE's version of a dance called bamaaya, he told me, "I noticed that the drumming had changed. They [the GDE] had brought a damba beat into bamaaya, which I didn't understand. It was hard for me to join them. I tried to explain to them that that beat is not part of bamaaya; it is part of damba" (2007). Occasionally, directors have also used songs within dances that are of completely different ethnic/language groups. For example, when Oh! Nii Kwei Sowah assumed the reins of the ensemble in the late 1990s, he was known to have infused *nmani* – a northern Dagbamba dance – with Ga songs of the Accra region. Similarly, when discussing the Ewe agbekor, Apetsi Amenumey explained that "in the dance ensemble they just bring any song out. They even bring agbadza songs and put it inside [agbekor]" (2006). When I asked him if anybody would ever do that in his hometown, he replied, "No, because they have agbekor songs; they have agbadza songs. These people [GDE], they don't learn enough songs." When I questioned additional ensemble members about this practice, they typically stated that they did not have enough time to learn many songs. In other words, pragmatism – the pressure to learn a large repertoire in a relatively short period of time – had significantly altered these cultural forms, pushing them further into the category of artistic representation rather than representations of local culture.

Stage performances, as Diane Thram's (1999) work in Zimbabwe shows, also often de-emphasize ritual/religious aspects of particular dances, shifting their intention from spiritual efficacy to secular entertainment. Although this ethnography argues that the GDE's dances are much more than entertainment, as they serve to further the ideological goals of nationalists and help participants achieve personal goals (artistic and non-artistic), Thram's argument is applicable here, because as religious/ritual dances are performed by the GDE, their spiritual aspects are often suppressed. For example, the GDE often performs a ritual dance called *akom*. Prior to the ensemble's representation of it, akom was enacted only in Akan communities to encourage spirits to possess practitioners, thereby bringing the blessings and healing powers of the metaphysical realm into the corporeal world. In the context of stage performance, however, spirit possession is not necessarily viewed as a blessing. David Amoo recalled:

> One time we [the NDC] did akom for about thirty minutes, and there was a person there that got possessed, so we had to take her out. So we told her that the next time we do that dance, she has to be taken out, because in the theatre we don't have time to waste on pampering one person like that. We maybe only have five minutes, and you need to move along with the program.... She can get possessed within a second, so we have to tell her to go away, or we have to take her backstage and do what we need to do. (2006)

Spirit possession, in other words, was seen as a burden within the theatre because it disrupted the "program." Although this example attests to the retention of spiritual efficacy despite the ritual's transference to a stage context (see Hagedorn 2001), the religious aspects of the dance (and other such dances) were de-emphasized in order to suit the aesthetic expectations of a theatrical/national stage environment.

Costuming, Form, and Sanitizing

In order to suit the aesthetic demands of the stage, GDE choreographers have refashioned "traditional" dances, significantly modifying costuming. Contouring the visual sense, this ensemble has strategically manipulated the regalia of its traditional repertoire. Often costuming is used that is brighter than what is worn in community contexts, so as to have more visual impact. The amount of clothing worn is also transformed. Recalling the sterilization of culture through the fashioning of Africa (see Allman 2004) that was part of the "civilizing mission" of Christianity and colonialism, more clothing is often worn for certain dances, particularly to cover sexually provocative body parts. Sikyi is a particularly dramatic example of this refashioning. Conventionally, when women performed this dance they wore only small pieces of cloth held in place by waist-beads, called *sekyi* in Twi; these garments concealed only the private parts (see Younge 2011, 193–97). In order for this dance to be "presentable," Opoku clad female dancers in modest *kaba* dresses, which covered most of the body.[15] On the other hand, the GDE's costuming practices can be more revealing. For instance, in the Asante royal *fontomfrom* dance, chiefs conventionally have danced in full pieces of kente cloth that cover their torso and legs. Within the GDE, during the performance of this dance, often artists imitating chiefs will fold the top half of their kente cloth down to reveal their torsos; such action reportedly gives performers more flexibility to dance in a more vigorous, "exciting" manner (PURL 2.9). However, as one dancer explained, "a chief would never reveal himself like that. It would be considered profane, disgraceful, and disrespectful" (Atsikpa 2007). Furthermore, performers' costumes are coordinated, implicitly advancing ideals of unity through visual uniformity.

Reinforcing this notion, movements are often synchronized while linear and geometric formations are created and added as choreographers craft pleasing works of art.[16] Although there are certain cultural expectations that inform the individual movements of dancers in local communities, there is often a sense of creative expression and freedom to move almost anywhere within these spaces. As one GDE dancer explained,

> In the village, we can dance anyhow. As long as you can hear the drum, then you can go wherever you want. And you can put your own creativity into your movements. In the dance ensemble, Opoku and other [choreographers] made us into lines. Sometimes they would make us into circles, even though the dance originally was not like that. He wanted us to all look the same way, so it would look proper onstage for the audience. And the lines and circles made the dances more exciting, more interesting for people to watch. (Seki 2006)

For instance, within many circle dances (for example, *bewaa,* damba, *takai*) drummers perform in the middle of a dancing ring, but the GDE has rearranged this, often placing drummers in straight lines behind the dancers (PURL 2.10). When asked about this decision, artistic directors often replied that they did this because it "just looked better onstage." While Opoku was the only formally trained visual artist of the GDE's many artistic directors, all have been educated (in Ghana and abroad) in choreography and staging practices, resulting in their cosmopolitan sensibilities used to geometrically formalize the nation's dances.

Senses of Spectacle

In all, while GDE choreographers have attempted to retain the essence of various community dances, these cultural forms are nevertheless compressed, hastened, amplified, magnified, dramatized, formalized, secularized, and sanitized – in short, sensationalized to increase their persuasive power as spectacles of nationalism. More precisely, these modifications have emphasized the dances' audiovisual qualities, which the modern theatrical context invites. The theatre, certainly at least since the advent of the first true "modern" proscenium stage in the seventeenth century, conforms to norms stemming from the European Enlightenment. In general, like the Western museum, which developed subsequently, the theatre is a relatively sterile environment, elevating the audiovisual sense while marginalizing what Kant calls the "lower-senses" – taste, smell, and touch.[17] For instance, the separation between a non-participatory audience and performers acts as a protective glass that eradicates the tactile sense for spectators. Like a museum, "traditional" dances within a theatrical setting often conform to an expectation for quiet reflection in which there is an increased valuation of the visual object, its compartmentalization, and its intellectual evaluation. Bodily ways of knowing (at least for audiences) are, consequently, suppressed. In sum, within the GDE, dances are adapted to cosmopolitan aesthetics – sensationalized to appeal to the audiovisual senses while they are simultaneously anesthetized or alienated from other sensory modes.

Thus, like museums and world's fairs, the GDE is a product of the "society of the spectacle,"[18] or voyeur culture, which, as Walter Benjamin has noted, developed in the Romantic period as a type of window shopping where a variety of goods are to be viewed and only occasionally sampled (1973). The GDE provides audiences with a diversity of music and dances to hear and view. Only in rare instances do audiences sample, or participate in, GDE performances directly. In other words, in displaying the essence of various dances, choreographers ironically marginalize an essential component of African performance: the participatory aesthetic. That is, GDE audiences' full range of senses is only occasionally stimulated. It is precisely due to this partial anesthetization, I propose, that choreographers are encouraged to spectacularize, or sensationalize, dances' audiovisual qualities in an effort to compensate for the diminished role of the other sensory modalities.

CONSEQUENCES OF ARTISTIC TRANSFORMATION:
"CULTURAL POLLUTION," CREDENTIALS,
AND THE EXPANSION OF AUTHORITY

Spectacular, sensational stagings of preexisting cultural traditions often invite critique as audiences draw comparisons between these newly constructed theatrical versions and their source material in local communities. While the GDE has been largely successful in creating pow-

erful spectacles that persuade performers and audiences to go beyond
ethnic and national boundaries, for some the essence of the various "traditional" dances has not been adequately preserved. That is, Ghanaians
have occasionally questioned the authenticity of the GDE's "traditional"
repertoire while others defend its preservation practices. Exploring these
contestations reveals the politics of authentication within this troupe. A
narrative by former GDE dancer Sulley Imorro highlights the cosmopolitan power dynamics within the troupe:

> In 1995, the GDE was performing in the [National] Theatre, and people from the
> north came to see. And these people told me that I am spoiling their dances.
> But I said it was not me; it was others who came before me. There were many
> that came and taught northern dances. The takai [Dagbamba dance] they do is
> different. The nagla is very different. One time I was called to the radio station to
> speak about what we are doing here [at Legon]. So I come out clear and people
> called and said, "You are the people who are spoiling the dances," until the direc-
> tor came in [to the radio studio]. He was the director of the Center for National
> Culture. He said, "*Sulley have no power* to do what he went there and joined
> them for. Those people have their own choreography." He said, "Sulley has done
> nothing. Sulley has been trying to change it." Me, I don't go to high school or
> university to get up and fight for all these things. I told them, they have to come.
> They have to write letters to the Center for National Culture and say that they
> shouldn't call damba/takai *tora*. Because damba has its own. Takai has its own
> dance. Tora is also its own. It is a woman who had been betrayed by a man. It's a
> long story. So you can't bring that dance into takai. So the northern people were
> angry. Why they don't call [the Ewe] agbadza [dance] agbekor [a different Ewe
> dance]? Why did they call ours different? I've been fighting for this. (2007)

The heart of this controversy was that Opoku had combined a number
of Dagbamba dances into one stage arrangement. Following principles
of modern reformism and time compression, three distinct Dagbamba
dances – damba, takai, and tora – made up a single choreographic work
by Opoku known as the *Dagomba Dance Suite* (PURL 2.11). Similarly,
Opoku's damba/takai was a combination of two distinct Dagbamba festival dances. Zachariah Abdellah, a senior member of the ensemble and
a descendant of reputable Dagbamba griots in northern Ghana, told me
that "this would never happen in the village, and it is not correct.... It is
cultural pollution!" (2005). A similar assessment was held by other GDE
performers I interviewed who corroborated that damba/takai does not
exist outside the ensemble.

Despite the criticism, many did not voice their concerns to the artistic director because they "have no power" and/or did not possess the necessary "credentials." Abdellah explained:

> Some of us, we have sat back and we've watched events and we realize that there are some areas that are a problem. Before you can talk for people to understand and listen to you and take instructions from you, you must have paper, a certificate. That makes you an authority. Then everybody can bow. You can't tell him [the artistic director] how it should be, because he is a professor, and you don't even have a PhD. If I get my PhD . . . [then] I have every right to come and stop you. For now, any changes to the dances have to come from the artistic director. (2005)

Although none of the GDE's artistic directors have held PhDs, Abdellah's comments allude to the practice of requiring advanced formal education to hold this position. For example, in addition to his royal Akan status, Mawere Opoku held arts degrees and certificates from a number of different Ghanaian, British, and American colleges and training institutions.[19] Francis Nii-Yartey, who was chosen by Opoku to lead the GDE in 1976, was selected not only for his abilities in dance but also for his formal education in Ghana and the United States. After receiving his diploma in dance from the University of Ghana, Nii-Yartey later earned a master's degree from the University of Illinois at Urbana-Champaign. E. A. Duodu, who took over the company at Legon after Nii-Yartey decided to move to the newly constructed National Theatre, holds a diploma in dance from the University of Ghana and a master's degree from Wesleyan University in Connecticut. Taking over the reins after Duodu decided to step down, Oh! Nii Kwei Sowah graduated with a master's degree in dance from the University of California, Irvine, after receiving a diploma from the University of Ghana. The director of the GDE (at Legon) during my fieldwork – Ben Ayettey – holds a master's degree in dance from Arizona State University. Similarly, the artistic director of the NDC (at the National Theatre), David Amoo, has also received a master's degree from an American university.

Within the GDE, these "credentials" have given artistic directors authority to suppress critique, authenticating their own artistic work and the ensemble in general. Thus, as they are in many parts of Africa, cosmopolitan markers of authority have proven to be particularly ef-

fective within the GDE. It is not surprising given that "the enumera-
tion of the slightest educational achievement is one of the postcolonial
codes of prestige, with special attention given to distinctions attained
in Europe" (Mbembe 1992, 27), and that the GDE is situated within the
European-initiated institution of the University of Ghana. In this context, Western forms of authority typically trump indigenous ones such as
family history, gerontocracy, and chieftaincy. While discussing university performance groups, Ricardo Trimillos writes, "Authority in these
. . . ensembles usually derives less from the lineage of teachers and more
from Western credentials" (2004, 41).

Compounding these Western credentials, local forms and practices
of power are significant in authenticating dances within the GDE as
they strengthen the status and authority of artistic directors. For instance, C. K. Ladzekpo, an Ewe master drummer and original member
of the GDE, was critical of the ways in which Opoku had rearranged the
Ewe agbekor. Opoku had broken this dance into several pieces. Ladzekpo, however, did not voice his concerns because, as he states, "in our
culture, in our tradition, in Ghana, you don't criticize your boss" (qtd.
in Hirt-Manheimer 2004, 55). Similarly, Von Salifu (a Dagbamba chief)
remarked that in Ghana, "when you are a smaller man and you think you
know, people don't take kindly to it" (ibid.). As I spoke with participants
about their criticisms of the GDE's "traditional" dances, they often ref-
erenced Ghana's "culture" and "tradition" of deference to elders, chiefs,
and "big men" as reasons to "keep quiet." Thus, while artistic directors
rely on cosmopolitan credentials, they simultaneously rely on local cultural practices to authenticate the "traditional" repertoire of the GDE.

Encouraged by the new trans-ethnic identity of postcolonial nationalism, these cosmopolitan modes of power have also acted as a bulwark
for an expansion of authority as directors have asserted claims over traditions with which they did not self-identify. For instance, Opoku – an
Akan and particularly an Asante – rearranged Ewe, Dagbamba, Ga, Lobi,
and other dances. Opoku then proceeded to claim ownership of these
dances, seizing power from provincial chiefs and elders. This precedent has persisted within the ensemble. Taking over the company in
1976, Francis Nii-Yartey, a Ga, has maintained Opoku's choreography.
Additionally, Nii-Yartey has made claims of ownership over his rear-

rangement of nagla, a northern dance of the Paga people. Each of the subsequent artistic directors has been given the authority to maintain or change the entire multiethnic repertoire of the GDE, despite their self-identification with only one ethnic group.[20] Such authority is rarely challenged openly by ensemble members. Criticism is repressed, sometimes inviting indignation. As one Ewe drummer of the GDE told me, "The director, he is a Ga. When he tells me something about Ewe dances, I will say yo [okay], bye. I know what is in my head. I won't say it. I have to show respect. If I say anything they will sack you. But I know my tradition" (Tekpa 2005).

When I asked Nketia about this power dynamic within the GDE, he stated that "because *we* were Ghanaians we were dealing with *our* cultures so we could do it the way we wanted" (2005). Political nationalism, in other words, had created a new sense of "we" and "our," and this new identity as a Ghanaian translated into *expanded authority* to represent the dances of multiple ethnic groups, as long as they were within the national boundaries. Due to the powerful ideologies and institutions created specifically by nationalism, artistic directors have become "Ghanaian dance experts," maintaining an expansive authority to represent and authenticate the dances of various ethnic groups found within their nation. In all, as artistic directors do so, they manage nationalism, harnessing its geographies, logics, and practices to preserve their own power and further their professional artistry.

"DON'T TOUCH MY WORK!" THE POWER OF ART AND COPYRIGHT

While encouraging new forms of cosmopolitan power, contact with the West and changing global dynamics have also informed notions of cultural ownership in postcolonial Ghana. As one of the GDE's senior drummers noted, "Modernity can bring a lot of things. Traditionally dances are created for the community. There is no owner or composer. That is why copyright is a problem. Before, it was all 'we, we, we'" (Abdellah 2005). Supporting this claim, Nketia noted that certain styles of Akan court dances are "copyrighted" by particular villages (1963). In such instances, it is not an individual who claims this right, but a group.

Throughout Ghana, although there are examples of the individual creation and ownership of songs (see Dor 2004), music and dance forms
are often *collectively* "owned" by the respective communities that claim
to have created them. Consequently, it is the leaders (chiefs and elders),
on behalf of these communities, who often maintain the right to control
the use of these forms.

Following this customary law, the GDE, in order to gain permission
to use various dance traditions, often performed its choreographic creations for local communities. As Nketia recalled, "We took the ensemble
all over the country to show our dances to the communities. We wanted
to get their approval to make sure we were going about things in the
right way. With few exceptions, the communities embraced us, even the
elders and chiefs" (2005). By dancing admirably for local authorities,
Opoku and other artistic directors have effectively "registered" their
works, because, in oral tradition, "public performance . . . serves as a
loose equivalent of publishing or registering such works, with connotations akin to copyright" (Dor 2004, 31). That is, local (Ghanaian) markers of authority, such as chieftaincy and gerontocracy, were significant
in creating a matrix of power, which served to authenticate the artistic
creations of the GDE's choreographers.

While deferring to traditional authority, GDE choreographers simultaneously instituted a new practice of attaching their individual names
to community-owned dance forms. William Diku, a senior dancer and
promotions manager for the GDE (Legon), recalled,

> When E. A. Duodu was the artistic director [after Opoku], he instituted his
> way of [performing] Akan ceremonial dances that Opoku designed. When he
> [Duodu] came, he presented it in his own way and didn't even call it the *Akan
> Ceremonial Dance.* He called it *Duabo,* which means a Durbar situation – kings
> and queens. . . . He did it while Opoku was still alive. Nevertheless, Opoku didn't
> take light to it though. He [Opoku] said, "No, why did you touch my work?"
> Opoku took offense of it. He didn't like Duodu tampering with his works. (2005)

Similarly, while discussing his attempt to reimagine Opoku's staging
of an Ewe dance, Duodu himself explained,

> He [Opoku] did it [Togo atsia] with three people. When I took over I used seven
> people and sometimes five, and he got mad. So I got Professor Nketia, and I asked
> him. "You are a musician; somebody's musical composition, you can rearrange

it." And he said yes. I have also rearranged it. The music is the same; the dance movements are the same. It is only that I have increased the number. Nketia said, "Don't mind him. Go ahead." So I called mine "Togo atsia II" and left Opoku's as "Togo atsia I" to keep him at ease. . . . So when you are performing Togo atsia II, my name will be down as the arranger. When we are performing Togo atsia I, Opoku's name will be there. I left his work intact. (2007)

Opoku had developed a sense of individual ownership over a group of community dance traditions, which hindered further innovation within the ensemble.

Such practices of authorship have persisted within the ensemble. Following Duodu's retirement, Oh! Nii Kwei Sowah assumed the GDE's artistic director position in the late 1990s. When I asked him if he had made any changes to the ensemble's "traditional" repertoire as director, he replied, "I decided not to change the traditional dances, because, I won't say 'trademark,' but that was the dance ensemble style. I didn't interfere with Opoku's works; I just made sure that I got the people to perform in a certain kind of spirit, to keep it going" (2006). Like Western art, individuals' names became attached to local, community-based dance forms. A performance program dated July 7, 1993, illustrates this practice (PURL 2.12). In general, speaking about the GDE's artistic practices, Diku remarked, "We all agree that we don't try to destroy somebody's works" (2005).

Ensemble choreographers, therefore, have primarily not considered the GDE's "traditional" dances to be re-presentations of local forms but rather distinct artistic creations. This is unsurprising given that, as Nketia has claimed, "our goal [with the GDE] was not to present an anthropological specimen. It was to create an art" (2005). In other words, artistic transformation has been an explicit aim of the ensemble since its inception; choreographers did not exactly re-present "the village" onstage but instead intended to create a unique art form. Affirming such a position, performance programs used throughout the 1980s claimed that a Ghana Dance Ensemble performance is "an experience separate from all others."[21] Such practices are not unique to the GDE, as the "reclassification of ethnographic materials as art has been instrumental to [the] process" of legitimizing state authority and the existence of the nation, in many cases (Kirshenblatt-Gimblett 1991, 81). Through this process, I

suggest that "art" may also be wielded rhetorically to buttress the authority of particular individuals, elevating their singular status along with
securing their personal power and legacy. In short, the cosmopolitan
poetics of "art" also serve to legitimize the self.

Opoku and other artistic directors have used "art" as a discursive
strategy to deflect criticism. A story by Sulley Imorro attests to this practice. Imorro explained that Von Salifu – a chief from his home village
near Tamale – attended a performance by the GDE and was so outraged
by the dance called *bamaya*[22] that he demanded that Sulley return to his
home village to be punished. Sulley pleaded with his chief, arguing that
he was not responsible for this portrayal of the dance, that he was merely
a performer, and that the director was the one responsible. Nevertheless, the chief reminded Sulley that he had an obligation to maintain
the integrity of his traditions. In general, Salifu stated that "we weren't
happy with the way they [the GDE] handled our dances, and we protested to the authorities at Legon. In reaction, Opoku changed the name
of bamaaya . . . to 'Bambaya'" (qtd. in Hirt-Manheimer 2004, 56). With
this rhetorical maneuver, as ethnomusicologist Isaac Hirt-Manheimer
correctly contends, "he [Opoku] deflected the criticism by claiming the
'bambaya' was an original work of art distinct from bamaaya" (ibid.).

This invocation of "art" and individual copyright by Opoku and
other GDE choreographers is evidence of the cosmopolitan networks
in which they operated. Opoku, like other directors, trained and traveled extensively in the United States and Britain, where notions of individual copyright and property ownership had been firmly established.[23]
Reinforcing such practices throughout the GDE's existence, Western
notions of intellectual property have taken hold in Ghana. The British Imperial Copyright Act of 1911 became the de facto statute in the
colonial Gold Coast. This law remained in effect until the first significant postcolonial state law regarding copyright in Ghana was enacted
in 1961 (a year before the GDE was formed). In 1985, PNDC (Provisional
National Defense Council) Law 110 revised and expanded this law to
include literary and other artistic work, including choreography. In 2005,
PNDC Law 690 repealed and replaced the former law. While these laws
reflect global trends in copyright legislation, much of the language found
in Ghanaian copyright law has been based particularly on that of En-

gland and America, as well as on precedents set by the World Intellectual Property Organization (WIPO). Particularly, a 1989 WIPO report was cited by Dr. Ben Abdallah, chair of Ghana's Commission on Culture, in his speech inaugurating the Folkloric Board of Trustees in Ghana[24] and subsequently by John Collins (1993), who is a founding member of this board.[25] Like Western copyright laws, Ghanaian counterparts are primarily concerned with preserving the rights of individual artists in regard to their own work, ensuring they receive fair compensation for their artistic efforts. As these laws have been publicized and debated within Ghana, individualized notions of ownership have been reaffirmed within the GDE.

Despite choreographers' awareness of the increasing controversies surrounding copyright law in Ghana (see Boateng 2002; Collins 1993), none have formally applied for copyrights of the ensembles' "traditional" repertoire. Thus, the aforementioned claims to copyright made by Opoku and other artistic directors have been communicative gestures with no direct legal consequences. Furthermore, according to Ghanaian copyright law, in order to be eligible for copyright, an artistic work must be "original in character" (Date-Baah 1972).[26] To obtain copyright, GDE choreographers, therefore, would have to prove the originality of these "traditional" works, which would be difficult given their extensive use of preexisting material and names (the bamaaya/bambaya example above appears to be the only case of an explicit name alteration to avoid criticism). Nevertheless, Opoku and other GDE choreographers have used the rhetoric of copyright to silence critique, preserving the ensemble and their own artistic rearrangements of Ghana's dance/music traditions.

In this way, choreographers have attempted to claim individual ownership in the face of long-standing local practices and federal laws that reinforce community ownership of "folk" culture, upon which much of the GDE's "traditional" repertoire is based. Since the 1961 copyright law has no provisions for folklore and is rather concerned only with work in a tangible fixed medium, Opoku technically was not transgressing any legal statutes. By performing for local communities, he was acquiring a customary copyright. Yet, his attachment of an individual name to these preexisting dances violated cultural norms.

Subsequently, however, PNDC Law 110 addressed the issue of folklore, stating that the Republic of Ghana maintained the rights to such
cultural products as if the Republic were the original creator (4).[27] That
is, although provincial authority was becoming usurped by the postcolonial nation-state, the copyright for Ghanaian folk music/dance remained
collectively held. Decades later, PNDC Law 690 stated that the rights
of folklore are vested in the president on behalf of the nation (5). While
further divesting provincial authority, this law mimics the role of chiefs
as custodians, or guardians, of culture by rendering the president as the
ultimate chief who acts in the interests of a collective. Despite such provisions, choreographers regularly informally subvert these and customary laws by claiming personal ownership over various community-based
dance traditions.

In all, Western notions of art and copyright have migrated to Ghana,
interacting with local social dynamics to create new power relationships
that further essentialize this nation's culture. Chieftaincy, gerontocracy,
and the particular hierarchical structures of the GDE have coupled with
notions of artistic ownership drawn from international (often Western)
sources. This cosmopolitan matrix of power, in turn, legitimizes and
perpetuates the interpretations of culture created by a few select individuals. In short, the "we" of the community and the nation has been
filtered through the "I"/eye of Opoku and other artistic directors. This
practice is not surprising given that nationalist ideologies often promote
a singular, often essentialist, national identity, de-emphasizing the pluralistic attributes of populations. For artistic directors, "copyrighting"
their "art" is a tactic for managing nationalism and the demands of the
state, acting as a strategy for mediating between collectivist ideologies
and a desire to achieve individual recognition.

"DON'T CALL IT TRADITIONAL!" CONTESTING ESSENCE

Along with cosmopolitan credentials and the rhetoric of copyright and
art, within the GDE's "traditional" repertoire, the discourse related to
"tradition" itself is an important point of contention. Labeling culture
as "traditional," the ensemble imbues it with special meaning that links
it symbolically to the past (Gilman 2004, 33; Hymes 1975, 353–54) – a

past that is often constructed as immemorial, ethereal, and mythical. As such, the discourse of "tradition" becomes a powerful tactic that is strategically employed to reinforce the authority of the state, and others, by disguising politically "invented" cultural practices as self-evident, indisputable truths (Herzfeld 1997, 39). While designating culture as "traditional" can serve to quell debate in this way, this marker can also elevate its status and visibility, rendering it a target of fierce debate. Given the artistic transformation and prominence of the GDE's "traditional" repertoire, it is not surprising that Ghanaians have questioned its authenticity as they compare these dances to their counterparts in local communities. What is remarkable is that this critique has occasionally come from foreigners. Focusing on one American in particular who made a lasting impression on the ensemble, this section further highlights not only the cosmopolitan politics that inform the authentication of culture in the GDE but also the ways in which individuals manage nationalism while debating the essence of culture. That is, it examines how artists mediate the rhetoric of "tradition" by deploying the logics and discourse of nationalism to serve their interests.

In 1967 a young dance choreographer and educator named Drid Williams came to Ghana to carry out field research in order to augment her studies of dance in the United States. She witnessed the Ghana Dance Ensemble in its seminal years, befriending many at the University of Ghana (Legon), including members of the troupe itself. After observing the GDE for several months, she asked one drummer in particular—Mustapha Tettey Addy—to join her in her sojourns through Ghana to examine dance performances in local towns and villages. As she engaged in intensive field studies throughout the country, she began to take note of the differences between the various local dance forms and the ways in which they were represented by the GDE. When she returned to Legon, she confronted Opoku about his rearrangements of "traditional" dances. Addy recalled:

> Drid Williams was telling Opoku, "You are [bringing] American modern dance steps into agbekor; it's wrong. You are using American dance choreography in agbekor; it is wrong. Agbekor is already choreographed by the people, originally. You don't need to do anything to it. You just have to bring it from the village to the stage—the way it is. You take something from the village and you put it on stage." This is the main argument. And Opoku would say, "Get out of here." (2007)

Illustrating the intensity of their debate, Addy later added that "she [Williams] fought with Opoku a lot. They nearly fought physically."

To further her side of this contestation, Williams, in her article "Traditional Danced Spaces," provides a detailed account of the differences between Opoku's staged version of agbekor and the performances of it that she observed in Ewe communities. She points out that the choreographed representation does not maintain certain spatial relationships of the "original" agbekor. She additionally notes that drummers in the GDE do not perform the slow procession or carry drums on their heads as they do in the village. Moreover, she explains that while dancers in the GDE turn away from the drummers to face the audience, in the village context dancers "would never *ever* turn their backs to the master drum. . . . Such an act in that [village] context would constitute an intolerable insult" (1997a, 257). She implies that the GDE's representations of dance traditions do not maintain the "essence" of these cultural forms.

Williams recalled that when she confronted Opoku with these reservations, her comments were quickly dismissed. Williams writes that Opoku justified his position thusly: "I (Williams) wasn't an African and therefore had no business saying anything about it at all" (259). She replied, "You may be African – specifically, a Ghanaian, but you're an Ashanti, you're not Ewe, therefore why do you think you know any more about it than I do?" (259). In other words, Williams critiqued the "expanded authority" that Opoku assumed under the politics of nationalism. When she continued to press him about how he choreographed certain Ewe dances, Opoku replied, "The way I stage these dances is the way that will please foreigners. I studied modern dance in New York. I went to Rockefeller Center. I know what they like to see" (qtd. in ibid., 259). While Opoku deployed his cosmopolitan credentials in an attempt to quell this criticism, Williams (a foreigner), however, apparently did not want to see what Opoku assumed she would.

Spurred by this debate, in 1969 Williams formed her own local dance group in Accra called Adzido, which included several former members of the GDE. As Addy recalls, "Adzido [dance company] was formed by Drid Williams here in Ghana to compete with the Ghana Dance Ensemble. . . . We perform original. Dance ensemble never carried agbekor drum.[28] But when Adzido was coming to perform, we carried agbekor drums on our head, everywhere. We can carry it from Arts Center [central Accra] to Osu [section of Accra]. And we used original costume and everything" (2007). Addy's comments imply that Williams and her ensemble's choreographies of various Ghanaian dances were more "authentic" – more faithfully capturing the essence of the dance – than those of the GDE. This example illustrates a clash of aesthetic expectations and a "clash of essentialisms" (van Ginkel 2004, 82) as differing conceptions of authenticity and tradition competed with one another, neither of which exactly re-presented the "village experience." While Opoku presumed to know what foreigners wanted to see, Williams showed that not all foreigners have the same aesthetic expectations or tastes. In other words, as Ghana's dances were essentialized, the tastes of audiences were similarly essentialized and stereotyped. Despite this essentialism, the GDE's performances have been largely accepted by audiences in Ghana and around the world. Nketia told me that it was because Williams had a particular training in dance and anthropology that she was critical.

Fundamentally, Williams's polemic regarding Opoku and the GDE rested on the concept of "tradition." She claimed that Opoku wanted to "re-create traditional Ghanaian dances as they were performed in the villages where they originated. . . . If the Ghana Dance Ensemble *had not claimed to present traditional dances,* my argument would be considerably weakened or non-existent" (1997a, 257). In short, she writes, "don't advertise one thing and produce something else" (262). Williams's overall assessment of these stage choreographies was that they were largely "counterfeit" and were thus "fairly worthless" (263). Although Williams was writing about these issues in the 1990s, her critique of the dance ensemble was based on a static conception of tradition, which had been outmoded in scholarly circles for decades. More recent scholarship has shown that tradition is a dynamic, ever-changing, emergent process, always in the making of the here and now, shaped by and shaping the contemporary (see Glassie 1995; Hobsbawm and Ranger 1983). Thus, if one adopts this conceptualization of tradition as dynamic and fluid, then the GDE's choreography can be interpreted as traditional because it is an extension of local forms and therefore does not need to exactly mimic indigenous practices to be considered as such.

Furthermore, it was *never* the explicit goal of the ensemble to create exact representations of the village or community context. Speaking with me about Williams, Nketia remarked, "There was a dancer [Williams] who had some anthropological training and started making a loud noise about 'Oh, this is really not authentic.' You know, because they are not carrying the drums on their head and so forth" (2005). I interjected, "But that wasn't the goal of the ensemble, right?" Nketia replied, "Right! Well, you see our goal was not to present an anthropological specimen. It was to create an art." Answering Williams's claim that the GDE's dances are "fairly worthless," he explained that "the dances don't lose meaning in the new context. That was the old way of thinking about it, sentimental perhaps. The dances acquire another meaning in the context in which it is being performed. And for us the national meaning is extremely important." Williams was locked in an "old way of thinking" about tradition and authenticity. Her views are aligned with those of an older generation of anthropologists and folklorists who took an objectivist view of authenticity – eternally searching for origins of culture rather than attempting to understand their contemporary constructions or reinventions (see Bendix 1997).

While Williams's assessments of the GDE may be characterized as outmoded and insensitive to those who value the national significance of these forms, Addy noted that "she was a strong person" (2007), and her lasting impact was evident as I spoke with past and present GDE members and staff. She had a particular influence on the conceptions of authenticity held by Francis Nii-Yartey:

> Drid Williams really had a case, and I agreed with her, but she presented the thing with some malice. And that's what really worried me, because she and Opoku had had some confrontation. And you could see that smelling from that article ["Traditional Danced Spaces"]. But she had a point that you cannot call anything that you take out of context what it is. And I totally agree with that. That's my thing right now. People don't use the new thing here [Legon]. I use it. I say [that] what the dances are, which are done in the two companies and in amateur groups, are *new traditional* dances. They cannot be traditional dances, because if you put everything on a scale of 100 percent, you begin to deduct, and you find out what is left is not what it is. It's a semblance of a tradition it cannot claim to be. . . . These are rearranged things; they are not even choreography. It depends on the extent to which you go with these things. It has some resemblance, but *please don't call it traditional dance.* Don't call things by names

which don't belong to them. And it's all right, just let people know that you are taking this thing somewhere. . . . So for lack of a better term at that time, Opoku and others were still calling it traditional dance, because they were the closest thing to the original. But I'm sure if you sat down with Opoku today, if he were alive, he would have agreed that, of course, he did some stuff to the dances, and therefore they couldn't represent fully. He might have added some things to enhance, but also he deducted some things. So *to be safe*, you say, this is a *new traditional* dance. Even though traditional dances are there, and they change all the time. The dances are not static; in fact we know how, historically, the dances were created. They were not just given from the sky, like the Golden Stool,[29] but they were actually done by people with the same sensitivities and the same faults as we all have. And each generation brings its own stamp, puts their own stamp on the dances. It's something we could debate until the end of time – authenticity. "This is a traditional thing, therefore it is authentic." Nothing exists like that, because the traditional people have to change anyway. (2006)

Although Nii-Yartey acknowledged the dynamism of tradition, in order "to be safe" from future criticism he elected to use the term "*new* traditional." This qualifier presumably deflected the GDE's detractors from condemning the ensemble's representations of local cultural practices. In short, Nii-Yartey used a discursive strategy to avoid critique.

Despite Nii-Yartey's alignment with Williams, members of the GDE often dismiss Williams's comments. In the summer of 2012, before a performance, I overheard a conversation between director Benjamin Ayettey and GDE members in which they joked about the Williams/Opoku controversy, noting that it was absurd that Williams, a foreigner, thought she could tell Opoku how to choreograph Ghanaian dances. Reminiscent of Opoku's defense, Williams's views were disregarded because she did not qualify as a "cultural insider." Such an unsolicited conversation attests to the persistent presence of Williams and the salience of authenticity within the GDE. Nevertheless, the ensemble has continued to call "traditional" choreographic works by their preexisting names. This practice remained a source of debate during my field research. While some derided the troupe, claiming that it performs "polluted," or "adulterated," re-presentations of culture, others maintained that the GDE has created meaningful artistic expressions of nationalism. Others further claim that the ensemble's "traditional" works offer accurate portraits of the nation's dances and thus a "real grounding" for the authentication of self.

Although the GDE has had its detractors over the years, it has often served as an authentic basis for many individuals. My conversation with former director E. A. Duodu attests to this position.

> Paul: What would you say to people who criticize the dance ensemble and say that the dancers are not authentic, or maybe that they are making counterfeit dances?
>
> Duodu: If you go to statistics, I would say that 90–95 percent of Ghanaians would not ascribe to that criticism. Because everywhere we go, they accepted it wholeheartedly. If you go to Asante and you do adowa, they are excited. Those who criticized that [the dances] had been adulterated are few people. A few intellectuals, because they have learned to criticize.... Those who criticize are those that don't know how to dance.... Nobody has adulterated the dance; it was a new form, a new concept. Opoku challenged them, he challenged me, and I was never annoyed with him. (2007)

Therefore, despite the criticisms of the GDE, Duodu implied that the ensemble has acted as a felt authentic grounding for many individuals who *believe* that the dance troupe's representations of cultural forms are "real" and/or "correct." Why and how do people maintain such beliefs? What is their "grounding"? This section explores the various ways in which the GDE has upheld its reputation as an "authentic" source for "traditional" Ghanaian culture.

Since its inception, founders of the ensemble made great efforts to retain the "essence" of the dances without destroying their cultural integrity. Referring to the early days of the group, Nketia remarked, "It was very important to ensure that the [dance] movements [used in the GDE] were correct, and that the dancers who were trained could dance in the village and be judged authentic" (2005). Nketia's extensive field study of nearly every region in Ghana (primarily conducted between 1952 and 1961), coupled with the cultural expertise of Opoku and the GDE staff, provided a basis for the confidence that the ensemble's representations would be judged favorably by local audiences. In the early 1960s, the GDE staff was hand-picked by Nketia and Opoku as they traveled to various communities to find the most reputable performers in each area. They presumed that this recruitment method would allow the ensemble's representations to remain close to the source. The ensemble also invited cultural specialists from various regions to teach at the university. To further ensure the ensemble's authenticity, Opoku and Nketia frequently made excursions to observe local dance practices and occasionally took the ensemble as a whole to important cultural sites to see dances in their idiomatic cultural context. Especially in the early years of the ensemble, according to Adinku, "they [the GDE] visited the Manhiya Palace of the Asantehene Sir Nana Osei Agyeman Prempeh, who made it possible for them to be exposed to the kete dance and music. Members also visited Asante-Mampong, Sekondi, Krobo Odumasi, Akropong-Akupim, Winneba, Kpong and Anyako to observe dances" (2000, 133).

Around this time (early 1960s), GDE members also traveled to seek local validation of their "traditional" repertoire. For instance, they went to the University of Cape Coast, where one professor found the ensemble's performance "so enriching" that he was brought to tears (Coe 2005, 73). Furthermore, Nii-Yartey explained that periodically,

> the traditional people watched [the GDE]. They had their criticism, but also they had their enjoyments. One time I remember, we went on a tour of Ghana, and one thing that a traditional ruler said that stuck to my mind was something mentioned as they [GDE] were doing the takai dance. We had taken it from there, gone here. We had reorganized it, cleaned it, you know, with a touch of modernity, but it was the same dance. But you see, takai takes a long time to perform. Opoku's thing was to cut the things, to shorten them – all of the dances. And so the traditional ruler was sitting there saying, "Oh, they're really good." And the thing finished, and he called Opoku and said, "When I was beginning to enjoy the thing, you stopped," which is a legitimate thing for a person like that to say. Which means also in a way, he [the chief] is *putting his stamp on it* – this is good, it should have gone on for a while. So his criticism was really exonerated. So, the traditional people did not complain, and the chiefs are the custodians of culture. (2006)

Approval by local authorities, recruitment of reputable local experts, and comparative observation of indigenous communities served as strategies to authenticate the ensemble's repertoire. Employing these tactics, the ensemble has attempted to transfer the authenticity of "the village" onto the stage.

The ideology and practices of preservation have often served to reinforce the feeling that the GDE's representations of culture are authentic. Paradoxically, the GDE's traditional repertoire is presented as both a "relic of cultural excavation and a modern expression of the nation" (Askew 2002, 215). That is, while preservation has always been one of the ensemble's key objectives, Opoku "modernized" these traditions to suit cosmopolitan expectations. Yet, the focus has been on the former. As such, the ensemble has been implicitly charged with the task of acting as a "performing archive" (Schauert 2007b), maintaining cultural "essence" through the various tactics previously described. Additionally, lack of funding for new research compounds such practices. Consequently, although most of Opoku's artistic work was created in the early 1960s and was based on even earlier research, his choreography has remained authoritative in the ensemble. Occasionally new versions of existing dance repertoire come into the ensemble, but as they do Opoku's works are not discarded, and the result is only an addition to the repository of the GDE. Recall that when Duodu rearranged Opoku's version of Togo atsia, he called it Togo atsia II to appease Opoku. Over the years the ensemble has re-created new versions of dances but "preserved" the older choreography. For example, the GDE's repertoire includes bamaaya I, II, and III; *borborbor* I and II; and so forth. Serving as an archive, or museum, the GDE provides documentation and display of various Ghanaian dances, giving audiences and performers a sense that they are experiencing the music and movements of previous eras. In this way, the GDE becomes a kind of "time capsule." However, in performance, the history of these dances is concealed, as they are often presented without explanation. Thus, these dances gesture toward, or capture, an undefined past, which seems to reference a time before the state and a time before colonialism, creating what Michael Herzfeld calls "structural nostalgia" (1997). That is, because the GDE's "traditional" repertoire works on the principle of resemblance, "iconicity serves the interests of nationalism by rendering its contingent claims as eternal realities by removing them from the domain of social practice to that of cultural essence" (140); by decontextualizing and dehistoricizing dance, the state and nation become imagined as eternal.

While working to secure the endurance of the state and nation, these preservation practices have created a contestation over the GDE's authenticity by perpetuating notions of cultural stasis. Some, like William Diku (senior member of the GDE), are "worried that the dances in the villages have taken on new dimensions" (2005) and that what the GDE performs onstage does not accurately reflect these contemporary changes in the communities. For instance, Ben Ayettey stated that "the *bawa* [a Dagara dance] that we [the GDE] perform now, if you go to the Upper West [Region of Ghana] and ask them, they will say, 'Oh, we haven't seen this before.' It is because they [the GDE] researched on that one in 1962" (2005). Yet others point precisely to the ensemble's acts of preservation as the basis for its authenticity. As a former member of the ensemble stated,

> the ones we [GDE] are playing at the theatre, they are the *old ones,* the typical ones. See, but the recent ones in the village, the young guys did not learn the better ones from the forefathers. Because of this global village, the way things are moving, we don't even have time to ask questions. So at the end of the day, you think you are doing the best one, but it is not like that. . . . What we [GDE] know is good because of Mawere Opoku. You know they started it in the 1960s. In the '60s, we don't have much churches and other things. In those days, when you see an African you know he is an African. So those ones are the typical ones, the ones they are still using. So if you learn it, it's good. . . . So if you learn anything from them [GDE], it is good. It is correct. (Azadekor 2007)

Many GDE artists have shared similar sentiments. They claim that, contrary to critics, the GDE performs "more correctly/authentically" than local communities because these communities are considered corrupted by Christianity and globalization. Thus, whether for ideological or pragmatic reasons, the GDE's "preservation" of dance choreography from the 1960s reaffirms the ensemble's authenticity for many participants as it has perpetuated Opoku's legacy well after his passing in 2002. Like Nkrumah, Opoku "never dies."

Due primarily to the GDE's research and preservation practices, other local performance groups have viewed it as an authentic source for Ghana's dance culture. Throughout Accra (and Ghana) there are hundreds of local amateur culture groups. These ensembles, which began to form shortly after the GDE's own founding (1962), take the GDE as a model for their performance practices and perform a multi-ethnic repertoire of dances that highlight their artistic features and "essence." Not only do these amateur groups use the GDE as a model, but they also often use, or "steal," its choreography. While discussing amateur ensembles, Diku remarked, "They hang on the windows, they peep, and just pick movements . . . and they go and present it anyhow. Therefore destroying the dances" (2005). Mercy Ayettey's description of her experience in a local amateur group near Accra supports Diku's claims: "So, we amateur people, we will come and stand at the window, watching them [GDE] here (see fig. 2.1). Then we have been stealing the simplest movement that we can do. So our dances are not like the dance ensemble's. We just took some small, small movements from it. And then we mention the name, but it's not all the movements that we used to do at the amateur group" (2007). To follow up on such comments, I asked why these groups went to the state ensemble to learn traditional dances. As one dancer explained, "They [GDE] have been going to do research for the dances. I think the dances here are more correct than amateur groups'" (Amotonyo 2005). Mercy Ayettey agreed, stating, "Yes, this [GDE] one is better [than amateur groups], because they [GDE] used to go do research" (2007). While the GDE is often considered "more authentic" than these so-called amateur groups, many, as noted above, also consider the ensemble's "traditional" dances to be more authentic than those found in local communities, which are assumed to be corrupted by modernity. In short, by observing the GDE and "stealing" its movements, amateur groups seek to embody the perceived authenticity of the national ensemble. In this way, the GDE, with its reputation for careful research, often acts as a felt authentic grounding for these local amateur groups.[30]

Due to this research, many ensemble members refer to the GDE's repertoire as the "original." For instance, as Jennies Darko, senior dancer and promotions director of the GDE (Legon), explains,

> I am saying "original" because we [GDE] went to the village to learn and adapt certain things to stage here with the help of our late Professor Mawere Opoku. That is why I am saying "original." And if you go to town and watch other groups perform the dances that we do here, you will see a big difference. To them, they don't understand the meaning of the movements. So they will just do it and add things to it. . . . But with us, we understand the movements that we do. It was Opoku and [William] Adinku who mostly taught us the meanings, and then taught it to Willie Diku, and they have passed it on to the young ones. (2007)

For many local culture groups, the GDE serves as the "original" source for learning Ghana's dances. Like others, Darko points to the research

2.1. Individuals watching the Ghana Dance Ensemble (Legon) through windows of the dance hall.

of Opoku and other founding members of the ensemble (such as William Adinku) as the basis for her belief that the GDE's representations of cultural forms is authentic. Generally, ensemble members often have used the term "original" to emphasize the authenticity of the GDE's "traditional" repertoire. As such, the GDE has become a type of "new" original where individuals come to learn the "authentic" versions of Ghana's dances, seizing this role from local communities.

While both the GDE (Legon) and the NDC (National Theatre) are typically viewed as "more authentic" than local cultural groups, when the two national ensembles are juxtaposed, discrepancies and contestations emerge. As a senior dancer at Legon explained, "The difference is, if it comes to the tradition – deep tradition – Legon people are the best. Though theatre people, they also do tradition, but not too much. . . . The reason I am saying that Legon is good [better] in tradition than them [NDC] is just simple. They [GDE] follow the *real* tradition. But at the National Theatre, Nii-Yartey used his mind to change certain things" (M. Ayettey 2007). Her comments were echoed by many members of both national ensembles and their audiences. The GDE, based at Legon, was often considered the "better" source for "real" Ghanaian cultural traditions. Such a reputation impacted the choices made by prospective members regarding which ensemble to join. A former member of the

Legon group, Solomon Agyari, told me that, "if you want the tradition, you have to go to Legon. You have to go to the GDE before you get it. There is no group that dances more of the tradition than Legon. I *believe* that. I know that the *real traditional* movement, everything that they do, that is the real thing" (2007). Agyari later explained that several members of his amateur group based in Accra joined the GDE (Legon) for a three-year time period specifically to learn "traditional" dance. When I asked him why he chose the Legon group over the ensemble at the National Theatre, he replied, "Nketia and Opoku had done the research. [They] were professors at the university. . . . They do the right movements. I trust them." Conversely, many members of the national ensembles and local culture groups claimed that Nii-Yartey had added "modern" dance and ballet movements to the NDC's "traditional" repertoire and thus had "spoiled," or inauthenticated, these dances.

SHIFTING SANDS: MANAGING RELATIONAL AUTHENTICITY

Far from being merely sites of inauthentic "fakelore," this discussion has shown these national folkloric troupes to often be bedrocks for authenticity. As they act as a "felt authentic grounding" for many individuals, this ground may shift like sands beneath a dancer's feet. That is, this discussion has shown authenticity to be not only discursively constructed but also subjective, dynamic, and *relational*. Given the sensational staging, or artistic transformation, of local dance forms, many Ghanaians and even foreigners consider the ensemble's "traditional" repertoire to be inauthentic when compared to preexisting community practices. However, directors have used a discursive, or rhetorical, strategy to avoid the critique that often accompanies such direct comparisons. By simply giving the GDE's "traditional" dances a slightly different name from those in local communities (for example, bamaaya being called "bambaya") or by adding the qualifier "new" to their creations, directors have shifted these dances from "inauthentic" re-presentations of culture to "authentic" choreographic works of art. In some cases, the GDE's versions of "traditional" dance forms are perceived to be "more authentic" than those from "the village" because the ensemble's versions are based on material from a half century ago, which, according to some, had been presumably less affected by Christianity and other foreign influences. Finally, when juxtaposed against amateur groups, the national ensembles are often viewed as "more authentic," but when directly compared, the ensemble at Legon shifts to become the "more authentic" source for the "real tradition." Therefore, as artists perform the essence of traditions onstage, the essence – or authenticity – of these traditions also moves as it changes positions with various partners such as "the village," amateur groups, or other national ensembles. The authenticity of the GDE and its "traditional" repertoire is thus relational, shifting but not completely melting into air. Performers become dancing essences as the essences of cultural forms dance.

Negotiating this relational authenticity is instrumental to managing nationalism. Engaging in a complex cosmopolitan politics of authentication, participants strategically choose to partner with particular orientations of authenticity to suit their interests and needs. Participants deploy a discourse, or lexicon, of authenticity – including terms such as "real," "pure," "traditional," "original," and "correct" – to buttress their own positions and achieve personal ends. As the nation and the state look to "authentic" local traditions to ground their legitimacy and stand out in the global order, individual artists similarly look to ground their realties and legitimize themselves as artists through the reputation and authenticity of the ensembles. For instance, as choreographers use the GDE as their personal canvas and archive for their artistic work, they manage authenticity by relying on cosmopolitan modes of power to authenticate these creations and achieve individual recognition. Paradoxically, then, preservation of national culture within the GDE has been accomplished through personal initiatives to protect and promote the works, reputations, and legacies of particular individuals, primarily artistic directors. In other words, it is the preservation and promotion of self that serve to archive the essence of the nation. Artistic directors and members of the national troupes simultaneously use a discourse of authenticity to legitimize the existence of these ensembles while delegitimizing competing groups; consequently, national artists increase their individual viability within the highly competitive environments of Accra, Ghana, and the international market. As such, by deploying such tactical artistry, the nation, nationalism, and the state become resources for self-improvement.

While strategically managing nationalism by using discursive tactics to secure their personal positions, many individuals claim to believe in the authenticity of the GDE and its "traditional" repertoire. Thus,
the authenticity often ascribed to "the village" has been successfully
transferred to the GDE. This transference allows the ensemble to serve
as a "mosaic of villages" where Ghanaians have come to seize this authenticity for themselves. Such a phenomenon resonates with Richard
Handler's observation that "contact with authentic pieces of culture in
museums or, better, the possession of such objects in private collections,
allows us to appropriate their authenticity" (1986, 4). Similarly, individual participation in the national ensembles provides those who believe
in the genuineness of their repertoire an opportunity to *embody* the authenticity of these forms, "incorporating that magical proof of existence
into what we call our 'personal existence'" (ibid.). In short, authenticity
is not merely discursive; rather, the perceived authenticity of the GDE's
cultural forms may penetrate the consciousness and bodies of artists,
providing a basis for individuals' felt authentic groundings as it becomes
a salient part of an individual's embodied sense of self.

The postcolony is a particularly revealing, and rather dramatic, stage on which are played out the wider problems of subjection and its corollary, discipline.

ACHILLE MBEMBE, 1992

THREE

Soldiers of Culture

Discipline, Artistry, and Alternative Education

ONE AFTERNOON IN THE SPRING OF 2007, I CAME INTO THE dance hall at the University of Ghana just before five o'clock and sat down on a bench that was on an elevated stage overlooking the dancers. They were milling about, their exhausted bodies waiting to close another workday. The director entered, and the scattered group came together to listen to his comments, as was common at the end of the day. Seated at a school desk at the top of the stage, he began to scold them; shame ran across their faces. He was angry or perhaps more disappointed in the group and punished them at his discretion. As one dancer summarized later, "We have to stay after today, because some of the dancers were misbehaving. They were eating during rehearsal. Others should have controlled them, but they did not" (Amotonyo 2007). Consequently, the entire ensemble was required to stay several extra hours (until about 7:30 PM) for this rehearsal/punishment.

Later that same year, an American student came to the university dance hall and asked one of the members of the Ghana Dance Ensemble if she could video-record him performing a selection of the ensemble's repertoire. Without obtaining the necessary consent from the director, the dancer agreed. Knowing this was a violation of ensemble policy, the dancer waited until the director left campus that afternoon to run errands. Subsequently, the dancer proceeded to perform for the American in an open space adjacent to the GDE's rehearsal hall. As he danced, others kept watch, promising to warn him if they saw the director return from town. Although engaging in illicit behavior, this dancer was willing to risk his job, eager to supplement his inadequate income with the relatively large fee he was promised (three times his weekly salary). Despite the ensemble members' best efforts to conceal their actions, later that day the director received word of this incident and punished the dancer by suspending him without pay for several days.

Such incidents of discipline and punishment are common within Ghana's national dance ensembles. As I observed, a significant portion of ensemble members' days were spent negotiating the political machinery that surrounded them – looking over their shoulders and attempting to avoid the gaze of superiors, the threat of reprimand, and the physical punishment that could accompany it. A comment by one of the ensemble's dancers offered an analogy for such practices. When I asked him if the troupe had any performances scheduled for the upcoming week, he replied, "We are like soldiers. When they call us into battle, we just go" (Atsikpa 2007). His comments alluded to the intense field of militaristic discipline in which he and his colleagues operated. As musicians and dancers, members of Ghana's state dance ensembles may be more precisely considered "soldiers of culture," defending the national heritage, advancing the government's ideologies, combating global and local prejudice, and battling to maintain national unity and sovereignty through expressive performance.

Extensively employing the work of Michel Foucault, this chapter highlights the imported nature of these disciplinary mechanisms and the notion of professionalism itself. Following anthropologist Cati Coe (2005), who has shown how Western-style disciplinary regimes have been cultivated in Ghana's public schools, and historian Frederick Cooper (1992), who has shown how European labor practices of disciplined "clock time" aided in colonizing Kenya,[1] this discussion points to the continual postcolonial adaptation of such foreign practices by Africans. While Foucault's language is deliberately invoked here to capture the restrictive aspects of discipline, my work also recognizes the agency of individuals who use their tactical artistry to assert control over such mechanisms and to harness state institutions for personal ends. The implementation of discipline within the GDE is not merely analyzed as a sinister, draconian imposition of power; rather, I show that it is intended to be part of the professionalizing process, designed to empower young musicians and dancers. As Nketia remarked, "We wanted to make sure that performers would have the right attitude [and] know the expectations of certain contexts and the appropriate ways of acting in those contexts so that they could be successful; they should be prepared to engage in *professional* settings – schools and government institutions – here in Ghana and overseas. For this, they need to be disciplined in accordance with modern standards" (2005). In short, discipline prepared musicians and dancers to engage more fully in modernity and cosmopolitan domains. Instituting multiple forms of surveillance, ranking, time management, and physical training, the GDE has created professional cultural soldiers who not only propagate the ideologies of the state but also manage to employ such methodology to propel their individual artistic careers.

DISOBEDIENT DANCERS AND MISCHIEVOUS MUSICIANS

In 2007, while searching the GDE office files at Legon, I came across an undated document titled "Special Conditions of Service,"[2] which shed new light on the disciplinary practices of Ghana's state dance ensembles. After outlining the major goals of the GDE, which aligned with Kwame Nkrumah's notion of African Personality, the document stated: "For the Company to achieve these aims and objectives, it calls for performers with a high sense of discipline, loyalty, and the right frame of mind to meet these challenges. There is the need more than ever before to have a code of conduct that would guide performers in maintaining this high sense of discipline, which is a prerequisite in the achievement of the above ideals" (1). Discipline, therein, was intimately linked with achieving the objectives of the ensemble and, by association, of nationalism. My discussions of this document with ensemble staff showed that these conditions of service, which were reportedly developed in the 1960s, continued to dictate the policies and practices of Ghana's national troupes. One senior staff member remarked:

> We are trying to put some kind of discipline in the group, because each and every one is coming from different homes. We are not like the institution where you wake up from your hall and then you go to work or school. We all come from different homes, so definitely each person has her own *character*. So when we meet as a group, we try to put things that are not right – you try to correct it. So at least the group can work as a group. And you use discipline, so that someone from outside will see that the group is disciplined. (Darko 2007)

Discipline was viewed by the staff as necessary for the ensemble to function, because it molded the character of individual drummers and dancers into a unitary, respectable, manageable, and obedient form.

Perpetuating such practices, the GDE is a testament to Nkrumah's legacy. As members carry out their duties with rigorous discipline, the ensemble is a remnant of his broader cultural project to create an ordered socialist society that reflected his vision for a modern Ghana. That is, the GDE was not the only state organization to promote discipline. The adolescent members of Nkrumah's Young Pioneers and Workers/Builders Brigade similarly compared their experiences to those of soldiers as they were trained to follow a strict protocol.[3] Wearing military-style uniforms, saluting their comrades, and marching in drill formations, they extended the colonial legacy of "disciplining the body" (Mitchell 1988). As these practices marked continuity with a colonial past, they ironically also signaled political change. These organizations displayed discipline and order to "showcase the political, social, and cultural revolution taking place in Ghana ... [and] demonstrate the state's control over a new socialist way of life" (Ahlman 2011, 90). Along with the Young Pioneers, the Builders Brigade, and other similar organizations, men and women in the GDE became cultural soldiers prepared to promulgate the interests of Nkrumah, his Convention People's Party, and Ghana. However, after Nkrumah's overthrow in 1966, the Young Pioneers, the Builders Brigade, and other similar organizations were dismantled.[4] Nevertheless, by linking discipline with culture and the development of the nation, Nkrumah set a precedent that has been followed by subsequent Ghanaian governments, most notably that of President J. J. Rawlings (Nugent 1998). In particular, the GDE and its disciplinary regimens have remained, proving once again that "Nkrumah never dies!"

With the specter of Nkrumah as a backdrop, from the moment prospective drummers and dancers enter the dance hall for their auditions they are situated within a "field of surveillance" (Foucault [1975] 1995, 189); they are observed and judged not only for their artistic skills but also for their moral conduct or "character." They are subject to a machinery of discipline and punishment that attempts to control, shape, and produce professional soldiers of culture. One day in 2007 I had the opportunity to witness an audition firsthand. Inside the dance hall at Legon, the director and senior staff sat on the elevated stage overlooking the dance floor and called the dancer to the center of the floor. "Do a traditional dance," the director said. The dancer paced about, appearing to be pondering what dance to choose; he then performed a section of *agbekor*, an Ewe dance. After a few minutes, the director told him to stop. The dancer gave the director a confused glance. The director asked if he knew any contemporary styles. The dancer nodded and proceeded to perform a Nii-Yartey-esque dance solo. A few minutes passed. "Fine, fine," the director said. And then, after a few more questions about the dancer's performance background, he and I were asked to exit the dance hall so the staff could assess his abilities. After rehearsal that day I was fortunate to see the dancer sitting, waiting for the results of his audition. I asked him how he felt about how he had done. He answered, "It was hard. Many people were there watching me. I had to dance by myself. I don't like to do that. They are the big men. They know dance very well, so you have to do your best for them. They know the right things."[5] It was obvious that this was a stressful process for the young dancer. His dance abilities were being put under a microscope. Exploiting the power of the gaze, this audition process subjects hopefuls to a "compulsory visibility" (Foucault [1975] 1995, 187), which, as Foucault has argued, is crucial to the implementation of appropriate disciplining. Eventually, the young dancer was told that the company could not take him at that time.

Even if he had made it into the company, the road ahead would have been arduous. Initially, performers who pass the audition phase enter into a one-year probationary period, after which, according to the "Special Conditions of Service" document, "a performer will become eligible for confirmation of his/her appointment subject to a report of satisfactory work and conduct from the Artistic Director. Training in the various disciplines of the company's repertoire would be undertaken during this period" (3). According to staff and other participants of the GDE, this system was still in place when I conducted my research. I learned that initiates enter into an intense probationary period in which staff and co-members closely observe their artistic skills, social attitudes, and moral conduct. If after this period the performer is considered worthy of entry into the group, the artistic director must then write a letter to the vice chancellor of the university, in accordance with part 1 of the "Special Conditions of Service." The vice chancellor, unseen by the young performer, transforms him or her into a member of the dance company with one stroke of his pen. This process illustrates Foucault's statement that "disciplinary power . . . is exercised through its invisibility" as it simultaneously subjects individuals to its system of visibility – or surveillance ([1975] 1995, 187).

After becoming formally accepted into the group, a performer gains a rank of class III and then may move up to class II and class I. A participant may eventually be promoted to senior drummer or dancer, dance instructor, promotions manager, assistant director, and finally, at the top of the pecking order, artistic director. According to the SCS, "No performer shall be considered for promotion if his/her performance has been unsatisfactory" (3). Performance here refers not only to an individual's artistic performance but also to his or her moral character. If promoted, performers receive increased wages and status. These promotions, however, are often difficult to attain and may take years to receive. Indeed, as Foucault notes, "discipline is an art of rank" ([1975] 1995, 146) and, in this case, "a learning machine that [is] also a machine for supervising, hierarchizing, and rewarding" (147).

I spoke to one dancer who had been in the company for "five good years" and had not received a single promotion. He told me that a performer is assessed at least every three years to determine if he or she is deserving of a promotion. Despite his hard work and good disciplinary record, this dancer had been passed over for promotion twice, he told me. He added that even some of the drummers and dancers who had been in the company for decades were still only a class III or class II rank. They should have been a class I or a senior instructor at least by now, he remarked. It was misconduct and "queries," he said, that the staff cited as their reasons for not granting him a promotion yet. These disciplinary actions have a profound impact on the experience of cultural performance onstage. The dancer continued, "Because of these things, you don't feel to dance; you just go onstage and don't really feel anything. These people are vampires. They are using us" (Badu 2007).

Conduct, Queries, and Apologies

As performers attempt to move up the ranks, the ensembles use an elaborate system of queries and apologies to keep tabs on their members' conduct. According to section II of the scs, titled "Discipline," "Any act of misconduct or negligence on the part of a performer is an offence which may render him liable to disciplinary action" (4). Some of the expectations are outlined, but overall the document seems vague, leaving the artistic director the ability to use his own discretion to make a judgment as to whether or not a particular behavior is worthy of disciplinary action. If there is such an offense, "the Artistic Director or his representative shall query in writing a performer whose work or conduct he has reason to be dissatisfied with" (7). The following is an example of such a letter:

Ghana Dance Ensemble–University of Ghana

I write to warn you about your attitude to work. Be reminded that two more of such warning letters to you will necessitate a disciplinary action against you.

Date _____ Artistic Director _____

One of the most common offenses is absence from work. A section of the scs titled "Absence from Duty" states that "performers are expected to be present during working hours, and are not to leave the University without permission from the Artistic Director" (6). Furthermore, "performers will not receive salary for time of absence . . . [and a] performer may be dismissed [fired] after habitual warning of unexcused absences" (6). Because this offense is particularly common, directors have found it helpful to have a form letter prepared for such an offense. The following is taken from such a letter, which appeared on university letterhead during Francis Nii-Yartey's tenure as artistic director:

Dear   ,

Would you explain within one hour why you were not at work on the following days (space for dates) and give reasons we should not advise the Finance officer to deduct the (#) days pay from your salary for the month of (blank).

Yours Sincerely,
Francis Nii-Yartey

Performers caught in violation of the GDE codes of conduct and who receive a query letter must then respond in writing with a letter of apology. "If [this] explanation is considered satisfactory," according to the SCS, "no further action shall be taken. If it is not satisfactory a decision shall be recorded in writing against him" (7). This practice not only helps to discipline and likely humiliate the dancer/musician but also serves to confirm the power and authority of the artistic director. Letters of apology often reaffirm the power dynamics that are present in the GDE's hierarchical system. The following is an example of a letter of apology on university letterhead:

Dear Sir,
Letter of Apology

With reference to your letter Ref. No. DNC.23/Vol.2/241 dated 20th March, 1974, I wish to write and apologize to you, the Committee, the Institute [of African Studies] and the University authorities in general for my unfortunate behavior at the G.N.T.C. shop recently.

I also vow not to repeat such a thing again, not only for the minimum period of 12 months, but for the whole time of my stay with the Institute.

I am very much thankful for your kind treatment of this case.

Yours faithfully,
[Name omitted by author]

The formality is evident, almost palpable, with the use of coded numbers and language such as "vow." This system has been in existence since the early days of the GDE and was employed regularly throughout my

research. Often, when I asked of the whereabouts of a particular performer at lunch break, other members would tell me that the individual
had gotten a query from the director and was busy writing an apology
letter to him. And often, while I was sitting in the GDE (Legon) office,
ensemble members would come to give a letter of explanation or apology
to the director.

Many of these apology letters have been written in regard to the code
that prohibits drummers and dancers from performing with or teaching
individuals other than those in the GDE. This teaching/performance
may involve foreigners, as in the second of this chapter's two opening
vignettes. Or, more often, it includes performance with local so-called
amateur groups. In 2007, such a case came to light. While I was standing with members of the Legon troupe outside the National Theatre
waiting for a performance to start, one of the dancers approached me
and started complaining about a warning letter he had received earlier
that day. It was from the artistic director, who was upset that this dancer
had engaged in a performance outside of the GDE. This unauthorized
performance had been broadcast on television and seen by the director. The television camera had acted as a surveillance tool, observing
him, preserving him, for the watchful eyes of the director. The dancer
performed a small act of defiance, joking to me that he would "use the
warning letter to wipe after going to the toilet." This was the fifth such
letter that he had received, but he was confident, he said, that the director would not fire him because the director knew that he was one of the
strongest dancers (in my opinion, he surely was). The director, however,
suspended him from the ensemble for a few weeks. He was not allowed
to engage in rehearsals or performances but nevertheless had to report to
the university during normal work hours (nine to five, Monday through
Friday). Thus, although this type of flagrant insubordination was rare, in
some instances performers subverted expectations and defied the rules
if they thought they were in a position to do so.

Countless times during my fieldwork in Ghana performers would
remark that they were dissatisfied with the ensemble, primarily because it precluded them from performing in other troupes – mostly local
amateur culture groups.[6] Drummers and dancers frequently broke this
rule in order to supplement their inadequate government/university

salaries. Often they were caught and queried, necessitating a written apology.

With such letters, disobedient dancers and mischievous musicians perform an act of written deference, virtually bowing to their superiors and affirming their place as subordinates within the national ensembles. In this way, such action is reminiscent of Togolese "peasant" recipients of European aid who were forced to write and rewrite letters in French in order to receive aid during the colonial era. Letter writing, whether in colonial Togo or in postcolonial Ghana, as Charles Piot notes, is very much about disciplining and humiliation; "the letter-writing process is about the role of education and the superiority of 'l'homme du papier' (the person who knows writing)" (2010, 142). Similarly, Foucault, referring to the French educational system, contends that the "power of writing" constitutes an essential part in the mechanisms of discipline, transforming an "individual [into] a describable, analyzable object" ([1975] 1995, 190). The act of writing itself, in other words, is a manifestation of the principle of visibility, which is a necessary part of the machinery of discipline. "The examination," or in this case the query and apology letter, "places individuals in a field of surveillance [as it] situates them in a network of writing" (189). In all, there is a litany of written rules, along with many that are unwritten, found only in the cultural norms of Ghanaian society for which this system of queries and apologies serves to enforce.

THE CREATION OF CULTURAL SOLDIERS

Within the dance ensembles' machinery of rules and codes, the body also becomes a primary site of disciplinary action. In this way, as Foucault states, "the body is directly involved in the political field; power relations have an immediate hold upon it; they invest it, mark it, train it, torture it, force it to carry out tasks, to perform ceremonies, to emit signs" ([1975] 1995, 25). When I asked E. A. Duodu, a former artistic director of the GDE and initial member of the group, about his approach to discipline, he responded not only by describing his own approach but also by detailing how physical discipline had been used in the ensemble throughout its history:

> Duodu: When you are choreographing you treat them [the performers]
> as artists; you treat them as human beings. You don't shout at them
> or yell at them, which Opoku did. Nii-Yartey copied him. He would
> yell at people. But I never yelled or insulted anybody. Opoku would
> use dance to punish us. If you misbehaved he would ask you to stay
> after class and do the movement 100 times or 200 times. It becomes a
> punishment. I remember one time we went to Star Hotel midday on
> a tile floor. Very hot to rehearse barefooted! It was a punishment.
> Paul: He did it on purpose?
> Duodu: I should think so. It must have been intentional.
> He used that to punish us, definitely (2007)

Dance itself was used as a form of punishment – punishment for the body. This is not surprising given that "disciplinary systems favour punishments that are exercise – intensified, multiplied forms of training, several times repeated" (Foucault [1975] 1995, 179).

Within the G D E, corporeal discipline is not merely punishment but also a mechanism for professionalization. When I asked a former member of the ensemble if he recalled being disciplined, he responded:

> Very much. If you are a junior there, after the closing you have to stay and work.
> If you go home they will give you query. And the seniors will send you out. And
> you will go around and buy food for them. And if you misbehave, they will make
> you scrub the changing room. Scrub it all! You will be scrubbing it for about
> one month. You alone. Or, maybe they will throw a stick at you. Discipline is
> very high over there. But through that you learn to become a serious artist.
> (Azadekor 2007)

A "serious artist" was considered someone who was well prepared to perform at a high standard of professional excellence. Nii-Yartey's comments regarding a comparison to his predecessor, Opoku, reinforced such a notion of professionalism:

> We sort of agreed in a lot of ways; he [Opoku] believed in discipline, I also be-
> lieve in discipline. He also had a lot of friends, he was a giver, he shared a lot, and
> I think I have learned to do that. I was ready to take his discipline. Many people
> were not. They thought it was out of place, especially some of the physical pun-
> ishment. But we knew it was necessary for the ensemble to move forward. (2006)

Like Nkrumah, Nii-Yartey viewed discipline as a necessary corollary to progress; Nii-Yartey particularly viewed this dynamic as required for the artistic development of individual artists and the ensemble as a whole. Following Nii-Yartey and Opoku, subsequent dance ensemble directors have used various methods of physical discipline, ensuring that individuals would perform to a high artistic standard; in the process, the GDE has acted to transform performers into embodiments of nationalism as well as professionalism.

To meet these expectations, within rehearsals, participants' bodies are methodically trained and retrained. Attempting to minimize the amount of retraining needed, initially, in the early 1960s, Nketia and Opoku preferred to recruit "untrained" dancers because, as Nketia recalled, "we knew that older people are difficult to train" (2005). However, it has become increasingly difficult to locate such individuals because of the growth of local amateur culture groups, which train performers in Ghanaian/African music and dance. Once initiated into the GDE, these performers have been encouraged to forget versions of dances previously learned in these amateur ensembles and learn/relearn the GDE's standard choreography, resulting in a tightly coordinated collection of sound and movement that serves to project the ideology of national unity. As the "chief master drummer" at Legon told me, "Before I came here, I knew so many musics, but I had to leave those at the door. Dance ensemble plays one way. I had to learn that, and now my body has lost most of the old ways" (Ametefe 2005). Another GDE drummer added, "My hand is not like before: I cannot play slow kpanlogo anymore; because I have been playing the fast ensemble one, my hand is used to that now" (A. Amenumey 2006). As with drummers, GDE dancers also come to embody the aesthetics of the ensembles and nationalism through a meticulous process of corporeal training. In one instance, a senior staff member repeatedly came down from her chair overlooking the dancers to move a performer's arm from a bent to a straight position. Later, the dancer explained that the director wanted her body position to conform to that of others in the group.

To facilitate this pedagogical process, dances within the GDE have been compartmentalized into small units of gestures and sonic phrases. As Nketia recalled, "The stage presentation meant making certain modifications. This is where Opoku came in, having been trained in the tradition and visual arts and going to the U.S. and studying with Martha Graham; he had an analytical approach to the whole thing. So the dancers would be taught in stages" (2005). This practice is what Foucault calls the "temporal elaboration of an act . . . whereby . . . time penetrates the body and with it all the meticulous controls of power" ([1975] 1995, 152). In general, as participants are acutely observed, movements and music are meticulously imparted, corrected, and repeated to accelerate learning and, by extension, forgetting.

Time also figures into the disciplining/professionalizing of the body in additional ways. For both new and senior members of the ensembles, rehearsals begin officially at nine o'clock every Monday through Friday at Legon and at the National Theatre. Lunch is granted from about one o'clock to two each day, after which performers return to work until five. As I observed, after nearly constant strenuous activity, performers' bodies were exhausted by the close of each workday. But, as Mustapha Tettey Addy, one of the original members of the GDE, proclaimed, "If you want to be professional, you have to work hard, and this is how you have to behave. Like for example, he [Opoku] would tell us when he was in the [United] States, these people would work for eight hours a day – nine to five. He would say, 'Don't fight with each other. You have to be clean. You have to be punctual.' He pushed us very hard" (2007). While suggesting the importation of Fordist principles (the eight-hour day and forty-hour workweek), this explanation of professionalism alludes to Foucault's concept of a timetable and the incorporation of Western temporality into the daily routine of the dance ensembles. Emerging from the European Enlightenment, the timetable is "a time of good quality throughout which the body is constantly applied to its exercise. Precision and application are, with regularity, the fundamental virtues of disciplinary time" (Foucault [1975] 1995, 151). To make the most effective use of time, the dance ensemble is subject to a type of disciplinary time, within which the precise movements of the GDE's choreography are inscribed on performers' bodies. The SCS document states that the repertoire of more than forty dances should be learned within the performer's first twelve-month probation period (3). To achieve this ambitious goal, it becomes necessary to make what Foucault calls an "exhaustive use of time" to intensify the use of time and "accelerate the process of learning" ([1975] 1995, 154).

Overall, the dialectic of discipline and professionalism found within the GDE exemplifies Foucault's "paradox of subjectification," whereby "the capacity for action [and individual agency] is enabled and created by specific relations of subordination" (Mahmood 2005, 29). On the one hand, like soldiers, GDE performers' bodies are trained and retrained with rigorous detail in a daily performance and embodiment of the micro-physics of power. Performers become entangled in a system of discipline and punishment, which attempts to control, shape, and produce them. Whether in Foucault's descriptions of the creation of the French military or in my analysis of the GDE, there exists a "policy of coercions that act upon the body"; there is "a calculated manipulation of its elements, its gestures, its behavior.... Thus discipline produces subjected and practiced bodies, 'docile' bodies" (Foucault [1975] 1995, 11). Yet, docility here does not denote complete passivity or loss of agency but rather the ability to become teachable.[7] Through rigorous discipline, combined with the individual will to submit to such practices, the docile body of a soldier-artist can be constructed. These soldiers of culture are molded to fulfill a set of duties: promoting and defending (that is, preserving) national heritage while advancing the ideologies of African Personality and Pan-Africanism. However, like a volunteer soldier, GDE artists submit themselves to a rigorous disciplinary system not only to achieve state objectives but also to gain personal skills, performance competencies, knowledge, and contacts that aid in artists' pursuit of self-improvement.[8]

Hence, far from being merely restrictive mechanisms of power, the practices of discipline outlined above have become vital to furthering the professional careers of many former GDE members. Several have stated that the disciplinary education they received in the GDE has been integral to their development as artists. As Salifu Merigah, a performer who started with the Legon troupe and later moved to the National Dance Company, explained,

> In the village their bodies are not tuned. Here our bodies are trained with discipline. The dance profession has tuned my body to use it anyway I want it, and I understand myself through the body. At first it was difficult because my body didn't want to learn. Sometimes my mind would say something, but my body wouldn't listen to it. So it was a conflict between my body and my mind. Slowly, I came to realize that my body and my mind need to work in tune. It took me more than two years before I felt comfortable with my body, because

it was a new strange language to the body. So now I'm quick, and I have more expression myself, because of my profession. So when we all [he and those in his home village] meet to play the *gonje*[9] they see that I make more excitement and fun for all of us. And they see that this guy [Merigah] is in a professional company. They see that I have something extra that they say they can learn from. (2006)

Other ensemble members have acknowledged that the discipline/professionalization of the GDE has had a positive impact on their careers. After leaving this ensemble, Addy, for instance, built a profitable international recording and performance career while maintaining his own ensemble in Kokrobite, Ghana; he noted, "I use the professionalism that Opoku taught as a basis for running my own groups. I make sure my people are on time, work hard, and don't get out of line" (2007). Similarly, Bernard Woma, a former member of the GDE and NDC who has built a notable cosmopolitan career as a performer and educator, told me that "at first I didn't understand why all the strict rules. Only later I came to realize that you need them to become successful. You need to make good use of your time and carry yourself with dignity" (2013). Other former ensemble members who have achieved international recognition, including Gideon Alorwoyie, Kobla Ladzekpo, and George Dizikunu, acknowledged (in personal conversations with me) that while the discipline of these state ensembles is limiting in many ways, adhering to such practices has prepared them to work within the cultural structures (that is, time frames, rules) of contemporary (academic) institutions as they have managed their own groups in the United States and England. In other words, becoming familiar with Western-style disciplinary practices of the GDE has eased these artists' transition into Western domains. These former members of the ensemble have also often found such discipline useful in maintaining a professional level of performance, which resonates with audiences around the globe. That is, discipline has helped these artists to ensure their acceptance in international contexts, raising their professional profile while furthering their careers. In all, as these artists have managed culture to produce spectacles that adhere to cosmopolitan expectations for performance, they have participated in a culture of managing – mediating and seizing political institutions to achieve self-improvement.

DRILLING DISCIPLINE

Beneath the panoptic regulatory apparatus of the dance ensembles, scattered practices survive, which defy a totalizing subjugation.[10] Ensemble members use a collection of tactical artistry to manage these state institutions and nationalism in creative ways. In April 2007, I witnessed the GDE's (Legon) performance of an original choreography, called *Drill,* which embodied the metaphor of cultural soldiers as it satirized and challenged notions of discipline.

It began with only drummers onstage playing an Ewe set of drums, but I did not recognize the rhythms. The rhythms were stuttered, staggered, and halting and did not include the characteristic polyrhythm I was used to hearing from Ewe music. It sounded like a marching percussion piece transferred onto African drums. Then, from stage right, a member of the ensemble appeared dressed in a militaristic uniform. He shouted something back toward the drummers. Six dancers came from backstage, in a high-stepping march movement, carrying rifles and wearing military uniforms. They formed a line facing the audience and halted upon the command of the dancer who was stage right. These dancers then began a series of military exercises, moving in formation with precision and conforming to the steady pulse of the master drum. The dancer stage right called "about face," "right turn," and so forth. With stoic, expressionless faces, the dancers obeyed. The audience of mostly Ghanaians giggled. The dancers were then called to face each other and draw their weapons. The routine then included a series of spins and fighting movements, reminiscent of *atsiabekor* or *adzogbo.* The dancers pointed their rifles in each other's faces, hopped swiftly, and turned. The dancers were then called back into linear formation. They drunkenly moved into position. One of the dancers, however, was out of place. He looked sheepishly at the "sergeant." Realizing he was in the wrong position, he stumbled back into formation. The audience again laughed, realizing this was part of the show. The dancers continued their exercises, in precision with the drums. Then they halted, the drums stopped, and the sergeant addressed the audience. He gave an exaggerated salute and asked the audience for permission "to fall them out, sir!" The audience laughed and jeered. "No, no!" they chuckled. Despite these

3.1. Members of the GDE performing *Drill* in the dance hall at Legon.

objections, the dancers left the stage, exaggerating their movements as they exited (PURL 3.1).

This dance was choreographed in 1972 by E. A. Duodu, who was inspired by the precision of local police parades and the successive military governments that pervaded Ghana and much of Africa at the time. It was created shortly after the military coup by Ignatius Kutu Acheampong in Ghana. Duodu juxtaposed discipline with humor, he said, "to make it lighter, so people wouldn't be so concerned about it" (2007). In this way, its early performances poignantly captured and critiqued the hypocrisy of the Acheampong regime (1972–78), which promoted strict military and socialist economic discipline as a solution to Ghana's financial woes while it ironically engaged in widespread corruption (*kalabule*) as well as the liberalization of Ghanaian markets.[11] Given that Ghanaians were well aware of such hypocrisy, it is unsurprising that this comical dance was well received by audiences, including students at Legon who regularly engaged in political protests against this leader and thus "were among those who could claim political credit for the demise of the Acheampong regime" (Nugent 1998, 32); however, surprisingly, *Drill* has also been well received by Ghanaian governments, including Acheampong's and later the Rawlings regime. Duodu noted, "The first time this dance was performed for president [J. J. Rawlings], he laughed his head off. He couldn't control himself. He forgot he was the head of state" (2007). Jennies Darko, promotions director for the GDE, later added, "On some occasions, the president [either Rawlings or later J. A. Kufuor] would even join in the choreography, coming down to inspect the dancers himself in a kind of joking way" (2007). This dance has been performed annually at the Accra Police Academy graduation, where it has similarly been well received by guards and cadets who engage in the performance. Playing along with the joke, government officials attempt to neutralize critique while endearing themselves to the citizenry by showing their sense of humor.

Following a long history of satirical African performance, from pre-colonial reproach of local leaders and the mocking of colonial military to Fela Kuti's Afrobeat,[12] *Drill* is subversive as a type of legerdemain. Paradoxically, as participants quite literally become dancing soldiers of culture, they are, in fact, mocking the disciplinary training they have undergone to perform this choreography and embody such an identity. By inflecting discipline with humor, this piece furthermore comments on local sociopolitical practices. Thus, it is "a tactic [that] boldly juxtaposes diverse elements to produce a flash, shedding a different light on the language of a place" (de Certeau 1984, 37). Through it, new light is cast on the particular forms of discipline found in the Ghanaian military and police institutions as well as in the GDE itself. If we understand these institutions and the practices within them as informed by British colonial rule, this choreography takes on wider significance. By producing a temporary amnesia of roles, *Drill* unites citizen and state in an open mockery of foreign power and its presence in local cultural politics. In general, *Drill* creates a space in which subaltern voices, otherwise silenced by institutionalized, cosmopolitan power relations, can "speak" (Bhabha 1996; Spivak 1988). Consequently, it is not the dancers who are coerced into obedience by Duodu's choreography; rather certain modes of discipline – namely, those imported from the West – are drilled into submission. Thus, the "mimetic faculty" (Taussig 1993) is used here not only as a way to comprehend otherness but also as a way to assert mastery of it (Stoller 1995).

While *Drill* adeptly reproaches foreign and local forms of power, it also marks historical transformations in attitudes toward African/ Ghanaian postcolonial rule. When juxtaposed with other similar pieces in the GDE repertoire, it portrays the change in perception of African soldiers (and states) that took place between independence and the early 1970s. While Opoku's *Lamentation for Freedom Fighters* (1965) glorified the sacrifice of African soldiers in the struggle for independence, within a decade *Drill* had transformed this heroic figure into a bumbling buffoon. As they stumble, the soldiers in *Drill* act as symbols of the corruption and indiscipline that became associated with African governments by the time of the choreography's creation. Taken together, these two works chronicle the general social shift in the public perception of African states from optimism to disillusionment.[13] Subsequently, as the seat of Ghanaian power changed hands, this dance-drama took on new meaning. What was once a critique of the Acheampong regime (and military rule in general) served to underscore Rawlings' attempts to redefine the role of the military and police force in Ghana. On January 5, 1982, he gave a radio address that outlined his call for a new perception of the soldier: "The days of the colonial type of army are over. Soldiers are also human beings with needs and aspirations, not just the tools for some people's oppression. The Ghana armed forces are now pledged to be the Forces for the people, working in the interest of the people, not brutalizing them. We have now a People's Army, a People's Navy, a People's Air Force" (Rawlings 1982, 5).

Viewed in this light, *Drill* served at this time not only as a critique of colonialism but also as an attempt by Rawlings to humanize the military and police force, showing that they served the interests of the people. However, this choreography still retained its ironic comical quality. Given the persistent brutality and corruption that often characterized the Rawlings regime, citizens continued to interpret this choreography as a satirical reproach of the government's hypocrisy. Recognizing such ironies, one dancer explained, "Rawlings, the man tried, but he went about it with some force, sometimes beating the people. He claimed to be of the people but sometimes was against them. *Drill* makes a joke out of this" (Azandor 2007). Many GDE members noted that while Rawlings professed to command a less brutal military, he ordered it to carry out violent raids of Ghanaian market women, enforce strict curfews, and execute federal judges (see Nugent 1998; Shillington 1992).

In all, such mimicry particularly deconstructs and "ambiguat[es] hegemonic control over thought and action" (Hecht and Simone 1994, 107), not only of that which is imposed by the West but also of that which is posited by the Ghanaian government or other African states. As Duodu told me in the summer of 2012, "*Drill* is a piece about how the local military and police should lay down their weapons and stop harassing the people of Ghana and other African countries. They should rather dance instead, because dancing and music heals the soul." Through its tactical artistry, *Drill* blurs the roles of government and governed as they dance and act together, highlighting their convivial relationship as it produces an "elegant joke" about the "hollow shell" that is the postcolonial African state (Mbembe 2001). Because such satirical performances erode official power but fail to produce significant changes in the social order, they enact the mutual "zombification" of state and nation as neither is empowered by the display (111). If governments have the ability to command bodies, performances such as *Drill* demonstrate that their control is not total as artists manage the symbolic order, engaging in critique of their state/employer, ironically within the very institutions that the state has initiated.

"ALTERNATIVE" EDUCATION

Situated primarily at Legon, the GDE has been a type of school within a school, a training ground within an institution of higher education within a government bureaucracy. The National Theatre group, although not located in the university directly, similarly acts as a type of school, offering its members opportunities to gain specialized knowledge and skills while operating under the auspices of the state. Like schools, these ensembles, as we have seen, are powerful tools for creating disciplined social order, controlling the body and the body politic (Mitchell 1988). Recognizing this, both colonial and postcolonial African states have relied on similar practices and institutions to shape the bodies and consciousness of subjects and citizens, respectively. While colonial states often used educational institutions to impose their "will to civilize," postcolonial African states rely on such institutions to impose their "will to nationalize" (see Coe 2005). However, education is a double-edged sword. As schools trained individuals to serve the colonial interests, this education also empowered students to fight for independence, counter-

ing European hegemony. Postcolonial African governments have similarly recognized education as necessary for national empowerment and
(economic) development but are cautiously aware that educational institutions, particularly universities, can be breeding grounds for dissent
and protest against the state. Thus, Ghana's national ensembles have a
precarious position, simultaneously serving as instruments of the state
and sites of personal empowerment and expression. In short, both ensembles provide artists with an "alternative education," allowing access
to a realm of specialized resources. While fulfilling duties to the state,
ensemble artists manage these educational opportunities to open up
new possibilities for self-improvement.

When Nketia, a scholar and educator, was first tasked with setting
up a national dance ensemble, he envisioned it as an arm of the national
educational system: "At the time there were really no other African
dance companies that the GDE was based on. There was the Guinea
Ballet, but they were commercializing the dance. We didn't want to do
that here. We wanted to connect the ensemble to education. That's why
we located it at the university. This makes the GDE unique. No other
dance company has this sort of relationship with a university or education in general" (2005). Indeed, although there has been much written
about national dance ensembles (Castaldi 2006; Hagedorn 2001; Kaschl
2003; Shay 2002; Turino 2000), none has been linked so directly with
a state educational system as the GDE.[14] William Adinku, a founding
member of this ensemble, writes that "the beginning of dance education
in [Ghana] was linked to the formation of the Company [GDE]" (1994,
5). Bringing together experts from around the nation, the GDE became
instrumental in formalizing dance (and music) education in Ghana.
Thus, the ensemble was both a centerpiece of the government's National
Theatre Movement and an institution of higher education. Addressing
this dual role, Nketia intended for ensemble members/students to be
educated in traditional music and dance in order to teach in Ghana's
public school system, thereby disseminating African Personality and
Pan-Africanism.

Given the GDE's position within the university, Nketia initially required those who intended to become members to simultaneously enroll
in the dance diploma program at Legon (see Adinku 1994). Thus, the

initial cohort of these state ensemble performers were predominantly those who had finished secondary school. However, those who were handpicked by Nketia and Opoku as music/dance experts were often not required to meet this stipulation. For these artists, the GDE acted as an alternative route to higher education. A musician without much formal education thus could learn from Nketia, Opoku, and other scholars, becoming steeped in specialized knowledge that is only taught at the university as they took advantage of available resources and contacts. For instance, Mustapha Tettey Addy, who acknowledged that he never finished secondary school, recalled,

> You know what I used to do? I used to go into the classroom where they were learning the labanotation,[15] and I learned it and was teaching some of the students. I was fast. I learned everything very fast. So when Opoku was teaching I was listening very carefully and learned whatever he was telling us. . . . It was the best . . . experience for me. I learned a lot of things. I met so many people, so many people. And when I went back to my village, people would say, "Oh, you are the one." It was a big, big education for me. (2007)

Like Addy, many of the initial staff of the GDE did not have much formal education. Nevertheless, without officially enrolling at the university, these artists studied their craft with some of the country's most renowned performers. They never received diplomas, but their association with the GDE has acted as a "credential," leading to career opportunities domestically and abroad. Many of the former members of the GDE, despite the lack of a college diploma, teach at universities in the United States and Europe and around the world.[16] In addition to much of their drumming and dance knowledge, performers also have the GDE to thank for their exposure to prospective employers through public performance in Ghana and abroad. In short, most of the Ghanaian musicians/dancers who hold university posts in the West have been able to achieve this status due primarily to their membership in the GDE (see Dor 2014).

While many exceptional local artists became members of the GDE in its early years, many more were precluded particularly because they had not completed secondary school. Meeting this mark has been a consistent obstacle to many Ghanaians for a variety of reasons: lack of personal funds to pay for books and fees, parents not valuing formal education, family and other domestic responsibilities taking precedence. Conse-

quently, completing secondary school as a stipulation for GDE membership was dropped in the 1970s as the troupe became more autonomous.
This ensemble subsequently became a more viable possibility as an "alternative university" for those who otherwise were not qualified or could
not afford higher education. The following narrative of Salifu Merigah
provides an example of a person who seized the alternative education of
Ghana's state dance ensembles:

> I came to Accra in 1980 because my senior brother was working with
> the company, playing the gonje. My brother decided to leave the company, so
> Nii-Yartey said he needed a young boy who could play the gonje and learn
> how to dance. So my brother, knowing that I wasn't going to school – not
> really doing anything – called me to come and join the company. I never
> finished secondary school, because my parents didn't value it; they didn't
> realize it was a good investment in a person's future.
>
> I did an audition on what I could play. I have the inspiration in me
> already. I couldn't do the dance, but that expression of art, I have it in
> me already because my parents were artists. So I was quick and sharp
> and could pick things [up] quickly. I have the power in me, and I enjoy
> myself, and it helped me more in what I could not [do]. Most of the dances
> I haven't seen before. I had not seen any of the other ethnic dances be-
> fore – Ewe, Akan, etc. I didn't know them at all. Even things from the
> North, Upper East, and Upper West, like bima, nagla, lobi. I learned all
> that in the company.
>
> [The dance ensemble] enlightened me and made me who I want to be,
> myself – to be able to move to any rhythm, to be all over Ghana, and to be
> able to understand yourself better. I can express myself in any dance be-
> cause I have the feeling of all the ten regions.
>
> Opoku was strict. Opoku, he would always call me and tell me to do it
> this way; meanwhile, I didn't know he wanted me to be better in future. He
> would tell me, "You have what it takes to be what you want to be, but you
> don't know it." He saw potential in me, because I was not aware of the po-
> tential in me. He tried to help me. He put that pressure on me. I was lucky I
> listened to him, because he made me the artist I am today.
>
> In the traditional way, we just play for ourselves, looking down. He
> would tell me to raise my head up. Look at the person you are playing the

*thing to. Move closer to them, express yourself, enjoy yourself. Open your
eyes, laugh ... you can't turn your back to the audience. You need to lend
your face to the audience. This is what I gained from Opoku. It was a new
experience; I wasn't aware. I was playing in a different way. Some things
I didn't like. But I came to realize that it was good; he gave me the expression. He used to tell me, "You have to sing loud." In our tradition we didn't
sing too loud. He wanted me to move back, so people could see what I was
doing, and then project myself so people could hear.*

*I have been helped to understand how to create things in a very broad
way. I would have not understood this before. So the company has actually
tuned me to be what I want to be myself. I didn't know I had that potential
before; I was not aware. I wanted to be a lawyer; they would come in their
coats and look very neat, and I said, "Wow, I like them." And this job has
taught me that if I were a lawyer, I would have cheated myself. And I'm
lucky that I got into the job. (2006)*

Like Merigah, many GDE members whom I spoke with credit the dance
ensemble for educating them. Opoku, Nii-Yartey, and other artistic directors have been cited for helping ensemble members realize their own
potential as artists. By participating in the GDE, Merigah and others
have received a profound education at a formal institution with expert
faculty. Because most of these artists, like Merigah, have never finished
secondary school, such (higher) educational experiences would not have
been possible for them otherwise.

Cultural and Social Studies

The alternative education of Ghana's state dance ensembles has been
informed by its primary political directive to promote the state's rhetoric
of "unity in diversity." To this end, members of these ensembles have been
educated in a plethora of cultural traditions from their nation and around
the continent, encouraging them to go "beyond ethnicity" and "beyond
Ghana." In this way, as shown in chapter 1, artists learn to enact "chameleonism," in which a multiplicity of (ethnic) identities, or cultural styles,
are strategically deployed instrumentally through performative compe-

tencies. Ensemble members often remarked that their ability to perform a range of Ghanaian and African dance repertoire made them more sought after as local and international artists. In cosmopolitan contexts, which often value the aesthetic of variety, they have a distinct advantage over provincial musicians and dancers who usually can perform only their local traditions. In short, through the GDE's "cultural" education, artists have become professional national and "African" dance experts.

Given the nature of the state ensembles, it is unsurprising that participants should gain knowledge of cultural traditions within these institutions. What is remarkable is the way in which this alternative education goes beyond music and dance. Participants learn valuable communication and social skills that equip them with increased confidence. For instance, as one GDE musician at Legon explained,

> I was on the farm helping my family when I was called to go to Legon in 2003. I never went to school, only worked as a farmer and then as a gonje player. The dance ensemble has helped me a lot. Before I came, I did not even know how to speak English, so I couldn't talk to many people outside of Ghanaians. I learned English all from being in the GDE. It has been a great experience that has opened my eyes to so many things. The GDE is like the school that I never got a chance to go to as a child. (Abdullahi 2007)

Similarly, when I asked Mercy Ayettey, who has been a member of the GDE for over two decades, if she thought that her experience in the dance ensemble has changed her as a person, she replied,

> Yes, it has changed me a lot.... I have learned a lot from the group – how to talk to people. At first I can't even talk to somebody because I feel shy. But we have been going to state functions, and you have to know how to talk to people. It has helped me to become more confident if I want to do something. Because I have been performing in front of hundreds, even thousands of people, and you alone are performing, so how can I be shy? So you have to express yourself. Before, I didn't know much English, but the dance ensemble helped me with that. Now, I feel I can express myself in English. (2007)

Many other participants had similar stories, stating that they learned how to speak English and sometimes even Twi and Ga (indigenous languages) through the GDE.

E. A. Duodu's comments on other ways that the GDE has increased participants' repertoire of social skills:

> I was a shy person by nature. And my shyness died out when I came here, it died
> out completely. Because to face a full crowd, it drove away my shyness. It put
> confidence in me and made me respect people – authority. And it helped me to
> work in harmony. It reduced my anger. It made me believe in teamwork. My
> self was pushed aside. I don't feel fine [but] I know the group has to perform.
> If I'm not there to perform, it will hurt them. So I will suppress my weakness to
> go and dance. (2007)

Like Duodu, many GDE members noted that they were shy upon their
initial entrance into the group, but they gained confidence in their artistic abilities and in themselves more generally as they continued to perform. Not only did the dance ensemble help Duodu and others overcome
their shyness, but it also instilled in them the values of teamwork and
sacrificing for the "greater good" – two essential components of nation
building. While performing nationalism encourages this expanded sense
of self, individualism still remains; as a young dancer remarked, "[The]
dance ensemble teaches you how to become a family, but also how to be
strong in yourself, so you can accomplish anything you want" (Agyette
2007). In all, the GDE has empowered individuals by providing them
with an opportunity to learn and sharpen their social skills, build their
confidence, and allow them to communicate more effectively to a wider
(foreign and domestic) social network, thus increasing their opportunities to further their careers.

Study Abroad

On a cloudy day in the summer of 2006, I met one of my Ghanaian
friends at the U.S. embassy in Accra. He was waiting in a long, curving
line that wrapped around the imposing edifice. He, like so many others,
was awaiting a chance to plead his case to a U.S. official who would determine if he was worthy of receiving a U.S. visa. Despite having a letter
of invitation and a good reputation as a performer, he was denied – like
so many.

As they are in many African nations (see Piot 2010), U.S. visas are
both highly prized and elusive in Ghana. Many Ghanaians believe that
traveling to the United States will bring guaranteed monetary wealth
and earn them respect from their countrymen. As one former member
of the dance ensemble explained, "Our tradition does not benefit you in

this Ghana. But if you go out, you make a lot of money. The vision is we want to travel. We want to gain something. We want to showcase something" (Agyari 2007). While domestic markets for "traditional culture" have continually declined over the past several decades, due in part to the marginalization of such arts by neoliberal policies (Perullo 2011), foreign demand for African cultural performances has remained relatively robust (see Klein 2007). A senior dancer who is also a mother remarked that, "because of traveling, we have something for our family's future" (M. Ayettey 2007).

Although many individuals denied that foreign travel was one of their motivations for joining the group, many outside the group contended that it is typically the primary reason for participating in the national ensembles. Individuals within or close to the GDE know that these travel opportunities often benefit individuals in numerous ways. Through touring, a select group of Ghanaians receive foreign visas, which would otherwise be nearly impossible to obtain; subsequently, these individuals have a better chance at receiving visas on their own because they have the precedent proving to government officials that they will not "run away" but will return to Ghana after traveling abroad.[17] Additionally, the social connections that individuals make in foreign countries often lead to economic opportunities, including teaching at Western universities (see Dor 2014). These appointments frequently result in substantial increases in income. Furthermore, those who have traveled often gain status and reputation among their peers upon their return. In short, those who "study abroad" are typically empowered and enriched by their experience.

Although GDE members often return from their foreign travels, many have run away to seek "greener pastures"; as in the Canada trip outlined in the introduction, these individuals never come back to Ghana for fear of being prosecuted. Given challenging domestic economic conditions and the marginalization of the ("traditional") arts by the Ghanaian government, many GDE members view the national ensembles as a necessary "exit strategy" (Piot 2010) when "desertion . . . [seems] the only suitable response to the arbitrariness and the slovenliness of the State" (Bayart [1989] 2009, 258). Ironically, ensemble members manage nationalism and these state institutions to depart from their nation-state.

Business 101

At the University of Ghana campus, just south of the main entrance, there exists a shady, open expanse of land. This area, directly adjacent to the School of Performing Arts, is often referred to as "under the tree" by the many drummers who use it as both a practice space and a teaching studio. A typical scene, taking place almost daily here, is one Ghanaian man surrounded by a number of foreign (mostly white) students sitting on benches attempting to learn "African" drumming. Predominantly, the teachers are those employed by the university who are not members of the GDE. However, although they are forbidden by ensemble policy, its members often engage in this educational process as well. Dancers and musicians who perform in the GDE receive exposure to foreign students through their numerous on-campus performances, put on throughout the academic year. Their attachment to "the" Ghana Dance Ensemble makes them sought-after as instructors of traditional dance and music. I often heard exchange students boast that they were taking drumming and dance lessons from a member of the GDE. Their status as "national artists" allows them to charge a slightly higher than average rate (relative to others in the area), typically running between ten to fifteen U.S. dollars per hour. Consequently, national artists can earn almost half their weekly government salary for one hour as a private instructor. On the ensemble's lunch break, participants occasionally told me they could not do an interview because they "had business with someone under the tree"; this phrase was a euphemism for teaching private lessons. These individuals risked their jobs to supplement their income, capitalizing on the available (although illicit) resources and opportunities.

Within the compound of the School of Performing Arts, there is a large whitewashed building that houses the dance hall where members of the GDE (Legon) regularly rehearse. On most days, a group of ensemble members sit just outside the building working feverishly, carving wood under a sign that reads "Drums for Sale." This is the "storefront" of a shop run by Christopher Ametefe, the chief master drummer of the GDE at Legon (figure 3.2). He and his crew produce drums for customers all over the world. Through their performances with the GDE and high

3.2. Christopher Ametefe, master drummer of the GDE, in front of his shop at the dance hall at Legon.

visibility at the university, they have been able to build a vast clientele, both foreign and domestic. Not only does this ensemble connect Ametefe and his crew with clients, but it was through a former director of the GDE that Ametefe first received this business education. Oh! Nii Kwei Sowah explained,

> You know that sometimes the [GDE] salary is not the best, but I always try to encourage people to keep on with their work when I was the artistic director. I think the guy who is selling drums there now [Christopher] will tell you that he got the inspiration from me, and now that is helping him. So I always want to bring out the best in you. Just stay focused and bring out the best in yourself, and that's where you will get your recognition. (2006)

Indeed, when asked, Ametefe acknowledged that Kwei Sowah had given him this "business idea." Whether as dance/drumming instructors or as drum builders/sellers, these entrepreneurs have primarily received their business training from the GDE and have learned to use this national institution for their personal enrichment.

Several former members of the dance troupes have employed their business training beyond the ensembles, establishing "cultural centers" throughout the country. The best known of these are Godwin Agbeli's Dagbe Arts Centre in Kopeyia (Volta region), established in 1982, and

Mustapha Tettey Addy's Academy of African Music and Arts (AAMA), founded in 1988 in Kokrobite (Greater Accra region).[18] Such sites adopt the national and cosmopolitan practices of the state ensembles as a framework for their own business models. Bernard Woma, another former ensemble member, told me the story of how he came to found such a site:

> The dance ensemble made me into a professional. It gave me the idea to use my cultural skills as a career. I had not really thought about that before I came to the ensemble. Before, I would just play for food, beer, and *pito*.[19] But after some time in the ensemble, I began to demand money for performances in Accra. Some got mad. But I thought, I am equal to musicians in highlife bands who were paid to go onstage and play. . . . The ensemble also gave me leadership skills; it gave me discipline, which helped me to be more professional. (2013)

Subsequently, Woma acknowledged the GDE for "putting him on the pathway to where [he] is today"; Woma is an internationally renowned artist who stated that he owed his career to both Opoku, who urged him to audition for the ensemble in the 1980s, and the troupe's master drummers at the time: Foli Adadae and Solomon Amoquandoh. He particularly credits the dance ensemble for his ability to profit (monetarily) from his artistic talents:

> The ensemble introduced me to the idea of teaching *gyil* to people. White people came to the university and wanted to learn. So I began to think about how to teach Westerners. And I began traveling to culture centers in Ghana and teaching gyil to both foreigners and even Ghanaians. From this, I came to the idea that I wanted to start a music center. I asked Nii[-Yartey] if it was a conflict of interest. I had to get his approval, because dance ensemble rules will not allow you to teach their repertoire outside of the group. I didn't want to do anything they call *mo kye de* [you all have done something from behind, or under, the table]. I succeeded in convincing Nii that I was doing something different from the dance ensemble. So I established the Dagara Music Center [DMC] in 2000. (2013)

Since its inception, the DMC has grown into a major site for cultural tourism in Ghana, attracting students from America, Europe, and Asia. At the DMC, tourists/pupils learn a diversity of dance and other cultural traditions such as kente weaving, batik, tie-dyeing, drum making, and blacksmithing. Woma considers himself a cultural ambassador of Ghana and recognizes the dance ensemble for inspiring him to take a nationalistic approach to his work. That is, although the name of the center is taken from his own ethnicity (in the Upper West region), Woma promotes it as a site for the transmission of "Ghanaian" culture. The broad repertoire of dances Woma and others learned in the ensembles has allowed them to appeal to cosmopolitan desires for variety. In all, Ghana's state dance ensembles have given Woma and others the tools (including cultural knowledge, discipline, and leadership skills) to manage their business ventures and achieve their professional aspirations.

Sociology of Ghanaian Music and Dance

Ghana's national dance ensembles have also participated in transforming Ghanaian music and dance into more respectable professions, allowing performers to pursue these artistic activities as occupations with increasing ease. Whereas musicians and dancers have long occupied respected positions in local (rural) communities, dance has acquired less favorable associations in "modern," cosmopolitan, urban settings such as Accra. Speaking about Accra in the 1940s, Duodu recalled, "We didn't have professional musicians. And you would only find them at drinking spots, palm wine spots. And people would buy wine for them, and most of them were drunkards. Nobody would want his children to become a musician. In those days people did not allow their children to dance. They thought that it would lead them into temptation. . . . They think it will lead them to prostitution, that a musician or a female actress is loose" (2007).

Even into the 1960s, such stigmas still existed, as Grace Djabatey's personal struggle attests: "When I started on this course, my family didn't like it at all; they didn't want me to be a dancer. Those days, people were looking down upon dance. At that time, this striptease thing was going on, and people thought that dancers were prostitutes. Because of the family I come from – they are Christians, and they are educators – they wanted me to do law or science or something like that" (2006). After years in the ensemble, "now they [my family] are so proud; they say, 'Oh sister Grace, can you bring your group to perform here or there?' . . . They feel proud because I proved to them that a dancer is not a prostitute. A dancer can also be a good housewife or have good behavior." Grace defied her parents, often an empowering experience on its own, to create a successful career as a dancer. Moreover, at the time of my research she had risen through the ranks to become the first female assistant artistic director of the NDC (the first for either ensemble).

Drummers and dancers in the ensembles often transgressed the wishes of their parents, risking alienation from their own families to pursue their passions. Caroline Yeme's story is one particularly dramatic example of how the GDE has helped change Ghanaian attitudes toward dance as a profession:

I wanted to dance, but my father encouraged me to join the police service. And I even went and did some of the training. But I quickly realized I couldn't do that. Through my friends in the GDE, I learned that they were looking for dancers. I had to make a decision whether to complete the police training or join the group. I loved dancing, so I didn't care what my father said. In 1988 I came to Legon and started work with the dance company. But my father didn't like it when I stopped the training, so there was this confrontation between my mother and father. I was trying to convince my father all this time. I went on my first trip in 1990 or '91 to Canada. Still he said I was not doing the right thing. I came back, he says I am not doing the right thing. I didn't have it easy, as far as my parents coming together. My father wanted one of his children to take over for him [as a police officer]. And he knew that I was good in school, and all my teachers were pushing me. And I was a straight person. He didn't want me to deviate from whatever he wanted me to do. So it had become a big problem with my parents; my father wouldn't talk to my mother.

My first production with the dance company was Atanga. It was very nice. Prof [Opoku] said that we should write a letter to all our parents to come and watch the show. So I went to my father's house to drop the letter, but he was not there, so I just left the letter there. Later, when he came home he saw the letter and called me. He got angry and he said there was no respect in it, going and showing yourself to people. He started asking me if they wanted money. I said no, they just want you to come and watch, because the first show was free for parents and friends. So he came to the show. Before the show he was always calling me and talking about the police service and saying things to convince me to leave the dance. But when my father came he said, "Eh! This girl is not joking." So since then, no more phone calls like that. That was my first relief. I was performing onstage, trying to convince my father that I wasn't joking.

So my father from then was telling everybody about the show and saying, "Come and watch my daughter, jumping" and all that. Now my father helps me, and he will do anything to support me in dance. If we are going for a tour or whatever I need, he will assist me. And he will come to the dance hall from time to time. He is very happy. (2006)

Throughout her struggles with her father, not only did Yeme deal with this unpleasant situation offstage, but her family concerns entered into her experience of dancing onstage as well. She was not merely dancing for the nation but simultaneously performing to earn the respect of her father. Her story reflects the broader social change in views on music and dance as a profession. Encouraged by the GDE, this shift has paved the way for future generations to pursue their dreams with less ridicule or conflict. As a young dancer told me, "One thing I want people to know is that it is respectful if you work with your national group. You become more respectable to your family and friends. Now when I go home they give me some respect. So I think it is a blessing to be in the Ghana Dance Ensemble" (Agyette 2007). By fostering respectability for music/dance as a profession, Ghana's state ensembles have helped establish a new path to power and personal enrichment, which allows individuals to capitalize on their artistic talents in ways that were not available to previous generations of Gold Coast or Ghanaian citizens.

ARTISTRY AND SUBJECTIFICATION

As members of Ghana's national dance ensembles are rigorously disciplined with militaristic detail, they become professional soldiers of culture, prepared not only to advance the ideologies of the state but also to further their individual aspirations. Reflecting Foucault's "paradox of subjectification," participation in Ghana's national dance ensembles subjects members to harsh disciplinary restrictions but simultaneously professionalizes them and offers them opportunities to gain specialized knowledge, skills, and contacts. Embodying disciplinary mechanisms, for instance, has prepared national artists to transition into careers outside of the ensemble.

In all, artfully managing the resources of the ensembles, state, and university (Legon group only), troupe members take advantage of an alternative education to acquire social and communication skills, study abroad, make business transactions, and transform the reputation of dance to their advantage. In this way, soldiers of culture use tactical artistry to "seize on the ... possibilities that offer themselves at any given moment ... [and] vigilantly make use of the cracks that particular conjunctions open in the surveillance of the proprietary powers" (de Certeau 1984, 37), poaching them and creating surprises within them where they are least expected, including satirizing the very disciplinary mechanisms that have both restricted and enriched them. Dancing in between regulatory codes, ensemble members create and exploit fissures in the nationalist façade, molding state machinery to suit their needs, turning public employment into a private resource (Chabal and Daloz 1999, 7). Throughout its history, members of Ghana's state dance ensembles have harnessed artistic and educational opportunities to achieve personal enrichment as they pursue their own self-improvement.

Every modern state needs the legitimacy of nationalism.

THOMAS TURINO, 2000

Modern states . . . are ultimately beholden to their citizens
and must publically perform their "stateliness."

KELLY ASKEW, 2002

FOUR

Speak to the Wind

Staging the State and Performing Indirection

ON JULY 24, 2012, GHANA'S SITTING PRESIDENT – JOHN ATTA MILLS – died suddenly in Accra. Although rumors of his battles with throat cancer had been swirling for months, including speculation that his recent trips to the United States were for medical treatment, this news nevertheless came as quite a shock to Ghanaians and others around the world. That morning, I was with staff of the National Dance Company at the National Theatre in central Accra, observing a rehearsal for an upcoming event on health care. In the middle of the afternoon, after this meeting had concluded, I entered a taxi to make the return trip back to my flat. Immediately the driver said, "Did you hear the news, our president is dead!" I was stunned. I offered my condolences before my attention was grabbed by the blaring car radio. The broadcaster was announcing a special emergency meeting of Parliament, asking all the MPs to report to the statehouse as quickly as possible. Traffic was flooding the streets as we passed the military hospital where the president had spent his last moments. Mourners clad in black and red lined the perimeter of this compound. As we inched along the congested boulevard, several motorcades of black SUVs passed us, sirens blaring from their police escorts. Urgency mixed with melancholy and disbelief as Ghanaians, and I, began to process what had happened.

Later that evening, my wife and I sat in a local restaurant watching the coverage of the parliamentary session on television in which the vice president, John Mahama, was sworn in as president. It was evident that Mahama was still in shock as he mourned for his longtime colleague and friend; he struggled to perform protocol. After being handed a golden machete, he had to be reminded to sit in the gold-plated throne in the center of the hall following the recitation of the oath of office. The next day I returned to the National Theatre, but no rehearsal was taking place. Due to the president's death, the NDC performance had been canceled.

Subsequently, the morning of July 26 I received a phone call from the Ghana Dance Ensemble (Legon) director telling me that the troupe had been asked to perform a special tribute to Mills for the Ghana Broadcasting Corporation (GBC). I met the director on campus, and we proceeded to the GBC studios in downtown Accra. When we arrived, the ensemble was already backstage, getting dressed in appropriate black and red funeral regalia. As we exchanged greetings, some dancers and drummers were called off to put on makeup and have their hair done; the men particularly teased each other about this. When the producers were ready, the ensemble and I filed into a small, quiet, dimly lit studio, where *fontomfrom* and *kete* instruments were already in place. Three large cameras stood at the back of the room, plus one on a balcony, amid a plethora of lighting and scaffolding. The GBC director discussed the plans for filming with the ensemble. She was, in a sense, choreographing the performers' choreography. In addition to arranging the dances for this particular space and lighting setup, she later told me that she wanted to be sure that each of the ensemble's four pieces – *atenteben, adenkum, kete,* and *fontomfrom* – would last only seven minutes (PURL 4.1). (Time compression in action, I thought.)

After the recording was finished, the performers quickly packed their instruments and headed outside to wait for their bus back to the university. As we waited, I asked them about this experience. One mentioned that during the performance, while she was thinking about the president, she also thought of her sister who had passed away a few years earlier. Another told me that while he was mourning for Mills, he was also thinking about making sure he performed kete well; he wanted to be certain that when people saw him on TV playing the lead drum, they would recognize his talents. This, he said, might encourage someone to pick him to tour abroad. In other words, performers did not lose sight of their own personal aspirations and concerns as they staged the state. In the following few days, GBC broadcast this half-hour tribute to the

4.1. Members of the GDE (Legon) at the Ghana Broadcasting Corporation Studios in Accra.

late president several times as part of its *damirifa due*[1] programming. Performers were excited to see their own images on TV, and, while they noted that it was an honor to pay tribute to Mills, some also mentioned that they hoped to obtain copies of the event to promote themselves.

Weeks later, Mills's funeral was held in Accra. On the first two days, August 8 and 9, his body lay in state. Scores of Ghanaians, dressed in black and red, queued around the statehouse for the public viewing. After dignitaries had viewed the body, the general public was allowed inside. Mourners were ushered in by the thunderous sounds of the fontomfrom drums, performed by members of the GDE (Legon). Subsequently, on the evening of the ninth, an all-night vigil was held; numerous eulogies were given by various dignitaries and clergy from across the nation. Later, around 2 AM, there was a performance by a group comprising dancers and musicians from both national ensembles and Noyam (Francis Nii-Yartey's contemporary dance troupe). Choreographed by Nii-Yartey, this piece involved a sea of dancers dressed in flowing white robes, slowly processing while carrying a life-sized likeness of Mills draped in kente cloth and holding an Asante royal sword; the dancers ritually slumped, clutching their stomachs and sobbing as they performed a swaying, step-slide movement.

While a reverent mood understandably pervaded these funeral rites, reproach of the Mills government had been commonplace among ensemble members earlier in the summer of 2012. Participants were frustrated with its lack of support for the arts and blamed it for stagnant wages, rampant unemployment, and increased inflation. They often noted that although Mills had overseen Ghana's new foray into oil extraction, the wealth generated by such operations did not "benefit the people." However, following Mills's passing, when I asked about such issues, their previous critiques were silenced as they reverently participated in the staging of the state.

In Ghana, a parliamentary democracy, criticisms of the government are unsurprisingly common as its citizens exercise their rights through various forms of civic engagement – openly lambasting their leaders for political corruption, low wages, inadequate utility services, and so forth. While participating in this democratic process, members of Ghana's national dance ensembles, however, are in a precarious position. On the one hand, they are employed by the state, consequently having an implicit duty to uphold its ideologies and legitimize its power. Yet these artists remain citizens, often actively joining fellow Ghanaians in condemnation of political authority.

While outlining a brief history of how the postcolonial Ghanaian state has been staged, this chapter also offers an anthropology of it. Such a perspective "allows us to pay careful attention to the cultural constitution of the state – that is, how people perceive the state, how their understandings are shaped by their particular locations and intimate and embodied encounters with state processes and officials, and how the state manifests itself in their lives" (Sharma and Gupta 2006, 11). Adopting this "view from below," the subsequent discussion examines the ways in which Ghanaians come to understand their government, and their relationship to it, through "embodied encounters" of music and dance performance. Although previous chapters have shown how state ideologies such as African Personality and Pan-Africanism have been enacted by the ensembles, here I more closely explore the direct, and indirect, interaction between government officials and performers.

Most notably, I focus on the clever and often surreptitious ways in which participants in Ghana's state dance troupes manage to "voice" their indignation with their government even as they perform under its direct observation. Performers mediate this situation by enacting a strategy of communicative "indirection," which is pervasive throughout West Africa (Obeng 2003; Tarr 1979; Yankah 1995). For generations, individuals in West Africa have used indirection as part of various "politeness strategies" (Obeng 2003) to "save face" (Goffman 1967), softening the impact of communication that may offend authority (such as chiefs, elders, and the like), invite reprimand, or tarnish personal reputations and relationships. For instance, instead of directly addressing authority or the Supreme Being, the Akan choose to "speak to the wind"; engaging in such practices, Akan (and other) highlife musicians often sing metaphorical lyrics to indirectly reproach political leaders (Yankah 2001). In all, indirection and its corollary, ambiguity, create a type of *thick communication,* which encompasses multiple layers of meaning as it additionally provides a protective coating/coding that cushions the force of expressions that have the potential to endanger the "speaker."

Within Ghana's national dance troupes, performers draw on the familiar practices of indirection, which allow them to avoid overt conflict while still managing to express dissatisfaction with their government/ employer. Thus, while artists stage the state, upholding expectations of compliance and unity, their use of subtle gestures, intentional silences, and coded reconfigurations of nationalist rhetoric is carefully calculated to slip under the radar of public officials, insinuating veiled indictments of a government that is often unable to meet their needs. In this way, indirection becomes a communicative tactic – an artful way of managing, or dancing in between, multiple positions as state employees, artists, and critically engaged citizens in a democratic society.

While this chapter further explores the mediation of multiple (postcolonial) identities – or subjectivities – it illustrates that the relationship of citizen-artists to their government defies a resistance paradigm as it is both "convivial" (Edmondson 2007; Mbembe 2001; Nyamnjoh 2002) and dynamic, regularly shifting. That is, citizens and the state are involved in a mutually reinforcing, and disempowering, dance: the two converge in moments of tangled conviviality as they are unified in purpose and rely on the other for support; yet, in certain instances, they diverge when at odds with the other's practices, views, or goals. By examining various case studies that span multiple Ghanaian regimes (Nkrumah, Rawlings, Kufuor, and Mills), the following discussion offers a diachronic analysis of the differing dialectics between particular governments and their people. I particularly analyze the GDE's role in a number of state "dramaturgies of power" (A. Apter 2005), because "public cultural representations and performance of statehood crucially shape people's perceptions about the nature of the state" (Sharma and Gupta 2006, 18). Overall, this chapter shows that as the state wields the nation's culture to legitimize its power, artists often similarly harness these political instruments – ironically, in some instances – transforming them into subversive tools to reproach their government.

SEIZING THE SANDALS OF THE CHIEF: NKRUMAH'S APPROPRIATIONS OF ROYAL SYMBOLISM AND POWER

Throughout his political career, Kwame Nkrumah was well aware of the ability of cultural performance to galvanize the masses. Arguing for the centrality of culture in the battle to end colonial rule, Kofi Agovi writes, "The 'culture people' – concert party artists, guitar bands, poets and playwrights of the forties – teamed up with [Nkrumah's] C. P. P. 'Verandah Boys'² and aroused the whole people of Ghana to fight for independence" (1989, 15). At public rallies leading up to his presidency, Nkrumah regularly employed highlife bands, such as E. T. Mensah and the Tempos, to perform. Aside from popular music, particular neotraditional ethnic styles, such as the Ewe *borborbor* and Ga *kpanlogo,* were also frequently used at political rallies. Nkrumah capitalized on the established popularity of these forms to gain the support of the populace of the Gold Coast, which was vital to further his quest for an independent nation-state and his own ascendance to power.

After independence, Nkrumah, as president, continued to use various types of culture to promote his, and the state's, authority. He also found culture to be a vital tool for nation building and for furthering his particular politico-cultural objectives (see Botwe-Asamoah 2005). Namely, as explored in previous chapters, Nkrumah mobilized cultural forms to further his ideologies of African Personality and Pan-Africanism. These state cultural displays also served to combat anti-Nkrumahist groups such as the National Liberation Movement (NLM), Ga Shifimo Kpee, and others who attempted to depose the leader, occasionally through violent means. Nkrumah's legitimacy as head of state was also challenged by the traditional authority of chiefs and community elders. In an attempt to attenuate this challenge, "within weeks of independence," Richard Rathbone writes, "the government was demonstrating that it was in firm command. In mid-April it suspended the Accra Municipal Council and only days later suspended that of Kumasi" (2000, 100). Overall, in the first year of Nkrumah's presidency, his government took a variety of measures that "tightened its control over the [nation-] state" (103) in an attempt to "show where power lies" (J. B. Danquah qtd. in ibid., 100). In other words, Nkrumah attempted to demonstrate the post-independence shift of power from local community and colonial leaders to the newly formed national government.

Throughout the remainder of his term in office, Nkrumah expended much of his energy quieting the authority of traditional Ghanaian chiefs because of its significant threat to his own authority. As Cati Coe notes, "Nkrumah attempted to undercut independent chiefs by taking away their judicial and administrative functions, to align chiefs with the national state, and to use symbols of chiefly authority to legitimate his own" (2005, 61; cf. Rathbone 2000). Asante kente cloth, royal stools, state umbrellas, *okyeame* (Akan state linguist), adinkra symbols, gold decoration, jewelry, and casts were all regular features of state ceremonies, because chieftaincy, according to George Hagan, was seen by Nkrumah as "the embodiment of the highest cultural values of the people . . . [and] he sought to surround himself with the symbols of chieftaincy. And he enjoyed it" (1985, 11–12). In short, because chiefs are widely understood in Ghana as the primary "custodians of culture" (Hagan 1985; Coe 2005), such symbolic displays, Nkrumah predicted, would give the impression that he was the "ultimate chief" of Ghana. In addition to material art forms, "culture," as Coe (2005) has carefully shown, has often been synonymous with the performing arts in Ghana, particularly "drumming and dancing"; Nkrumah considered them to be the most powerful artistic tools with which to proclaim his authority and legitimate his rule. For instance, in his book *I Speak of Freedom,* Nkrumah remarked that "my arrival at Parliament House was heralded by the beating of traditional drums . . . [and] State horns – *Mmenson* – were sounded by the Juaben State Ntahera" (1961, 238–39).[3]

To affirm his role as the new leader of the nation, Nkrumah was careful to select particular music and dance that carried the weight of traditional authority. Although there were a plethora of ethnic groups throughout the nation, each with their own music and dance traditions, Nkrumah primarily relied on the music and dance of the Asante court. These cultural forms were already imbued with deeply imbedded connotations of hierarchy, royalty, and chiefly authority, which Nkrumah sought to imitate and usurp. While many ethnic groups had hierarchical political organizations prior to independence, they were not necessarily equivalent. David Apter notes that, for instance, the Ewe have "the least tribal hierarchy among coastal groups," while the Tallensi of the Northern Territories "have almost no recognizable formal political authority" (1963, 81). And, while Apter recognizes the "highly articulate forms of chieftaincy" of the Dagbamba, he maintains that it is the Asante who have the most "highly developed" systems of chiefly authority (ibid.).

Additionally, the Asante had a long history of dominance in Ghana, as they conquered many areas, bringing various groups under the Akan umbrella (see Wilks 1993). At the time of independence, the Akan made up over half of the entire Ghanaian population. The size and scope of the Akan enabled the Asante-led NLM to provide the strongest anti-Nkrumahist movement during the early years of nationhood. Therefore, it is not surprising that Nkrumah most frequently used the symbolism of the Asante royal court in his own performance of power, because it was already imbued with the historical weight of the Asante. Moreover, including Asante traditions in postcolonial state ceremonies may have been a way for Nkrumah to appease the NLM, creating a sense of inclusiveness. In all, I assert that the Asante court most closely resembled the hierarchical structure that Nkrumah sought in his formation of a state system for Ghana because it stood as the most powerful and "highly developed" state system previous to independence.

Nkrumah also adopted Asante music and dance, I propose, particularly because it already had acquired a multiethnic identity, which reinforced the state ideology of "unity in diversity." As evidence of the Asante's powerful influence, particularly in regard to their political organization, many ethnic groups in Ghana have adopted Akan court music/dance and have subsequently developed their own variations. The Ga, Ewe, and Adangme all borrow the Akan *atumpan* twin drums for their court music, and while the Ga have *obonu*, the Ewe have *vuga*, which are their versions of the Asante fontomfrom (see Nketia 1962, 19). The Ewe also perform their own version of the Asante kete royal music/ dance and, like the Ga and Adangme, have adopted the royal horn music of the Akan. The royal court music of the Asante, thus, was poised to become a national symbol because it had cut across ethnic lines well before independence.

Given its associations with Asante power and trans-ethnic connections, it is not surprising that Nkrumah often utilized the Asante royal court, or "state," music/dance of kete and fontomfrom. Kwabena Nketia uses the term "state" to indicate that, until the twentieth century, although these music/dances were adopted by neighboring ethnic groups, they remained directly and exclusively associated with chieftaincy. He explains, "In the past many of the drums and drum ensembles of the chiefs could not be privately owned or played without permission of the chief; nor could they be played at any time other than that laid down by custom and tradition. To order fontomfrom, for example, to be played for you privately or to keep a set of these drums for private use meant elevating yourself to the position of chief. It was regarded as an insult and an offense" (1963, 119). Furthermore, the type and size of drum that a particular chief could possess was limited by his general status in relation to the entire Asante nation (120). In general, only the most powerful chiefs – not village headmen (*odikuro*), for instance – could own large state drums such as the *twenekesee*. Additionally, there were strict customs governing the adoption of court music/dance variations from other areas. A chief had to obtain permission from another to borrow "new drum creations," including both instruments and musical innovations (121). Due to their coveted status, the drums of another village captured in battle were highly prized as they became "war trophies," symbolizing the "humiliation" of the defeated chief; their status also made the drums of the court a valuable gift or reward in honor of outstanding achievement or to mark significant events (121).

These customary laws were amended as Nkrumah appropriated the court music/dance of the Asante for his own purposes. Although he was

Nzima, an ethnic group within the Akan, Nkrumah was not a descendent of royalty and thus did not have the "traditional" status as a chief. Performing kete or fontomfrom for Nkrumah, in other words, marked a significant departure from customary Akan law. Although it is not clear if Nkrumah initially obtained permission to use these drums to signify the national state, there is evidence that at least some Asante eventually allowed Nkrumah, and the state, to use these specialized instruments beyond the royal court context. Fontomfrom, atumpan, and other Akan drums were donated to the state by Opanyin Kwasi Boateng of Akomadan (Ashanti region) in a ceremony at the Flagstaff House in July 1962, in which the minister of information accepted the gift on behalf of the state (see fig. 4.2).

Throughout his term in office, even before this particular ceremony, Nkrumah used the fontomfrom and kete to mark significant national and state occasions, including his own arrival to many such events. For instance, a set of fontomfrom drums has resided in the Ghanaian houses of Parliament since independence; the drums are sounded to signify the opening of a new legislative cycle or special session. Particularly, it is appropriate that the fontomfrom drums, not any other Akan court instruments, are kept in the Ghanaian Parliament because, as Nketia notes, this is the "most important of all state orchestras" (1963, 136). The kete, for example, is played for "minor" occasions, while the fontomfrom is performed only for "major" events (137). This hierarchical relationship of the Asante court music is often maintained in the national state, as the large fontomfrom drums are beaten only for the most significant of political ceremonies.

Within fontomfrom there are several sections, each with a particular meaning and function. Typically, as I learned from members of the GDE, in matters of the national state it is the *nnawea* that is performed. Nketia describes this music as the "best-known" of all the sections; it functions as a "music for a dance of joy, a triumphant music, which may be performed behind the chief when he is returning to his palace after a celebration, or when he is seated during a state assembly" (1963, 138). Many in the national dance ensembles confirmed this assessment, stating that they performed this music because "everyone" knew this variation and could dance together. During this variation, the fontomfrom

4.2. Article from
the *Daily Graphic,*
July 12, 1962.

drummers beat a rhythm that has lexical meaning. In a deep, resonant "voice" the drums pronounce:

Efiri tete.	It is an ancient truth.
Banin ko; banin dwane.	A man fights; a man flees.
Okoko dammirifua.	Condolences, warrior.
Banin ko; banin dwane.	A man fights; a man flees.[4]

As it is performed for the national state, the drum language originally intended for an Asante chief is reinscribed to refer to the Ghanaian president. The message of the drums equates the president to a warrior and effectively lauds him as he who fights for the nation. The meaning of fontomfrom is thus expanded as the drums praise and affirm the authority of not an Asante chief but the political leader of the entirety of Ghana. This drummed statement also reinforced Nkrumah's self-proclaimed title: Osagyefo, which is often translated from Twi as "warrior," "savior," and/or "redeemer." Nkrumah viewed himself as a man who fought to save and redeem the nation. Additionally, this drummed statement, originally exclusively intended for Asante chiefs, stands as another example of the many ways in which Nkrumah appropriated the symbolism of chieftaincy to serve the nation and trumpet his own authority. In all, the performance of fontomfrom (and other indigenous court music/dances) for the Ghanaian government signified the historical shift of power to the national state as local chiefs and elders were "destooled" – abdicated – from their former positions of authority in numerous ways, metaphorically having their "sandals seized from under their feet" (Hagan 1985, 9).[5]

CULTURAL POLICY AND PERFORMING FOR NKRUMAH

Clearly, Nkrumah recognized the importance of culture in the process of galvanizing political support and building a viable nation-state. Nkrumah appropriated the symbols not only of chieftaincy but also of popular cultural forms, such as highlife, to promote his bid for president and legitimize his authority after independence. Due to Nkrumah's charismatic push to promote culture, which set a strong precedent for subsequent Ghanaian regimes, Ghana has had a remarkable history of cultural programming (Coe 2005, 9). Given his extensive mobilization and manipulation of cultural forms, it is surprising, however, that Nkrumah did not promulgate an official cultural policy during his presidency. Similar to other scholars (Coe 2005; Hagan 1985), I have found no references to cultural policy before a 1975 UNESCO document that states, "African Personality . . . [had been] the guiding principle of Ghana's cultural policy from the time of independence to the present" (Cultural Division 1975, 9). His lack of policy has led some to characterize Nkrumah as a cultural "non-interventionist" (Hagan 1985, 12). However, while his primary aims were political and economic, Nkrumah took great interest in cultural affairs, playing an instrumental role in establishing such institutions as the Institute of African Studies at Legon, the Arts Council, the National Dance Company, the National Archives, the National Theatre Movement, and the National Museum, most of which have continued to play significant roles in the trajectory of cultural nationalism in Ghana. Marking a significant intervention, he worked to "traditionalize" highlife, requiring some bands to receive training from Ghana's Arts

Council in traditional music (such as *agbadza* and fontomfrom) before they could perform for the state (see Plageman 2012). Yet, in select cases, like the GDE, he often adopted a "non-interventionist" approach, allowing African Personality to act as an "invisible hand" to guide its cultural practices. Unlike highlife, the GDE, by its nature, possessed knowledge of "traditional" culture and was explicitly ideologically aligned with African Personality.

Because he had played a significant role in the initiation and philosophical foundations of the national troupe, subsequently he often adopted a hands-off approach to it. On an administrative level, as Nketia stated, "once Nkrumah helped established the company, he mostly left us alone to do our work" (2005). Corroborating such remarks, Mustapha Tettey Addy recalled,

> He didn't get too involved in the dance ensemble's affairs, except to say that he wanted different ethnic dances to be performed for him. Usually we play the [Dagbamba] *damba*. Sometimes we play the calabash drums, and we play kete a lot, and fontomfrom. When he's coming from a plane, usually we play damba with the *breketes* and *dondons*. When he comes to Legon we usually play kete, or sometimes *sikyi*. He liked the highlife ones a lot. But he liked all the pieces we played. Nkrumah is not a tribalistic man at all. (2007)

Another ensemble member who performed for Nkrumah, Foli Adadae, also acknowledged that at such occasions, "[Nkrumah] never said anything much to us. He didn't criticize us. He just praised us to go on and continue our work" (2006). While attesting to Nkrumah's non-interventionist approach to the ensemble, the previous comments indicate that he, conversely, strategically used a wide variety of "ethnic" dances to reify the state's rhetoric of "unity in diversity," which was a crystallization of African Personality. In this way, throughout his tenure as president, Nkrumah primarily only indirectly shaped the practices of the GDE.

However, there is one instance in which Nkrumah and his government directly intervened in the practices of the national ensemble. In the 1950s, a new music/dance style called kpanlogo was gaining popularity in Accra. It was created by Ga musicians as a recreational music/dance form and quickly became popular with urban adolescents, who often added sexually provocative movements to it, including hip gyrations in close proximity to one another; in addition, males danced behind females, pressing themselves against the females' buttocks. Due to its sexually suggestive movements, the state considered banning kpanlogo altogether. Government authorities requested to see the dance firsthand to judge for themselves. In 1964, Otoo Lincoln, considered to be the creator of this dance, was brought before the Arts Council and questioned about the dance. Subsequently, he and his group were invited to perform at the national stadium in Accra for Nkrumah and others who would decide the fate of this dance form. After some deliberation, Lincoln enlisted the help of the National Dance Company (GDE). Mawere Opoku, aware of the controversy surrounding the dance, rearranged it, putting space between the dancers, which effectively removed the sexual connotations of the movements. Staging this refined version of kpanlogo at Ghana's national stadium later that year, the ensemble secured approval from Nkrumah, who praised the dance. Incidentally, this official performance facilitated kpanlogo's growth in popularity and "established the guidelines for creative innovations that would be culturally accepted" (N. Thompson 2000, 65–67). While performances of kpanlogo in community settings often still include suggestive movements, its sanitized version has become one of the most popular "traditional" African dances on Ghanaian and international stages. Thus, despite the lack of an explicit cultural policy, Nkrumah's regime has profoundly shaped the performance and representation of national culture in this way.

Aside from his impact on the representation of cultural forms, I interrogated the experiences and views of those who performed for Nkrumah. I expected a range of contentious responses given Nkrumah's infamous abuses of power. Nkrumah became increasingly suspicious of the Ghanaian populace and ever more dictatorial throughout his tenure as he feared assassination and coup attempts from oppositional groups. Most notoriously, Nkrumah created and aggressively pushed through Parliament the Preventive Detention Act in July 1958, which "empowered the government to arrest and detain for five years anybody suspected of or found acting in a manner prejudicial to the security of Ghana, and to her relations to other states" (Asirifi-Danquah 2007, 29). Nkrumah made liberal use of this act, detaining as many as three thousand Ghanaian citizens during his term. Moreover, throughout Nkrumah's presidency, Ghana's economic situation steadily worsened and was "on the brink of national bankruptcy" (66), encouraging thousands to flee the country. Nkrumah's corruption also worsened, as he regularly took bribes and used state funds for personal expenses. In all, according to Asirifi-Danquah, "Nkrumah's policies at home caused so much distress to Ghanaians of all shades of life that all Ghanaians including ordinary members of the CPP were crying onto their 'gods' for a change of government" (68). Unfortunately, records of ensemble members' experiences and views regarding performing for Nkrumah could not be found from this period. And already by the 1970s there was growing nostalgia for Nkrumah (Nugent 1998, 30).

As I explored this topic in interviews, compounding such nostalgia was a pervasive nationwide euphoric reverence for Nkrumah as Ghana celebrated its fiftieth anniversary in 2007. Given this, it is not surprising that GDE members did not express criticism of Nkrumah even when pressed on the aforementioned issues. When I asked how it felt to perform for him, the few remaining founding members of the GDE generally remarked that it was an honor. They did not express indignation regarding Nkrumah, despite the president's questionable actions while in office. If ensemble members felt anger or resentment toward Nkrumah, it remained hidden. When discussing subsequent regimes, however, as the following sections will illustrate, participants more openly expressed dissatisfaction with their employer/state. While performers were often candid in private interviews, they were careful to mask such reproach during performances, subtly and indirectly "voicing" critique of the state as they staged culture under its direct supervision.

RESTORING THE NATION: ECONOMIC AND CULTURAL RECOVERY IN THE RAWLINGS REVOLUTION

With Ghana on the verge of economic collapse and Nkrumah's corruption and human rights abuses becoming increasingly intolerable to the public, he was overthrown on February 24, 1966, in a bloodless coup d'état led by the Ghana Armed Forces and the Ghana Police. A military council, the National Liberation Committee (NLC), replaced the deposed leader and remained in power for nearly three years. Ghana's economic situation continued to decline after Nkrumah's overthrow, leading to political instability. In 1969, following a democratic election, a civilian government took the reins, with Dr. K. A. Busia as the prime minister. After attempting unsuccessfully to revive the Ghanaian economy through a concentration on rural development, Busia was ousted by another military coup within three years of taking office. Under the new leadership of Colonel Ignatius Kutu Acheampong, prices of goods rose as they became increasingly scarce. Corruption and government secrecy also spread. Many Ghanaian citizens commonly referred to this period (1974–79) in the nation's political history as the time of *kalabule* (Hausa word literally meaning "keep it quiet" or commonly understood as "corruption").[6] Failing to stem Ghana's economic woes, Acheampong's state was overthrown by General F. W. K. Akuffo, who lasted less than a year in office before he was similarly overthrown.

In May 1979, Flight Lieutenant J. J. Rawlings of the Ghana Armed Air Forces organized a dramatic attempt to oust Akuffo but, after a hail of gunfire, was captured and detained. Rawlings was later tried in a court tribunal, which became a boon for his political career. At the trial, Rawlings became a "national hero overnight" (Asirifi-Danquah 2007, 119) because his court testimony courageously decried government corruption and its ineptitude. The nation largely sympathized with his statements because he voiced opinions that were "deeply rooted in the minds of Ghanaians" (119). After he was released from custody, Rawlings and his Armed Forces Revolutionary Council (AFRC) soon grabbed the seat of power from Akuffo's unpopular Supreme Military Council party. In 1979, Rawlings and the AFRC oversaw democratic elections and honored the results, making Dr. Hilla Limann the head of state. After little more than two years in office, Rawlings and his supporters, who formed a new party called the PNDC (Provisional National Defense Council), remained unsatisfied with the progress and direction of the country. Therefore, they staged a second coup, known as the December 31st Revolution, to regain leadership of Ghana. Rawlings's second term in office lasted for nearly twenty years (1981–2000) and had significant impacts on the economy as well as on the trajectory of cultural policy and development in Ghana.

Rawlings's second term of office, as Cati Coe accurately notes, "reinvigorated the push to promote 'Ghanaian culture'" (2005, 9). Discussing the early days of Rawlings's second administration and its promotion of the arts, Ben Abdallah – a key figure in the cultural policy development under Rawlings – told me,

> When Rawlings's government came to power, they put together a think tank that looked at every sector of the country – education, finance, roads, port, mining, health.... They came up with what they called the "PNDC Policy Guidelines." When it came to culture, [this document] was saying that culture was the basis of our own development, and that we cannot begin to see where we are going until we understand where we are coming from and who we are as a people. (2007)

Like Nkrumah, Rawlings recognized the importance of culture in building a strong nation. Abdallah acknowledged that Rawlings's emphasis on culture was reminiscent of and inspired by Nkrumah's conceptions of African Personality and Pan-Africanism. And, like Nkrumah, Rawlings readily appropriated the symbols of Asante chieftaincy to simultaneously usurp and diminish provincial authority while promoting his own.[7] For instance, Rawlings commissioned local artist James Akyeampong (of the Kumasi Cultural Center) to carve an elaborately decorated, oversized set of fontomfrom drums; their enormity dwarfs conventional fontomfrom drums (figure 4.3). Given that increasing size often represents higher degrees of authority in Ghana, these enlarged drums signified the continued transfer of political power from local chiefs and elders to the postcolonial national state. In all, after what Abdallah called a period of "free for all" (1966–81) riddled with coup d'états and a declining economy, Rawlings's administration oversaw a reassertion of African Personality. That is, culture was seen by Rawlings as a way to both restore the dignity of the Ghanaian people and help return this country to economic prosperity.

As he followed the precedent set by Nkrumah, Rawlings attempted to go beyond the work of his predecessor by formalizing the Ghanaian government's relationship with culture. Rawlings did so by calling for the drafting of a detailed cultural policy. Ben Abdallah, who served in Rawlings's administration in a number of capacities since 1983, helped to compose the document, which would serve to guide the promotion and development of culture in Ghana. This policy encouraged the elevated status of culture vis-à-vis the state, because it established, in 1989, a

4.3. State drummers playing the *sika fontomfrom* drums during the inauguration of newly elected president John Atta Mills of Ghana at Independence Square in Accra on January 7, 2009. *PIUS UTOMI EKPEI/AFP/Getty Images.*

government body solely dedicated to the promotion and development of the arts – The National Commission on Culture (NCC). With Abdallah as its first chairman, the NCC worked to implement the propositions outlined in the new cultural policy. Regional cultural centers that had been idle since Nkrumah's time were revived and new regional cultural centers were established across the country. Most important for this discussion, despite this new government policy and "the several changes of government, each new regime recycled and expanded on the ideas of its predecessors. Thus we see [in Rawlings's cultural policy] an increasing association of culture with drumming and dancing" (Coe 2005, 57). Consequently, the dance ensemble was a key component of this cultural policy. With this focus on drumming and dancing, additionally, the GDE remained a vitally important cultural symbol of state authority. As such, Rawlings continued to include this dance troupe in national events and used it in the state's pageantries of power. In general, as the testimonies of my consultants implied, the cultural activity, particularly in regard to drumming and dancing, was spurred by this cultural policy as it encouraged increased activity in Ghana's "traditional" arts during Rawlings's tenure. That is, while popular (highlife) musicians generally regard the Rawlings period as one that precipitated the decline in live music, due to the imposition of curfews that led to the closing of many nightclubs in Accra, "traditional" artists often noted that there were always plenty of performances at the time; one drummer told me, "We always had work when Rawlings was in power. He did a lot to promote the arts" (A. Amenumey 2006). However, the new cultural policy and government body (NCC) had one particularly adverse indirect effect on the GDE: they led to its bifurcation, which caused frictions between the two ensembles. Nevertheless, ensemble interviewees did not appear to blame Rawlings for this event but rather generally revered him for his promotion of the arts, often citing that he had overseen the construction of the National Theatre (see chapter 5).

Performers also noted Rawlings's direct involvement with the ensembles, which served to endear him in their memories. As one NDC dancer recalled,

> Rawlings was somebody who liked dancing. He and the first lady would come to the National Theatre and watch rehearsals. He would like to see how we were going about things. And he would write us letters, saying, "Let's get together and do something for this program or that." Also, after a performance he would even come to the backstage and shake hands with you.... Rawlings even invited the dance ensemble to his house twice.... Rawlings also came to dance sometimes, and if you are a performer it makes you perform well when you see that. (Yeme 2006)

Another dancer added, "Because the man [Rawlings] will dance with you, that is why I like him. If someone does not dance, then you might think they are hiding something" (M. Ayettey 2007). Other performers noted that invitations to the president's home and his willingness to dance served to partially inform their overall positive impression and trust of Rawlings. In other words, music and dance performance was a significant way in which individuals came to understand the state and their relationship to it through embodied encounters. These actions served to reify the president's claims that he was indeed a "man of the people" leading a "people's revolution"; however, although such actions may have endeared him to the GDE members and perhaps audiences, while reaffirming his calls for "people power" and putting control of Ghana back in the hands of ordinary citizens, most of the national decisions were still made by a small group of PNDC functionaries in Accra "who were not accountable to anyone" (Nugent 1998, 48).

Nevertheless, throughout my time in Ghana, I found considerable support and reverence for Rawlings. He remains a national hero in the eyes of many Ghanaians despite his numerous questionable policies and actions. Under Rawlings, the government expanded its ability to detain citizens and suspended the writ of habeas corpus. As Asirifi-Danquah notes, Rawlings had the "worst record of human rights abuses in the history of independent Ghana" (2007, 217). Yet, due to the dire economic circumstances in Ghana, this populist revolutionary, against the ideology of many of his socialist supporters, reluctantly embraced controversial IMF and World Bank policies and led Ghana to becoming a "model pupil" (220) of structural adjustment. While it remains debatable whether these particular policies brought recovery about, Ghana emerged from official economic decline as its national GDP grew exponentially during Rawlings's watch. As J. L. Adedeji notes, "Many Ghanaians believe that Rawlings, more than any other individual in the country's history, by leading them through the difficult years of economic recovery, has given them back their self-respect and national pride" (2001, 1). Echoing this sentiment, when asked about Rawlings in general, GDE members often remarked that he was a "great man," "he tried," and "he did something for Ghana." As with the discourse surrounding Nkrumah, if there was criticism of Rawlings, it remained predominantly hidden.

A few comments made in interviews, however, revealed a point at which the dance ensemble diverged from the protocols of the state. When asked about performing for state events, Ben Abdallah surprisingly remarked,

> Personally as an artist myself, as a playwright who includes dance in his performances, I was always angry. I used to tell Nii[-Yartey], "Don't let these people [state protocol] turn the NDC into a piece of entertainment for politicians who say, 'Come bring the dancing boys and girls,' and they are eating their dinner and you are dancing for them." I said that my perception of a national dance company is way above. I would not want my national dance company to do that kind of thing, because it cheapens the art. Maybe a special performance, they should bring the visitor, like if Nelson Mandela came they should take him to the theatre. Let them do a special performance for him. But not this kind of per-

formance where you have idiots who have no idea and look upon them [perform-
ers] as entertainment, and they'll be talking and laughing while the performance
is going on. I know Nii-Yartey resisted that [kind of dinner performance] as
much as he could. Sometimes if a state dinner would come, he would say, "Why
don't you get the Legon group for that?" I think Nii-Yartey has succeeded in telling those people [at state protocol] to leave them alone. (2007)

As in Tanzania, "cultural officers and state-sponsored musicians do
not always see themselves as agents of 'the state'" (Askew 2002, 270).
By suggesting that the Legon group, not his NDC, be called upon for
state dinner performances, Nii-Yartey was engaging in communicative
indirection. Employing such tactics, the NDC's absence at many of these
types of state functions was a strategic silence, indicting the policies
and practices of the Rawlings government that often marginalized the
ensembles during state dinner performances. In this way, Nii-Yartey
and Abdallah were participating in a pervasive "culture of silence" that
existed during this period. Rawlings's intimidation and suppression of
dissent led to such a situation in which Ghanaians "protested indirectly
through silence" (Obeng 2003, 136). In all, Nii-Yartey and Abdallah deployed a clever communicative strategy, managing nationalism by surreptitiously expressing their dissatisfaction with the state as they preserved their jobs and senses of artistic integrity.

REVERING RAWLINGS, CRITICIZING KUFUOR:
SUBVERSIVE SMIRKS AND SILENCES

After nearly twenty years in power, Rawlings honored the outcome of
Ghana's 2000 democratic election and handed over the seat of the state
to J. A. Kufuor. A member of the New Patriotic Party (NPP), Kufuor ran
on a platform of "Positive Change" with the slogan "Ghana Incorporated," which indicated his focus on neoliberalist economic development
of the nation through a businesslike approach to government. Kufuor
succeeded in bringing new international investment to Ghana, encouraging Ghana's GDP to grow enormously while stabilizing inflation. He
has presided over the longest reign of civilian rule and economic growth
in the nation's history, and for his efforts he was democratically reelected
in 2004. Despite many positive aspects of his presidency, ensemble mem-

bers voiced criticism of Kufuor, much more so than of Rawlings or of any previous Ghanaian head of state. GDE participants regularly expressed dissent, disapproval, dissatisfaction, and indignation with regard to Kufuor but did so indirectly.

Yet not all drummers and dancers expressed dissatisfaction with this president. When asked about performing for Kufuor, one dancer stated,

> It's a blessing, because it's not everybody who has the opportunity to perform for the president. And I had the president shake [my hand] for a dance. I did *gome* and he shaked me for that. I did *bamaaya* and he came and shaked me for that. When I was doing a performance at the state house he told his people to give me some money, and then he shaked me and said *"Ayeko* [congratulations]!" When I got back, my mom called me and said, "Hey, I have seen you shaking the president." It's a blessing from God. It's not everybody that has the opportunity to talk to the president or perform for the president or get near to the president. It has been a great opportunity for me. (Agyete 2007)

Due largely to this encounter, the dancer remarked, "That is why I don't have a problem with Kufuor, because he came and shaked me and praised me for that dance. He respected me for my work, so I will also respect him." When confronted by his colleagues' criticisms of the president, in the course of informal field conversations, he often held up this example as the basis for his positive assessment of the Kufuor regime. Thus, the dancer's opinion of Kufuor was significantly informed by his direct embodied interaction with the state via dance.

The aforementioned dancer's affinity for Kufuor appeared to be in the minority, however, when compared with the onslaught of criticism directed toward the president by GDE performers. When I asked one former drummer of the ensemble, who had performed under Rawlings and Kufuor, if he did anything differently when performing for each of these leaders, he explained,

> Oh, I didn't do anything different as such, but you know me, I hate Kufuor. During Rawlings's time, if you see me playing fontomfrom, you will see people jumping on drums; you will see that something is happening. But now Kufuor come. Sometimes Rawlings will come and stand and dance. But Kufuor, he will just walk fast. Rawlings many times, he will be clapping, so you see that it is fine. It makes you know that my presence is considered. But just sitting down and talking to people [like Kufuor], no. It's like you are hating me and what I am doing. So me, I haven't played praises for Kufuor before on the drum. But Rawlings, if I am welcoming him on the atumpan drums, I will play *"Akwaaba*

[welcome], President Rawlings," [two high tones with flams followed by two low tones], "*Akwaaba!*" [high tone, low-low], and "*Wayedee!*" [you have done well] [high-low, high tone with flam]. . . . Kufuor, he's not thinking about anybody; he's only chopping [consuming] the money. Kufuor will just stand somewhere far away, but Rawlings will come and make sure he knows what is going on; he takes more interest in it. (Seki 2006)

I then asked, "So when you see Kufuor, do you insult him on the drums?" He replied, "No, but in my head plenty!" Several other drummers later echoed this disdain for Kufuor, explaining that while they did not play insulting phrases on the drums, they deliberately neglected to perform any praises for him. Drummers could not insult him directly because, as one explained, "after all, he is the president. For that thing [insult], you just keep it in your mind and do your job" (Agyari 2007). While their occupation, cultural norms of deference, and duties to their nation and government kept these drummers' criticisms silenced, their neglect to play praises for Kufuor was a subtle tactic with which to indirectly express critique. Thus, as it is for Guinean popular musicians and others,[8] for GDE drummers, silence is not merely an absence or an "un-thought void or submission" but can be a deliberate "dense presence" wielded by artists to mediate power as they "manage their lives and careers in highly volatile contexts" (Dave 2014, 18–19).

Several dancers similarly participated in this discourse of disapproval for Kufuor. A conversation with one senior dancer elucidates some of the key issues that created this indignation in general and the ways in which she indirectly performed her political views of the Ghanaian state through dance:

Paul: Do you like Kufuor as a president?

Yaa: Me, personally, no, I don't like him.

Paul: So do you ever feel to insult him when you are dancing?

Yaa: Oh, I feel to, but I can't do that, because there will be chiefs following him. Me, I will just dance, collect my money, and go. Me, I like J. J. [Rawlings]. Can't you see [a picture of] J. J. in my room? I like J. J. because the man is straightforward. He sacrificed for people to have low prices for goods. But now, *gari*, the cheapest food in Ghana, is 12,000 [cedis]. It used to be 4,000. Kufuor has been raising things [prices]. And they [Kufuor government] are chopping all the money over there. It is not a small money. But workers, their salary is very, very poor. Right now I am getting no pay, because they take it for my house and light bill. I went to the bank today. No money in my account. And now look at me, my sister is sick. In Ghana, if you are sick and you don't have money, you will die, because nobody is ready to help you. In Ghana, we are suffering. Can't you see my business is coming down?

Paul: Do you blame the government?

Yaa: Hey, yes, it's a government problem, because things are not correct. Look at the petrol now. Before, he [Rawlings] was beating it down. Me, I didn't vote for Kufuor [an Asante], because the Asante people like money. So the moment that the man will be sitting there, the man will grab the money, and then he will owe a lot.... So the man is killing us slowly.

Paul: So you say you are not happy with Kufuor and the government. How do you feel when you are performing at state functions?

Yaa: At times I feel bad, but it is my job. It is the job who pays me, so I have no choice. But if you know my head, oh, the way I will insult the man [Kufuor]. One day we need time to talk to the man – the president. We need to tell him we need a bus; we need costumes, because this is a national group. Kwame Nkrumah's time, he is moving, and dance ensemble is moving. The same thing with J. J.; he moved, the dance ensemble moved. Even when it's not the president, we would go with the vice. We went to Botswana with the vice, and they were saluting us like something. Dancers are ambassadors. So, we are the ambassadors for the president. So, you have to raise the group – give us costumes; give us something. Push us forward. Right now, he [Kufuor] doesn't care for anyone because the man has money. Especially the Asante people, they like money serious.

Paul: And when you are dancing for state functions?

Yaa: If I go to a cocktail and people are drinking, then they have to smile [laughs].

Paul: So you will do something funny?

Yaa: Yes, I will do this [motions with one finger to come]. I am inviting Kufuor to come and dance. It means "I like you" or "I love you." I am inviting him to come and dance. Meanwhile he doesn't know what is in my head. At times he used to come, but now he will just do this [makes V praise symbol with two fingers]. But J. J. will dance. Hey! That's why I like the man. J. J. can dance with me [laughs]. The man is free. If he is talking to you, he will take you like a son or a daughter. And the day he shook [hands with] me, he was talking to me, saying, "My children, I am meeting you all the time. We have to find time and invite each other and talk to each other." And then some man came and took a picture, and that picture is in my room now. You see how I am happy there [in the picture]. But now you won't see me like that. When I dance for Kufuor, the smile is not like that. You see the way I squeeze my face. (Asari 2007)

The subtle difference between a smile and a smirk marked an indirect expression of indignation with the state as the dancer attempted to avoid possible reprimand. Corruption, inflation, and the lack of attention for the arts were the primary criticisms of Kufuor for a number of participants, leading to many other instances in which performers employed indirection to artfully, and surreptitiously, express their grievances with

4.4. GDE dancer
performing
adowa at a state
dinner. Note her
facial expression.

the state.[9] In general, performers' understanding and opinions of the state were significantly informed by their close interaction with state officials through embodied encounters of music and dance. While performers cited Rawlings's participation in dance and their direct conversations with him as reasons for their trust and general affinity for this leader, Kufuor's neglect to dance at state events was taken as a sign of disinterest or disrespect and added to artists' negative impressions of this president and a mistrust of his administration's actions.

"THEY GIVE US THE CRUMBS"; OR, OF MARGINAL IMPORTANCE: INDIGNITY AND INDIGNATION

In June 2006, while attending a GDE (Legon) performance for a visiting Beninese delegation at the Accra Conference Center, I witnessed a dramatic interaction between performers, Kufuor, and government officials that revealed some of the sources of indignation ensemble members expressed in regard to their state/employer.

On the evening of the performance, I approached the entrance of the conference center, where a line of expensive BMWs waited in the circle drive, carrying dignitaries and VIPs who were arriving at this state dinner for the Benin diplomatic delegation. At the entrance, members of the GDE (Legon) were performing kete with one female dancer. With permission from the artistic director, I filmed the ensemble but was promptly told by security to stop recording. I was ushered through the automatic sliding glass doors and into the main hall of the building.

Once inside this giant room, I noticed the GDE drummers were still setting up. I went over to them and overheard one of the event organizers saying, "Please don't set up near the high table. The noise will be too much for them." The official then led the drum ensemble off to the side of the hall, away from the high table, and into the margins of the room. The drummers expressed dissatisfaction at this repositioning and told me that now they would be too far from the dancers, which would negatively impact the quality of their performance. I was reminded of a similar incident that had occurred just a week before, when the Chinese delegation was received at a state dinner in the conference center. The drummers had begun to set up at the front of the hall but were promptly moved by officials to a more marginal position. "You see this?" one senior dancer pointed out. "This is how they treat us. The government does not respect us."

After the drums were positioned, nearly out of sight of the high table, the senior ensemble staff and I took seats well behind the drummers. We sat in plastic chairs that we had hunted for ourselves, because the officials offered little help. From the sidelines, I could see guests continuing to arrive in their tuxes, suits, and formal evening dresses. They sipped wine and champagne as the police band, seated in a balcony above our heads, played a few highlife numbers. The drummers, staff, and I waited in our seats, which were under a stairway leading to the balcony, nearly out of sight of the arriving guests. For more than an hour we sat there, watching as the guests mingled about and eventually took their seats at various reserved tables decked in white linens. I could still hear the faint sounds of kete being played outside to welcome the guests. Suddenly the police band began to play Benin's national anthem to signal the arrival of this nation's president. Moments later, Kufuor arrived to the fanfare of Ghana's national anthem, also performed by the police band. Everyone stood and watched as he took his seat at the high table. Flanked by his vice president and the leader of the Ghana Armed Forces, he sat with them and the president of Benin at a long, elaborately decorated table, facing the sea of guests.

After those at the high table took their seats, the drummers from outside ran inside carrying their drums. They needed to quickly change costumes for the next performance. Kufuor then gave a speech, welcoming everyone and affirming diplomatic relations between Benin and Ghana. When he finished, an emcee asked the GDE to "give us some entertainment." In a show of solidarity with their African neighbors, the ensemble performed *adzogbo,* a dance from Benin. Later, as dinner was served, the ensemble performed the Asante *adowa,* which was, as one dancer told me, Kufuor's favorite dance. Although the artistic director had planned a set list of seven dances, these were the only two that were performed due to time constraints. After Kufuor had finished his meal, he promptly exited the building, joined his long motorcade, and was gone.

Around nine o'clock, the drummers and dancers were tired and hungry. Although the staff and I had been allowed to eat the catered food earlier (after the guests had taken their share), the performers had not eaten since the afternoon. Several dancers asked their director if they could eat the remaining food left at the buffet. After consulting with an event organizer, he told them they could. However, once they got to the buffet, the performers discovered that there were no clean plates or silverware. They asked for clean utensils but were told that there were none available. Many decided to go ahead and eat from dirty plates or on small napkins. Some ate only with their hands, while others used the unclean silverware. Because the tables were being torn down, they had to stand or sit on the floor. As they quickly gorged on the food, knowing they had to vacate the building soon, I overheard grumbling (and not that of their stomachs). One GDE staff member remarked, "They give us the crumbs. They [the government] don't care about us. It is not correct. We come and play for them, and this is what we are left with." A number of other ensemble members echoed these sentiments, feeling they were mistreated and disrespected regarding their work.

A dramatic form of the politics of the belly, this narrative also enacts Achille Mbembe's metaphor regarding the African postcolonial state; he notes that "the autocrat is a hole, a sort of bottomless, endless excess, with a voraciousness that is quite insatiable. It is very well for the people to cry out 'We want to eat! We want to eat!' He asks them to wait 'until I have finished first'" (2001, 160). Along with this performance of power, Kufuor's actions were a direct contradiction of his cultural policy, which stated that one of its primary objectives was "to promote . . . human dignity . . . [and] the dignity of labour" (National Commission on Culture 2004, 4). Literally marginalized by the state, which characterized the GDE's presence as "noise" or, at best, "entertainment," the drummers were forced to compromise their performance. Consequently, dancers said they did not enjoy these state dinner performances because they could not properly hear the drums. Several drummers also remarked that their sets were often cut short, and this was not the first time that ensemble members were forced to eat the "crumbs" left by the state and its guests. While concealing these frustrations and maintaining dutiful composure during their state performance, after Kufuor and the guests had left, ensemble members did not hesitate to criticize their leader. Although music and dance were important to the state, enlivening and emboldening its performance of power, ensemble members felt that they were marginalized – not duly recognized for this role or for their talents. Apparently, not much had changed since Abdallah's and Nii-Yartey's similar complaints about these state dinner performances under Rawlings. In all, the "insults and slights to human dignity" generated by the state's practices of domination and exploitation invited an indirect expression of indignation that was hidden from the government's gaze in an offstage, or backstage, conversation (Scott 1990, 11).

STAGING "GHANA @ FIFTY": HIDDEN AMBIVALENCE AND THE STATE OF THE ARTS UNDER KUFUOR

As I witnessed in 2007, during Ghana's celebration of its fifty years of independence, the performances of nationalism and state power were abundant. On March 5, the morning on the eve of Independence Day – fifty years after the country had first attained its freedom from colonial rule – the deep, powerful bass tones of the two enormous fontomfrom drums echoed through the chambers of the Ghanaian Parliament as President J. A. Kufuor, dressed in colorful kente cloth, led a procession of dignitaries to their respective seats at the front of the room. Two young drummers from the National Dance Company stood on stools and lifted their sticks above their heads in order to beat the drums that towered over them as the president took his seat on an elaborately decorated golden throne, modeled after the Asante golden stool.[10] This special session of Parliament was formally opened as the drums sounded their praises for Kufuor. The Duke of Kent took his position as the guest of honor, representing Queen Elizabeth II. This session commemorated the Duchess of Kent's historic 1957 presiding over the final legislative session of the colonial state. This pageantry of power filled the hall with the bright colors of Ghanaian and European symbolism. Special kente cloth adorned the chamber and Akan royal symbolism decorated the throne and seats of the high order, which were backed by the Ghanaian coat of arms painted on the chamber wall. Adinkra symbols were etched into the drums, and military officers, dressed in European-style uniforms, stood behind the diplomats.

Around 10:30 PM I began to watch the festivities at the Kwame Nkrumah mausoleum (in central Accra) on television. I saw several groups entering the grounds, one from each region. The ensembles, each comprising around twenty to thirty people, performed a dance that was representative of their area as they processed up to the main stage. Once onstage, each group was featured for a few moments before the next took its place. Performing hyper-condensed and compressed versions of culture, the Ewe group danced agbadza, the Ga group did kpanlogo, and so on. This was followed by a reenactment of Nkrumah's famous 1957 speech by the Actors Guild of Ghana. The actors played the parts of the "big six"[11] and even the cheering audience members. The man playing Nkrumah went through the whole speech, although without as much passion as Nkrumah. The whole thing seemed a bit bizarre and surreal. This was followed by a fireworks display, lasting about fifteen or twenty minutes. I could hear the booms from my apartment, a few miles from the activities.

Subsequently, music groups – mostly pop and highlife style – continued to perform all through the night. I decided to go to bed, to rest up for the next day, which was sure to be packed with celebration.

On March 6, Independence Day, I left for Independence Square at around 7 A M. A few friends and I took a taxi to central Accra but had to stop before getting to the square because there was too much traffic. Swarms of people lined the streets, all moving toward the square. Once we got closer, I could see that the stadium-style grounds were overflowing with people. It was a vast sea of bodies draped in the colors of the Ghanaian flag – red, gold, and green. People handed us free paper flags as we entered the square, and a group of about four people, two or three playing dondons, came up to us. One of the drummers had his whole body painted red, gold, and green. He was carrying a small clay pot on his head for donations. They played right in front of me for a few moments, and I felt obliged to give them a few cedis. Commerce was everywhere. The entrance was filled with sellers of mostly Ghanaian national memorabilia.

People had been at the square since the previous night just to get a spot. Thousands of Ghanaians lined the seats, singing, cheering, and waving their flags with pride. We entered the seating area, but there was no room to sit. We tried to stand in the aisles but could not see anything from our vantage point. After about thirty minutes of surveying the scene, we decided to go to a nearby bar to watch the events on television.

The president was hauled around in a small pickup-type truck, almost like the Popemobile, and he had two heads of defense with him. After circling the grounds a few times, he eventually got out to light the eternal flame at the center of the square. This was followed by a presentation of schoolchildren. A few hundred boys ran around with red, gold, and green flags and did some formations with them; then the girls came out with colored flower wreaths and made some formations. This took about twenty minutes. Next the military came out and paraded around, conducting complex exercises and a number of large formations. Later there was a performance of kete by a young girl and boy who had won competitions earlier that year for the honor to perform for the occasion. Although dance was included in the program, to a small degree, there was the conspicuous absence of either national dance ensemble at these events. In fact, most of the NDC members were overseas in India during the entire week of Ghana's independence.

The next afternoon, I arrived at Independence Square around 3 PM with the GDE. The stadium looked virtually empty compared with the crowd yesterday. Overall, the spectators seemed exhausted from the last few days of activities. We milled about in the hot sun and took refuge under the large balcony where the dignitaries would sit. After nearly an hour, the program began with the announced arrival of various important guests, members of Parliament, and the vice president. Then, preceded by a long police motorcade, President Kufuor and the Duke of Kent arrived. They stood on a covered, decorated podium in the center of the square as the military band played the national anthem. They were escorted to their seats, high above us, directly overhead in a special loft area. Then the GDE (Legon) and the military band performed together in the center of the square. As the loudspeakers announced the various dances, the drummers played the rhythms while the band played arrangements of melodies of the various musical/dance styles. Dancers came from behind me and spent only a few minutes on each dance as the emcee announced each one. It was a hyper-intensified medley of dances from each major ethnic group. They went through about five dances in ten minutes – *agbekor,* bamaaya, gome, adowa, and *kundum.*

After the GDE finished, one of the military band members did a lengthy ragtime-style xylophone solo (a little sloppily). This was followed by an extensive gymnastics display. A troupe of about twenty Ghanaians did a routine of acrobatics. Then came an extensive presentation of military exercises. Before starting the drills, the leader of these exercises came to the center of the square. Dwarfed by the enormous structure that housed the president and dignitaries, the soldier looked up, gazed far above his head, and asked for permission from the president to start the exercises. In a performance of power/authority, from his lofty perch towering over the soldiers, Kufuor stared down and gave the permission to start the drills. As the soldiers marched in formation around the infield, I could see the audience was as bored as I was, talking on cell phones and not making any sounds of appreciation for this display. Next was a presentation of Scottish bagpipers with a drum and fife group. Again, the audience seemed unenthused. The military band, subsequently, took the stage and performed a number of short arrangements. This was followed by a repetition of the Ghanaian national anthem as the president and dignitaries exited the square in their black limos. Last, there was a gun salute and a brief fireworks display (PURL 4.2).

These events were the highlight of a yearlong state-sponsored calendar of activities (including lectures, concerts, and films) officially titled "Ghana @ 50," designed to commemorate Ghana's fifty years of independence from British rule. During such events, while Ghanaians generally rejoiced and reveled in the accomplishments of their nation over the last half century, "behind the scenes" there was an undercurrent of ambivalence and even dissent among the nation, which was directed at Kufuor and the Ghanaian state. Many were upset that a number of the scheduled events were eventually canceled, fostering a string of privately sponsored events, known as the "alternative Ghana at fifty." Offering an explanation for these disruptions, Ghanaian newspapers and media were flooded with accusations that the government's "Ghana @ 50" Committee had mismanaged resources allotted for the celebrations. For instance, the government had purchased over two hundred new luxury vehicles to ostensibly transport visiting dignitaries when, according to many journalists, only sixty-four cars were needed. Furthermore, many Ghanaians argued that the vast sum of money (about 20 million U.S. dollars) that the government dedicated to these celebrations could have been better spent on building the country's infrastructure and meeting the basic daily needs of its many citizens who had not benefited from Kufuor's neoliberal policies. While the country's GDP continued to grow and foreign investment was evident from the numerous construction projects I saw everyday in Accra, this wealth did not trickle down to a majority of Ghana's people. This general critique of Kufuor's state was evident throughout 2007 as I conducted fieldwork.

The major roadways of Accra were adorned with colorful banners on the streetlights and with giant billboards congratulating Kufuor and Ghana for its fifty years of nationhood. City buses were painted with national symbols and the "Ghana @ 50" logo. This state-sponsored symbolism and rhetoric was, however, reinterpreted by individuals in a type of "personal nationalism" (A. Cohen 1996) that offered an indirect critique of the state. For instance, as Apetsi Amenumey and I were

4.5. State-sponsored billboard on Liberation Road in Accra for Ghana @ 50 celebrations. *Photograph by Jennifer Hart.*

standing at a bus stop, I saw a double-decker bus that had a picture of the "Ghana @ 50" emblem on it (the "o" had a Gye Nyame symbol inside) with Nkrumah raising his fist on one side in black and white and Kufuor, in color, throwing his hands up in a relaxed fashion on the other. Apetsi commented that Nkrumah wasn't smiling and was raising his fist because "he was a fighter, someone who fought for the people." Kufuor, he argued, "just likes to wear nice clothing like you see in the picture, and get lots of money. You see how we are suffering while our government gets fat" (2007).

Of the many billboards commemorating Ghana's jubilee celebrations, one received particular attention from a number of participants. Through the magic of modern photo technology, it depicted a black and white image of Nkrumah and Kufuor sitting together next to the official "Ghana @ 50" emblem and a statement that read "Ghana: 50 Years of Leadership"(fig. 4.5). As I traveled with the GDE, passing the sign numerous times throughout 2007, several ensemble members commented that Kufuor should not have been depicted to appear larger than Nkrumah. In Ghana, size matters because it is a cultural indication of status. One dancer remarked, "Look at Kufuor all big there, more than Nkrumah. He [Kufuor] is no Nkrumah!" (Asari 2007).

Similarly, the slogan "Ghana @ 50" was reinterpreted. For example, after the GDE's portion of a dress rehearsal at the National Theatre for its upcoming performance for the Education Reform 2007 unveiling ceremony, I sat with a number of ensemble members and watched the remainder of the groups prepare for this event. A young girl, probably about seven, took the stage to practice a recitation of a poem she had written about the benefits of basic education. The poem praised the government for such reform. Meanwhile, ensemble members sitting next to me mocked the speech. One remarked that if he had to give that speech, he would say, "Hey Mr. President, look at the way we are suffering – no lights, no water, no pay. We are a professional group, a national group, and we can't even pay for transport or buy decent costumes. Ghana is suffering. Ghana at fifty [in a sardonic tone]" (Mihesu 2007).

His sarcastic use of the Ghana @ 50 slogan was often echoed throughout the year. For example, one evening as I sat waiting for a friend on the steps of the School of Performing Arts at Legon, the lights went out. Not a second later, a voice cried out, "Ghana at fifty" in a disdainful tone, as if to say, look at this, look at Ghana, here we are fifty years after independence and we can't even manage to have basic services in the capital. Throughout most of 2007, there was a load-shedding program in effect that limited the use of electricity in Ghana. In Accra, the city was divided into sections, and a given area would be without power for twelve hours of every forty-eight. The only exception was during the week of Independence Day, when the government graciously decided to suspend the program. "Ghana at fifty" became a running commentary, sardonically uttered by Ghanaians throughout the year as lights went out, water stopped flowing, or people were generally unhappy with the state of the country. As Cati Coe writes, "Thus, people draw on discourses that compete with those of the state in order to create meanings other than what the state intends within the very spaces that the state creates" (2005, 6).

While members of the ensemble joined in the national critique of Ghana @ 50, they additionally criticized the Kufuor government for its lack of attention to the arts. When asked to compare Kufuor to the previous Rawlings administration in regard to the arts in Ghana, Francis Nii-Yartey stated, "I don't think Kufuor's line is like Rawlings's line. We haven't done much for his government. His line is not like the previous ones who had worked with the arts. He hasn't commissioned me to do anything. I haven't seen anything serious since he came. His orientation is different. He likes football [American soccer]. I don't think he's a dance man or an art man as much as he is for football" (2006). Supporting this claim, Kufuor had pushed for the African Cup (soccer/football) to be held in Ghana in 2008. Additionally, in 2007 I attended the CAF (Confederation of African Football) awards. This was the first time the

CAF awards had been held in Ghana. Echoing Nii-Yartey's statements, Ben Abdallah, who was no longer the chairman of the NCC, remarked, "I think perhaps the new government does not even understand the role of dance, theatre and the arts. I could be wrong. If it does, maybe it does not want to put any emphasis on it for one reason or another. But if you listen to what people say, they will say things have gone down" (2007). Abdallah later criticized the NCC at the time for its lack of organization and inability to effectively promote the arts and artists in Ghana. Affirming this position, many drummers and dancers had noted that there was less artistic activity in Ghana during Kufuor's regime as compared with Rawlings's time because they claimed Kufuor had concentrated his efforts on the promotion of football to the detriment of other forms of culture.

This criticism seemed ironic given the state's adoption of its first official cultural policy. Although Rawlings had encouraged the establishment of the NCC, which drafted a cultural policy document in 1991, as George Hagan (chairman of the NCC under Kufuor) states, this "Draft Policy... did not receive assent then" (National Commission on Culture 2004, x). Hagan continues in the preface to the cultural policy document commissioned by Kufuor that the NCC "identified the absence of a Policy as a major hindrance to the aspirations of the people of this country" (x). Therefore, in 2001, the NCC reviewed the older cultural policy document and drafted an updated version, which was officially authorized by Kufuor in 2004. In conjunction, Kufuor established a Culture Trust Fund that would "give financial backing to the promotion of Ghana's diverse culture" (x). Overall, this nearly fifty-page document details the state's pledge to promote the cultural diversity of Ghana by encouraging the development of the arts and the creative efforts of individual artists. Despite these efforts, artists vociferously complained that Kufuor was "killing the arts" and "did not care" about artists. Moreover, in terms of the arts, many performers shared the sentiment that "things were better under Rawlings" (A. Amenumey 2007). It appeared that, despite the lack of an official cultural policy during Rawlings's time, his government had prevailed over Kufuor's in the minds of many artists regarding the state's support of the arts. This issue, as well as the overall discontent with Kufuor's (and the state's) failures, was expressed by the sardonic tone of GDE members as they satirically uttered the phrase "Ghana at fifty," indirectly articulating indignation with their government.

This frustration with the Ghana @ 50 celebrations, coupled with negative assessments of the Kufuor regime's attitude toward the arts, insidiously seeped through the year's performances of nationalism and the staging of the state. In 2007, as a GDE dancer was preparing to perform in one of the anniversary events, he told me, "Ghana has been free for many years, but what do we have to show for it? Lights are off, people are suffering, artists are suffering. Ghana @ 50, no, we shouldn't be celebrating like this; the government is chopping all the money and doing nothing for us artists" (Agyette 2007). He went on to perform in the anniversary event; as I watched, it appeared that his enthusiasm was low, and my suspicions were confirmed when he subsequently told me that he did not enjoy the performance. He explained, "You see, I perform that way so the people will know that we are suffering." Yet, he added, "I still performed well enough, so I won't get in trouble; but if you see the way I perform before, you'll know that the one today was not my best." Like many other GDE artists, he expended efforts beyond the enactment of music and dance alone during a state event, carefully managing his performance to indirectly express reproach of the government under its direct observation.

THICK PERFORMANCE AND THE STATE

Embodied encounters involving music and dance are primary ways in which artists understand and negotiate the postcolonial African state and their relationship to it. While artists work to avoid the surveillance of the dance ensembles' internal disciplinary apparatus, this chapter has shown that performers often must additionally mediate the gaze of the state. As ensemble members are employed to legitimize state power and propagate its ideologies, they strike a delicate balance between duty to their nation/state, maintaining the integrity of their craft, job security, and rights to freely reproach their political leaders. To navigate these often-competing objectives and interests, artists engage in a kind of multilayered, or thick, performance. They simultaneously perform musically, kinesthetically, and theatrically, including a type of surface acting, or "emotion work" (see Hochschild 1983; Schauert 2007a), in which they conceal their negative feelings and opinions of their employer – the state. Indirection is a vital component of this thick performance. Manifested in the form of silence, smirks, sardonic reimaginings of state slogans, backstage grumblings, and unenthusiastic performances, indirection is a tactic for managing; it is subtle and ambiguous enough to avoid negative consequences while still satisfying the needs of individual citizens to vent their frustrations. In all, indirection is a crucial way in which non-elite artists reconfigure the logics, rhetoric, and institutions of nationalism to serve their personal interests and needs, managing the Ghanaian state, nationalism, and their precarious positions as both government employees and citizens in a democratic society.

FIVE

"We Are the Originals"

A Tale of Two Troupes and the Birth
of Contemporary Dance in Ghana

SINCE ITS ESTABLISHMENT IN 1962, THE GHANA DANCE ENSEMBLE has been based at the University of Ghana in Legon. In 1990, under the Rawlings regime, a state law was passed that implied that the ensemble should become the resident group at the newly constructed National Theatre in downtown Accra. The proposition of moving the ensemble sparked a host of heated public and private debates between the Ghanaian government, university officials, and troupe members. The GDE became a political battleground for discussions of tradition, modernity, development, and the relationship between the state and the arts. As these contestations persisted, personal loyalties, private fears, and political affiliations were exposed, challenged, and solidified. After years of debate, as a compromise the company was split into two groups – the Ghana Dance Ensemble, which remained at the university, and the National Dance Company, based at the National Theatre. This separation had ramifications for the trajectory of (national) dance in Ghana as well as for individual and group identities. Exploring these consequences, this chapter further illustrates how artists and the state have managed the cosmopolitan power dynamics of nationalism while staging culture in Ghana, representing the nation, and forming individual senses of self.

After the formal split in 1992, the tensions that brought it about continued to inform the relationship between the two competing ensembles. Each developed its own identity, which is reflected in the groups' rhetorical and performative practices. Members of the GDE, based at Legon, collectively proclaim, "We are the originals" and bolster this assertion by carefully preserving the traditions of choreography that have existed since the time of the ensemble's first director in the early 1960s. On the other hand, the NDC, with its progressive leader, Francis Nii-Yartey, while continuing to perform "traditional" dances, has pushed the artistic boundaries by electing to focus on the "development" of "contemporary African dance." As it explores the birth of contemporary dance in Ghana, this chapter also shows how the NDC's concentration on this mode of expression reifies its pronouncement that it is "moving forward." While their rhetorical and performative practices have helped the ensembles differentiate themselves from each another, both ensembles are considered national dance companies of Ghana; thus, their differences express competing ideas of nationalism and the nation.

This chapter will examine how these ensembles compete in Ghana and abroad as they represent their nation in distinct and overlapping ways and, in the process, construct both group and individual identities. To explore these issues of identity, I build on the theories of Stuart Hall, recognizing identity as a continual and relational "process of identification" (1996, 344) in which individuals and groups can come to understand themselves only vis-à-vis an Other (345). Regarding group identity, I explore the ways in which these national ensembles employ both rhetorical and performative strategies in relation to a local Other (that is, each other) to ensure their viability, survival, and coexistence within Ghana – a highly competitive environment. While these groups carve out their identities, this negotiation impacts the ways in which individuals construct their own sense of self and understand the possibilities for their artistry. Most notably, my examination of the split highlights additional ways in which artists (and others) manage nationalism as they attempt to use Ghana's national ensembles to advance their own political, ideological, artistic, and pragmatic interests by choosing to support and/or join a particular state dance troupe according to their individual needs.

FORESHADOWING THE SPLIT: TWO ENSEMBLES FROM THE START

The ensemble's rupture that occurred in the 1990s did not create an entirely new situation in Ghana. Since the GDE's founding in the early

1960s, there had been another national dance ensemble in Accra, which was established and supported by the Arts Council of Ghana. This Arts Council ensemble, like the GDE, received a government subvention and was considered a national performance troupe. Although it was reportedly not officially founded until 1965, there is archival documentation of its existence dating back to at least 1962 (the same year the GDE was founded), a fact corroborated by numerous interviewees, including Kwabena Nketia (2007b). Under the leadership of Robert Ayitte, an Ewe master drummer who was brought to Accra by Nketia, the group rehearsed at the Arts Center in central Accra, which was the headquarters of the Arts Council of Ghana.[1] This forty-member ensemble, referred to in documents as the Arts Council Ensemble, the Arts Center Troupe, or, most often, the National Folkloric Dance Company of Ghana, performed a repertoire of dances similar to that of the GDE.[2] Like the GDE, the Folkloric Dance Company (FDC) also performed for local schools throughout the country, at national and local festivals, and for corporate events. It also held public workshops to teach music and dance to the citizens of the nation.

For several decades there was enough demand for music and dance to sustain both groups, and they were able to coexist. Yet, according to Nketia, "there was competition between the two groups, only because the Arts Center people thought that the Legon people got better salary and more opportunities to travel" (2007b). Although Nketia stated that Ayitte was "a good leader and managed the group well . . . he [Ayitte] didn't have the charisma, knowledge, or skills of Opoku" (2007b). Perhaps due to this, the GDE was often seen by interviewees as the "stronger" of the two groups. They noted that, given its reputation, the GDE performed more often for state functions and received more opportunities to travel abroad. Wisdom Agbedanu, an Ewe who was a member of the FDC, however, remarked that in some ways the FDC "was stronger," representing certain dances more faithfully than the GDE did. In particular, he stated that the FDC performed Ewe dances such as *agbekor* and *adzogbo* "more like how they do it in the village," but "the Akan dances were performed better by the Legon group because Opoku was Akan" (2007). Such comments highlight the centrality of authenticating symbolic forms in legitimating these performance ensembles, which continued to be a point of contention between the GDE and NDC. Ultimately, the FDC was dissolved when, in 1985, the Rawlings government decided that having two national dance ensembles was causing confusion and undermined the ideology of national unity (Agbedanu 2007). The government encouraged the members of the FDC to join the GDE, but many of the FDC members preferred to resign.[3] These events foreshadow the later controversy that took place surrounding the split of the GDE and illustrate that state officials were concerned with how culture was representing the nation and their own political objectives.

THE NATIONAL THEATRE CONTROVERSY

At least since 1959, there is evidence that the Arts Council of Ghana was agitating for building a national theatre in central Accra.[4] This plea continued to gain momentum throughout the 1960s with the advent of the National Theatre Movement. Architectural plans were commissioned and can be found in the National Archives of Ghana. Nketia told me, however, that the theatre that was proposed in the Arts Council files was never built, and "it had to wait until Abdallah came along and got the Chinese involved" (2007b). Nketia's remarks refer to Dr. Ben Abdallah, who, as we shall see, played a major role in the events that resulted in the splitting of the GDE; thus, his biography is worth noting.

Abdallah was, from his childhood, an extremely gifted student who was interested in language and teaching. After completing his secondary education, he attended Wesley College in Kumasi, where "his interest in drama was ignited" (Yankah 1993, 21). After teaching literature and French at Prempeh College, he enrolled in the University of Ghana's School of Performing Arts, where he obtained a bachelor of arts degree before traveling to the United States to pursue his doctorate in drama at the University of Texas, Austin. Upon his return to Ghana, he was offered a position as a senior staff member at the School of Performing Arts. While at the university, Abdallah was tapped by the Rawlings government to be the deputy minister of culture and tourism in 1983. After serving in this position for three years, he became the minister of education. Most notably for this discussion, in 1989 he was appointed to chair the newly formed National Commission on Culture, which he helped to formulate (see Yankah 1993). Throughout his tenure in these various government posts, Abdallah was extremely influential in shaping the national culture of Ghana and was a primary figure in the controversy that unfolded regarding the GDE.

When asked about the building of the National Theatre by Kwesi Yankah, Abdallah remarked, "The national theatre project was formulated as far back as 1986, when the Head of State [J. J. Rawlings] went to China, and signed an agreement with the Chinese Government to construct a national theatre" (qtd. in Yankah 1993, 23). Abdallah was instrumental in bringing about this state agreement between the Chinese and Ghana. As Francis Nii-Yartey told me, "It was through his [Abdallah's] efforts that the National Theatre was built. He prevailed on Rawlings to build the National Theatre [when] they were going to build a stadium" (2006). After nearly three decades of agitation, Abdallah as deputy minister of culture and tourism helped to persuade the Ghanaian government to finally make a plan to construct the National Theatre. Shortly after this agreement had been made, and before construction on the theatre had even begun, debates surfaced regarding the relocation of the GDE. Many individuals argued that the National Theatre should become the new home for the national performing ensembles of the country, while others contended that the GDE should remain at the university.[5] This debate took place primarily between those at the University of Ghana and those attached to Ghanaian government bodies working with culture (such as the Ministry of Culture and Tourism, the NCC, and the Ministry of Education). This contestation reveals the complex power struggle that ensued as individuals negotiated pragmatic, artistic, and ideological concerns vis-à-vis the GDE and Ghana's national culture.

With few exceptions, most notably Nii-Yartey (the GDE's artistic director at the time), those at the university were opposed to moving the ensemble to the National Theatre. A university memo dated July 1, 1986, addressed to the commissioner (presumably Abdallah) outlines the basic tenets of their argument. This document states, "Events have proved that the University is the right training ground for our genuine Ghana dance culture and its presentation as seen by dance troupes throughout the country."[6] The memo continues by making the point that the university was interested in educating students about their national heritage and implies that many at the university feared that this focus would be lost if the dance ensemble moved to the National Theatre. The connection to an educational institution, recall, was paramount in Nketia's formulation of the ensemble from its inception; such a partnership, he argued, would ensure that national culture could be shared with the public through education. Nketia also maintained that the ensemble's location at the university would guarantee that research could be conducted and transferred directly to the GDE, thus presumably ensuring that the cultural traditions represented onstage would closely resemble those practices found in local communities. In this regard, an appendix to the memo includes a portion of Nketia's inaugural speech: "The training [of the GDE] could not have been devised effective[ly] without previous research into music and dance. And it is in this regard that the link with the Institute of African Studies [at the university] has proved beneficial" (2). In short, Nketia and others saw the GDE's connection to the university as a way to ensure the authenticity of the ensemble and its repertoire. Along these lines, the memo argues that previous dance ensembles in Ghana disappeared because "they did not present *genuine* Ghanaian dances. The danger is that the Ensemble, uprooted from its home and the University's aura, may either fade away or present dances which do not reflect our *Grass-root* dances" (3; emphasis mine). The terms "genuine" and "Grass-root" here could be exchanged for "authentic" (see Handler and Linnekin 1984), and, as such, the above statement consequently reveals that many at the university, including Nketia and Opoku, feared that if the GDE was removed from this institution, the authenticity of Ghana's national culture would be in jeopardy.

Along with authenticity, another point of contention centered around the issue of artistic "development." The memo continues by making the claim that "Mr. Nii-Yartey seems to be under the delusion that the Ghana Dance Ensemble is [only] a research group" (4). This statement is a response to Nii-Yartey, Abdallah, and others who argued that the GDE could not adequately grow or "move forward" within the context of academia; they contended that those at the university were concerned only with research, not "development." Attempting to counter this claim, the memo continues, "The University finds it hard to understand why it should transfer . . . [the GDE] for its further development when the Uni-

versity is able, with its experience, to effect this. As long ago as 1967 the
. . . first Artistic Director [Opoku] had foreseen such development and
collaboration with other theatrical presentations" (4). The document
then cites Opoku's collaboration with the Accra drama studio in his 1967
production of Wole Soyinka's *The Lion and the Jewel* as evidence for the
GDE's ability to develop Ghana's dances in a theatrical manner within
the university. Furthering this argument, the memo states that "we [at
the university] have approached our task as a creative experiment" (2).
This phrase is an indirect reference to Nketia's inaugural speech titled
"A Bold Experiment" in which he stated that the ensemble stands for
tradition as well as creativity (Nketia [1967] 1993, 14). Individuals at the
university contended that they were not opposed to creative development of Ghana's cultural traditions but had been advocates of it from
the ensemble's inception.

The concluding remarks of the memo reveal another primary concern of those arguing for the GDE's retention at the university: "The University does not see any necessity of acting [as] a research and training
ground for the National Theatre Dance Company whose ideas on development of our [Ghanaian] traditional dances may be radically different
from our [Legon] conception of the subject" (4). Hence, this document
not only maintains that the university was capable of encouraging creativity but also implies that the *ways* in which Ghana's culture might
be developed outside the purview of its expertise might denigrate the
nation's heritage.

Opoku also feared that if relocated to the National Theatre, the
dance ensemble would become overly politicized – too entrenched in
governmental politics; he presumed officials would have too much influence over the ensemble's artistic direction. In an interview, he commented, "When you go up there [to the National Theatre] – then it becomes political. . . . Because they begin to give you orders – that . . . would
not have to do with anything with the arts" (qtd. in Schramm 2000, 56).
Opoku also voiced concern that the ensemble would become commer-
cialized if it were attached to the National Theatre. In another interview,
referring to the GDE's relocation, he stated, "You don't sell things you
believe in that cheaply. Not when you're doing dance" (qtd. in K. Fabian
1996, 11).

Echoes of these remarks were still present during my research. Participants expressed concern that the National Theatre had cheapened the dances and that Nii-Yartey had taken the company there only for financial gain. As one drummer at Legon claimed, "The reason Nii-Yartey moved to the National Theatre was so he could make money. If he was at the university he was under African studies, which meant that the money for performances went to them [the university], not Nii-Yartey. So he [Nii-Yartey] struck a deal with the minister of culture [Abdallah]" (Kofi 2006). These comments allude to the close social relationship between Nii-Yartey and Abdallah, both of whom strongly advocated that the GDE should relocate to the National Theatre.

Countering the stance outlined above, Nii-Yartey, Abdallah, and others refuted these assertions regarding the lure of financial profits and the loss of authenticity, arguing instead that the National Theatre was the right place for the ensemble to grow and develop. Regarding the relocation of the GDE, Nii-Yartey explained:

> The whole university was against it. They thought it was political the way the government did it. But I was looking at things completely different. . . . For the first time, we [Ghanaians] had a national theatre, and I could do my work. And I started producing, creating dance-drama, dance-theatre, more correctly. I need a big space. I needed to *move forward*. So I took it as an opportunity because I was having some frustrations here, with discipline with the dancers. The university to me was inimical to the development of the arts. This is the way I saw it; I stand for correction, but . . . I saw the company as a whole department. But apparently those who came after Nketia and other people [at the university] didn't see it that way. To them it was just a little thing inside the Institute [of African Studies]. To me, dance should be developed, and develop beyond what it is, or what it was. . . . If you keep using us in there [at the university], we will not grow. And that is not correct, because dance is a complete discipline. But nobody was listening. I fought with a lot of them [at the university], because they didn't understand. (2006)

In Nii-Yartey's opinion, the university's facilities, or lack thereof, inhibited his ability to "move forward" artistically. Moreover, Nii-Yartey noted that his university colleagues did not share his vision of what dance could become in Ghana, alluding to his perception of the university faculty as too conservative in regard to the arts.

Nii-Yartey additionally claimed that his artistry was hindered by the university's bureaucratic system:

> The university system was difficult. I had to write a letter to the university. Then
> they had to write a letter to the administrative secretary. Then the administra-
> tive secretary had to write to the director. Then the director had to write to
> the top.... Anyway, all these things were there, and I couldn't discipline the
> people the way a dance company should.... They were treating the dancers as
> they would treat anything in academia, and that is not correct for a professional
> company. So I was being frustrated. (2006)

In our discussions, Nii-Yartey continually stressed that he was not concerned with financial rewards or government politics; rather, his primary motivation for moving the company was the artistic development
of dance.

Reinforcing these sentiments, Abdallah's ideas regarding "development" closely aligned with Nii-Yartey's, and together they proved to be
a powerful force in advocating for the relocation of the GDE:

> When Nii and I were students together, I watched him very closely try to do this
> work of preservation and at the same time [understood] very clearly that you
> cannot imprison the culture of a people in a time capsule. And that can be a way
> of reintegrating the nation. You take different dance forms from different re-
> gions that don't recognize any boundaries. And that is what he began to do with
> some of his pieces. There is pure traditional dance and contemporary African
> dance that goes beyond and does incredible things. (Abdallah 2007)

Abdallah was an advocate of Nii-Yartey's artistic vision for the development of Ghanaian dance. As he told me, "He [Nii-Yartey] probably was
one of the few people who really understood the role of dance in national
development and the need for the development of African dance. These
are two very important things." Abdallah also recognized that there were
pragmatic obstacles to "development" at Legon:

> I also happened to know that on the Legon campus, there was also a problem with
> space, that there was a conflict all the time between [the] Dance Ensemble and
> the rest of the School of Performing Arts, always vying for rehearsal space. Facili-
> ties at the theatre here alone help the national companies to be able to *fulfill their
> potential*.... We assumed it was obvious.... You don't have a national theatre and
> then put your professional national companies somewhere else, especially in our
> case where *the National Theatre is the best equipped* for what they are doing. A lot
> of work has gone into providing for the dance company, for example, one of the
> most modern dance studios in Africa. (qtd. in Yankah 1993, 23; emphasis mine)

In short, like Nii-Yartey, Abdallah stressed that the GDE and Ghana's
culture needed to develop and "move forward"; he contended that the

5.1. National Theatre of Ghana, Accra. *Photograph by Jesse Weaver Shipley.*

best place to realize the artistic potential of the troupe was in the new, "modern" National Theatre. Designed by Chinese architects to resemble a boat, the National Theatre (see fig. 5.1) incorporates modernist architectural elements, while the Legon dance hall (fig. 5.2) recalls its colonial construction. The difference in physical structures and architectural style is emblematic of the distinctions participants make between the two companies. That is, while the National Theatre's contemporary lines suggest modernity and development, the dance hall projects continuity with the past.

While opposed to many at Legon, Abdallah, Nii-Yartey, and others agitating for the GDE's relocation to the National Theatre were nevertheless open to the concerns of the university. Abdallah explained:

> When the theatre was being built, I said, "Let's have a discussion." I said this would be an opportunity for the dance company to emerge and really come into its own. Then there were all kinds of arguments [and those] who said, "No, they are not going anywhere." . . . I wanted to move [the GDE] to the National Theatre, but I would also want a relationship between the theatre and the IAS [at the university] so we could continue to improve and work on our research. (2007)

5.2. Dance hall at Legon. *Photograph by Jennifer Hart.*

Nii-Yartey's recollection of these discussions between the university and government illustrates the difficulties in achieving such a relationship:

> I proposed that the university and the government should come together to run the National Theatre, because the university trains the people, all the people. My argument was, and I said it several times, the university could easily, with its training and knowledge, influence this thing [National Theatre]. But some people were playing politics with it. The university administration then did not like the government in power [Rawlings's National Democratic Congress party]. And the government in power was a revolutionary government. The university had a system of doing things, which contradicts revolution. And those at the university thought this was going to make the arts suffer. I told them I wanted the university to see me as a link between this institution and the National Theatre. (2006)

Nii-Yartey shared the university's concern that those in government would not have the knowledge and experience to develop the arts in a sensitive manner:

> So what is stopping some [government] administrators who know nothing
> about the arts to dictate to us how we should go about this [artistic develop-
> ment]? We should leave the National Theatre in the hands of people who
> couldn't handle things? We needed to try to balance things, and take personali-
> ties [egos] out of it, and look at the arts. . . . The university should train people
> to oil the wheels of development in the system. The university is the only place
> in this country that can provide the manpower, needs, and knowledge for that
> place. And the university had all the power to send people to [the National
> Theatre], but because the university people did not agree with some of the
> government's politics, the university said no. (ibid.)

Nii-Yartey and others offered a solution, a compromise, and a place for
the university at the National Theatre in which to influence the direction of new cultural developments; but, according to Nii-Yartey, faculty
refused primarily on political grounds.

After a thorough debate between the university and government,
a law was passed that eventually led to the bifurcation of the GDE. In
1990, Provisional National Defense Council Law 238 repealed Law 232
and established the National Commission on Culture (for which Abdallah became its first chairman). Among other responsibilities, this
law solidified the NCC's direct control over the National Theatre, which
included the GDE as one of its resident companies (see Botchwey 1993).
Abdallah noted, however, that "[this] law just established the authority
of the NCC. It didn't say they [the GDE] had to move. It just said that the
NCC is responsible for it" (2007). Moreover, Nii-Yartey noted that "the
university said we don't regard the law" (2006). As Krista N. Fabian
remarks, "Opoku and Nketia, standing firm in their belief that the company must be linked to an educational institution, refused to move, in
spite of the lure of financial rewards" (1996, 11). Nii-Yartey, on the other
hand, was eager to relocate the GDE to the National Theatre. He told me,
"I'm a good citizen, so I had to regard the law. And, I wanted to develop
so bad" (2006). The ambiguity of the law required further negotiations
to resolve this tension, as Abdallah explained: "Eventually we [the university and the government] came up with a compromise. We said those
who wanted to could stay at the university and do their research, and
those who wanted to be in a more stagy theatre environment could do
that" (2007). According to interviews, about half of the thirty members
decided to stay at Legon, while the other half chose to leave for the Na-

tional Theatre. Only seven years after the government had merged the FDC and the GDE (in 1985) in order to create less confusion and a more coherent sense of national unity, Ghana, once again, had two national dance ensembles.

A FORK IN THE ROAD: PRAGMATISM, IDEOLOGY, AND AGENCY

When the National Theatre was nearing completion in 1991, GDE members were given the opportunity to decide once and for all which path they were going to take – the National Theatre or the University of Ghana.[7] The 1986 university memo states, "The University is of the opinion that its employees are free to choose where they would like to work" (4). According to ensemble members at this time, Nii-Yartey initially told them that they had three weeks to decide but then surprised them by asking for their decision after only three days. Most performers were caught off-guard, and if they were not sure, Nii-Yartey just had them stay at Legon (see Schramm 2000). The following section will explore the experiences of ensemble members who had to wrestle with the prospect of leaving the university. This discussion reveals the ways in which musicians and dancers managed the ensemble's initial split, balancing national service, personal loyalties, artistic aspirations, and pragmatic quotidian objectives while attempting to maximize this situation to suit their interests and needs.

As E. A. Duodu, who became the artistic director at Legon after Nii-Yartey left, recalled, "When the ensemble split, the National Theatre enticed [the performers] with better salary structure. And at the time there were some problems at the university and [performers] were not getting the salary. But still some remained. They were too adamant to go, and I am glad" (2007). From discussions with participants, the current salaries within the two companies do not differ dramatically. The NDC performers on average make about ten U.S. dollars more a month than their counterparts at Legon. Many in the theatre troupe still complain about their low wages and struggle to cover their everyday basic expenses. But at the time of the split, performers were promised a larger, more significant pay increase if they moved to the National Theatre. According to some interviewees, salary played at least a small role in the performers' decision-making process.

Closely linked to salary, job security also informed individuals' decisions about which career path to take. Patience Kwakwa remarked, "The group that left was more adventurous and willing to take a risk. Things were safe here at the university. There was the possibility that the one at the theatre might be disbanded, but here [Legon] you can't destroy things just like that" (2006). Some who were at Legon at the time of the split claim that "when Nii-Yartey left, he tried to confuse us. He tried to say that he was still the director [at Legon]. But how can you be the director at two places at the same time? By telling people he was still director at Legon, he was trying to force people to come to the theatre and threatened them with fear of losing their jobs if they did not move to the National Theatre" (Asante 2005). On the other hand, there were reportedly some at Legon who were attempting to convince dancers that if they left for the National Theatre, they would run a greater risk of losing their jobs there. Ben Abdallah explained:

> There was also a certain perception of job security, which was pumped into the young dancers. At the time they were [saying] "If you move there it is a political thing; you are under a ministry and if tomorrow there is a coup and there is a change in government, you don't know what will happen, but here [Legon] you are part of the university system and you are protected." I don't think Opoku or Nketia were the ones who were pumping those ideas in. But everyone was pumping their own political inclination. (2007)

Some of those with influence over the dancers used job security to further their own political objectives. The performers became caught in the middle of this political battle. Whether propaganda or not, many performers who chose to stay at Legon noted that the National Theatre was new, which invited uncertainty. Participants explained that one could easily see how government might destroy it or might mismanage it. No one knew if the National Theatre could be sustained in Ghana, whereas the university and the dance ensemble at Legon had been in existence for decades.

Although pragmatic concerns such as job security and salary weighed heavily on the minds of those who had to decide which national ensemble to participate in, ideology and personal loyalties also played a role in this process. The most senior drummer of the GDE at the time of the split, Foli Adadae, remarked, "This place, I've been here for a loooong time. So I can't just leave this place and go to another one anywhere. No, you can't do like that. You stay in one place and do your work, and when you retire, you retire. Opoku and Nketia were like my fathers; they treated me like their own child" (2006). Adadae felt a sense of loyalty to the university and its staff, which had helped him in numerous ways. Similarly, there were those who felt this same sense of loyalty to Nii-Yartey and other members of the GDE staff who decided to leave for the National Theatre. When I asked Caroline Yeme about her decision to leave Legon, she told me it was because "my director, my stage manager, my production manager, my costume designer all decided to come. Some of my friends have been with Opoku for a long time; when I joined, [however,] Nii-Yartey was the director" (2006). Her remarks indicate a generational factor that informed individuals' choices at the time of the split. Namely, older members of the GDE, who had started under the direction of Opoku (like Adadae), overwhelmingly were the ones who decided to stay at the university. The younger members of the group, who presumably did not have as close a connection with Opoku, Nketia, and the university, made up the majority of those who relocated to the National Theatre. The result was an overall younger group of performers at the theatre, which seemed to mirror the NDC's emphasis on progress, development, and newness. This left an older, more conservative group at Legon, which similarly mirrored the concentration on the continuity of tradition by the ensemble based there.

This is not to suggest that pragmatic concerns alone inevitably produced an ideological division between the GDE and the NDC. In fact, some participants I spoke with explained that their choice of ensembles did take into account the ideologies of "development" and "tradition." Duodu remarked that "some [performers] said they were not going; for the love of the university, for the *love of continuity*, and for the love of the art they decided to remain" (2007). Many ensemble members at Legon told me that, in addition to their personal loyalties to Opoku, Nketia, and the staff at the university, they remained because they believed the university was better suited to preserve the "continuity" of Ghana's national heritage.

Others chose to follow Nii-Yartey to the theatre because they assumed that it would be a better context in which to "develop" and "grow" as individual artists. Evelyn Akowian, who chose to move to the theatre, explained it this way: "That time Nii was the director. And he likes things different, different, different. And he likes contemporary and ballet. So, if I stay at Legon, I will be in the same cup, but me, I want a different cup. I see different things. I see an improvement in myself. If you dance contemporary, you can do everything; you are not lazy on it. It will help to improve yourself, and you will know more" (2006). Similarly, Salifu Abubakari Merigah, who also decided to move to the National Theatre, told me, "I chose to come [to the National Theatre] because I was serving the nation. I wasn't serving the university. I was serving myself and the nation because I was a citizen. And also the theatre had some facilities that the university doesn't have, but I wasn't looking at that. I was looking at myself, because [I wanted] to *grow* myself more into art" (2006). Speaking broadly about the performers who left for the theatre, Merigah stated, "The dancers wanted their own space, so we could build our repertoire and *develop* more as artists." Like Merigah and Akowian, many NDC members noted that they came to the theatre in order to develop their personal artistry. They also predicted that the theatre would offer increased economic opportunities, primarily through travel.

In all, a combination of pragmatic and ideological factors contributed to performers' decisions. Predominantly, the younger members who placed emphasis on personal and cultural "development" followed their progressive leader, Nii-Yartey, to the National Theatre, while an older, more conservative group remained at the university. Not necessarily concerned with the nation as a whole, both groups carefully considered their options, working out which path would best suit their personal interests and needs. Many who left for the theatre did so to develop their artistic talents and pursue prospects for creative and economic enrichment. Similarly, many remained at Legon because they saw it as the more attractive social, artistic, and financial decision. Asserting their agency in this way, ensemble members mediated this schism and strategically managed the institutions and practices of nationalism to pursue their own definitions of self-improvement. Once these decisions had been made, a rift between these two ensembles occurred as each took a different approach to the staging of national culture, competing for the attention and resources of the nation and the state.

STRUGGLING FOR SURVIVAL: PERSPECTIVES FROM LEGON

Funding and Travel Opportunities

At the end of 1992, Francis Nii-Yartey took those who wanted to move and relocated to the recently completed National Theatre. Participants at Legon told me that Nii-Yartey had taken many of the costumes and virtually all of the drums with him to the theatre, leaving the GDE in disarray. As one GDE drummer bitterly remarked, "Nii crippled the group" (Kofi 2006). Nii-Yartey's departure also left the university without an artistic director. To remedy this situation, the university called upon a founding member of the GDE, E. A. Duodu (who worked at the university at the time), to step into the artistic director position. While commenting on this period, Duodu stated, "At that time Nii-Yartey had left for the theatre, and the dance ensemble was virtually dying" (2007). Given these dire circumstances and driven by his deep devotion to the GDE, Duodu sacrificed his sabbatical to nurse this group back to health. This section will examine the perspectives of those who chose to stay at Legon at the time of the split as well as of those performers who chose to come to the GDE following this separation. This exploration not only reveals additional ways in which these artists managed but also further elaborates on previous discussions of authenticity, tradition, and the reimagining of the self.

Duodu and the GDE faced many obstacles at Legon in the wake of the separation, not the least of which was the issue of funding. According to Krista Fabian, who did research with the GDE for several years, "Abdallah, leading the government to believe that the Ensemble received its subvention from the culture half of the Ministry of Education and Culture [when in fact it received it from] . . . the education half, transferred all government funding to the company at the National Theatre, leaving the original Ghana Dance Ensemble of the University of Ghana struggling to regain its name and its funding" (1996, 11–12). Regarding this transfer of funding, one of the senior dancers at Legon remarked,

> When Ben Abdallah split the group, he wanted to make sure this group [GDE] would sink.... It's serious. The man [Abdallah] cannot talk to me. He can come and pass as I am sitting here. He knows me. But he can't talk to me, because the man is so wicked. He is wicked! He [Abdallah] made all sorts of photocopies that said this [GDE] group is basing at the National Theatre. So we [at Legon] had to wake up and also write our letters that still the Ghana Dance Ensemble – the group that they know – we are still in Legon. We didn't move anywhere. ... So because of that people have been inviting us for programs. If we didn't do that, they would have thought everybody went to National Theatre. So we have had to fight! (Asari 2007)

These types of spirited comments were common among those I interviewed at Legon, as members of the GDE continued to harbor resentment regarding the actions of Abdallah and Nii-Yartey. After the split, the GDE had to "fight" to regain a viable level of financial support. Thanks to the backing of the university and private clients who have continued to hire the GDE for performances, this group has been able to persevere.

This lack of funding and government support had other lasting consequences for the Legon ensemble. The production manager of the GDE, Jennies Darko, explained how this affected the Legon group: "Because they [the NDC] are right under the Commission on Culture, they have money for their costumes. So their costumes are A-one compared to us. We are working with an institution [the university]. You know how it is. Even asking for money to buy a nail to nail something is very difficult. You need to write a lot of letters for people to approve and so on" (2007). Moreover, Nii-Yartey's close personal relationship with the chairman of the NCC, Ben Abdallah, according to those at Legon, led to an overall increase in performance and travel opportunities for the NDC and conversely a decrease for the university-based ensemble in this regard. A senior drummer at Legon stated, "Nii-Yartey has stolen many opportunities [from] the GDE. A lot of the gigs that were supposed to come to the GDE have gone to the NDC" (Kofi 2006). Another GDE (Legon) member later added, "They [the NDC] even took our trip that we had been planning for years. They took all the funds to the National Theatre.... We hear they've gone to U.S. and Russia. We know that they are enjoying our trips" (Asari 2007). During my research with the ensembles, the NDC traveled abroad much more often than the Legon group. This disparity in travel and performance opportunities, in turn, exacerbated the financial difficulties that the university ensemble faced. Despite these obstacles, the Legon group forged ahead, rebuilding drums from scratch, sewing new costumes, and agitating for financial support from the university and other patrons. Funding and travel are only some of the numerous obstacles that have threatened the existence of the university-based troupe.

Two Ghana Dance Ensembles: Naming Rights

Nii-Yartey, in addition to moving performers, resources, drums, and costumes to the National Theatre, took the original group's name with him. Thus, the ensemble at the National Theatre was also referred to as the Ghana Dance Ensemble. Kwesi Yankah, a lecturer at the university in the period just after the split, commented that "the resultant duplicity of nomenclatures is one of the most anomalous spin offs the Abdallah regime has bequeathed to the arts" (1993, 23). This duplicity was, and remains to some degree, a source of controversy between the two ensembles, causing confusion among audiences and state officials, which, in turn, has had significant consequences for the individuals in the national troupes.

According to many at Legon, after the split the troupe at the National Theatre was to be referred to as the National Dance Company (of Ghana), while the Legon group would retain its title of the Ghana Dance Ensemble. This differentiation presumably would avoid confusion between the groups, allowing audiences to distinguish between the two. This was not always the case, however. Mercy Ayettey, a member of the GDE since the time of the split, recalled:

> There was confusion at times. At times we used to fight. We used to fight with them [the NDC] ... [because] at times they would play and they would mention our [the GDE's] name. It's not fine. They [the audience] have to know who is performing. That is the reason why J. J. [Rawlings] joined the groups [the FDC and the GDE], and now look. When they [the NDC] bring the name like this, we have to make the phone calls. "Oh, we saw this on tele[vision]," and they mention this name. The announcer thought there was only one group. That is what they know. So, now they have divided in two, and it has created confusion for the people. (2007)

Nii-Yartey commented on the situation in a 1997 *Weekly Spectator* interview:

> We [at the National Theatre] are aware of the ambiguities that are being created ... and how embarrassing sometimes it is both for us and our colleagues at the University.... [Therefore] those of us at the National Theatre are slowly moving towards having us called the National Dance Company of Ghana ... but it is a legal matter. We would have liked to have changed the name immediately but the law must be respected. (qtd. in Abdulai 1997)

Nearly a decade later, Duodu, who was retired and did not frequent the university campus, contended that Nii-Yartey had completed his "move towards" a new naming practice: "The conflict has died down. Now there is a clear distinction between the two. They [the NDC] were using 'Ghana Dance Ensemble,' and the university was also using that name. But now they [the NDC] have seen the logic and have changed to the National Dance Company" (2007). William Diku, however, noted that "they [the NDC] are still pirating the name. They have not yet given up fully on the name. They write it in brackets. Because of that we have been losing money for our trips. They capitalize on it" (2005). By examining a number of the NDC's programs (1995–2007), I have observed a progressive shift: earlier programs featured the name "Ghana Dance Ensemble," while subsequent programs show the adoption of the name "National Dance Company of Ghana" but still retain the "Ghana Dance Ensemble" below in brackets or in smaller print. Finally, around the year 2000 the NDC began to use solely the title "The National Dance Company" in their program notes. However, illustrating the continuing confusion and controversy over its name, the theatre troupe is referred to as "The Dance Company of Ghana (Ghana Dance Ensemble)" on the NCC's website.[8]

The university ensemble's ongoing struggle for recognition and the retention of its name was evident in a 2006 performance at the statehouse in central Accra. The group had been performing for state officials and dignitaries for nearly an hour, without much audience response, when the members began to perform *gome*. After watching this comical and sexually provocative Ga dance, the crowd reacted enthusiastically, laughing and applauding loudly. A staff member of the GDE quickly took the floor after the dance ended to announce, "You are watching the Ghana Dance Ensemble from the University of Ghana, Legon." He felt it necessary to state this, he told me later, because "the people have to know which group they are watching. They have to know that Legon is here, and we are good" (Abdellah 2006). The continuing debate over the names of the ensembles has caused confusion for audiences – the citizens of the nation – and invited rivalry between the two groups. This contestation, ironically, serves to undermine the goals of national unity for which the ensembles are commissioned to propagate.

Tradition, Authenticity, and Identity

When I asked participants in the university ensemble if there were any differences between their group and the one at the National Theatre, the common responses were, "Legon is the original group," "We are better at the traditional dances," and "We use the correct movements." This section will unpack these responses to reveal the ways in which these claims help those in the GDE (Legon) to maintain their political viability when confronted with direct competition from their counterparts at the National Theatre. In other words, given the financial difficulties outlined above, I explore how these claims counter the anxiety of annihilation and ensure the survival of the Legon group and its members. Furthermore, I ask: How do individuals re/negotiate their own identities and that of the GDE in light of the advent of a competing national ensemble?

When I asked the promotional manager at Legon if there was one thing that people should know about the GDE, she responded, "I want people to know that this is the *original* group. If you go out into town and ask them when their group was formed, they can't say 1962" (Darko 2007). Her statement implies a definition of originality equated with the source of some idea or object from which copies have been made. Participants at Legon often referred to the NDC as a "copy" and stated "We are the originals" to imply that their group was not only older but more authentic. The university troupe is historically the original national dance ensemble of Ghana, but its members also claim that their dances offer a "better," more "authentic/correct" representation of the nation's "traditional" heritage. Many Legon ensemble members remarked that they do "original movements" based on the careful research and reputations of Nketia and Opoku while claiming that the NDC (primarily Nii-Yartey), on the other hand, has profoundly altered "traditional" repertoire, resulting in a loss of authenticity. In all, such discourse illustrates the politics and poetics of authentication, attesting to authenticity's relational and subjective social construction as drummers and dancers at the university argue that Legon better represents the "real traditions" of their country.

These claims of authenticity not only are internal reassurances of the university ensemble's sense of itself but also have generated a wider reputation among its audiences and the NDC. Remarking on the direct contact between the two ensembles, a senior dancer at Legon stated:

> When they [the NDC] see us, they salute us.... Anytime we meet, they will say, "Oh, the elders are here." So we should leave them to do it. At times we can meet at a program and they will tell the promoter that "there is no need for us here. Because the dances we are coming to do, their [GDE] dances are better than ours." So they will leave the program for us. It has happened before with the National Dance Company at the Golden Tulip [Hotel in Accra]. We saw the names there: National Dance Company and then Ghana Dance Ensemble, wooo! We are happy, because this means they are going to perform first before we do. And they said no. The reason we are last all the time is, because, as I have told you, our dances are correct. People want to stay and look at it. And the foreigners, they like it. So, they [NDC] went and told the promoters that they had an emergency somewhere. This dance ensemble [GDE] is here, so they should do it. Then you will see them packing their drums. Then they moved to leave the performance for us. They can't compete with us. (Asari 2007)

Her statement implies that members of the NDC respect the GDE members' abilities and often defer to them as "their elders," refusing to compete with them directly. This dancer also recalled a time when Nii-Yartey invited the GDE to participate in a joint performance with the NDC at the National Theatre. As her statements indicate, Nii-Yartey's gesture had an ulterior motivation: "We agreed to do the performance, not knowing that it was our dances that they [the NDC] wanted to learn. He [Nii-Yartey] wanted us to do only the traditional dances, and the dance company did the contemporary ones. When we are dancing then he is recording, because he wanted to take our dances to teach his group" (ibid.). According to this dancer, Nii-Yartey wanted to record the university troupe's performance because "our [Legon's] dance is the correct one. They know it!" Like those who peer in the windows of the dance hall, Nii-Yartey had devised a strategy to appropriate the authenticity of the Legon group for himself.

"They [the NDC] don't know the traditional dances," she continued, "because we are teaching them. We haven't finished. The dances that we have been giving to them, they didn't get all the movements before they left [for the National Theatre]" (ibid.). Due to the NDC's focus on contemporary African dance (discussed later), many at Legon argue that the theatre ensemble has allowed the "traditional" dances of Ghana to "escape them" (Agyette 2007). While participants often acknowledge that the NDC is more proficient at contemporary African dance, the GDE, they claim, is more adept in the "traditional" aspect. The artistic director at Legon told me that "the NDC can't compete with the GDE when it comes to traditional dances" and further remarked that he would "gladly have a competition with them anytime to see who is the better company at traditional dances. The GDE would win without question" (B. Ayettey 2007b). While members of the Legon ensemble often make claims of their prowess in "traditional" Ghanaian dance, many also acknowledge that the NDC has more expertise in contemporary African dance. One GDE (Legon) dancer described the basic perceived distinction between the two national ensembles succinctly when he remarked that "when it comes to traditional dance, the dance company [NDC] doesn't come near us. When it comes to contemporary dance, we don't go near them" (Agyette 2007).

With its gestures toward authenticity and tradition, the GDE's reputation as "the originals" not only forms a grounding for a sense of self for existing members but also plays a significant role in ensuring the survival of this troupe by attracting a steady flow of new recruits to replace outgoing members. As one young dancer at Legon told me, "I wanted to join this group [the GDE] because they are good in the traditional dances. . . . They have been going to do the research and [therefore are] better than the National Theatre group in the traditional things. National Theatre, they don't do the traditional dances that well. They come to learn it here and take it there. I want to do the correct thing, so I came to Legon" (Amotonyo 2005). As further evidence of this distinction, recall the example in which several members of a local amateur culture group intentionally joined the Legon ensemble specifically to learn "traditional" Ghanaian dance, while other members of this same group went to the National Theatre to learn "contemporary" dance. Broadly,

William Diku stated that "as the research wing at the Institute of African Studies, we have been concerned with the traditional dances, and those who prefer traditional dances come to the GDE, not the National Theatre" (2005). The GDE (Legon) and its members' reputation as "the originals," or the "better" purveyors of "authentic traditional" Ghanaian dances, has contributed to the ensemble's survival as it continues to attract new members who are particularly interested in learning and performing this type of dance form.

This reputation has additionally helped the Legon group to procure clients, including corporate and government patronage. As the ensemble receives little funding from the university, these clients are vital to its survival. Many at Legon contend that audiences prefer "traditional" dances to "contemporary" ones. Referring to the joint performance at the National Theatre mentioned above, a GDE dancer recalled, "So we [the GDE] did the traditional dances, and then they [NDC] came to do the contemporary dances, and people [the audience] started leaving, because they like the traditional dances. So we will do the contemporary dances first, because people will wait to see the traditional dances. So we will perform last. Because, for our dances, people will stay" (Asari 2007). Moreover, when I asked the promotional director at Legon how she would respond to criticism that the university group was not developing because it focused too heavily on the "traditional" dances, she replied, "But people love it. It's not the same old thing. People love the culture. They love the original movements. . . . People like the tradition – the roots where it came from. If an Asante comes to see the *adowa*, he will say, 'Oh, this is the adowa, this is where I come from,' and they will like it. If you keep on doing things from outside, people won't like it. That's why we have kept our tradition" (Darko 2007). This preference for "traditional" dances has encouraged many clients to choose the GDE, rather than the NDC, for certain occasions. For instance, during a 2006 GDE (Legon) performance at a corporate event in Accra, I asked the organizer why he chose the university group instead of the National Theatre troupe. The organizer told me that he wanted "some traditional culture to make our event powerful. We know that the university has the old people who do the traditional dances, not like the theatre – they do mostly contemporary."[9]

Regarding government patrons, the GDE's identity as "the originals" additionally aids the group's viability. Although some at Legon argue that state officials do not know the difference between the two groups, choosing Legon only because "that is the group they are most familiar with" (Duodu 2007), others note that the Ghanaian state recognizes and calls upon a particular troupe based on the traditional/contemporary distinction between the two ensembles. Speaking about state protocol performances, the promotional manager at Legon commented:

> They [the state] call us when they need us. They know we [the Legon group] are the elders. They know our performances are clean. They know we compose ourselves. They know how we are. So normally when there are big, big functions they call us to perform for them.... They like us better because we are most into tradition. We didn't throw away our culture. We didn't throw away our traditional dances that we have, unlike the other group.... When the separation came, the elderly people – the ones who knew the traditional dances – stayed. So, the tradition is more here than there. And we do the original thing. Theirs [NDC] is a photocopy. They [the government] know very well that that [NDC] group came from this [GDE] group. We call ourselves the original group. (Darko 2007)

Corroborating this assertion, a government official at the state protocol office stated, "When we need a traditional thing, we normally call the Legon people. We know they are good in the tradition. If we need a contemporary thing, we will call the theatre people."[10]

In all, the university troupe members' identity as "the originals" reinforces their favorable reputation regarding the "correct/authentic" performance of "traditional" dances. The Legon group and its members embody this identity through performance. As such, given the lack of support from the university and fierce competition from the NDC, "We are the originals" becomes a vital *performative strategy* that ensures the sustainability of this troupe. By continuing to articulate their abilities in maintaining the continuity of Ghana's national culture, the GDE (Legon) and its participants have additionally used this phrase as a *rhetorical strategy* to carve out a unique identity, or niche, in a highly competitive atmosphere. By claiming and performing their identity as "the originals," members of the Legon ensemble ensure that they succeed in their struggle to survive by using this rhetorical and performative strategy to manage nationalism, relying on it to ground their sense of self and further their individual pragmatic pursuits.

"WE ARE MOVING FORWARD": PERSPECTIVES FROM THE NATIONAL DANCE COMPANY AND AFRICAN CONTEMPORARY DANCE

When I began intensive field research for this project in the summer of 2004, I initially only worked with the GDE based at Legon, due primarily to my tether to the university for language courses. While sifting through archival material at the university, I came across Krista Fabian's work, in which she writes, "While . . . Mr. Duodu and his ensemble keep to their original aim of ensuring the continuity of tradition in African dance . . . Nii-Yartey's company at the National Theatre has taken a more contemporary angle to Ghanaian dance" (1996, 12). As I began to work with the NDC in 2005, I attempted to explore if and how this "contemporary angle" was realized in this troupe and how its members viewed their relation to the GDE.

While the NDC continued to perform "traditional" dances, the repertoire of which is nearly identical to that of the Legon group, Nii-Yartey had often taken a "more contemporary angle" to these dances. As a former dancer of the NDC explained, "Though they [the NDC] do tradition, Legon is good [better] in tradition than them [because] . . . they [the GDE] follow the real tradition. But at the National Theatre, Nii-Yartey used his mind to change certain things to make it more stronger than how Legon is" (Azadekor 2007). Another NDC dancer gave an example of why he thought the university troupe was "better" at the "traditional" dances: "Legon goes into details on the traditional dance more than National Dance Company." When I asked what kind of details, he replied, "The movements. Although the National Dance Company too is doing the movements, because of Nii-Yartey, they [the NDC] do it a contemporary way. In terms of agbekor turnings, at Legon they do the traditional turning, but Nii-Yartey changed it slightly. The traditional way has an extra step in the turn, but Nii's is faster" (Mensah 2007). The dancer then demonstrated Nii-Yartey's version, which uses a quick pivot on the right foot without planting the left foot until the body completes a 360-degree turn. Legon performs the agbekor turning phrase with an extra step halfway through the turn, which, the dancer stated, was the "traditional way." I asked, "So, in Anyako [an Ewe village], they don't do the fast one?" He replied, "No you have to take time. But Nii-Yartey, because of the contemporary, has changed it. . . . It's faster." Although the dancer could not give another example at the time, he assured me that Nii-Yartey had made similar alterations to other "traditional" dances of the NDC.

Regarding these types of modifications, Nii-Yartey has stated, "Modern life has shaped our way of looking at time. . . . When those traditional dances were created . . . things were slower, life was slower and a lot more relaxed" (qtd. in Schramm 2000, 78). The hastened pace of modern life has influenced Nii-Yartey to create faster, more streamlined versions of "traditional" repertoire. More broadly, while "traditional" dances have been transformed since Opoku's rearrangements in the 1960s, and occasionally criticized for these artistic developments, Nii-Yartey has further modified "traditional" choreographies to suit his ideas of contemporary aesthetics. This continued transformation, he also contends, reflects the tastes of modern audiences in Ghana and abroad. Although Opoku had also modified dances, often increasing tempos and omitting movements, his choreographies in general are often cited by practitioners as "more real/authentic" than the NDC versions.

Yet, taking a "contemporary angle" to Ghana's dances involves more than the modification of "traditional" cultural forms. When I questioned a senior drummer/dancer with the NDC about the differences between the two national ensembles, he stated, "We go forward more than them. We are doing more modern dance here. They are still doing the old, old dancing" (Atsikpa 2006b). Another dancer similarly responded, "We are far ahead of them [the GDE]" (Akowian 2006). Echoing this statement, Daniel Moffatt, the public relations manager for the NDC, has stated, "These people here at the National Theatre are far ahead of the ones at Legon" (qtd. in Schramm 2000, 63). While many individuals in the NDC reaffirm Legon's claims of supremacy in regard to "traditional" Ghanaian dances, they often proclaim that they are "moving forward" and are thus "ahead" of Legon because the National Theatre group is "developing" dance as an art. When asked about how the NDC is developing dance and moving ahead of Legon, a senior dancer at the theatre explained, "We are not in Gold Coast time. We are in Ghana, and the world is moving. And the choreographer [Nii-Yartey] realized that, because Ghana is moving, we need to move the dance. So we are moving into *contemporary dance*. You need the contemporary because we are *developing* our lives and ourselves" (Merigah 2006).

Generally, many in the theatre ensemble equate "development" with the performance of contemporary African dance. While both ensembles include these types of dances in their repertoire, some individuals in the NDC were not aware that Legon was practicing this style of dance. Or, if NDC members did acknowledge Legon's forays into this genre, they maintained that those at the National Theatre focused more on contemporary African dance and were thus more "developed" than those at the university. From observations of rehearsals and performances, it became evident that the NDC concentrated more effort on contemporary African dance than did the GDE. Thus, in order to understand the distinction between the two groups, it is vital to explore the nature and practices of contemporary African dance in Ghana, including how it is distinguished from "traditional" dance and how its performance relates to the identity of the NDC, its members, and the nation.

Contemporary African Dance in Ghana

Although "contemporary African dance" is a phrase used to describe a number of performance troupes and pieces throughout the African continent and the diaspora, there is little literature that adequately addresses this dance genre per se and its development (see Loots and Young-Jahangeer 2004). Thus it remains loosely defined and ambiguous in scholarship. This academic ambiguity reflects the complex and various ways this concept is deployed and defined by participants with whom I have worked. In all, there does not seem to be a consensus definition of contemporary African dance among scholars or my consultants. While a comprehensive historical account of contemporary African dance is sorely needed, it is beyond the scope of this project. However, as this section explores how this dance form arose and was developed in Ghana, it will reveal the ways in which Francis Nii-Yartey was part of the broader emergence of contemporary African dance. As such, this discussion will historicize the ways in which those at the NDC differentiate themselves from their counterparts at Legon as they present their own form of nationalism through contemporary African dance.

In Ghana, "contemporary" often becomes conflated with "Western." Many Ghanaians argue that all GDE and NDC repertoire is contemporary because it has been modified – infused with foreign, mostly Western, influences. Individuals with this view often take a conservative position in regard to the artistic development of indigenous dances, often considering contemporary African dance as a corruption of Ghana's heritage. This relatively small group of so-called cultural purists is typically at, or associated with, Legon. Overall, NDC members conceptualize contemporary African dance in particular ways to support their contention that what they do at the National Theatre is "completely different" from what the GDE or any other group in Ghana does. This distinction serves to reaffirm their identity as those who are "developing" or "moving forward." It is necessary, therefore, to examine the nuanced ways in which participants conceptualize contemporary dance to understand how these individuals re-create individual identities and various forms of nationalism.

To understand contemporary African dance in Ghana, it is important to explore its historical emergence. If one assumes the broad definition of contemporary African dance ascribed to by the "cultural purists," which includes any dance in this category that even hints at foreign/Western modes of expression, this genre could be traced back at least to Mawere Opoku. Receiving a significant amount of dance training in the United States and Britain and working with such noted "contemporary" artists as Martha Graham, Opoku's rearrangements of Ghanaian dances, as we have seen, were done with the cosmopolitan artistic sensibilities developed partially from this training. In other words, with this broad conception of contemporary African dance, even the so-called traditional repertoire of the dance companies becomes enveloped in this genre. Most individuals with whom I have worked, however, do not subscribe to this viewpoint. Overwhelmingly, individuals call dance forms "traditional" that are predominantly based on indigenous forms, use familiar titles (*kete,* agbekor, and the like), and intend to "authentically" represent local cultural practices.

Adding to the complexity of defining contemporary African dance, there is another genre of dance performed by the national ensembles known as "dance-drama," or, to a lesser extent, "dance-theatre." This genre of dance, while drawing on local dance forms, does not explicitly attempt to re-present these dances. As such, the names of these dance-dramas do not reference community dances. Additionally, these dance-dramas use a minimal amount of foreign elements to express narratives through dance, music, and pantomime. These narratives comment on contemporary local and global issues. One of the first in Ghana was *The Lion and the Jewel,* choreographed in the early 1960s by Opoku and based on a story of the same name by Wole Soyinka. Opoku's most famous dance-drama is called the *African Liberation Dance Suite* (often referred to as *Lamentation for Freedom Fighters* or simply *Lamentation*), created in the 1960s as a social commentary on, and tribute to, Africans who had recently fought for their nation's independence. This piece later inspired Nii-Yartey to produce his first dance-drama, *The Lost Warrior,* in 1976, which enacted the story of a wife losing her husband in battle. Subsequently, Nii-Yartey has continued to produce dance-dramas, which have been the hallmark of his career.[11] Moreover, a number of other Ghanaian choreographers, such as E. A. Duodu and William Adinku, have also created dance-dramas.[12]

These particular dance-dramas, however, are largely not considered contemporary African dance in Ghana

> because in Opoku's time we were basing our dances on the traditional dances. He [Nii-Yartey], like Opoku, also did dance-dramas, like *The King's Dilemma* and *The Lost Warrior.* But he does use some of the traditional movements to create these dance-dramas. For instance, in *The King's Dilemma* you see the *takai* [Dagbamba harvest festival] movements and the [Dagbamba] butcher's dance, but in a story form. Later, Nii-Yartey introduced these contemporary dances. (Djabatey 2006)

"Opoku's time" here refers to the time period when his career was most active (1960s–early 1990s). Although the dance-dramas of this period incorporated foreign elements of staging, aesthetics, and so on, these particular pieces were primarily based on, and featured, indigenous music and movements familiar to many Ghanaians. For example, as Grace Djabatey explained, "*The Lost Warrior* wasn't a contemporary dance. It was based on the traditional dances that already existed, like agbekor.... It was a dance-drama because it used the traditional movements. The contemporary dance was a new form here, so at least we have moved forward." While a few individuals consider dance-dramas to be a form of contemporary African dance, Nii-Yartey is often credited (particularly by those at the theatre) with introducing it to Ghana many years after these dance-dramas were first developed.

Nii-Yartey drew inspiration from several other choreographers and dancers who had been previously experimenting with contemporary African dance for many decades. While it is difficult to pinpoint the exact origins of this type of dance, there are several sources that have fed into its development. One stream of origin for contemporary African dance can be found in the works of Americans such as Alvin Ailey, Pearl Primus, and Katherine Dunham who drew heavily on African material to develop their expressive, experimental styles, most notably in the 1960s; however, these artists are often considered participants in the "modern" dance era centered primarily in America. When discussing the history of contemporary African dance in Africa, scholars often point to two women as pioneers of the genre: Sylvia Glasser and Germaine Acogny. Born in South Africa, Sylvia Glasser studied dance and anthropology in the United States and Britain in the 1960s and 1970s. She later founded the Moving into Dance Mophatong (MIDM) in her native country, where she developed Afrofusion, a hybrid of European, American, and African dance styles and techniques. In West Africa, Germaine Acogny, often called the "mother" of contemporary African dance, was developing her own experimental dance hybrids. Born in Benin but spending most of her life in Senegal, Acogny studied in Paris and New York as a young woman. When she returned to Senegal, Acogny established her first dance studio in Dakar in 1968. Between 1977 and 1982 she directed the dance company Mudra Afrique, in which she developed both traditional and contemporary forms of African dance. While living in Brussels, after the closure of Mudra, she developed solo works such as *Sahel* (1987) and *YE'OU* (1988); touring these pieces, she started to build international recognition for contemporary African dance.

Throughout the early 1990s, the prevalence and global visibility of contemporary African dance increased dramatically. In Nigeria, Peter Badejo founded Badejo Arts in 1990. This company developed contemporary African dance, blending traditional Nigerian dance with British contemporary dance.[13] Meanwhile, Glasser continued to choreograph pieces in South Africa, working with her protégé Vincent Mantsoe, who formed his own African contemporary dance company in the early 1990s. Similarly, another one of her students, Jackie Mbuyisela Semela, after training at MIDM, formed the Soweto Dance Theatre in 1989 and performed contemporary African dance throughout the 1990s. In East Africa, dancers Opiyo Okach and Afrah Tenambergen cofounded the first contemporary dance company in Kenya, La Gàara Company, in 1996.

While anglophone African countries played a role in the proliferation of African contemporary dance on the continent, francophone African nations have been the most significant sites for the development of this genre. This dominance has been driven by postcolonial international politics. The French saw the cultivation of contemporary African dance as part of their foreign diplomatic policy as they employed it to strengthen political alliances and contain African migration to Europe by giving youth artistic opportunities within Africa itself (Kringelbach 2013, 150–51). As part of this political strategy, in 1995, France financed Rencontres choréographiques de l'Afrique et de l'Océan Indien, a biennial dance competition first held in Luanda, as a strategic political tactic to further France's oil interests in Angola (152). That same year, the French also sponsored Danse l'Afrique danse!, another competitive biennial event, which firmly established African contemporary dance in the global market as it brought this dance genre to wide international attention. Further exemplifying this French influence, Compagnie Cie Salia nï Seydou was formed in Burkina Faso by Salia Sanou and Seydou Boro in 1995, two years after living in France and working with French choreographer Mathilde Monnier at the Centre Chorégraphique National in Montpellier.

Although Ghana is often absent from scholarly discussions of contemporary African dance, Nii-Yartey both influenced and was inspired by this genre's larger continental and global community. He has particularly noted the following artists as having an impact on his own contemporary work: Germaine Acogny; Alphonse Tierou; Adiatu Massidi of Côte d'Ivoire; Kofi Koko of Benin; Elsa Wollianton of Kenya; Achille N'Goye of Congo; Sylvia Glasser; Salia Sanou, Seydou Boro, and Irène Tassembédo of Burkina Faso; Peter Badejo; and American Kariamu Welsh Asante (Nii-Yartey 2009). When I asked how contemporary African dance came to Ghana, a senior drummer in the N D C told me that "Nii wanted to put new things inside. He brought contemporary dance to Ghana" (Atsikpa 2007). Although he had produced similar pieces (for example, *Solma, Musu: Saga of the Slaves, The King's Dilemma*), Grace Djabatey noted that "*Sal-Yeda: Fate of Man* [created in 1997] was Nii's first contemporary piece" (2006). She and others cited this particular work, I argue, because a significant portion of the dance movements and music used in this choreography are not based on recognizable "traditional" Ghanaian forms that are largely familiar to local audiences. Conversely, *Solma, Musu, The King's Dilemma,* and other previous works were largely based on identifiable "traditional" forms. For instance, after watching *Solma* and *The King's Dilemma,* art critique Nii Kwei Danso wrote, "It set me wondering. Is it a new dance? No, it's the same old dance only well polished and more exciting" (1995). Similarly, Ghanaian music/dance scholar and performer Kwesi Brown noted, "*Musu* used all traditional movements. I can see them and know where each of them came from" (2009).

Unlike these pieces and other dance-dramas, *Sal-Yeda* marked a categorical break largely because it incorporated a broad range of elements that were not necessarily discernible as "traditional" Ghanaian cultural forms. For instance, regarding the musical accompaniment of *Sal-Yeda,* dancers improvise fluid movements to a mix of Beninese singer/songwriter Angélique Kidjo's Afro-pop-inspired compositions and cuts from the 1995 album *Lambarena,* which fuses Bach violin excerpts with various African acoustic music. Regarding movement, although Nii-Yartey's piece incorporates Ghanaian/African styles and gestures, *Sal-Yeda* primarily features artistic dance styles and techniques, which have developed from Nii-Yartey's local and foreign (mostly Western) training in dance (for example, modern, postmodern, ballet, tap, jazz, and so on). Nii-Yartey uses a large palette comprising numerous contemporary local and global influences to express a narrative in which "man must seek the intervention of 'Asaase Yaa,' the earth's custodian, to help rejuvenate him and his environment."[14] Given its organization around a storyline, *Sal-Yeda* is thus both a dance-drama and an example of contemporary African dance, illustrating that these two genres are not mutually exclusive.

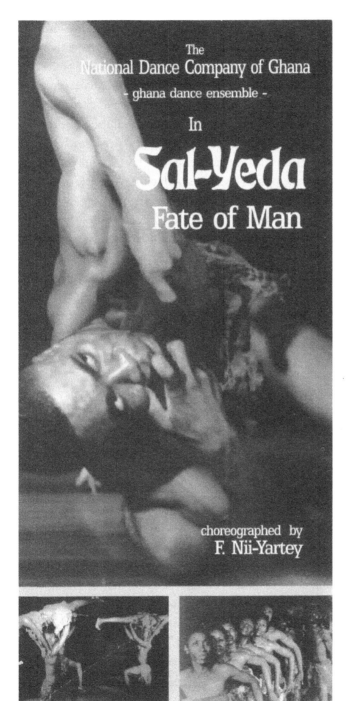

The
National Dance Company of Ghana
- ghana dance ensemble -

In

Sal-Yeda

Fate of Man

choreographed by
F. Nii-Yartey

5.3. *Sal-Yeda* program.

Distinguishing contemporary African dance from dance-dramas and other forms of Ghanaian dance is ultimately an inter/subjective process of negotiation that relies on a participant's recognition of certain performance elements. The absence of recognizable Ghanaian cultural forms of expression typically moves a particular piece of choreography toward the genre of contemporary African dance. Additionally, the degree to which contemporary dance techniques and styles, primarily borrowed from the West, inform a particular choreographic work influences the ways in which participants classify the companies' repertoire. While contemporary pieces use a broad vocabulary of dance movements drawn from both foreign and indigenous inspiration, they often modify local elements to such a degree that renders them unfamiliar to most Ghanaians. Similarly, musical accompaniment for contemporary choreographies is often a form of cosmopolitan hybrid such as Afropop or "World/Afrobeat" and is prerecorded. "Traditional" dance repertoire, on the other hand, is often accompanied by cultural expectations for performance practices, limiting the musical and movement vocabulary available to choreographers in this genre to that which is typical of provincial practices. Within contemporary dances, artists often use improvisation to create new dance forms that are often based on their everyday movements. In particular, artists consider improvisation a "technique" that is a hallmark of contemporary African dance. As a senior dancer explained, "It [contemporary African dance] is like dance technique. People just created their own movements and then put them together, that's all" (Agbedanu 2007). Furthermore, these "techniques" help to create a distinctive identity for NDC members; as one asserted, "We have dance technique here [National Theatre]. They [at Legon] don't have it" (Akowian 2006).

Contemporary African dance, therefore, is not simply Africans performing forms of dance borrowed from the West. The qualifier "African," when placed beside "contemporary dance," does not denote merely who is performing the dance but *how* these dance forms are created and enacted; they are performed in ways that reflect African perspectives and influences. "It is important to say 'African,'" a young dancer asserted, "because we mix some of the traditional dance movements with the foreign ones. It is not modern dance. Modern dance is like the European ones. We do contemporary, African contemporary" (Agyette 2007).

Similarly, many dancers in both companies regarded "modern dance" as foreign, equating it with such styles as ballet, hip-hop, and salsa, and distinguished it from contemporary African dance. Supporting this claim, in a "Statement on Contemporary African Dance" Nii-Yartey has written that these dances are "dance forms which express *our unique* [African] history and socio-economic situation *today*. . . . [These dance forms are] relevant contemporary dance productions, which have their roots in our African traditions, but which also reflect the reality and relevance of the current African situation."[15] Reaffirming this point, in regard to his contemporary choreography, Nii-Yartey explained that "with these dances I put an emphasis on the new things. But I don't do the new things without going back to the traditional dances, because otherwise I am not doing anything African" (2006).

Contemporary *African* dance, thus, while borrowing from foreign sources, is generated locally, taking into account local sensibilities and situations. As a young dancer explained, "African contemporary dance is made from our everyday life. Everything we do, we put into the dance. We change it and make it our own, and it goes into the dance" (Agyette 2007). As Nii-Yartey further clarified,

> Every society, every time has its own contemporary elements. Even a different geographical area has its own contemporary feeling, because of the process of socialization. The needs and other structures that are available at a certain time in a particular area may determine how people perceive this contemporary stuff. The definition will be determined by your own circumstances. New York contemporary is not Kumasi [city in central Ghana] contemporary. So when people say "contemporary," they think New York or London. It is because the way the word is used in those places. But it could also mean that we have it here, but our definition of it is different than the way others define it. So we need to put things in contexts; then we can appreciate it without the semantics around it. (2006)

Contemporary African dance is, consequently, a cosmopolitan phenomenon that is both "discrepant" (Clifford 1992) and "vernacular" (Bhabha 1996), having many centers and being somewhat distinct from contemporary dance in other parts of the globe. That is, contemporary dance is "widely diffused throughout the world" as it is "always localized" (see Robbins 1992) and "shaped by, and somewhat distinct in each locale" (Turino 2000, 7). Perhaps, then, it is better to label *Sal-Yeda* and similar pieces as contemporary *Ghanaian* dance, instead of the broader designation "African," in order to both avoid essentialist implications and more accurately reflect vernacularism.

Understanding definitions of contemporary African dance is not merely a semantic exercise of taxonomy but reveals ways in which participants construct their sense of self. Like popular music in Zimbabwe, contemporary dance styles and techniques borrowed from foreign sources are *deeply internalized* or embodied in Ghana, becoming part of the performers' "repertoire" (see D. Taylor 2003) or bodily ways of being-in-the-world. Furthermore, contemporary African dance often involves the creation of new movements, which emerge from individual quotidian experiences. This embodiment and creation of contemporary dance re/shapes those who engage in such practices and gives certain individuals a way to establish and maintain distinctions between the NDC, the GDE, and their members. Namely, many individuals in the theatre troupe proclaim that they "do contemporary," while Legon dancers do not; or, if they do acknowledge its presence at the university, members of the theatre group maintain that the Legon group is not as proficient. NDC members make such claims despite the fact that the GDE has performed contemporary African dance choreographies (such as *The Map*) and has had a number of young dancers who have performed this genre with expertise. Nevertheless, the performance of contemporary African dance provides the basis for the assertion of many NDC members who claim that they are "moving forward" or "developing." In turn, this discursive strategy significantly contributes to NDC performers' individual constructions of self, particularly their ability to differentiate themselves from those at the university.

Funding, Resources, Travel

As indicated by the earlier comments of Legon ensemble members, once the theatre troupe was established, state resources and attention were directed toward it. This is not surprising, given the ideological shifts in government at the time and the ways in which these aligned with Nii-Yartey's artistic innovations. In the 1980s, the Rawlings government started to reorient its conception of culture, widening it to include "the total way of life of a people"; simultaneously, the regime also promoted the rhetoric of "culture for development," a slogan it adopted from the World Bank (Coe 2005, 94). As Rawlings adopted policies and practices and drew economic support from the IMF and World Bank, he increased emphasis on the marketing of Ghana through tourism. He also adopted these international organizations' neoliberal reforms, and with them came a renewed emphasis and urgency regarding notions of "progress" and "development," inviting a more forward-looking vision for the nation.

Not only did Nii-Yartey's progressive artistry and focus on "development" align with Rawlings's politics, but it also reinforced the ideologies of other key officials in government. While Nii-Yartey told me that "tradition is like a flowing river; it is always moving, so why fight the current? Just jump in and go with the flow" (2012), Ben Abdallah has similarly remarked:

> Culture is dynamic, it moves. So when you look at the rhythms, the movements, the energy of the National Dance Company it must represent . . . the spirit of the nation, what it's going through. And that includes influences from all over the world which are being used in its *movement and development*. . . . If you look at Ghana generally what is in danger of not happening is the development of the courage to move into the future, to take a glimpse into what Ghanaian dance can become, what contribution it can make to the world of dance, what contribution it can make to world culture, so [that] it can go beyond itself. And the only place where you see that really happening is with Nii-Yartey's company. (qtd. in Schramm 2000, 147; emphasis mine)

It is evident that personal and ideological bonds informed Abdallah's decision to transfer the GDE's (Legon) subvention to the National Theatre and to contribute to the government's propensity to support the NDC. While the theatre troupe's artistry reinforced Rawlings's political agenda, subsequently, in the twenty-first century, the NDC has implicitly promoted J. A. Kufuor's "progressive" (neoliberal) vision for the nation through its concentration on contemporary dance. This alignment, in turn, has significantly contributed to the theatre ensemble's financial and political survival. With this government backing, Nii-Yartey has had the resources to realize his artistic vision. The theatre's facilities and space have allowed him to create elaborate sets on which to perform more complex dramatic spectacles that, as he has stated, "championed the development of African contemporary dance, and moved Ghanaian dance forward" (2006).

This government support is also evident in the forms of publicity and travel for the theatre troupe. When I met Grace Djabatey for the first time, I asked her if I could speak with her about the NDC. She advised that I read some of the group's promotional material first and handed me a number of its full-color, glossy pamphlets. The university troupe does not have such promotional materials. As I perused the pamphlets, it became clear that the NDC had more financial resources at its disposal. Additionally, under the rubric of "Cultural Institutions and Agencies" on the NCC website,[16] one finds a detailed description of the NDC. After only a brief mention of the NDC's beginnings at Legon, the website's description then focuses on the development of "Dance Theatre" by Nii-Yartey, which is unsurprising, given that he was primarily responsible for composing this text. The website's narrative also reveals the increased travel opportunities that the theatre troupe has received while under the National Commission on Culture, detailing the various international tours that it has participated in since moving to the theatre.[17] Beyond this list, the NDC embarked on numerous international tours during my research period (2004–12). The Legon ensemble, on the other hand, traveled outside Ghana only once, to Malawi, in this time. This disparity in travel opportunities and promotion reflects the Ghanaian state's alliance with the dance ensemble based at the National Theatre.

The NDC's reputation and ability to perform contemporary African dance has additionally contributed to its endurance by attracting Ghanaian and international audiences as well as young performers. As David Amoo told me, "Since we have started with this contemporary thing, it has shifted a lot of the audience to our side, because these people have seen the traditional dances before and they want to see more of how you can use the traditional dances and create something new" (2006). Or as Grace Djabatey stated, "Ghanaians are fed up with these traditional dances, because every Ghanaian has his or her traditional dance and can do it. So they like to see something new" (2006). Staff of the NDC had mentioned a number of instances where patrons specifically requested their services because these clients wanted to "see something new." Government agencies and private patrons often commission work from the NDC based on its, and Nii-Yartey's, reputation for contemporary African dance.

Similarly, young drummers and dancers are aware of the NDC's and Nii-Yartey's reputation for African contemporary dance and often intentionally audition for this ensemble based on this perception. For instance, when I asked a former NDC member why he joined that particular group rather than the one at Legon, he told me, "I wanted to learn traditional dances, but I also wanted to learn African contemporary dance. Legon, they used to not do contemporary dances. . . . The National Theatre people were the ones who first were experiencing the contemporary dance; they are stronger in it, so I just wanted to go and join them" (Mensah 2007). Despite the GDE's performance of contemporary repertoire, patrons and prospective performers often hold the perception that Legon either does not perform contemporary dance at all or does not do so as proficiently as the theatre ensemble. This perception/reputation significantly contributes to the NDC's ability to exist in the face of direct competition with the GDE. Performers and patrons often make deliberate decisions based on the reputations of the two companies.

By placing emphasis on contemporary African dance, both through performance and rhetoric, members of the NDC collectively proclaim, "We are moving forward," reinforcing their claims to a group identity as those who "develop" national culture more effectively than the GDE. This suggests that the NDC's focus on "development," the perpetuation of this discourse, and its enactment through performances have significantly contributed to the continuing viability of this troupe. Perpetuating this discourse, the theatre ensemble has been able to garner support from the Ghanaian government as well as local and international audiences while attracting young performers who are particularly interested in learning contemporary styles. Last, through the performance of contemporary African dance, individual NDC members have embodied the rhetoric of "moving forward," reshaping and renegotiating their sense of self in relation to their counterparts at Legon.

RHETORICAL AND PERFORMATIVE
STRATEGIES OF SELF/OTHER

One morning in June 2007, I awoke early to a phone call from my research assistant. "The Dance Company [NDC] is here," he said. "Come down and bring your camera." I quickly gathered my equipment and made my way from my campus flat to the dance hall, remembering that the NDC was to be on campus today for the funeral of a former member. I could hear the music as I walked down the road. When the dance hall was in view, I saw that both GDE and NDC members were contributing to the sounds I was hearing. Members from both groups were also dancing and adding to the lively, yet ultimately somber, atmosphere. Drummers and dancers from both groups later marched through campus, performing agbekor in a processional manner. Afterward in the dance hall, GDE and NDC members, young and old, participated in the performance of Opoku's *Lamentation for Freedom Fighters*. Performers circled around the open casket of the deceased, some weeping as they danced, while drummers from both groups provided a heartfelt rendition of Ewe rhythms and textures. Often divided by politics and competition over gigs as well as by the attention of the state and nation, these two ensembles could at least come together to mourn the loss of a beloved friend (PURL 5.1).

While infrequent, such performances illustrate that the divisions between Ghana's two state dance troupes are not insurmountable. Furthermore, since retiring from the NDC in 2007, Nii-Yartey has taken an appointment back at the university; he continues to work tangentially with both companies and encourages collaboration between the two. As this chapter outlines, however, participants in these national ensembles make marked distinctions between the groups. Like nations, the individuals and organizations that comprise them carve out distinct identities to ensure survival and viability as well as to achieve political and pragmatic objectives. This "carving out" is a dynamic and intersubjective "process of identification" (Hall 1996, 344) in which one's sense of self is continually reformed and renegotiated in relation to contemporary circumstances.

For Ghana's state dance ensembles, this process of identification is both discursive and performative, existing at both the individual and group level. Distinctions between the two groups were invented, solidified, and strategically employed to ensure the sustainability of both troupes within a highly competitive environment. On the one hand, the performers at Legon maintain that they are "the originals," invoking this

5.4. Members
of the GDE and
NDC performing
Opoku's
*Lamentation for
Freedom Fighters*
in the dance hall
at Legon around
the casket of a
late member
of the GDE.

statement to imply both that they are the progenitors from which the
NDC is only a "photo/copy" and that their performance of "traditional"
repertoire is superior – more "authentic" – than that of their counterpart.
Members of the theatre ensemble, on the other hand, collectively proclaim that they are "moving forward," citing their performance of contemporary African dance as evidence of their perpetual "development."
In both cases, these rhetorics have been reified through performance
practices. Although both groups perform "traditional" and "contemporary" repertoire, each receives support from various patrons (government, business, tourists, and so on) and new membership based largely
on the particular reputation for, and specialization in, the performance
of particular repertoire. Consequently, the proclamations of "We are
the originals" and "We are moving forward" act as both a discursive
and a performative strategy through which these ensembles, and their
members, renegotiate and differentiate their identities as they engage in
managing nationalism.

Like the ensembles writ large, individual members of Ghana's national dance troupes primarily negotiate their identities through the
rhetoric of "authenticity," "tradition," and "development." Individuals
within the GDE often use the statement "We are the originals" to reaffirm
their own identity as those who maintain the continuity with Ghana's
national heritage by performing the "real traditional" dances. Similarly,

"We are moving forward" provides a way for NDC participants to express their focus on "development" and professed dominance in the idiom of contemporary African dance. In other words, "We are the originals" and "We are moving forward" are narratives in which individuals come to understand their positions; as Stuart Hall writes, "identity is a narrative of the self; it's the story we tell about the self in order to know who we are" (1996, 346). Hall further states that "only when there is an Other can you know who you are" (345). In the case of Ghana's national dance ensembles, the two opposing narratives outlined above reveal key aspects of the ways in which participants *perform* and articulate their individual sense of self in relation to a local Other.

These discourses, furthermore, are embodied and enacted onstage and off to meet the pragmatic and creative needs of artists. By navigating the bifurcation of the dance ensembles, participants have mediated the dancing politics of nationalism, reshaping and instrumentalizing them to suit their contemporary needs. During the run-up to the split, while ensemble staff, state officials, and university faculty used the GDE as a platform to debate their political positions, performers in Ghana's state dance ensembles strategically chose one particular group to serve their individual interests. Subsequently, prospective members have often carefully chosen which ensemble to audition for based on their personal interests and aspirations. Those who seek "traditional" knowledge and "love the continuity of tradition" often are attracted to the GDE, while those who are interested in "developing" their skills in "contemporary" dance often gravitate toward the NDC. This assertion of agency is a type of artistry, a way of managing nationalism as artists harness the machinery of the state to serve their needs for self-preservation, "self-improvement," "growth," and personal enrichment.

Music [and dance]-making in Africa are above all
occasions for the demonstration of character.

SIX

Politics of Personality

*Creativity, Competition, and Self-Expression
within a Unitary Matrix*

MICHAEL HERZFELD KEENLY OBSERVED THAT "NATIONALISM is directly predicated on resemblance, whether biogenic or cultural. The pivotal idea is that all citizens are, in some unarguable sense, all alike" (1997, 27). Given this, he notes that a primary objective underlying nationalism is "uniting all citizens in a single, unitary identity" (1992, 6). Regarding such practices, Anthony Cohen has similarly remarked that "nationalism . . . seems often to have expressed the extreme massification and subordination of the individual whose only significance was a mere cipher of the nation." Although, as he continues, "nations obviously differ in the extent to which . . . they attempt to press individuals into a national matrix" (Cohen 1996, 803), nations and states nevertheless are always seeking to some extent to "press" individuals into this "national matrix."[1] It is not surprising then that state-sponsored dance ensembles often perform a "highly essentialized portrait of their respective nation-states" (Shay 2002, 1), underscoring the state's objective of promoting national unity. In this pursuit, Anthony Shay notes that "state folk dance companies stress and emphasize the group: 'the people's' art" (38) rather than individuals. What place then does the individual have in the "massification" brought about by nationalism? Is there space in this national matrix to express individual creativity?

This national matrix, as this work has shown, is a complex, cosmopolitan latticework of competing interests. Artists adeptly manage a political matrix composed of local and global structures and strictures, including intersecting internal modes of discipline, state and provincial politics, and institutional practices of the university, as well as cultural and familial expectations. While this ethnography has illustrated ways in which individuals pursue self-interests by using their artistry to manage the state apparatus, this chapter particularly focuses on how this is accomplished to express individuality and develop personal creative talents in the face of a national matrix that often seeks to "massify" artists into a unitary identity. Most notably, Nkrumah's interpretation of African Personality has sought to unify Ghanaians within the nation and across the diaspora. While this study has previously explored the subjective embodiment of this ideology, here I ask: Does this call for unity invite uniformity of artistic expression? Has this essentialist ideology informed the degree to which artists are able to cultivate their own creativity or personalities within national institutions such as the dance ensembles? In other words, how does African Personality inform the artistic expression of individual personalities? Or, how might artists give nationalism and its ideologies the "impress of their own personalities" (Sapir 1934, 412)? By exploring such questions, this chapter continues to examine nationalism as a discretely mediated experience and expression, investigating how it simultaneously participates in the construction and staging of culture as well as of the individual self.

"PUT SOME *PEPA* IN IT TO MAKE THE DANCE SWEET": CREATIVITY IN THE "TRADITIONAL" REPERTOIRE

Regarding "traditional" African dance in general, Patience Kwakwa, scholar and former member of the Ghana Dance Ensemble, notes that creativity occurs within a culturally defined limit or movement vocabulary (1994). Amplifying this claim, Nikko S. Thompson's study of *kpanlogo* concludes that "cultural norms . . . dictate socially acceptable movement patterns" (2000, 25). In relation to African music, John Chernoff similarly notes that "truly original style consists in the subtle perfection of strictly respected form" (1979, 112). These forms, norms, and vocabularies are culturally constructed. That is, "traditional" dances are "intertextual" (Bauman 2001a) as a competent community evaluates each performance in relation to previous performances of a particular dance genre (kpanlogo, *agbadza,* and so on); this evaluative process produces a "horizon of expectations" (Todorov [1976] 2000) for the normative enactment of each piece. As part of these strictures, "traditional" music and dance phrases and gestures often have lexical meaning, requiring that dancers and drummers create in particular ways to ensure that the rhythms, tones, and movements are meaningful or communicate to local audiences and are appropriate to specific social occasions (see Chernoff 1979; Locke 1978, 1990; Nketia 1962, 1963).

In this way, "traditional" dances in Ghana generally can be understood as genres, each with their own framework of socially constructed expectations for performance and creativity. Although local dances have often taken on "new dimensions," innovations occur in accordance with cultural norms that ensure that change, or creativity, happens in ways and at a pace that can be grasped by members of a given community. In all, as Oh! Nii Kwei Sowah remarked, "There is a certain amount of individual freedom that is allowed [within traditional African dance], but it is done within the *cultural sanctions* of a particular dance" (2006). Similar to dances performed in local communities, the "traditional" repertoire of the GDE is subject to critique by the community and is informed by cultural expectations, or boundaries, of a given "genre" of dance. Recall that Mawere Opoku often sought the approval of various local communities within the nation for his arrangements of dance forms.

There are, however, additional restrictions on creativity within the context of the GDE due to its particular practices, power dynamics, and national character. Speaking about the Dagbamba *takai* dance, Salifu Merigah explained how the creative processes in the GDE are distinct from those in Ghanaian communities:

> Everybody there [in the village] expresses themselves in their own way. And they will change the rhythms everyday. But in the ensemble we have a pattern we follow. In the village they can change it anytime they want. They keep renewing the dance. They keep renewing the expression. They keep renewing the dancing. They keep renewing the drumming. In the village you can just dance anyhow, for yourself, but *onstage* you can't dance anyhow. We have to arrange ourselves in a *uniform* way. They have individual showmanship, and we have a more collective showmanship; we try to do things together. In the village it's more of an individual expression, individual prerogative. And so you have more freedom in the traditional way. *Things done in a professional way have to have regulations and be disciplined.* (2006; emphasis mine)

The professionalism, stage aesthetics, and discipline practiced in the
GDE have encouraged uniformity, or collective expression, thus informing the ways in which individuals can express themselves within Ghana's
national ensembles.

The quest for authenticity additionally shapes the expression of individual creativity within the national ensembles. When asked about
personal creativity within the state ensembles, the GDE's promotional
manager replied,

> Because we are human beings, someone might teach you a movement, and you
> might add your own to it, and it may not be included. If you want to keep to the
> original you must keep to what you have been taught [at Legon]. If someone
> does their own movement and then teaches someone else and then they also add
> their own movement, at the end of the day we will not get the right movement,
> the *original*, which we have learnt already. That is also part of discipline. We try
> to have them keep to the original movement that we [GDE] have, for them not to
> add any other thing. (Darko 2007)

As discussed earlier, the state ensembles, particularly at Legon, rest their
reputation on members' ability to perform "original" movements, which
are often presumed to preserve the authenticity of local practices. And,
authenticity of the ensembles' "traditional" repertoire is largely based
on the research and reputation of Kwabena Nketia and Mawere Opoku.

The GDE's attempt to "preserve" the "authenticity" of the nation's
heritage in turn informs the degree to which individual performers are
allowed to put their own creative touch on these dance forms. Many in
the state ensembles, when asked about creativity within these groups,
remark with some disdain that the GDE plays "one way," referring to
the practice of performing/preserving a set pattern of choreography
that has been well established. Performers' frustration with the GDE's
"traditional" repertoire originated because these conservative, or preservationist, practices depart significantly from those found in local communities, where artists generally have more freedom to create music and
dance according to the needs of a given context and their own artistic
will. Several drummers and dancers told me that when they came to the
dance ensemble, they "forgot" the versions of dances they previously
knew, suppressed their creative impulses, and performed "the dance
ensemble way." Most of the "ways" of performing the GDE's repertoire

are based on Opoku's arrangements from the 1960s and, as previously explained, have largely persisted due to notions of copyright and art, lack of funding for new research, and the dances' proven reputation as accepted and effective forms of national culture/spectacle. Many performers criticize the GDE for such practices, arguing that the national ensembles do not accurately reflect new performative dimensions found in local communities. Nevertheless, the intention and authority of artistic directors to preserve the authenticity of cultural forms, coupled with the conservative practices and pragmatic difficulties found within the national ensembles, create a powerful obstacle that significantly limits the ability of individual drummers and dancers to imbue the GDE's "traditional" repertoire with their own creative sensibilities.

As such, "traditional" dances within Ghana's state ensembles have been primarily arranged through the decisive authority of Mawere Opoku and other artistic directors, subordinating the creative role of drummers and dancers within these groups. In general, during the troupe's seminal years, as C. K. Ladzekpo (one of the founding members of the GDE) recalled, he and other artists had "limited involvement in the choreographic process" (qtd. in Hirt-Manheimer 2004, 7). Supporting this claim, when I asked Nketia about the role of drummers and dancers in the creative processes of the GDE, he replied, "To create new dances is a difficult thing. We don't expect the dancers to be doing this. It is the [job of the] people in charge [artistic directors]" (2005). This limited role of drummers and dancers in the choreographic process of the GDE's "traditional" repertoire receives significant attention in the work of Isaac Hirt-Manheimer (2004). Overall, he argues that performers were marginalized in the process by which "traditional" dances were staged. The author attributes this lack of involvement to two primary factors, the first of which was a communication gap. Von Salifu, a northern chief, recalled that "they [the GDE] mostly hired illiterates, people who couldn't read or write, who could just sort of communicate with them [Opoku and the GDE staff] sometimes through signs. And they [the performers] taught them [the GDE] how to dance" (qtd. in ibid., 54). Zachariah Zablong Abdellah's comments and criticism of the early choreographic process corroborate Salifu's remarks. Speaking about his uncle Idrissu Alhassan, who was hired as the GDE's first Dagbamba drummer, Abdellah stated,

"My uncle was an illiterate. That was one big problem. When he played something that the artistic director liked, he [Opoku] said, 'OK let's use this.' Then you play another thing, and he says, 'OK let's see how we will arrange it and join them together'" (qtd. in ibid., 55). While their skills were vital to the formation of the GDE's "traditional" repertoire, performers were involved in the creative/choreographic process only as much as they provided a demonstration of music and movement. The creative work was primarily accomplished by Opoku.

This practice was brought about by the second limiting factor: social conventions of authority within Ghana that transferred into the ensemble. Cultural practices of deference to authority (such as chiefs and/or elders) carried over into the GDE, which created a "hierarchical relationship that existed between the artistic director and the performers" (ibid., 55). For example, recall that when Mustapha Tettey Addy, founding member of the GDE, attempted to compose his own musical fusions in the 1960s, these creative efforts were abruptly stopped by Opoku. More recently, this hierarchy was evident as interviewees stated that any changes to the "traditional" repertoire had to come from the artistic director. This hierarchical relationship is compounded by Western "credentials" and notions of art and copyright, which together serve to limit the creative efforts of drummers and dancers in the GDE. That is, the global and the local have coalesced to create cosmopolitan, yet idiomatic, modes of power within Ghana's state dance ensembles, which have significantly informed the creative choreographic processes of the GDE.

In sum, performers in the national ensembles appear to have had little involvement in the processes by which the "traditional" repertoire was created. Along with the hierarchical cosmopolitan modes of power and the "communication gap," performers' creativity within the GDE's "traditional" dances is additionally constrained by the cultural expectations, or "sanctions," of particular dance genres that inform "traditional" dance more broadly in Ghana. Further limiting individual creativity within the ensembles is the national groups' quest for authenticity (such as to preserve the GDE's "original" choreography), adherence to stage aesthetics, and "professional" discipline. When taken together, these practices appear to leave little room for creativity or personal expression by individual performers within the "traditional" repertoire of Ghana's national ensembles.

Yet, "there is something about the African," Patience Kwakwa remarked. "We can't all do it the same way. There is this individual personality that is imparted to dance that nobody can take away from you. Therefore it doesn't make all the movements the same. Therefore they might look a little different on each person" (2006).Individual personality was allowed to surface in the GDE, but such expressions were calibrated: "Not that we could create something new, but *we could do little things to make the dance sweet.* For example, in *agbekor* some people go with the bell, and some people go only once for every two beats. And that's something we saw, and so even though you have not been asked to do it, you could do it.... He [Opoku] never complained about things like that, because he too liked to see something more exciting than the ordinary." Similarly, senior dancer Mercy Ayettey explained, "Sometimes I make my face a certain way, so that people will understand what I am doing. You have to put your own style inside so that the thing is good. When I am dancing *adowa,* I can put my own style inside" (2007).

In general, Nii-Yartey described, "it is impossible to do it [dance] the same way, because the people who come to dance all dance in a different way. Those who come, come with their own touch" (2006). For example, the lead drummer at Legon explained, "I put my own something small in it ["traditional" music], but it is not a change. I just put some *pepa* [pepper] in it to make the dance sweet" (Ametefe 2005). While the master drummer noted that he could bring his own style to the dances, he said, "I won't change it, because if I change it then the next person who comes changes it; then it will be lost. In the GDE, from 1962 up to today, it's the same." His statements illustrate his awareness of the preservationist practices of the GDE and the ways in which his style or creativity is informed by such practices. Broadly, although restricted in a number of ways, drummers and dancers manage to do "little" or "small" things to put their own style inside the GDE's "traditional" repertoire, thus rendering these dances, and nationalism, expressive of their own personalities.

Although Ghana's state dance ensembles inhibit creativity in a plethora of ways, the GDE's role as the *national* troupe provides particular opportunities for creative expression within "traditional" dance

idioms. A memo from 1967 simply titled "Ghana Dance Ensemble" lists
the objectives of the group at the time: "As a repertory company the
Ghana dance ensemble will perform not only African dances in the old
traditional style but also artistic presentations of these dances as well as
original compositions based on African dance forms" (emphasis mine).[2]
Such a statement is directly in line with Nketia's inaugural remarks that
the GDE stands at once for "creativity and tradition" ([1967] 1993, 14).
This creativity, however, has occurred in particular ways and primarily by certain individuals in relation to "traditional" dances. Namely,
artistic directors such as Opoku, Nii-Yartey, and others were chiefly
responsible for developing these "original compositions" called "dance-
dramas" – creative works that enact a narrative based on "traditional"
forms. Some examples (previously mentioned) are Opoku's *Lamentation for Freedom Fighters* (based on Ewe *yeve* cult music and dance),
Nii-Yartey's *Lost Warrior* (based on Ewe traditions), and Ben Ayettey's
Peace and Unity, which combines Ewe and Asante traditions found in
local communities. Based on numerous conversations, it appears that,
similar to the development of the "traditional" repertoire, performers
had little, if any, creative input in the choreographing of these dance-
dramas. Again, this illustrates Nketia's remarks that "it is the people in
charge" who are expected to create new dances. Although drummers
and dancers often have little creative voice regarding the construction
of these forms, these dance-dramas are an example of the unique ways
in which the national ensembles have provided creative opportunities at
least for the artistic directors. In other words, the *national* context of the
ensembles provided a special platform for these choreographic creations
to come into existence.

First, nationalism, and its ideologies and practices, provided the thematic inspiration for these particular works and several others that have
been performed by the national dance ensembles (for example, national/
African independence inspired *Lamentation for Freedom Fighters;* na-
tional/African unity informed *Peace and Unity*). Moreover, the explicit
call to "develop" Ghana's culture for nationalistic purposes gave directors the artistic license to creatively transform indigenous practices in
ways that likely would have been difficult in local communities. Within
these dance-dramas, artistic directors have combined several distinct

dance forms (such as *damba*/takai, fast and slow agbekor), which, as we have seen, is a practice that often encounters resistance in local areas. This is not to claim that musical practices are not adopted by neighboring groups throughout Ghana, for one could find numerous examples (for instance, Ewe *brekete* adopted from the northern part of Ghana, *dondon* drums from the north adopted by the Akan, the Akan *atumpan* adopted by the Ewe, and so on). Choreographers (artistic directors) of the GDE, however, put this array of dance and musical idioms in direct contact with one another in various ways, according to their *own* artistic vision – personality. Recall Ben Abdallah's comments that "traditionally a dance was created by a community," and it did not have an individual's name attached to it. Whereas in provincial contexts creativity is often achieved through community interaction (see Dor 2004), wherein individuals may bring their own "style" (see Thompson 2000; Chernoff 1979) to a preestablished genre of performance, the GDE provided a context in which the entirety of a dance could be considered an expression of an individual.

Thus, "those in charge" have found the genre known as dance-drama to be a productive site in which to express their own creativity and personality. While maintaining a close relationship with dances in local communities, dance-dramas are not expected to strictly adhere to "original" local practices, because their new titles suggest a categorical break from such dance forms. Within these dance-dramas, Opoku, Nii-Yartey, and other artistic directors have created space for their own voices and personalities to emerge as they harness the ensembles to develop the art of dance and attain individual recognition. While not their primary motivation, both Opoku and Nii-Yartey have received numerous national and international awards and honors for their innovative choreographic work, including their development of these dance-dramas.[3] Thus, creative expression within dance-dramas becomes a way in which these directors use their artistry to manage nationalism, turning state directives into platforms for individual achievement.

Despite the ability of artistic directors to develop personal expressions of nationalism within the GDE, the creative prospects for other members appears limited. As the following section will illustrate, however, within the category of contemporary African dance the social dynamics of creativity shift. Artists, while adhering to similar internal power structures of the ensemble, are not subject to the same degree of cultural expectations/sanctions attached to the ensembles' "traditional" repertoire. New dance forms invite different artistic relationships that allow performers, no matter how low in the hierarchical structure, to more fully participate in creating national culture. Contemporary African dance provides an imaginative space in which performers are able to imbue nationalism with their own personalities and sensibilities.

"CHARTING NEW GROUND": STRUGGLES IN THE INITIAL DEVELOPMENT AND RECEPTION OF CONTEMPORARY AFRICAN DANCE IN GHANA

As the South African choreographer Gregory Maqoma states, "African contemporary dance marks a new wave of choreographers who are breaking barriers" (qtd. in Loots and Young-Jahangeer 2004, 29). As part of this class of choreographers, Nii-Yartey has pushed and broken the boundaries of possibility in regard to African dance. His creative works have challenged audiences to reimagine Ghanaian and African dance, to interpret them in new ways, and, in so doing, to reevaluate their place in their contemporary nation and world. This simultaneous reassessment of self, state, and nation has produced a struggle against the tide of tradition. The creation of a "new thing" – contemporary African dance – brought controversy as audiences debated its relevance and merits. While this ethnography has previously explored definitions of contemporary African dance and its role in the differentiation of identity, the following discussion will illustrate this genre's initial creative development and reception, providing an exploration of the dancing politics that accompanied Nii-Yartey's assertion of his own personality and creativity within a national matrix.

Since the 1980s, Nii-Yartey had been "developing" Ghanaian dance forms in creative new ways through his innovative choreographic dance-theatre productions such as *Musu, The King's Dilemma,* and *Solma.* These works, as I have shown, were not considered contemporary African dance, however, because they were primarily based on recognizable local traditions. As such, they were largely well received with little need to justify their importance or relevance. Nii-Yartey's subsequent "contemporary" choreography, developed in the 1990s, however, invited questions and controversy because it was largely an unfamiliar form of expression to Ghanaians. When asked about the initial reception of Nii-Yartey's forays into the contemporary genre, Grace Djabatey recalled, "Oh! There were a whole lot of comments . . . [because] it was a new thing to some of us [Ghanaians]" (2006). Nketia elaborated:

> By going into [contemporary] dance and making the thing abstract, [Nii-Yartey] is bringing in new forms but creating a lot of problems for us. Because even if he has a story we are not always sure how the story is being translated into the dance forms; the references are not so obvious. Why are they falling down all the time? Fall and recovery is nice in Western dance, but to find fall and recovery in every dance puzzles people. Why are we throwing the women and doing it that way? They do it in Western theatre. Is it necessary? (2005)

Many Ghanaians, like Nketia, were "puzzled" by some of Nii-Yartey's work and questioned its relevance. Particularly, Nii-Yartey's frequent use of a Western dance concept known as "fall and recovery" (popularized by noted American dancer/choreographer Doris Humphrey) was foreign to most Ghanaian observers. Although Nii-Yartey's choreography also incorporated local and other African elements that were familiar to many Ghanaians, for some, his use of foreign and "abstract" elements overshadowed these contributions, inviting confusion and contestation.

As Nii-Yartey recalled, this debate significantly affected his personal relationships and created difficulties for him:

> When I started the [contemporary] dance theatre here, some of my colleagues, not within the dance field but here [in Ghana], were attacking me. They were saying the same things that were said to Opoku. They would try to discourage me and try to instigate the dancers to go against me and not to do this. I went through a lot of things. *The gap between me and Opoku was too big.* When I took over, I was trying to do things in a way that people were not expecting. They were saying I should just do what Opoku was doing. But *I was my own person,* and I wanted to add to what Opoku did. *I was charting new ground.* I was touching on people's sensibilities, so I had to be careful. I had to enter into that world. It affected my family. My extended family was nonexistent. I lost a lot of friends. Up till now I don't have any real friends outside my own area. Anybody, if you are committed to doing something, you are bound to sacrifice something.
>
> In the end I was able to champion the development of dance theatre in this country and move into the contemporary African dance. Now dance was lifted from that level of traditional dances to a more spectacular thing that people

come to actually sit down and watch and have something to talk about beyond
what existed. So I paid a price for it, though, because I had a lot of difficulties
with the university, and I had a lot of difficulties with my friends. And I nearly
didn't come back into the system because there were people that hated me so
bad. They took things personal. (2006)

By "charting new ground," Nii-Yartey was attempting to develop his
own artistic ideas and personality to distinguish himself from Opoku,
but he paid a price for this, primarily because the "gap" between him
and his predecessor was "too big." While Opoku's works were generally
recognizable by Ghanaians, Nii-Yartey remarked that critics "did not
understand [his contemporary works], because they did not have a *reference point*" (2006). In order for "new" forms of culture to circulate, they
"must be recognizable to those in whom it is designated to kindle interest" (Urban 2001, 16). Thus, Nii-Yartey's contemporary choreography
needed to "make reference to a range of prior . . . [familiar] cultural elements. Without those temporal referents, the new entity would have little
prospect of further motions or future circulation. It would simply be
incomprehensible" (5). Although these cultural referents are subjective,
many Ghanaians were not familiar with contemporary African dance,
including its modern, postmodern, "abstract," and foreign elements.
Thus, a large portion of Nii-Yartey's primary audience (in Ghana) often
dismissed and condemned his innovative accomplishments. Similarly,
African choreographers in Burkina Faso and other African nations have
encountered resistance and miscomprehension by local audiences in relation to their contemporary works (Gukhière 2007; Mayen 2006; Speer
2008). Like other contemporary African choreographers, Nii-Yartey has
recognized that in order for his progressive artistic vision to be accepted,
he needed to educate his audience. Writing in the program notes for his
first "contemporary" work, *Sal-Yeda* (1997), Nii-Yartey remarked that
"[an] African audience is therefore being cultivated at a very fast pace
. . . thus ensuring a receptive and sympathetic audience for the future."

Although his artistic work "charted new ground," the criticisms and
controversy surrounding Nii-Yartey's contemporary choreographies
were not entirely unprecedented. As Nii-Yartey stated, "Opoku at first
had the same problem; when he started putting the dances onstage, people blasted him! [Critics] said, 'You are bastardizing some of the dances'"

(2006). Whereas Opoku had modified "traditional" dance forms, Nii-Yartey had pushed the boundaries of acceptability in Ghana even further in regard to the nation's culture. His innovations did not come without sacrifice, as he lost friends and endured attacks on his family by numerous critics, all in the pursuit of his artistic vision. Eventually, however, the tide turned in his favor. As Nii-Yartey remembered,

> I explained the situation, and later I managed to get them [critics] into the system. They became my supporters. One of them actually became a resource person for me. Some of these people who were saying, "Don't go to the National Theatre and do contemporary dance," then came and saw what I was doing. Then they would wait for an hour after the show just to talk to me and say, "Oh, I didn't know I was wrong, and I only have a few weeks left; can you help me? I want to do something with the group." So I helped them. (2006)

After a long and hard-fought battle, Nii-Yartey, like Opoku, was able to achieve a degree of respect and acceptance for a new form of cultural performance in Ghana.

However, contemporary African dance has continued to face challenges with its acceptability abroad. While France and other nations often host contemporary African dance workshops, competitions, and festivals, several GDE artistic directors have noted that when the ensemble travels outside Africa, it performs mostly "traditional" African dance because, as Ben Ayettey stated, "this is what foreigners like to see. They never seem to respond well to the new things. They like to see the old traditional ways" (2007a). As Kathryn Speer has noted, "African artists who wish to evolve their traditional forms face opposition not only from their own countries where the assumption is that traditions should not change, but also from outsiders who pigeon-hole African art as primitive and traditional"; particularly, she continues, "Marie de Heaulme, manager of *Salia nï Seydou,* finds that French audiences hold in their minds a cliché or representation of African dance as primitive, full of high energy, and sexually charged. When they see a performance of *Salia nï Seydou,* she confided that many leave feeling either surprised or disappointed" (2008, 15). Contemporary African art/dance is often caught between a rock and a hard place. On the one hand, it is frequently confined by Western expectations for stereotyped images; on the other, because the notion of contemporary art has often been considered a

Western invention despite the tremendous influence of Africa on its initial development, contemporary artistic/dance innovations in Africa are often seen as Western adulterations.

In developing African contemporary dance in Ghana, Nii-Yartey's primary objective was an artistic one and only secondarily nationalistic:

> I felt a calling not for Ghana, but for dance, and by extension for Ghana. The art form was first in my mind, and that's why I chose not to be outside the country but from within the country.... I chose to operate from home, against all odds. I've gone through hell here ... [but] if I hadn't have stayed here I wouldn't have been able to influence people in the way that I have. I've been able to influence a whole generation of dancers.... Just like Opoku, if you [went] to any town in this country when he was here, every dance group was copying his work. Now everybody is doing mine. We are influencing a generation of people, keeping the torch burning; it is very important. In that sense I'm being nationalistic for being here. (2006)

Despite Nii-Yartey's leadership role in an explicitly nationalistic institution, nationalism was only a by-product of his primary aims of developing the art of dance, his own creativity, and his own reputation as an artist. In this way, his use of the state dance ensembles was, for him, primarily instrumental to the development of the self and only secondarily concerned with that of the nation. Institutions of nationalism may not necessarily always be intentionally, or primarily, directed toward achieving the ideological aims of nationalism. As I have argued throughout this work, while building a collective national identity is ostensibly one of the primary goals of the GDE, artists frequently subvert this objective by utilizing this organization for individualistic interests. Mediating a national matrix with its intense scrutiny and visibility, Nii-Yartey managed a variety of dancing social politics to create a "new thing," which balanced the needs of the nation with his own artistic objectives.

Nii-Yartey's artistic innovations have prevailed, influencing the next generation of Ghanaian dancers and choreographers, including their contemporary expressions of the nation's culture. As my research assistant confirmed, "The amateur groups – the culture groups – started creating their own things like that. Now if you go around you will see other people doing the contemporary dances" (Amenumey 2006). This was evident as I witnessed several amateur groups from around Accra performing Nii-Yartey-esque contemporary dance pieces throughout my research tenure. Nii-Yartey's influence was also evident as I watched various "contemporary" choreographies of the GDE at Legon. Nii-Yartey's struggle for self-expression against the demands of the public and the state produced, and introduced, new forms of dance that have proliferated throughout Ghana. As the following section will illustrate, his resolve consequently also popularized new *methods* of dance creativity in Ghana, which fostered their own brand of dancing politics as artists harnessed these tools in an attempt to express their individual personalities within a national matrix.

"IT'S NOT ONLY THE CHOREOGRAPHER WHO
CREATES": COLLABORATIVE CREATIVITY AND
CREDIT IN CONTEMPORARY AFRICAN DANCE

Speaking at a conference on African contemporary dance at the University of KwaZulu-Natal in 2004, Ntombi Gasa noted that "in this contemporary African dance . . . the process of making dance is what makes it so exciting" (in Loots and Young-Jahangeer 2004, 47). Recognizing this, Adrienne Sichel, South African theatre and dance critic, later added, "We urgently need to interrogate, research, and document the creative processes, the conditions, the intellectual and philosophical underpinnings of this [African contemporary] choreographic repertory, which is being produced on the continent [Africa], and we need to do this not from a distance, but here in Africa" (ibid., 24). While Sichel's comments mark an invigoration of an urgently needed academic conversation on this topic, the conference proceedings do not mention the contributions of Ghanaian artists to this genre of dance. This is unsurprising, given that much of the research and discourse on contemporary African dance has been focused on francophone nations (see Loots and Young-Jahangeer 2004; Kringelbach 2013; Speer 2008). In response to Sichel's call, the subsequent discussions investigate the creative processes involved in producing contemporary African dance in Ghana, paving the way for future research in this area.

This section, in particular, examines the choreographic process of artistic directors such as Nii-Yartey and Ben Ayettey along with members of Ghana's national dance ensembles to understand the creative processes by which contemporary expressions of the nation and the self are co-constructed and contested. Initially, I suggest that Nii-Yartey introduced innovative creative processes, or methods, into the dance ensembles and the nation. Subsequently I ask, who creates these choreographies? And who has received the credit for their creation? Exploration of such inquiries reveals the particular artistry and politics within Ghana's state dance ensembles as individual performers (not just artistic directors) attempt to contribute to the creation of national culture, imbuing nationalism with their own sensibilities and personalities as they manage contemporary forms of expression to suit their artistic and pragmatic needs.

Arranger or Choreographer?

In regard to creativity, Nii-Yartey marked a significant departure from his predecessor, Opoku. The local debate over the titles of "arranger" as compared with "choreographer" illuminates the distinctions between these two individuals and highlights Nii-Yartey's creative innovations within Ghana's national dance ensembles. As E. A. Duodu recalled,

> Opoku told me that when he went to the U.S. he had never heard of the word "choreography." He saw his name in the papers and it said "African choreographer." So he had to grab a dictionary. He didn't know he was choreographing. He knew he was arranging.... Opoku, I don't call him a choreographer. I call him an arranger. He himself didn't call himself a choreographer. But if you create a storyline, you create the movements, you create the music, the props, the costumes, then you are a choreographer. If you take adowa, it is not yours; it is theirs [the local people's].... Say [you are] going to choreograph adowa. To me, you are going to arrange, organize, twist, expand, limit. Opoku, I don't know any dance that he created. When you are talking about choreography, then you are talking about original. I don't see Opoku as a choreographer; I see him as an arranger. (2007)

This distinction was replicated by many that I spoke with, including Kwesi Brown, a former member of Abibigromma, the resident theatre group at the School of Performing Arts at Legon:[4] "Opoku was not a choreographer; to be a choreographer you have to create something new. Opoku just took the things from the village and rearranged them for the stage. So he was an arranger, not a choreographer. All his dances were based on traditional movements" (2009). Because Opoku had primarily worked with preexisting material, many I have worked with and talked to did not consider him a choreographer.

This local definition aligns closely with other established conceptions of choreography. Doris Humphrey articulates this notion in her seminal text on the subject, *The Art of Making Dances,* wherein she writes, "One of the famous definitions of choreography is 'the arranging of steps in all directions.' But we are going to set about the problem in a different way and from a different direction, which will lead to *composing,* not arranging" (1959, 46; emphasis mine). This perception of choreography remains pervasive among Ghanaians and other dance scholars who see composition, or the creation of new material, as the hallmark of being a choreographer. Although Opoku occasionally created new movements (most notably, for instance, within his "arrangement" of *sikyi*), he primarily used preexisting local forms of cultural expression and thus often received the title of "arranger." Nii-Yartey, on the other hand, is most often referred to (verbally and in print) as a choreographer. This is not to diminish the importance of Opoku or the impact he had in Ghana and abroad, but this signifier illustrates individuals' recognition of Nii-Yartey's distinct creative innovations within the national dance ensembles. Most notably for the present discussion, as Nii-Yartey pioneered contemporary African dance in Ghana, he introduced the country to an array of innovative *processes* by which to create and stage music and dance within a national context.

Collaborative Creativity, Cosmopolitanism, and Credit

In regard to the "traditional" repertoire, individual drummers and dancers were often marginalized in the creative processes by which these particular dances were rearranged for the stage. These performers were constrained by hierarchical power structures of the ensembles as well as by socially constructed expectations for performance circumscribed by categorical or generic boundaries. Within contemporary African dance, however, Nii-Yartey had introduced methods of choreography that rely heavily on the creative talents of dancers, drummers (to a lesser extent), staff, and others, resulting in a type of collaborative creative process. Nii-Yartey adopted these methods of creativity from his training in Western dance. In the United States and Europe, he was exposed to concepts propagated by Doris Humphrey, a pioneering figure in American contemporary choreography, as well as by several other similar artists who used thematic improvisation to create their choreography. Humphrey writes about having dancers improvise in one-bar segments of $\frac{4}{4}$ time signatures. She instructs readers (and students) to do about nine of these movement phrases and then "string" them together (1959, 47). She later states, "Students are given themes to work with, single ideas, which are neutral; capable of various interpretations" (60). This method of creating dances has become commonplace in the Western dance community and many parts of the world, including Africa (see Kringelbach 2007, 2013), particularly when composing so-called contemporary choreography. By adopting and adapting such choreographic methodology from foreign sources, Nii-Yartey fostered a type of cosmopolitan creative practice within the GDE as Western modes were not merely imitated but deeply embodied, becoming part of the self.

While collaborative, or "communal," creativity has existed in Ghana for generations (see Dor 2004), the methods by which this creativity occurred in the GDE marked distinct cosmopolitan innovations. The introduction of such practices into Ghana's state dance troupes resulted in an increased creative role for performers. Nii-Yartey's use of thematic improvisation provided a framework in which drummers and dancers could significantly impress their personality onto the nation's culture. Given this process, it is not surprising that members of the ensembles often refer to these "contemporary" choreographies as "creative dances." As David Amoo, artistic director of the National Dance Company, told me, "Each and every one has an area, so we all come together to choreograph the contemporary dances" (2006). When discussing the creation of a short contemporary piece called *Solokor,* senior dancer/drummer of the NDC Afadina Atsikpa told me that "Nii asked everyone to contribute to the dance. Nii said that we should each go home and think of something and bring it back to the dance. He didn't want traditional things. He wanted something different – new" (2007). Katharina Schramm also encountered this practice in her study of Ghana's dance ensembles. As one of her consultants told her, "Nii asked us to create something for ourselves and then he would watch it and pick this movement, that movement. So it is not only himself who is doing it [creating the work]" (Kwaku qtd. in Schramm 2000). Or, as Apetsi Amenumey put it, "It's not only the choreographer who creates" (2007). In other words, Nii-Yartey wanted performers to improvise in order to generate music and movements that would not be recognizable as "traditional." This improvisation also took place at rehearsals. As Kwesi Brown recalled, "Nii-Yartey will tell you to improvise during warm-up and then pick movements from that. Opoku didn't work like this, because all his movements were from traditional styles" (2009). Departing from his predecessor, Nii-Yartey used directed improvisation as a primary method to engage the ensemble in a collective creative process with the intention of developing new dance forms.

Taking cues from Humphrey and other contemporary choreographers, the improvisation that Nii-Yartey encouraged was based on themes. As NDC dancer Evelyn Akowian remarked,

> Nii, sometimes he says, "Do 'fucking.' Tell somebody 'fucking' [like an insult]. 'Go you' [go away], but don't use your mouth." And you have to think about it and then come and do it. Maybe you use your hand or body, and then he will say yes, or maybe he won't like it. At first it was difficult, but now if you tell me something like that, I can do it [snaps her fingers]. At times he will say something like, "Do *akwaaba* [welcome]." And then you and your partner would do something. And in thirty minutes he will come and see it. And then he would come, and everyone would dance akwaaba one by one, and if yours is good he will say yes, or maybe he will tell some people to work on theirs and then he will come back and see it again. . . . So *we had freedom to come out with our own thing.* (2006)

As Apetsi Amenumey's remarks indicate, themes were not always based on emotions or concepts: "He [Nii-Yartey] will give you an assignment. Do something. Bring out some movement. He will be telling you things like, 'Make like snake,' and everyone will be doing it, and he will say this one is fine [points]. And then he will put all the movements together and make like a dance-drama – the contemporary" (2006). Although Ghanaian dancers in local communities may improvise based on thematic concepts, the particular type of *formalized and directed* improvisation outlined above was introduced by Nii-Yartey. Regarding this aspect of Nii-Yartey's creative process, dancers of the GDE have commented that they were not familiar with such practices. Since many performers are well versed in local community dance forms, their remarks indicate that such creative processes and practices were new to Ghanaians in the GDE and in general.

Speaking about the creative role of the dancers in the NDC, Akowian later explained, "See, *we [dancers] make the movements,* and he [Nii-Yartey] came and saw them and would say, 'This one is good; this one is no good,' and then he would come and choreograph it" (2006). During my fieldwork in 2007, I had an opportunity to witness this process in action as the GDE worked to create two contemporary pieces: one called *The Map* (the performance of which is described at the beginning of chapter 1) and the other an unnamed introductory piece (PURL 6.1). Both, as mentioned earlier, were performed for the Ghana Education Reform unveiling ceremony in April 2007. The following excerpts from my field notes in March and April 2007 illustrate the relationship between the artistic director and performers, their roles, and their individual contributions as they engaged in the process of creating a contemporary African dance. Because these events took place at Legon with Ben Ayettey as the artistic director, this example underscores two points: the methods and style of choreography introduced into the national ensembles by Nii-Yartey have indeed influenced the "next generation" of choreographers and dancers, continuing to inform the creative processes by which these contemporary cosmopolitan dances are produced, and the university ensemble in fact performs contemporary African dance.

I went to the dance hall around two. Talked to Mihesu. I asked him about the new piece [The Map] the ensemble was working on for the 11th [of April]. He said that he and Leslie [another dancer] came up with most of the movements, and that Christopher [dancer] brought the music (sounded like Baba Maal; it was definitely Senegalese). He said that Leslie came up with the movements for the female dancers in the first piece who were doing the calabash in a semi-circle. And Mihesu came up with most of the movements that were inside that. (Where does he get his inspiration? They look similar to things Nii-Yartey has done.) The dancers spent most of the day in a dance practice studio, experimenting in small groups, working out their ideas and arrangements. Ben came in later in the day, and they started rehearsal. They worked on a particular sequence where Christopher was supposed to do a forward roll movement, then into a backward spin, with arms moving in and out, finally into a leap, with three male dancers catching and lifting him up. This all happened in the space of about 8 counts. Dance counting. This is certainly Western influenced, "5, 6, 7, 8. And ah 1 and ah 2," etc. The dancers were not even rehearsing with music; it was only with counting. They were timing the movements just according to counting. Mostly the sequences were done in 8-count segments, and then they would sometimes switch to counting repetitions of certain movements. Rarely they counted more than 8. Ben was commenting on the leap, and trying to get Christopher's movement look more fluid, and make sure he could go smoothly from the backwards spin to the leap, and jump on 7 and up on 8. (field notes 3/21/07)

[A few days later at a rehearsal in the dance hall.] Did two run-throughs starting around four o'clock. Ben had to correct some jumping, Rose was not jumping with the calabash at the beginning correctly. Ben had to demonstrate what he wanted. Jennies had to run down to correct Afia, who was not bending her arm in the same way that the other girls were at a particular point in the second part of the suite. Yet, when they ran through it again, and Jennies was not there, Afia still was holding her arm straight (did she just forget, or was it a deliberate attempt to be different?). Ben worked on one sequence for a while, trying to get a transition smoother between movements.

After rehearsal, Ben showed me what he wanted for the music. I spent some time this evening mixing together a Youssou N'Dour and Salif Keita piece so it would have a smooth transition, like a DJ. (field notes 3/26/07)

[The following week at the dance hall.] GDE rehearsing contemporary [introductory] piece, adding a new part at the beginning, working on the choreography that Morgan, Julius, and other dancers designed the other day. Also, Mihesu, Leslie, and Christopher came up with some additional dance movements to add to the other trio's steps. Ben came into the dance hall around 4 PM, as usual, to polish the movements. He tried to get things to move smoother – connect movements – make sure there is a flow, the timing is right, and it looks clean and together. He wanted to make sure

the dancers are coordinated well, so they look in sync. Sometimes he will
straighten someone's arm, or a foot, making sure it is pointed straight for-
ward, for instance, while sitting with legs crossed, like today for instance.
(field notes 3/30/07)

   At National Theatre, day before performance. Rehearsal for tomor-
row's performance for the national education reform of 2007. Dancers spent
time with Ben adjusting the spacing of their choreography to fit the large
stage. Ben would ask the dancers to do a sequence and often the dancers
were too close together. Ben either told them to move, or grabbed them and
moved them into the place he wanted. Dancers also spent time getting used
to the rising platform, i.e., orchestra pit. (field notes 4/10/07)

   [Day after the performance.] Conversation with "Assembly Man"
[GDE senior drummer] about the new contemporary pieces. In this regard,
he was saying that the new choreographed piece, The Map, was a challenge
to the dancers and showcased their creative talents; he was pleased with
the result. It allows them to bring out things that others, and maybe even
themselves, may not have realized they had. Reveals hidden potential;
empowers individuals to be creative and to have confidence in their creative
abilities. He says that "the director would be nothing without the talents
of his performers, but most directors don't really give their dancers enough
credit." In the end, it is the director's name that is attached to the piece, not
the individual dancers that helped create it. At the performance yesterday,
the emcee announced a few times that the two pieces were choreographed by
Ben Ayettey. (field notes 4/12/07)

   But who really created these pieces – the dancers or the artistic director? And who should receive the credit? Based on my consultants' testimonies and my own observations, it is clear that the creation of these
contemporary choreographies was a collaborative effort primarily between the artistic director and the performers (dancers). Additionally,
the use of the map prop was an idea attributed to the event organizers.
Even I played a small role by editing the musical accompaniment for both
pieces. Hence, the overall process was collaborative. The dancers created
a majority of the movements and sequences, whereas the artistic director's role seemed to be one of "polishing" these movements and creating

6.1. Members of the GDE (Legon) performing a contemporary dance at Ghana Education Reform 2007, National Theatre of Ghana.

a "smooth" flow of action, or transitions between sequences. The artistic director also made sure that the final presentation looked "together" and was spaced appropriately for the particular stage. In all, dancers have contributed significantly to a "contemporary" performance of Ghanaian nationalism while developing their skills as individual artists. As GDE drummer Wisdom Zigah noted, this process "gives these young dancers confidence in their artistic abilities and propels them in their careers as professional dancers. The director would be nothing without the talents of his performers" (2007). Participation in these contemporary choreographies enriches ensemble members with skills and self-assurance that are instrumental to developing their sense of self.

Although dancers may have become empowered by these experiences, they were simultaneously disempowered. In the end, as Zigah remarked, "most directors don't really give their dancers enough credit." Although the printed program for the event lists no individual names associated with these pieces, as mentioned above, the emcee announced that Ben Ayettey was the choreographer and the GDE's artistic director. In short, credit for the pieces' creation was bestowed entirely on the choreographer/artistic director. This practice is not limited to the university troupe but is the case in the NDC as well. As Afadina Atsikpa remarked,

> Sometimes I suggest things. I can do that, and he [Nii-Yartey] will listen, and sometimes he will take it. There was a time when I used to choreograph some things. I created some movements. The only thing is they don't put our name there on the program. That thing has spoiled some of us. They only put Nii-Yartey's name there. He choreographed it. That's why some of us get discouraged. If they give us credit, then maybe I would bring new things, but they don't so I just keep quiet. I'm now just waiting for my pension. (2006b)

A number of ensemble performers made similar comments, expressing their dissatisfaction that despite their significant contributions to the creation of contemporary dance choreographies, their names were not included as collaborators or co-choreographers on programs. On many programs, however, dancers (drummers and staff) are listed, which at least gives them some degree of recognition. Yet the names of choreographers/artistic directors appear most prominently on the front page of these materials.

This practice of attributing credit solely to the choreographer or artistic director, despite the contributions of the individual dancers, has been common in many dance companies throughout the world. American choreographers I spoke with routinely dismissed such practices, stating, "That's just the way it is"; Western choreographers appeared more accepting of the practice than my Ghanaian consultants. To account for this disparity, Zachariah Zablong Abdellah pointed out that "traditionally dances were created by a community" (2005) and particular names were not connected to them. In the GDE, however, dances became "copyrighted" works of art, complete with specific names attached to them. This type of singular credit for the creation of dances conflicts with "traditional" Ghanaian practices of communal ownership, thus often producing dissatisfaction among artists in the GDE. Nevertheless, artists may feel compelled to adopt cosmopolitan notions of individual credit and copyright as a response to their implementation by the artistic director. Artists often argue that if such practices of credit are used, they should apply equally to all who create these works of "art." As one dancer remarked, "The names of the dancers and drummers who helped create the pieces should also be on the programs; and they should also mention us when they announce the pieces at performances" (Asari 2007). It is doubtful that choreographers deliberately neglect to credit performers; rather, they are following a widely practiced cosmopolitan choreographic convention. Nevertheless, this practice of attributing credit serves to underscore the power and authority of the artistic director and can even discourage creativity among some drummers and dancers who feel that their contributions to various "contemporary" choreographies are undervalued.

In short, while the process of creating contemporary African dances is collaborative, the credits often do not reflect such a practice. Given their cosmopolitan nature – embodiment of various provincial and global cultures – "contemporary" choreographies invite both cosmopolitan modes of creativity and credit, which result in a contentious politics of individual recognition and self-fashioning. While cosmopolitan creativity stresses the collective, cosmopolitan credit conversely highlights the singular hierarchical authority of only those individuals in relative positions of power.

Constraints on Creative Expression: Competition and Travel

Although contemporary African dance allows GDE performers a greater degree of creative input compared with the "traditional" repertoire, artists remain subject to the hierarchical relationships and other internal dynamics found within the ensembles. Such strictures are informed and compounded by broader social and political dynamics present in Ghana. As a former NDC member explained, "Over there [National Theatre] the leaders and the old members will not permit you to create what you like, because they know that if it comes to traveling they will pick you. So they will make every effort so that you will not be able to express yourself the way you like" (Azadekor 2007). Travel, particularly internationally, is highly prized by performers within the ensembles as it is more broadly in Ghana. Many drummers and dancers view travel as an opportunity to broaden their horizons, make social and business contacts, and gain status with their family and friends back home. Performers who travel also receive a small additional salary and save the per diem (by bringing their own food) in order to make a modest financial gain from these trips. As Mawutor Azadekor added, "The salary [in NDC] is not good. The only hope is to travel outside and make some small money. So you are happy when they select you, and if they don't you become mad" (ibid.).

Often, the artistic director chooses only a few performers to travel abroad. This invites "competition" among the performers as they vie for limited opportunities. Azadekor added, "It was my creativity that made me to travel about four times with the group [NDC]" (ibid.). In general, the "best" performers are chosen for these trips based on their artistic abilities, including an assessment of their creative contributions to the group. Rehearsals and public performances within Ghana then become domains in which to not only display national culture but also showcase personal artistry in the hopes of catching the eye of the ensembles' staff. Thus, performers carefully calibrate their attempts to "stand out" as they are encouraged to "blend in" to the national matrix.

In pursuit of the former, in order to ensure their creative talents outshine those of other ensemble members, performers work hard not only to develop their own skills but also to occasionally impede the creativity of their competitors/colleagues. Many performers noted that fellow members would "not teach them anything" for fear that they would be "outdone" by their pupils and thus be chosen to receive travel opportunities instead of their teachers – the senior members of the group. If individuals display their creative talents, they run the risk of being sabotaged by other members of the group. Several members of both the GDE and the NDC noted that in some instances, their colleagues would become "jealous" and fearful; attempting not to be outperformed, artists occasionally have resorted to supernatural forces, using juju to physically hurt their competitors. In all, creativity can be perceived as a threat among performers within the ensembles as some personalities overshadow others, precluding some from participating in scarce travel opportunities. In short, although fierce competition to travel can motivate creativity, it can equally inhibit the artistic expression of individuals.

While artistic directors often encourage ensemble members to contribute to "contemporary" choreographies by asking them to improvise and experiment to develop movements for these pieces, the artistic director may also stifle creative efforts of the performers. For instance, as I was preparing to leave Ghana in 2007, a small group of GDE (Legon) dancers were choreographing their own "contemporary" piece, not at the request of any state or local patron but rather, as one of the young dancers involved remarked, "to bring up my own idea, to try my brain, and show that I can put something together on my own" (Badu 2007). This creative endeavor did not work out the way he had hoped, however:

It all went dead because the director sometimes doesn't allow us to do something on our own. Even if you do something that you think is good for you, he will always change the thing into something else, and you always look stupid. Because what I cracked my brain to do is stupid to the director. So why should I worry myself to do anything again. But then I tell myself that I am not doing it for him; *I am doing it for myself.* If he says he doesn't want me to do it, I can do it on my own. I can use it to improve my talent that I have. I can improve myself in all things that I am doing without him. . . .

It's very frustrating when you have been in the group for five years without traveling anywhere. You don't even travel to Kumasi. So I have been discussing with my friends, . . . let's have a CD [DVD] so that when somebody comes to your home and asks what you do, you can show them. We've tried several ways, but I feel like we are being sabotaged by our director. So with this piece, I went to him and said, "This is what I want to do. I will present it to you, and if you like it then you can teach the whole company so that it becomes our own." So then I sat down with my colleagues and discussed about sewing costumes, and then we would give them to the company. So I took this proposal to him, and he agreed that I should go ahead and do it. Then it got to a time that he called me and asked me: What am I going to use the piece for? What is my intention of doing that piece? Because if I'm going to do it outside the group, then I should stop. I said, "I am not going to do it to seek for greener pastures or something." . . . And so he agreed. Then he talked to one of my colleagues and said if he sees us performing this thing anywhere else, he will punish us. Does it mean that our director doesn't trust us, he doesn't believe us or something? I just said, "Let's move on." So we continued with the piece.

But one day I came to rehearsal and my friends were sitting there, and I said, "What is wrong?" They said that the director had sacked [one of the young dancers involved] from the piece. So I went to the director and he said, "Yes, I have sacked him because the guy had an outdooring on Sunday and he didn't come to work on Monday." . . . He [the artistic director] has all the authority. . . . He doesn't want us to travel and make something more than him, so he sabotaged the piece. . . . It's not going to work. Yesterday I feel like crying. I almost cried. (ibid.)

Artistic directors have a responsibility to maintain group solidarity, and this is continually threatened by individuals who "seek for greener pastures" abroad. As I have shown, many individual members over the years have deserted, or "run away," to foreign countries in the pursuit of financial gain. In this case, the artistic director presumed that the young dancers' creative project was a strategic attempt at self-promotion in order to gain recognition from international sponsors who would then likely poach them from the ensemble. Although the young dancers assured their director that they would not use this piece to travel, he was not convinced and asserted his authority to stop the project. Individual artistry and agendas were stifled ostensibly to maintain the integrity of the dance ensemble; but this performer implied that the reasons for stopping this endeavor were not necessarily for the benefit of the group or nation but were imposed due to personal jealousy.

Competition runs through the ranks of the dance ensemble as artists attempt to manage the (travel) opportunities at hand to pursue personal aspirations. Performers are competing not only with each other but also with the staff and the artistic director. While such competition may spur creativity in some instances, it often impedes such practices. Personal politics, competition, and particularly jealousy regarding the chance to "make it abroad" significantly limit personal expression. As they are for many in Ghana (and Africa), travel, success, and accumulation are inextricably linked for performers. Success and wealth, while having the potential to benefit the self and the community, have long been considered suspicious; social mechanisms of shaming and sabotage are widely practiced and well known in Ghana and West Africa.[5] These cultural practices attempt to ensure that degrees of wealth stratification remain small, preserving the integrity of a community and social equilibrium. Within the contemporary repertoire of the GDE, these long-standing cultural and social norms regarding individual success serve to limit personal expression within this national matrix. This is not entirely surprising, given that such collectivist norms had informed (Nkrumahist) African socialist nationalism since before independence. This form of nationalism deliberately aligned with, grew out of, and reinforced such cultural norms. Despite Ghana's more recent trends toward neoliberal policies and practices, which invite a glorification of individual accumulation and achievement, these socialist political ideals along with traditional notions of collectivism have persisted, merging to inform the dancing politics of creativity within the national matrix of the GDE.

Cosmopolitan Creativity: An Artistic "Journey" of Appropriation, Translation, and Experimentation

While artistic directors have impeded creative projects in some instances, they also encourage creativity in the ensemble. There are numerous examples of artistic directors calling upon the talents of individual performers to create small-scale pieces for a variety of occasions. This creative encouragement has often occurred while collaborating with guest choreographers from abroad. This is unsurprising given that contemporary African dance often articulates a "transnational politics of belonging that transcends earlier discourses of post-independence African nationalisms of the 1950s and '60s [which were] stifled by a static notion of cultural heritage" (Sörgel 2011, 83–85). In Ghana, the GDE's early years reflect an attempt to solidify national identity by focusing on the "recovery" of indigenous cultural expressions. While relying on Western aesthetic practices and modern reformism, Opoku was careful

to conceal these foreign elements. By the 1990s, with Ghana on more secure national footing, having firmly carved out an identity for itself and
achieving relative stability despite political upheavals, Nii-Yartey was
able to more comfortably articulate a transnational artistic vision.

Contemporary African dance is often explicitly cosmopolitan in
character. While critics condemn foreign influence as corruption, accul-
turation, or Westernization, proponents and practitioners of contemporary African dance often see international collaboration as a productive
source of artistic inspiration. Generally, from Sylvia Glasser's Afrofusion
to Germaine Acogny's extensive work with French and Belgian choreographers to Salia Sanou and Seydou Boro's collaborations with French
choreographer Mathilde Monnier, cosmopolitan collaborations have
produced significant innovations in African contemporary dance. In
Ghana, Nii-Yartey worked with Germaine Acogny to create the contemporary African dance called *Images of Conflict* in 1999 and has continued
to collaborate with a number of dancer/choreographers from around
the world, such as Germaul Yusef Barnes from the United States, Jean
Françoise Duroure of France, and Monty Thompson from the U.S. Virgin Islands. These choreographers, and other such collaborators from
abroad, have encouraged creativity within Ghana's national troupes by
sharing their unique experiences and talents with members of the GDE
and NDC. Cosmopolitanism has been a creative force for the production of contemporary African dance as the global and the local "dance
together" to inform expressions of nationalism and the individual. In
this way, these collaborations also further the GDE's stated objectives:
"to contribute to the work in the area of international relations" (*The
Legend of Okoryoo* program notes) and to "enhance Ghana's cultural
image abroad both within and outside Africa."[6] While these objectives
have been vital components of furthering the nationalistic ideologies
of Pan-Africanism and African Personality since the inception of the
GDE, beginning in the 1990s African contemporary dance began to articulate these objectives in new ways.

Heeding Sichel's call for more scholarly attention to the construction processes of contemporary African dance, the remainder of this
section examines a particular case in which the GDE (Legon) worked
with a guest choreographer from the United States, illustrating how

The French Embassy and Alliance Française, in collaboration with the National Commission on Culture and the National Dance Company of Ghana, present

IMAGES OF CONFLICT
Contemporary African Dance

Choreographed by F. Nii-Yartey and Germaine Acogny

6.2. Program from an African contemporary dance co-choreographed by Francis Nii-Yartey and Germaine Acogny.

this ensemble adopts cultural elements from the international community to produce new artistic expressions of the nation and the self. This appropriation, in turn, facilitates Ghanaian nationalism's concurrent resonance with foreign and local audiences. In short, this creative collaboration increases the cosmopolitan character of the ensemble and the individuals within it. Through this cosmopolitanization, Ghana simultaneously carves out a somewhat unique identity as it reinforces its place as a nation among nations. Individuals, similarly, are caught up in a type of dual mandate for resemblance as they are encouraged to form a "unitary identity" vis-à-vis both their nation *and* the international community. How does the individual find space for personal expression within this homogenizing inter/national matrix? More broadly I ask, how has culture been appropriated, translated, and experimented with in order to produce contemporary expressions of both individuality and nation? As this process unfolds, this case study also reveals some of the aesthetic, compositional, and organizational differences between Western and Ghanaian musical and dance practices. Throughout, cosmopolitanism, or more precisely cosmopolitanization, is posited as a dynamic *embodied practice,* highlighting the ways in which performers strive to adopt new musical and bodily ways of being-in-the-world.

In May 2007, a guest dancer/choreographer from the United States, Brian Jeffery, came to work with the G D E (Legon). A university professor of dance, Jeffery is an accomplished contemporary choreographer noted for his innovative experimental work with XSIGHT! Performance Group, in which he brings together elements of theatre, dance, music, and visual arts. Ben Ayettey was enthusiastic about his arrival and told me that he "had been looking forward to Brian's visit. You see, this is what we need more of here. I want to expose the group to different styles – these modern and contemporary things" (2007a). Only a day after setting foot on the African continent for the first time, Brian began to work with the ensemble, which I observed:

Rehearsal at dance hall with Brian, 9 A M. Brian introduced himself to the group. Overall, the group seemed eager to learn. Brian asked the drummers to play some light music. The cool xylophone melodies and the percussive taps of a log drum provided a musical backdrop for the dancers as they began a warm-up routine. Sitting on the floor in a yoga-style position they began stretching, reaching with elongated fluid movements in various directions. Brian wanted them to feel the "wide positions of the body" and work on their balance – their relationship with gravity by supporting their bodies while slowly and gracefully exploring numerous positions of the body. It was obvious that some of the dancers had never done these types of stretches before.

These stretching exercises moved seamlessly into a collection of movements that later became part of the piece. The first movement involved a shift from a long, high, thin stretch, lifting up on the tips or ball of the foot, to a low, wide lateral stretch while moving sideways. I immediately recognized these movements as those Brian had been working out in his flat last

night as I and a few friends were chatting over dinner. The next movement
was more complicated, so Brian broke it down into small phrases and
performed it very slowly. He also used scat-style nonsense syllables to ac-
company the movements and had dancers recite them as they practiced the
sequence over and over until they were comfortable with it. The particular
phrase sounded like "bah-dah-shee-wha, bah-dah, bop, bop." "Bah, bop"
seemed to correspond to hops; "shee" accompanied slide-type movements.
I had suggested to him earlier that this may be a good idea because often
drummers and dancers learn Ghanaian music through a series of vocables,
or nonsense syllables.[7] The drummers, as I had hoped, picked up immedi-
ately on these vocables, accompanying the movements so one could hear the
dance steps through the drums. (field notes 5/16/07)

If one agrees with Bradford Robison's (2002) and Dick Higgins's
(1985) assessments that jazz scat singing is an African retention, then
Jeffery's use of scat-style singing to communicate with the drummers
and dancers becomes what scholar John Collins calls a "feedback loop"
(1987). Through transatlantic journeys, this African cultural practice has
migrated across the ocean and was reinvented and returned to the continent to be used again in new ways – as a tool to translate Jeffery's ideas
into a language that was mutually intelligible for him and the dancers.
This communication provided a conduit that allowed for the transformation of dance and the individual self.

This same rehearsal session revealed another aspect of translation
and cosmopolitanization as the ensemble worked to adopt/embody
practices from abroad.

It became clear that there was a noticeable difference between Brian's
movements and the GDE dancers' bodies. The dancers were having a bit
of difficulty grafting these new movements onto their bodies – they seemed
a little tight and needed to loosen up the flow of their bodies. There were
a few, however, that could do the movements with a fair degree of fluid-
ity. What I had been discussing with Brian and Jill [Flanders-Crosby,
another American dancer/choreographer/professor visiting Ghana who
was friends with Brian and me] became apparent – most African dance
tends to be closed, rigid, tight, in the torso. Brian was really trying to open

their bodies, or unbound them, from their seemingly constricted styles that they have been used to. As he stated, he was trying to "get them to use their whole bodies, from fingers to toes ... and get them to move in new ways." (field notes 5/16/07)

When I asked Jennies Darko why some of the dancers had difficulty performing Jeffery's movements, she stated, "With [Brian's] Western style they make more use of the hands and the legs, and it's more athletic – jump, extension. With traditional African dance we make use of our body, especially our upper torso. It's either a contraction or releasing, or a gyrating. It's not like these *open* movements [of Western style]. Africans don't do open movements; we do closed movements. Western style does open movements and extensions" (2007). Although a detailed examination comparing Western and African dance practices is beyond the scope of this project, suffice it to state that her comments align with several scholars who note these general differences between Western and African dance (Acogny 1980; Blum 1973; Knowles 2002; Welsh Asante 1996). It is important to note that in illustrating the translation and adoption of foreign cultural elements in African contemporary dance, the dancers' bodies were culturally tuned in particular ways, which corresponded to their training in African dance idioms, but had to be retuned to accommodate Western forms of dance expression. In short, for GDE artists, learning contemporary dance is a way of embodying cosmopolitanism. This process involves a rigorous corporeal retraining as individuals re-form their kinesthetic ontology, acquiring new ways of moving-in-the-world.

This process of translation also involved a restructuring of the auditory ontology for GDE members, Jeffery, and myself. After we had discussed the possibility, the following day Brian reintroduced me to the group as his musical assistant. He asked me to assist the drummers in constructing music that would reflect his dance choreography. For the first time in the three years I had been working with this ensemble, I had an opportunity to work with them in an artistic capacity. This creative collaboration revealed numerous issues regarding musical aesthetics and the translations of musical ideas within the process of cosmopolitanization.

So I had to fulfill a double role as an ethnographer and assistant drum instructor. I wanted to try more legato sounds to reinforce Brian's elongated fluid movements. At a point when I could stop filming, because the dancers were just repeating movements, I started scraping the gankokui [bell]. I told Ema to bring another xylophone. After playing with the bell for a bit, I said to Togbui [another drummer], "Do you ever play it like this?" He said "Ah huh," rather unenthusiastically, and then tried it a bit, but was not too amused. I started working with Ema. I played the kagan drum, and was playing with a stick and a hand, doing lots of rolls with the right stick and doing some tones and mutes with the left. Ema said, "Oh, you are doing some drum set stuff," because the pattern sounded like a kind of funk drum set groove but just with kagan. After that I experimented with a jazz ride pattern on the side of the kidi drum and then played what would be comping patterns with the left, holding the stick like a traditional jazz grip, and putting in some buzz rolls. Ema was eager to learn and started to try to play the buzz roll with one hand using a curved dondon stick. It wasn't working too well, so I told him to switch to a straight stick. Then he kept trying, [and] I was telling him how to use a fluid motion in the hand and arm and how to use the thumb and forefinger as a fulcrum to let the stick move freely, balanced on that fulcrum, so that the stick can bounce. He had difficulty with it, as any beginning drum student would; this made me realize that I could have something to offer the GDE drummers. I was so used to and so focused on learning from them, I never really thought to teach them anything, and they never asked, although Ema has recently asked about learning the drum set. Then Ema started playing two sogo drums with sticks, I was playing a kagan and sogo with sticks, and Assembly Man was playing xylo. We "jammed" for about 15 minutes while the dancers were on break; it sounded interesting. I was trying to get them to play more dynamically.

The drummers are so used to playing at one dynamic level for an entire piece, or even event! They rarely changed dynamics within a piece, certainly not in the ways a Western drummer would, like fast de/crescendos. They also rarely stagger entrances of parts; usually all the drummers play all the time, but Brian wants an arrangement that spans the dynamic range in one piece – loud/quiet, fast/slow, sparse/dense. There needs to be an orchestration of parts here. Brian likes to do rounds with dance movements, i.e., a movement that takes 8 counts, he will have two people do it, but one

will start 4 counts after the other. I thought to do this with the drums as
well; usually the drummers will just find one pattern that works, usually a
kpanlogo-type thing, and then everyone does that, based on the movements
of the first dancer. I want one drummer to follow each dancer, so that there
is also a staggering of entrances, a drum round, that reinforces the danced
round. Also I want to try some dondon rhythms tomorrow, maybe gome,
anything that has a pitch bend–type sound, creating a bounce feeling to re-
inforce the skip-like dance phrases. (field notes 5/17/07)

This initial "jam session" showed that, in order to meet the demands
of Brian's choreography and artistic vision, I needed to orchestrate the
drum parts and introduce the drummers to a few Western musical concepts. First, Brian wanted the music to swell and dip with energy in relation to the activity of the dancers. I immediately equated this with a sonic
de/crescendo but quickly realized that drummers were not familiar with
such practices. Additionally, most Ghanaian music involves instrumentalists playing simultaneously throughout a given piece, but I wanted
drummers to rest and enter at various times throughout the course of the
piece. In short, this excerpt reveals the process of embodying sensual
ontologies as performers attempted to hear the world in new ways.

As I was experimenting and collaborating with the drummers on
the musical accompaniment, a week after beginning this artistic journey
Brian began to rely more heavily on the creative talents of the dancers.
While overall, many of the movements were Brian's creations, he did
occasionally ask the dancers to improvise movements that later became
incorporated into the final choreographic work.

Arrived at the dance hall at 9:30 AM, just after the group's warm-up
routine. They started on a sequence of movements, where the dancers were
divided into five groups. Each group of three dancers was told to create
a movement on their own. They were given about 10 or 15 minutes. Each
group staked out a part of the dance hall and worked with their partners
on developing their ideas. Individuals collaborated with one another.
Slowly, movements and sequences emerged. Some movements seemed
vaguely recognizable as "traditional" movements. I could see a bit of kpan-
logo here, a bit of nagla there, but they were embellished, elongated, and

abstracted. Other groups worked out movement sequences that did not seem to reference traditional movements at all. However, I did notice that some of these movements resembled a creative/contemporary piece that had been performed a few weeks ago, before Brian's arrival. They were relying on a familiar vocabulary even though they were asked to create something new. This seems not all that different from a jazz musician who improvises, essentially putting together practiced techniques, phrases, and forms in relation to the demands of the moment. (field notes 5/28/07)

Inspired by both "traditional" elements and a familiar repertoire of "contemporary" styles they had previously learned, the dancers were making creative contributions to the overall choreography. In the final performance, this section of the choreography began with the dancers all aligned at the back of the stage, then one group (of three individuals) at a time would move forward to feature their movements for a few moments. Their individual personalities were singularly highlighted for a brief time within a collective work (PURL 6.2).

This portion of the piece, which involved five groups of dancers each featured at various times in close succession, inspired a particular musical arrangement, which mirrored this choreographic form.

Rehearsal with Brian. Remembering what Brian said, "the more dancers on stage should be reinforced by more sound," I wanted to layer the drum parts. The ensemble drummers predictably just played all at once, about seven parts. I assigned each drummer to a group of dancers (1 thru 5) and gave them each a number and pointed to the group for which they were associated. First the xylophone started with the first group, then bell, then gome, then another drummer on a kpanlogo drum, and then three other drummers and I on shakers and log drum. Once we were all in, then it was just a matter of changing dynamics to reinforce the actions on stage. Then I told them to watch their group, and when their group was at the front of the stage they should play louder and when they were at the back they should play softer. The dancing groups took turns at the front of the stage in sequence, with a bit of overlap. This seemed to work well, but towards the end of rehearsal the drummers got tired, and forgot to watch the dancers, and just played all one volume. (field notes 5/28/07)

Throughout the development of this piece it was obvious that this type of musical orchestration, which included drummers simultaneously playing at various shifting volume levels, was a foreign concept to these drummers. The concept of crescendo and decrescendo in particular took some effort to adopt, and when drummers were not concentrating enough, they fell back into familiar patterns of a more consistent dynamic across all musicians.

In my field notes I offered an additional explanation for the drummers' difficulty with this section of the choreography:

Particularly in regards to the concept of staggered entrances and dynamics – the last section where each drummer is assigned to a group of dancers . . . – it is the responsibility of each drummer to watch and interact with their assigned group of dancers. Some of the drummers weren't paying attention to the group they were assigned. They were just playing anyhow. This may be due to the practice that typically in Ghana the master drummer is the one who is primarily responsible for interacting with the dancers. Support drummers, on the other hand, are just used to taking their cues from the lead drum. So the support drummers were at first just interacting with the drums, and forgetting to watch the dancers, because they thought that it wasn't their responsibility. They had to learn that in this instance it was everyone's responsibility simultaneously to watch the dancers and interact with a distinct group. Also they had to learn to play dynamically [in the sense of loud and quiet]. It took one drummer at least four or five run-throughs to understand that when his group of dancers was at the front he should play loud, and when they were at the back he should play soft. So there are at least two elements here that needed to be learned by musicians, dynamics and shared responsibility – not just relying on the lead drum for cues. (field notes 5/28/07)

This creative "contemporary" context, in other words, challenged these musicians to perform music in new ways as they adopted unfamiliar practices.

Similar problems and processes emerged as I worked with the musicians on another assignment that Brian had given us the following morning.

Brian wanted us to do some singing. He gave us a basic melody, about five or six notes, roughly about two slow measures of $\frac{4}{4}$. Then he told us to make up something based on that, and we could build it up, and improvise. The drummers and I went into the room behind the dance hall, where the drums are kept. They wanted me to sing the melody for them; I did and then they responded in typical call-and-response fashion, but I knew this was not what Brian wanted. They also were reluctant to improvise. I had to coax them into making up variations. Mutellah (a Dagbamba) found an indigenous Dagbamba song that seemed to work with the melody; so, after some discussion, we decided to use that. Also Christopher made up some nonsense syllables to go with the melody [hey ya, mama, hey . . .], replacing the dagbani. I had to divide them into groups of two, and then give them numbers in order for them to come in, in a staggered entrance style (the same method I used for staggered entrance of the drumming). Once I did that, I was expecting each group to just come in, in succession at each new round of the song. However, each group waited an extra time, so that the lead singer sang solo again before the next number came in, giving a call-and-response-type feel. I assumed that this is not what Brian wanted. (field notes 5/29/07)

I later found out that I was correct in my assumption that Brian did not want a call-and-response style but rather a slow crescendo, or addition of voices, throughout. Further practice was needed for these drummers/singers to perform in this manner. As my field notes explain:

Brian wanted the song to come in with one voice, then build gradually. I told him my method of assigning numbers to individuals, and each time through the short song [hey mama, mama, hey mama, maaa, hey mama, mama, hey mama] the singers would enter in succession producing a crescendo effect. We rehearsed this a few times, and it seemed to work. We rehearsed it fine, and then when it came to the run-through with the dancers, it fell apart. Like yesterday, if I am not there to point at certain people to sing, then people revert back to a call-and-response-type mode, which is what they are used to, and all they really know, as far as singing style. It is going to take them another few run-throughs to get the concept of just building. The idea of de/crescendo is completely foreign to them, I believe.

Then Brian wanted to fade the voices out, not an abrupt ending like what
they naturally did. We had to again assign groups and tell them that when
a particular dancer started his run then the first group [out of three] would
drop out. Then the next time through the song the next group would drop
out until finally the last group dropped out. (field notes 5/31/07)

These passages illustrate the problems of translating musical ideas
across cultures. The foreign concept of round singing was coming into
contact with a call-and-response style that was deeply ingrained for these
drummers. It would take some time and effort for the drummers to learn
to sing in a new way.

This creative process invited questions regarding my role and the
degree to which I was influencing the artistic expression and character
of the piece.

Christopher [master drummer of the GDE] is still the leader. He is
the master drummer, and I don't want to usurp his power and role here. I
feel that it is my role to shape what is going on with the rhythms, but not to
necessarily invent new ones. Basically I am shaping dynamics and creating
some orchestrations, staggered entrances, and helping decide which instru-
ments should play when. For the most part I am letting the GDE members
come up with their own rhythmic patterns, which are brilliant. Interpreting
dance movements into drum patterns is second nature to these drummers
because it is common practice. (field notes 5/31/07)

Overall, by their use of various local instruments, rhythms, and melodies drawn from several regions of the country, the character of the
musical accompaniment was predominantly Ghanaian. Implicitly then,
while the work expressed cosmopolitanism, it equally staged a national
sentiment of unity, as individuals fused music from several ethnic areas.

All the sections of the choreography were complete. Brian and the
ensemble continued for another week to string the pieces together into
a coherent whole. The public performance of the piece occurred in the
dance hall for an audience of about forty people, including many of the
dance faculty at Legon, GDE director Ben Ayettey, staff of the university music department, and a group of tourists who happened to be on

6.3. Members of the GDE (Legon) rehearsing *Journey* in the dance hall at Legon.

their way through campus. William Diku introduced the piece, noting that the work – called *Journey* – was choreographed by Brian Jeffery (PURL 6.3). Thus, following cosmopolitan choreographic convention, credit was assigned only to the choreographer, despite the significant contributions of others. After the introduction, the piece then began and lasted about twenty minutes. As the performers showcased the hard work they had put in over the previous several weeks, the local and the global, the regional and the national, "danced together" in a contemporary cosmopolitan creation. As dancers imitated automobiles and airplanes to express the theme of *Journey,* this piece captured some of the essence of contemporary African dance and the hyper-mobility that often creatively fuels this genre and cosmopolitanism in general. After the final drum rhythm faded away, the audience cheered enthusiastically. Many individuals I spoke with afterward were impressed with the performance and praised it for its creative and innovative style, energy, and excitement as an engaging artistic expression. Subsequently, as several members of the university ensemble told me, this choreography has been performed at various state and corporate events and has been well received in Ghana as a "contemporary" expression of the nation. Members of the GDE (Legon) have also deconstructed *Journey,* rearranging and building on its various elements to create expressions of self and nation.

In all, "contemporary" expressions of nationalism in Ghana are often achieved in the ensembles through a rigorous cultural process of appropriation, translation, and experimentation. Although direct international collaboration is not a requirement for these types of expressions, they often rely on foreign elements. While these choreographies often use Western practices (such as orchestration, dynamics, thematic small-group improvisation, and "open" movements), I maintain that overall, through the use of indigenous rhythms, melodies, and movements, the African-ness or Ghanaian-ness of these pieces dominates, thus representing an Africanization of Western culture. In this way, international collaboration is one way in which Ghanaian artists navigate a basic paradox of nationalism, retaining distinctiveness while resembling others. By engaging in cosmopolitan creative processes, the national ensembles create an expression of the nation that is recognizable to, and resonates with, foreign nations; yet, the unique character of the Ghanaian nation is retained in the GDE through the artistic use of local practices. More precisely, it is the creativity of individuals that imbues these national expressions with personality, rendering them unique to the nation of Ghana. In turn, this process illustrates a way in which artists (both foreign and domestic) work within, or *use,* national institutions to express individual personalities, reforming nationalism by personalizing it.

Cosmopolitan creativity is a transformative experience for individuals. Through international collaboration, artists directly encounter, contact, and embody the Other. All parties involved in this process, African and non-African alike, become increasingly cosmopolitan. Embodying cosmopolitanism and nationalism involves a restructuring of the self and, more precisely, a re-formation of individual ontologies as artists adopt new ways of sensing and moving-in-the-world. These new ways of being-in-the-world are translated and transformed through the idiomatic vernaculars of personal habitus, giving rise to endless permutations and interpretations, ensuring that this creative process itself remains dynamic.

CREATIVITY AS COSMOPOLITAN COMPETENCY AND SOCIAL CAPITAL

In her study of dance theatre in Tanzania, Laura Edmondson notes that cultural nationalism theoretically suppresses creativity and innovation because it often relies on static notions of authenticity and tradition (2007, 48). In Ghana, African Personality, Pan-Africanism, and nationalism are premised on such essentialist ideologies, which attempt to conserve culture while encouraging individuals to adopt a unitary identity. It is unsurprising, then, that within the GDE, choreographers attempt to preserve the authenticity of the "traditional" repertoire; such practices, consequently, merge with the cultural conventions and sanctions for given dances, limiting individual creative expression within these pieces. That is, the structure and strictures of "traditional" dance are more formalized within the GDE as compared with its counterparts in local communities. While this framework is somewhat fluid in idiomatic domains, it becomes more rigid within the GDE. Compounding such constricting effects, Ghana's national dance ensembles rely on hierarchical power structures that promote discipline; such ordering combines with choreographers' quest for professionalism and artistic integrity, which favor cosmopolitan stage aesthetics that promote uniform movements. Consequently, within their "traditional" repertoire, Ghana's state ensembles produce highly regulated choreographic stagings of culture, which can limit self-expression. Yet, within this synchronized, formalized, national matrix, performers find "small" ways to give nationalism the impress of their own personalities. Through these creative acts, artists render African Personality and Pan-Africanism as uniquely situated expressions of the self. Such action includes not only a reimagining and refashioning of the self but also a re-formation of the nation and nationalism. Creative expressions act to personalize the ensembles' repertoire and, in turn, nationalist ideologies.

Such personalization of nationalism is more pronounced within the ensembles' contemporary repertoire. For, while "traditional" dances often leave little room for personal expression and artistic contributions, as Hélène Neveu Kringelbach notes, "the 'contemporary' approach, by contrast, uses the personality traits and experience of individuals as the creative 'raw material'" (2013, 170). Consequently, within such dances, African Personality becomes more personal as individual creativity is explicitly encouraged. As drummers and dancers "crack their brains" and learn to develop their creative ideas, they gain confidence in their own artistic abilities, becoming increasingly self-assured and competent as performers and entrepreneurs.

Cosmopolitanism becomes an engine for this simultaneous expression and transformation of nation and self. Contemporary African dance is an imaginative space that invites a collaborative, experimental mode of thinking, which often transcends nation as it paradoxically becomes an expression of situated nationalism. Through a rigorous retraining and reorientation of personal (sensory) ontologies, which occur as foreign practices are filtered through the idiomatic habitus of artists, cosmopolitanism is internalized by both individuals and the ensembles writ large. On the one hand, contemporary African dance marks a way in which Ghanaians attempt to fulfill a longing for global citizenship, which has become increasingly important after the end of the Cold War (see Piot 2010). While outward looking, as the local and global are embodied, cosmopolitanism within Ghana's state dance troupes becomes not only "rooted," "vernacular," and "discrepant" but also subjective. This cosmopolitanization transforms artists as they become enriched with creative skills, which they often use to further personal objectives. In brief, learning African contemporary dance is one way in which individuals acquire a cosmopolitan competency; through this acquired "cultural style," artists can operate in a variety of global settings, interacting and connecting with, as well as contributing to, the widely diffuse phenomenon of contemporary dance as they work to transform the social order to their advantage.

Throughout this process, creativity within Ghana's state dance ensembles becomes a form of social capital and a tactic to manage nationalism. Performers use their individual creative abilities to distinguish themselves from others in an attempt to gain access to international travel; such opportunities provide contact with foreign markets and capital,[8] which is often associated with status, success, and accumulation. Creativity becomes an existential competition, which both propels and discourages artistic innovation. Acts of personal creativity are, thus, instrumental in achieving social mobility; such individual aspirations often outweigh national concerns for performers. That is, although such practices seem to counteract the collectivist ideals for which the troupe was originally intended to promote, making a name for *oneself* through artistic innovation is often of the utmost importance to those within the national ensembles. Distinguishing themselves in this way, ensemble members reconfigure this state institution as a path to personal achievement. Receiving individual credit for creative efforts, therefore, provides coveted cachet, which artists transform into domestic and foreign professional opportunities. Artistic directors benefit from cosmopolitan conventions of attributing credit, attaching their own names to collaborative efforts and receiving much of the cultural capital earned by the ensembles. Nevertheless, although Ghana's state troupes have continued to at least ostensibly promote the collectivist ideologies of nation building and African Personality, performers attempt to stand out as unique artists, engaging in a politics of personality as they harness the state apparatus with their creative talents to forge expanded notions of self as well as provincial and even international careers.

Conclusion

Managing Self, State, and Nation

IN THE SUMMER OF 2012 I FINALLY HAD AN OPPORTUNITY, AFTER
five years, to return to Ghana. On the first morning back in Accra I traveled to the university to reconnect with the Ghana Dance Ensemble.
As I made my way from central Accra to Legon, the rapid transformation of this city became readily apparent. My taxi first passed the new
state-of-the-art U.S. embassy and blocks of gated extravagant estates
before running into traffic congestion around the recently renovated
Kotoka international airport. Beside this structure was "Airport City,"
which included a dense array of newly constructed high-rise "luxury"
apartments, soaring office complexes, and high-end hotels; these edifices
were surrounded by a myriad of cranes and scaffolding for numerous
construction projects that were progressing at alarming speed. Working
our way through a sea of cars, including more luxury sedans and SUVs
than I had ever witnessed on previous trips, we passed the recently built
Accra Mall (the first of its kind in Ghana); this sprawling testament to
neoliberal capitalism included an Apple Store, several boutique clothing
outlets, electronics retailers, a grocery, a bookshop, a food court, and a
movie theatre that screened mostly contemporary American films. Fu-
eled by the profits from recently tapped offshore oil reserves, it appeared
that the landscape of Accra had changed drastically in the last half decade, mirroring similar developments in other southern Ghanaian cities
(most notably Takorodi).

After fighting the morning rush-hour traffic, which was exacerbated
by the road expansion project near Legon, I exited the lorry near campus and darted across the half-paved road, dodging machinery and py-

lons along the way. Approaching the dance hall I saw several familiar faces. We exchanged greetings. "You dey, *chale?*" I asked. "Managing oh," several replied. "I dey run things proper," one said. I began asking the whereabouts of various other members. Although there was a core group of "elders" who remained, I was informed that many drummers and dancers had "stopped the work." When asked why, participants replied with explanations such as, "You know how it is here," "The salary is not enough," "They married a white," "They've traveled," "They went back to their hometown," or "They went back to their amateur [dance] group." Membership had dropped significantly, prompting the director to place a recruitment advertisement in the local and national media; this ad called on young Ghanaians between the ages of eighteen and twenty-five who had completed junior secondary school to submit an application; those chosen would then audition by the end of the year. As I sat with performers outside the dance hall, they noted that the number of performances had decreased, there had been no travel opportunities, and the overall activity of the group was nearly stagnant. As one dancer remarked, "This work is not helping us these days. We want to do the work because it is our passion, but things are difficult. The government is not supporting us as much as before, and the creativity has gone down. You see some people are enjoying these days, but we still struggle" (Badu 2012).

Across town in central Accra a few days later, I met with staff of the National Dance Company at the National Theatre. When I arrived, the troupe was rehearsing a new contemporary piece commissioned by Korlebu Hospital for the inauguration of its new burn unit. As opposed to the university troupe, the theatre group had little time to chat and exchange greetings. Later that afternoon I met with David Amoo and Grace Djabetey, who were preparing performers' visas for the ensemble's upcoming five-week tour in Japan. Amoo complained that Japanese officials wanted to see only "traditional" dances and were not interested in "contemporary" productions. It appeared that the Japanese government wanted to keep the performance of Africa in a stereotypical box, filled with antiquated notions of tradition. Our discussion quickly turned to the troupe's recent sojourn to South Korea to perform in a World Expo and to the communication problems encountered while abroad. These tales of touring stood in stark contrast to those told by Legon ensemble members, who bemoaned the lack of international travel. The N D C's . narratives articulated the government's ongoing trend of shifting its resources to the National Theatre, a practice that began soon after the split in 1992. Despite the N D C's demanding performance and touring schedule, its members recounted familiar tales of insufficient salaries and the necessity to hoard per diem allowances to support themselves and their families. Participants particularly noted the increase in domestic transportation costs (such as taxis and *trotros*[1]) and overall inflation that was straining their stagnant wages.

The symbols of affluence, change, "development," and prosperity that made up the Accra cityscape belied the relentless perpetuation of unemployment, poverty, inflation, power shortages, inadequate state services, and growing wealth inequality in Ghana. Although Ghanaian poverty officially had decreased overall in the last few decades, 11 percent of urban denizens remained below the poverty line, which was set at a mere average income of one U.S. dollar per day; and, while the country's unemployment had dropped to a national average of 3.6 percent, Accra's official figure was nearly 9 percent in 2012, with youth statistics in this regard even higher (see Obeng-Odoom 2012). Compounding these economic challenges, in 2007 the Ghana Statistical Services finally recognized what artists and other Ghanaians had been acutely aware of for years: this decline in poverty and unemployment was "offset by increasing [wealth] inequality" (17).[2] The influx of petrol capital that had noticeably altered the social, economic, and physical landscape of Accra clearly had not equitably benefited the nation, as indicated by artists' testimonies. In the 2008 presidential campaign, Atta Mills pledged that Ghana would not become another Nigeria,[3] stating that the potential oil revenue would largely be used to fund education and development projects throughout all ten regions of the country. Subsequently, during his time in office, Mills was lambasted for his inability to fulfill such promises. Despite their positions as state employees, ensemble members readily joined in this critique, particularly noting that Ghanaian oil had served only to increase inflation and decrease their quality of life.

Confronted with this frustrating calculus, ensemble members "manage." National artists strategically deploy a range of identities at various moments to navigate their positions as they seek self-improvement. Engaging in multiple forms of (tactical) artistry by adeptly mediating and manipulating a cosmopolitan matrix of power and possibilities, ensemble members dance in between identities and political strictures, eluding the surveillance of the state as they attempt to both blend in and stand out. Like nations in general, national artists must appear as both somewhat unique and universally recognizable to a larger cosmopolitan community. When it suits their interests and needs, these artists become chameleons, blending into their surroundings to express national solidarity. Musicians and dancers in the GDE are often encouraged by the state to transcend and conceal their ethnic, and even national, identities in order to promote unity in diversity and Pan-Africanism. These artists also find it advantageous to adopt an expanded identity as "Ghanaian" and/or "African" cultural experts as they travel abroad and strive to meet the often essentialist expectations of foreigners. While participants may ostensibly conceal their ethnic identities, they often remain deeply rooted in them. Although their individual identities are often pressed into a unitary matrix, the unique personalities and artistic talents of particular GDE participants are occasionally recognized, becoming instrumental in achieving their subjective ends.

Ensemble members also strategically use discourse as another way in which to manage. Artists in the GDE have deployed discourses of tradition, authenticity, essence, copyright, preservation, and art to further their personal objectives. While the state relies on rhetorics of tradition and authenticity to solidify its legitimacy and reify the existence of the nation, artistic directors have used these discourses to maintain their own positions of power and defend their creative choices. To deflect criticism that their artistic rearrangements of local dance forms do not accurately reflect community practice, directors maintain that their goal is not to produce an exact re-presentation of these cultural expressions but rather to create an artistic rendering while capturing the essence of each dance. As such, the GDE's "traditional" repertoire becomes a collection of authentic works of art. Like Western art, GDE choreographers have attached their individual names to these dances, claiming personal ownership over dances that are often considered to be community property. Directors deploy cosmopolitan modes of power as they "copyright" these works and maintain their authority to do so by pointing to a combination of local and global markers of status or cosmopolitan credentials. In all, these directors have used a discursive artistry to manage nationalism, ensuring the endurance of their own legacy and seeking individual recognition as they simultaneously work to promote the collectivity of the nation.

While these discursive tactics predominantly benefit artistic directors, nearly all ensemble members take advantage of an alternative education as they attempt to manage the resources and opportunities at hand. Through this education, troupe members enhance their cultural knowledge while developing skills in social communication, financial management, and entrepreneurship. Artists learn to stretch their inadequate pay, often supplementing it with external labor as they hustle for extra performance opportunities and navigate their professional careers, both locally and internationally. Like many Ghanaians, dance ensemble members often simultaneously participate in the formal and informal economy as they harness their particular situatedness. Although officially prohibited by ensemble bylaws, many become petty traders in the evenings and on weekends, selling cloth, food, drums, and/or their artistic talents. For instance, in 2012, Mercy Ayettey continued to own and operate a food stand, directly behind the School of Performing Arts. As she has for many years, she served clients from the dance ensemble and the university (including myself, who often ate lunch there during my fieldwork). In 2012 Christopher Ametefe and his crew still produced drums for local and international clientele, using the dance hall as their storefront; and, despite their explicit transgression of ensemble policy, artists (at Legon) conducted business as usual "under the tree," capitalizing on their status as GDE members – *national* performers – to charge a premium for private music and dance instruction. This alternative education had sparked interest in acquiring its formal counterpart. Spurred by economic necessity, curiosity, and proximity to academic institutions, several GDE (Legon) members had also been attending adult education courses at the university to try to "improve their positions."[4]

As performers navigate the internal regulatory codes of the ensembles and take advantage of the alternative education they offer, they simultaneously manage the state, including their direct interactions with government officials. In 2012 ensemble members continued to use indirection to conceal their indignation regarding the state of their nation. Although dancers and drummers complained bitterly that Ghana's new influx of oil revenues had not benefited them or the majority of the nation, such critiques were hardly evident as they performed for the state. While producing a reverent tribute to the passing of the late president Atta Mills, many ensemble members were not reluctant in their backstage conversations, blaming the Ghanaian government for their own financial difficulties and the underdevelopment of the nation. While this "hidden transcript" was apparent to those behind the scenes, it was hardly noticeable on stage. Artists used tactics of indirection to conceal such indignation and manage their emotions as they worked to promote the ideologies of the state and uphold public expectations for appropriate public displays of grief. Although employed by the state, many ensemble members do not consider their performances as expressions of direct support for the government. After his performance at a Mills memorial, Bernard Woma explained, "Ghana is set up for Ghanaians, not for any political party; when I play, I play for my country, not for any particular regime" (2013). His comments indicate the precarious position of ensemble members as they are situated between their duties as state employees and their responsibilities as citizens in a democratic society. This ambiguous position often produces veiled critiques of their government/employer. As this ethnography has shown, GDE members display their artistry not only by engaging in music and dance performance but also by staging clandestine expressions of dissatisfaction and disapproval (for example, *Drill*, smirks, silences, and so on), turning the instruments of state power ironically into subversive tools of reproach.

While mediating their direct interactions with the state, ensemble members have continued to negotiate the consequences stemming from the bifurcation of the GDE, which was brought about through debates between government officials and those at the university. In 2012, despite Francis Nii-Yartey's move back to the university and the increasing creative collaborations between the two troupes, reminiscent of the run-up to the initial split in 1992, ensemble members and staff continued to deploy discourses of tradition and authenticity to differentiate themselves from one another. The performative and discursive strategies that have characterized the Legon ensemble as the "originals" and the National Theatre group as "moving forward" remain a vital way for managing to survive in a highly competitive environment. New members continue to join while patrons often employ the ensembles based on their respective reputations. Such choices reflect artists' ability to manage this split, using the institutions of nationalism to suit their particular needs and interests in "traditional" and "contemporary" dance.

While making such intentional choices, participants additionally continued to manage nationalism by asserting their individual personalities through their creative artistry. In 2012 members from both ensembles told me that they were still discovering new ways to "put their own touches" on the so-called traditional repertoire while developing innovative contemporary productions. Although often constrained by internal political hierarchies, ensemble performers continued to view the troupes as domains of artistic experimentation, striving to discover and realize their choreographic visions. Musicians, dancers, and choreographers seek out new challenges, "cracking their brains" to "make for continual self-improvement." As choreographers balance stagecraft with statecraft, Ghana's state ensembles continue to act as laboratories for creative innovations as artists produce contemporary cosmopolitan expressions of state, nation, and self. Embodying new methods of creativity, artists add to their personal repertoire of skills, building their competencies, confidence, and character as they pursue self-improvement. In short, artists continue to use their creative abilities to manage nationalism, seeking positive recognition, (national) awards, travel, and further artistic opportunities, both domestically and abroad.

As this ethnography has focused on the art of managing nationalism, it has highlighted the transformation of both symbolic forms and performers. First and foremost, participants in Ghana's state ensembles become a dancing cadre of citizens. Managing the interaction of ideology, expediency, and identity, participants become unified, at least ostensibly; through shared experience and action they embody (to various degrees) African Personality and Pan-Africanism, staging such notions as instruments of the state. Within this process, a diversity of dance traditions is sensationalized – transformed into copyrighted artistic works that appeal to cosmopolitan aesthetics. Performers, thus, are drawn into the dynamic impressionistic canvases that constitute a dancing archive of Ghana's heritage. Engaging in this choreographic collapsing of history and geography, artists become biographers, cartographers, and archivists, solidifying the legacy of Mawere Opoku and other artistic directors as they stage re-imaginings of both the nation's past and its ethnic/geographic boundaries. Mediating a machinery of militaristic disciplinary codes and mechanisms, these participants serve as soldiers of culture, fighting to create and maintain Ghana's national identity. Seizing on the opportunities and resources of the state ensembles, including an alternative education that allows these performers to acquire a range of stylistic skills and competencies (Ferguson 1999), these individuals learn to become entrepreneurs, professionals, socialites, and cosmopolitans who capitalize on their talents to travel and build (international) careers. Last, musicians and dancers act as political satirists and critics, indirectly reproaching the state through mimicry as well as through subversive silences and smirks. Thus, ensemble members take on a host of forms as citizens, nationals, and cosmopolitans; biographers, cartographers, and archivists; soldiers, entrepreneurs, and professionals; socialites, critics, and satirists. However, ensemble members remain, above all, artists. Using a multidimensional artistry, musicians and dancers manage a surrounding matrix of power, becoming instruments of state nationalism as they instrumentalize it to serve their personal ends. While artists are transformed into virtuosos of movement and music, many also achieve mastery of social negotiation, dancing between self, state, and nation. In this way, artists not only manage to get by but also "run things" to improve their positions as well as ensure personal enrichment and success.

Through such artistry, members of Ghana's state ensembles have also transformed the social order. Like Ghanaian market traders, hiplife musicians, and bar women, state ensemble members "hustle" in their attempts to manage their surroundings to pursue success. And, like young men in Arusha Tanzania, the practices of GDE performers are "not just attempts to reproduce the sources of value in the wider world or pleas for full recognition by global society. Rather, they are attempts to transform the world so that what qualifies as value and belonging can be defined and established by these social actors themselves" (Weiss 2009, 36). Artists in the GDE attempt to change the world around them to suit their interests, needs, and values. They actively transform the meanings, values, and reputation of dance and music in Ghana and elsewhere as they also work to elevate the social and cultural value of "Africa" and Africans in the world. Such action requires a social competency that is learned and developed, in part, within the ensembles themselves. Through participation in the GDE, many artists become not only increasingly nationalistic but also cosmopolitan as they gain the stylistic skills that allow them to function and prosper in local and global domains. By hustling for gigs, doing their work, and manipulating the available opportunities and resources, performers provide for themselves, their families, and their communities as they pursue self-improvement. In this way, managing can be understood as an ontology, a way of being-in-the-world, that is both emergent and dynamic. Like crocodiles and chameleons, it is adaptive; it is a way for artists to not only dance-in-the-world but also dance-through-the-world as they rearrange the social order.

Nation building, statecraft, stagecraft, and self-fashioning are often concurrent processes. Such simultaneity inevitably results in dynamic tensions, for, as the proverbial conjoined crocodiles of the Akan illustrate, the nation comprises individuals who have both overlapping and competing interests. Thus, while studying the ways in which the nation is performed into being through collective action, it is crucial to comprehend the processes by which nationalism is subjectively embodied or reconciled within an individual matrix of memories, identities, and ontologies. As a disparate group of individuals dance together to per/form a nation, these individuals also strive to retain their unique sense of self. Such activity often requires that citizens strategically manipulate nationalism's cultural forms and institutions to their advantage.

Finally, it is important to note that nationalism in Africa began long before independence from colonial rule (see Chatterjee 1993) and did not end as sovereignty was granted by European powers. Focusing on Ghana's post-independence period, this ethnography has shown that nationalism and its representation, like the lives of individual participants, involve an ongoing process of updating to meet the demands and challenges of the contemporary moment. Thus, in postcolonial Ghana, nationalism remains instrumental – both significant and useful – for elites and non-elites alike who employ it to accomplish their objectives, no matter how quotidian or personal. If nationalism is a fiction invented and perpetuated by elites to serve their political and personal interests, it is equally maintained by non-elites who both play into it and play with it in ways that serve theirs. Nationalism and its cultural products endure not because the force of elite ideology overpowers the masses, but precisely because "the people" find purpose and function for them, weaving them into their own lives and aspirations as they manage them to seek for self-improvement. By negotiating nationalism, participants in Ghana's state dance ensembles not only continually imagine and reimagine the nation but also invent creative ways to both "ground" and enrich themselves within the maelstrom of modernity, strategically *using* the institutions, rhetorics, and logics of nationalism to inter/subjectively construct meaningful, satisfying, and productive lives. In all, managing nationalism entails a process whereby individuals employ multiple types of artistry to simultaneously stage (national) culture and pursue personal interests, mediating the dancing politics of a fluid and dynamic cosmopolitan matrix of power. Such action results in a relentless renegotiation, re-formation, and renewal of the nation as well as of the individual self.

Notes

Introduction

1. *Weekly Spectator,* June 24, 1989, 8.

2. Ghana Dance Ensemble performance program, July 20 and 21, 1989. Kpanlogo is a social music and dance of the Ga people in Accra; for further discussion of its history, see Collins 1992, 42–48; and N. Thompson 2000.

3. Kate Zimmerman, "Dancers Bring Africa to Life," *Calgary Herald,* July 21, 1989.

4. After this incident, Nii-Yartey instituted a policy whereby each member of the ensemble had to have his or her parents, legal guardian, or related property owner sign a document acknowledging responsibility for any such illegal immigration activity. This became known to ensemble members as the "obligor" document, referring to its obligation. According to Bernard Woma, who had recently joined the troupe, "This document put a lot of fears in performers who were traveling" (2013).

5. This was a common expression used by ensemble members.

6. Francesca Castaldi also notes that members of the National Ballet of Senegal similarly use this ensemble as a way to gain access to visas and travel abroad (2006, 96).

7. For further biographical information on Kakraba Lobi, see Ben A. Aning, "Kakraba Lobi: Master Xylophonist of Ghana," in "A Festschrift Presented to J. H. Kwabena Nketia," special issue, *African Musicology: Current Trends* 1 (1989): 93–110. For further discussion of GDE performers' integration into North American universities, see Dor 2014.

8. For further biographical information on Gideon Alorwoyie, see Davis 1994.

9. For a detailed discussion of Ghanaian market women in this regard, see Clark 1994.

10. For further discussion of hiplife artists and hustling, see Shipley 2013, 222–23.

11. John Chernoff (2003) provides a detailed exploration of hustling through his ethnographic life history of a Ghanaian "bar woman."

12. This Akan proverb expresses adaptability: *Odenkyem da nsuo mu, nso onnhome nsuo, ohome mframa.* (The crocodile lives in water, but does not breathe water, it breathes air.)

13. Although there are certainly many works that analyze the performance of nationalism, here I am particularly referring to work in Africa such as Askew 2002; Ed-

mondson 2007; Moorman 2008; Straker 2009; and Turino 2000.

14. For further discussion of instrumental nationalism, see Brass 1979; Gellner 1964; and Nairn 1977.

15. For further discussion of the "invention of tradition," see Hobsbawm and Ranger 1983.

16. Francis Robinson (1977) has also criticized Paul Brass and other instrumentalists' approaches to nationalism for their overemphasis on elites. Addressing this concern in his own work, Robinson is primarily concerned with the ways in which non-elites use nationalism to construct group identities and mass movements. Yet Robinson leaves space for the exploration of the ways in which individual non-elites instrumentalize nationalism to achieve pragmatic and artistic ends. Here I am conceptualizing non-elites as those with little formal education as well as minimal economic means and officialized political status.

17. For discussion of the politics of disorder in Africa, see Chabal and Daloz 1999.

18. For discussions of the instrumental qualities of religion in Africa, see Allman 1994; Comaroff and Comaroff 1991; Hodgson 2005; Landau 1995; Meyer 1999; and Peel 2000.

19. For discussion of the instrumentality of wage labor in Africa, see Akyeampong 1996; Allman 1996; Atkins 1993; and Cooper 1996.

20. For further discussion of the reductive and functionalist tendencies of instrumentalist paradigms, see Mbembe 2001, 6.

21. Being a "big man" in Ghana suggests that one has accumulated a high degree of status, wealth, and power. For a detailed discussion of the meaning of the phrase "big men" in Ghana, see Nugent 1998.

22. For further discussion of the politics of the belly in Ghana, see Hasty 2005.

23. For further discussion of Weber's concept of the "iron cage," see a collection of his political writings published in 1994.

24. For further discussion of Bourdieu's concept of "field," see a collection of his essays published in 1993.

25. For further discussion of performativity, including the concept of iteration, see Butler 1999.

26. Anthropologist Bob White has shown that "nationalism and cosmopolitanism can no longer been seen as antithetical" (2002, 681; cf. Cheah and Robbins 1998, 24–25).

27. For instance, see Appiah 2006; Brown and Held 2010; Cheah and Robbins 1998; and Feld 2012.

28. Some of the more prominent national dance ensembles in Africa include the National Folk Troupe and Mahmoud Reda Troupe (Egypt), both founded 1961 (see Shay 2002, 126–62); Heart Beat of Africa (Uganda), formed 1963 (see Hanna and Hanna 1968); National Dance Troupe in Tanzania, established 1964, disbanded 1980; Ballet National du Mali, established in the 1960s; Ballet National du Chad, established 1969; Ballet National de Côte d'Ivoire, established 1974; National Troupe of Nigeria, established 1989; Zimbabwe National Dance Company, established 1981, disbanded mid-1990s (see Turino 2000, 321–29); and Malawi National Dance Troupe, formed 1987, formerly the Kwacha Cultural Troupe.

29. See A. Apter 2005; Askew 2002; Coe 2005; Gilman 2009; Moorman 2008; Turino 2000; and White 2008.

30. See Bohlman 2004; Largey 2006; Moore 1997; Tuohy 2001.

31. "Fakelore" is a term coined by American folklorist Richard Dorson in 1950 denoting "inauthentic" forms of

culture that are constructed for strategic, often political and economic, purposes.

32. Regina Bendix (1997) clearly shows that this romanticization of folk and rural culture as "authentic" and "pure" grew from the ideals of the Enlightenment.

33. Yet a paradigm shift to a constructivist standpoint did not come without its detractors. As late as 1988, Richard Handler still had to ward off criticism from many of his anthropological brethren, particularly because his study of nationalism centered on folkloric culture (Handler 1988, 13).

34. Major works on African nationalism include Falola 2001; Freund 1998; Geiger 1997; Peterson 2004; and Shillington 1989, 373–421.

35. Major works on nationalism in Ghana include Allman 1993; D. Apter 1963; B. Davidson 1992; Rathbone 2000.

36. Michel Foucault has convincingly argued that "power is neither given, nor exchanged, nor recovered, but rather exercised, and that it only exists in action" (1980, 89). Like Kelly Askew, I take a performative approach to power, recognizing it as "a diffuse resource available to everyone everywhere (albeit to differing degrees) and never the exclusive domain of some over others" (Askew 2002, 12).

37. For further discussion of this concept, see Castaldi 2006.

38. See Erlmann 1996.

39. Jean-Paul Sartre has stated, "[Emotion] . . . is a mode of existence of consciousness, one of which it understands its being-in-the-world" (1948, 91). Martin Heidegger states, "[T]he possibilities of disclosure belonging to cognition fall far short of the primordial disclosure of moods" (1962, 127).

40. For a discussion of the false dichotomy between reason and emotion, see Damasio 1994.

41. A group of scholars known as "primordialists" have particularly highlighted the emotional intimacy of nationalism; for further discussion, see Smith 1986 and Herzfeld 1997.

42. For discussions of music and bodily motion, see Kubik 1977; J. Davidson 1993.

43. Thus, my conception of embodiment differs from Pierre Bourdieu's well-known theory of habitus, which is an *unconscious* set of bodily dispositions that can no longer be recalled (1977, 72, 124).

44. An exhaustive list of references on African music would be beyond the scope of this project. The sources listed here specifically address the relationship between African music and dance scholarship.

45. Agreeing with other phenomenologically grounded theorists, I note that history may be accessed by an individual through a reflective process in the present and can be reconciled with experiential modes of thought because, as Harris Berger states, "the historical past is a history for experience and a history in experience: history is there for experience inasmuch as past events, no matter their span, can potentially be grasped by a historically *reflecting* subject. . . . Taken in this way the currents of history can be understood as a cross-situational phenomenon" (1999, 247; emphasis mine). Berger derives this assumption from Anthony Giddens, who created the term *structuration,* which refers to the process by which "past intentional acts become objectified as the context for present acts" (Berger 1999, 23). Therefore, in addition to the immediately lived cultural context, an individual's experience is also informed by a horizon of his or her, and others', past experiences. Furthermore, it is a given that the world existed before the present

experience and that this present is additionally informed by the world of our predecessors (Schutz [1932] 1967, 207–14). Consequently, it becomes essential for scholars to examine certain historical elements that have influenced a participant's current lived experience, because "performances mediate not only across existential domains but also across gaps in time" (Bauman 2001b, 101).

46. For a critical literature review of the scholarly work on Ghanaian music and dance, see Schauert 2005.

47. For a discussion of cultural performance in Ghanaian schools, see Coe 2005.

48. For discussions of highlife and its developments, see Collins 1992, 1996; and Plageman 2012.

49. For a discussion of hiplife, see Shipley 2013.

1. Beyond Ethnicity, beyond Ghana

1. This statement was made by the emcee of this event as he introduced the ensemble.

2. African Personality is a phrase that is often attributed to seminal African nationalist Edward Wilmot Blyden (1832–1912) (see Falola 2001).

3. "The Midnight Speech," March 6, 1957. Transcribed by author from audio recording, accessed at http://ghanacon scious.ghanathink.org/audio/by/title /the_midnight_speech, on February 3, 2009.

4. National Archives of Ghana document, RG3/7/33, 66.

5. For further biographical information on Amu, see Agyemang 1988.

6. Legon is a particular suburb of Accra in which the University of Ghana campus is located.

7. It has become a commonplace assertion in scholarly discourse that African independence struggles were primarily

elite-driven movements (see Cooper 2002; Davidson 1992; Falola 2001; Freund 1998; Shillington 1989, 374–408). Recently, Africanists have begun to explore the ways in which national sentiment was subsequently transferred to the citizenry – the masses – in the postcolonial period (see Allman 2004; Geiger 1997; Moorman 2004; Peterson 2004).

8. The Ghana Dance Ensemble was known as the National Dance Company until its inauguration in 1967.

9. From "The Midnight Speech."

10. Population data according to the 1960 census: Akan (Twi, Fante, Nzema), 44.1%; Mole-Dagbani (including Dagarte, Frafra, Kusasi, Dagomba [Dagbamba], Mosi), 15.9%; Ewe, 13%; Ga-Adangbe, 8.3%; Guan, 3.7%; Gurma, 3.5%; Grusi, 2.2%; Yoruba, 1.6%; Mande, 1.4%; Hausa, 0.9%; Central Togo Tribes [sic], 0.8%; Tem, 0.7% (Gil, Aryee, and Ghansah 1964, xxxiii–xxxiv).

11. The *Akan Ceremonial Dance* is made up of two Asante court dances – the *kete* and the *fontomfrom*.

12. Richard Handler, studying nationalism in the Canadian province of Quebec, notes that when nationalists often prodded individuals to choose between identities, many participants responded by asking, "Why can't we be both Canadian and Quebecois?" (1988, 49).

13. The notion of "tribe" and its social construction has been the subject of much scholarly discussion. Early anthropologists, particularly of the functionalist school, often reified notions of bounded African "tribes" (see Tonkin 1990). Scholars such as Terrance Ranger and other so-called instrumentalists have argued that "tribes" were primarily "invented" by colonial officials to facilitate administration (i.e., indirect rule) and hegemony. Offering a corrective to this overemphasis on

instrumentality, J. D. Y. Peel (1989), argues that ethnicity must resonate with people's actual experiences and lived histories; similarly, Carola Lentz notes that ethnicity in Africa has often been the outgrowth of precolonial we-group associations (1995, 6). Countering the instrumentality of colonial officials, scholars (Bates 1974) have acknowledged that Africans themselves often strategically used the notion of "tribe" to consolidate their own authority as local leaders (chiefs), make claims to resources, and access the institutions of colonialism (Lentz 1995).

14. For instance, Akan day names have been widely adopted by Ewe and other neighboring groups.

15. For instance, Asante *adinkra* symbols and *ananse* (spider) folktales have become commonplace in Ewe and other neighboring communities.

16. Mustapha Tettey Addy has produced a number of recordings that feature his compositions, which fuse a variety of ethnic styles from Ghana and Africa.

17. Dance-drama is a term used by ensemble members to denote dance choreography based on a specific narrative, telling this story through dance, music, and pantomime.

18. If one includes literary works within the rubric of "artistic performance," then the pool of sources remains significant (see Hurley, Larrier, and McLaren 1999; Kanneh 1998); however, if one strictly searches for scholarship regarding Pan-Africanism's link to the performing arts, this pool quickly empties. Moreover, it is rare to find a discussion of the ways in which Pan-Africanism has been expressed through music (Richards 2001) and dance (Castaldi 2006) and subjectively embodied by individuals. Castaldi's work (2006) discusses the performance of Négritude in Senegal, which

has close ties with Pan-Africanism but is not necessarily synonymous.

19. These include, in chronological order: Britain 1968, Mexico Olympic Games 1968, Nigeria 1968, Italy 1968, Paris 1968, New York 1968, United States 1969, USSR 1969, Germany in 1970 and 1974, Jamaica 1977, Germany 1979 and 1980, Italy 1980, Paris 1981, Yugoslavia 1981, Paris 1983, UK 1984, London 1985, New Delhi and Bombay 1987, Guyana 1988, New York 1988, Canada 1989, Germany 1989, Holland 1989, Nigeria 1989, Switzerland 1989, Tokyo 1989, Zimbabwe 1989, UK 1989, Germany 1994, Japan 1995, and Korea 1995. Additionally, the *Spectator* includes reports on the GDE's participation in "Dance/Africa" in Chicago in 1996, "Images of Africa" in Copenhagen, Denmark, in 1997, and tours of Indonesia and the UK in 1995, Denmark in 1999, London in 1999, and Jamaica in 2003. Through personal conversations I also learned that the GDE (Legon) had toured Malawi in 2006, and the NDC had performed in India during the Ghana @ 50 celebrations (March 2007).

20. The AU developed from the OAU (Organization of African Unity), of which Nkrumah was a founding member.

21. Judy Rosenthal discusses how "chameleon capacity" is a foundational value of Ewe selfhood. She notes that Sunia Compo, a *gorovodu* spirit, appears weak but actually demonstrates great power by changing colors to meet the demands of its surroundings and situation. "This practice of camouflage," she states, "takes part in a larger aesthetic of masking and changing identities; and in Ewe selfhood it is 'masks all the way down.' Such masks, costumes, camouflage and makeup are not indications of artificiality but rather of diverse dimensions of agency and reality" (Rosenthal 1998, 81; cf. Geurts 2002, 141).

2. Dancing Essences

1. As Nketia's opening remarks from that evening state, "Traditional Ghanaian custom requires that when a baby is born it should be outdoored and formally named in the presence of relations, friends, and well-wishers. Our custom also requires us to take a look at the child again when it comes of age, and to celebrate this event in a fitting matter. To-night, we have come to perform both the official outdooring ceremony and the coming of age of the Ghana Dance Ensemble" (in Opoku 1968, 6).

2. Regina Bendix notes that the "longing for authenticity is oriented toward the recovery of an essence whose loss has been realized only through modernity, and whose recovery is feasible only through methods and sentiments created in modernity" (1997, 8).

3. Such as Sékou Touré in Guinea (see Straker 2009); Léopold Sénghor and his Négritude in Senegal (see Castaldi 2006); and Mobutu Sese Seko and his *authenticité* in DR Congo (see White 2008).

4. Here I am drawing particularly on Birgit Meyer's (2010) concept of the "aesthetics of persuasion," which relies on a broad Aristotelian notion of aesthetics that includes the body and its senses.

5. Michael Herzfeld reminds us that "distrust of essentialism in social theory should not blur our awareness of its equally pervasive presence in social life" (1997, 27). In other words, while authenticity remains an "intellectual red herring" for scholars, "the concept remains nonetheless entrenched in popular thought and is an emotional, political issue for indigenous peoples, particularly for those who are engaged in a struggle for sovereignty" (Linnekin 1991, 446).

6. These questions highlight the link between authenticity and authority, which recall the Greek etymology of the word

"authenticity" itself – *authentes* meaning "one who acts with authority" or "made by one's own hand" (Bendix 1997, 13) and *authenteo* meaning "to have full power over" (Trilling 1972, 131).

7. Karl Marx and Friedrich Engels, *The Communist Manifesto* (1848; Minneapolis: Filiquarian Publishing, 2007), 10.

8. Participants often use these two terms interchangeably.

9. "Traditional" dances, with quotations around the word, will refer to those that the GDE and its members label as such.

10. From the program notes for *Beating the Retreat,* March 6, 2007.

11. See Chernoff 1979; Locke 1978.

12. Nii-Yartey, Duodu, Kwei Sowah, and Ayettey have all acknowledged in interviews and casual conversations that they regularly watch and are inspired by these kinds of films. Nii-Yartey particularly mentioned his fondness for American westerns.

13. For a further discussion of Damba, see Locke 1990. For a further discussion of the aesthetic of the cool, see Chernoff 1979 and R. Thompson 1966.

14. Nagla was originally performed at funerals by the Paga people of Ghana's Upper East Region. It later became a social dance of the youth.

15. Similarly, in some cases, sexually provocative movements are often avoided on stage, such as kpanlogo; see chapter 4.

16. See Drid Williams (1997a) for a detailed account of the ways in which the Ewe *agbekor* dance has been choreographed using linear and geometric formations.

17. Immanuel Kant, *Anthropology from a Pragmatic Point of View,* trans. Robert B. Louden (Cambridge: Cambridge University Press, 2006), 46.

18. Guy Debord uses the phrase "society of the spectacle" to refer to "an

order that concentrates all attention, all consciousness, on the act of seeing the commodity" (1995, 92). Here, I would add that the society of the spectacle focuses attention on the auditory sense as well.

19. Opoku was a student of the Kumasi Government School from 1921 to 1930. He attended Achimota Training College from 1931 to 1934 and studied at the Achimota Special Arts School in 1939. He entered the Camberwell School of Arts and Craft in London in 1944 and did a specialist course in art at the Central School of Art and Craft in London in 1952. He later studied at Juilliard and at the Martha Graham School in New York. Opoku obtained the title of professor when he taught at the Kwame Nkrumah University of Science and Technology (KNUST). He was later awarded an honorary doctorate degree from the University of Ghana in 1991, among numerous other accolades (see Vieta 1992).

20. E. A. Duodu identifies as Adangbe; Oh! Nii Kwei Sowah is Ga; Ben Ayettey is Ga; and David Amoo is also Ga.

21. Performance program, Ghana Dance Ensemble, 1989.

22. Same dance as *bamaaya* but a different spelling.

23. Lyman Ray Patterson, *Copyright in Historical Perspective* (Nashville: Vanderbilt University Press, 1968). For further discussion of copyright and music in Africa, see Perullo 2008.

24. Speech at the inauguration of the Folkloric Board of Trustees, National Commission on Culture offices, September 12, 1991.

25. See WIPO's General Introductory Course on Copyright on Neighbouring Rights: Protection of Expressions of Folklore.

26. See also PNDC Laws 110 (referring to the Copyright Law) and 690 (referring to the Copyright Act).

27. PNDC Laws 110 and 690 do not explicitly define the term "folklore." It is assumed that this term refers to works that have no known individual author (see Perullo 2008).

28. On occasion, members of the GDE do process while carrying drums on their heads. I witnessed such an occasion at a funeral for a former ensemble member that took place at Legon in 2007 (PURL 2.13).

29. The Golden Stool is a cultural icon of the Akan that is said to be the source of their power. Akan oral tradition claims that the Golden Stool descended from the sky and was given to the Akan chief.

30. Inverting this relationship, occasionally so-called amateur groups have been considered "more authentic" than Ghana's national ensembles. Ephraim Ketsri, who founded the Nana-nom culture group in 1983 in New Town (Accra), noted that when his group performed a collection of northern dances at Independence Square in 1991, the ministers from this region remarked that it was the first time they had seen their dances performed properly in Accra. This was an implicit indictment of the GDE, which often performed these dances for these state officials but apparently not to their liking. Due particularly to this performance, Ketsri recalled that "state protocol began to call us for national performances because they knew some of our dances were more correct than what the dance ensemble was doing" (2012). He noted that Nii-Yartey sought out his help in choreographing these northern dances and would often attempt to poach his dancers. That is, the national dance ensemble had unconventionally looked to an amateur group for its felt authentic grounding.

3. Soldiers of Culture

1. Cooper builds on the classic work of E. P. Thompson (1967), who argues that the work rhythms of industrial capitalism were a product of European technological innovations in time measurement (e.g., clocks).

2. Although this document is not dated, contextual clues lead me to estimate it to have been produced in the 1960s, shortly after the GDE was founded.

3. For further discussion of the Young Pioneers and Builders Brigade, see Ahlman (2011).

4. The Young Pioneers and the Kwame Nkrumah Ideological Institute were disbanded shortly after Nkrumah's ousting, but the Builders Brigade did not fade away until the early 1970s (Ahlman 2012).

5. From my conversation with this individual on May 4, 2007, in Legon.

6. See p. 5 of the SCS.

7. Saba Mahmood points out that "although we have come to associate docility with the abandonment of agency, the term literally implies the malleability required of someone in order for her to be instructed in a particular skill or knowledge – a meaning that carries less a sense of passivity than one of struggle, effort, exertion, and achievement" (2005, 29).

8. Saba Mahmood notes that a virtuoso pianist "submits herself to the often painful regime of disciplinary practice, as well as to the hierarchical structures of apprenticeship, in order to acquire the ability – the requisite agency – to play the instrument with mastery" (2005, 29).

9. A *gonje* is a bowed stringed fiddle found in northern Ghana (see Djedje 2008).

10. To address such practices, Foucault, toward the end of his career, proposed "technologies of the self" that "permit individuals to effect . . . operations on their own bodies and souls, thoughts, conduct, and way of being, so as to transform themselves in order to attain a certain state of happiness" (Foucault 1988, 18). Yet these ideas beg further consideration and analytical development, and critics have been quick to point out Foucault's overall marginalization of individual agency within his theoretical work.

11. Jennifer Hart (2013, 392–93) has discussed the hypocrisy of the Busia and Acheampong regimes, noting that while they both called for a disciplined approach to rooting out corruption, their administrations engaged in dubious practices to enrich themselves.

12. For centuries, Ashanti rulers have sanctioned critiques from their subjects during the eight-day *apo* festival (Bosman [1705] 1967). Noting satire directed at foreigners, early explorers of the Gold Coast wrote about "Tshi" speakers who often improvised songs that ridiculed and mocked European practices (Cruickshank [1853] 1966; Ellis 1887). More recently, Konkomba bands of the 1930s reinterpreted British regimental music (Collins 1992). Similar practices that have satirized the European colonial military include the Hauka movement in francophone Africa (Stoller 1995) and *beni ngoma* along the Swahili coast (Ranger 1975). In postcolonial Africa, most famously, Fela Kuti has lambasted the Nigerian military mentality of blind obedience in his popular Afrobeat song "Zombie," mimicking and mocking soldiers' training regimen (Olaniyan 2004).

13. Similarly, Jennifer Riggan describes how Eritrean fighters, once thought to be icons of national service, became transformed into symbols of punishment and a punitive state by local teachers who were angered by their government transfers (2013, 757).

14. As I have argued elsewhere (Schauert forthcoming), this attachment to an educational institution has contributed to the GDE's longevity. While many African national dance troupes have disbanded (Edmondson 2007; Turino 2000), Ghana's groups have endured, due in part to Nketia's decision to link the GDE to the university at Legon.

15. Labanotation is a complex form of dance transcription.

16. Some former members of the GDE who have gone on to teach at U.S. universities are Gideon Foli Alorwoyie (University of North Texas), C. K. Ladzekpo (University of California, Berkeley), Bernard Woma (State University of New York; Indiana University), and Abraham Adzenyah (Wesleyan University) (see Dor 2014).

17. "Running away," or not returning to Ghana, is one of the major concerns of the Ghanaian government when issuing visas and is often cited by state officials for the denial of foreign visas to its citizens.

18. Godwin Agbeli was a member of the Arts Council's National Folkloric Company in the 1960s. He passed away in 1998.

19. *Pito* is an alcoholic beverage made from sorghum and/or millet; it is particularly prevalent in the Upper West region of Ghana.

4. Speak to the Wind

1. *Damirifa due* literally translates from Twi as "deepest condolences" and can refer to a series of tributes to a deceased person.

2. The CPP was Nkrumah's Convention People's Party. "Verandah Boys" was a term used to designate the group of poor youth who were generally considered to be "hooligans" and made up a large portion of Nkrumah's support. They earned this nickname because they were often homeless and slept on the verandahs of their

"political mentors" (Addo 1997, 102).

3. *Mmenson* is a set of seven horns made from elephant tusks. They are blown to signal important state/royal occasions in Akan communities. For further discussion, see Kaminski 2012.

4. From Nketia 1963, 138.

5. As George Hagan has noted, "For a chief to step on the ground with his bare foot was a sign of abdication or self-destoolment. A destooled chief has their sandals seized from under their feet" (1985, 9).

6. While ensemble members were predictably silent regarding this historical period, they did note that Acheampong had bought a bus for the troupe.

7. For a more detailed discussion of the relationship between Rawlings and local chiefs, see Nugent 1998.

8. Naomi Dave provides a brief review of the literature regarding the ways in which women have deliberately used silence as a form of personal protection and self-expression (2014, 19); the author notes Keith Basso's (1970) study of the Apache; Edwin Ardener's well-known work on women as a "muted group" (1975); Michael Herzfeld's article on women's subversive silences in Greece (1991b); Hélène Neveu Kringelbach's work on emotionality and dance in Senegal (2007); and Kay Kaufman Shelemay's study of Syrian Jewish women and their music (2009).

9. Kelly Askew provides an example of a state performance in Tanzania wherein two popular *ngoma* bands performed for their president. The first band sang a song, which included lyrics that "offered a scarcely concealed critique of local leaders" cloaked by "the thin veil of praise [song]" (2002, 228–29). This was followed later in the evening with another song that did not mask its criticism of local leaders as well. As the artist sang about how

government corruption and greed were
responsible for Tanzania's ills, it became
unbearable and unacceptable for the state
officials. Askew writes, "The band had
only reached the end of the third verse
when a high-ranking cultural officer surreptitiously disconnected the main power
line to the band's equipment" (229). Because the reproach of the state was not as
discreetly performed as in the Ghanaian
examples, the Tanzanian musicians were
literally disempowered.

10. See Lentz 2008

11. "Big six" was a phrase that referred
to six leaders of the United Gold Coast
Convention (UGCC) party who agi-
tated for an end to colonial rule in Ghana
throughout the 1940s and 1950s. Nkrumah
had been a member of this party until
he broke away to form the CPP in 1949,
citing that the UGCC had not been aggressive enough in its approach to gaining
independence.

5. "We Are the Originals"

1. The Arts Center in Accra was formerly the European Club, which existed
since colonial times. After independence
the Ghanaian government decided to take
it over and turn it into the headquarters
for the Arts Council.

2. Henceforth, I shall refer to this
group as the Folkloric Dance Company
(FDC).

3. Wisdom Agbedanu was the only
member of the GDE who came from
the FDC.

4. See "The Function and Constitution of a National Theatre" document
in the National Archives of Ghana,
RG3/7/59.

5. In addition to the GDE, the resident national performing ensembles at the
theatre include the National Symphony
Orchestra and the National Theatre

Troupe – called Abibigromma – which was
previously based at Legon.

6. From page 3 of the "Ghana Dance
Ensemble" memo found in the Ghana
Dance Ensemble office files, Legon.

7. According to Nketia,

There was a theatre already on the site
of where the National Theatre is now.
That land was owned by Efua Sutherland
[noted Ghanaian dramatist], and she
built a small theatre there that was used
by several companies, including the university since the 1960s. When the Chinese
agreed to build the theatre in the late '80s,
it was decided that the National Theatre
should be built on the site of Sutherland's
theatre, and the old theatre would have
to be completely demolished. So Abdallah also got the Chinese to agree to help
build a replacement theatre on campus,
which they did, and is now the home of
the Efua Sutherland Drama Studio. (Nketia 2007a)

8. See http://www.ghanaculture.gov
.gh/index1.php?linkid=331&page=2
&sectionid=661.

9. From my conversation with this
individual on July 24, 2006, in Accra.

10. From my conversation with this
individual on April 4, 2007, in Accra.

11. For example, some of Nii-Yartey's
other notable dance-drams include *Bu-
kom, The King's Dilemma, Atamga, Okoryoo,* and *Sal-Yeda: Fate of Man.*

12. E. A. Duodu has choreographed a
number of dance-dramas; his most well-
known is *Nsrabo,* which comments on Africans' use of Western medical practices.
William Adinku's *Orphan* is a well-known
dance-drama in Ghana created in 1992
(see Adinku 1996).

13. Badejo's piece *Sisi Agbe Aye (Opening the Gourd of Life,* a collaboration with
Paris-based Koffi Koko, toured to sixteen
venues throughout the UK during the autumn of 1995 and spring of 1996.

14. From *Sal-Yeda* program notes, 1997.

15. Ibid.; emphasis mine.

16. Again, see http://www.ghana culture.gov.gh/index1.php?linkid=331 &page=2&sectionid=661.

17. The website lists the following international tours for the NDC: "Images of Africa" in Denmark (1993); London International Festival of Theatre (1993); Expo '93 in Korea; International Trade Fair '94 in Germany; Art Summit Festival, Indonesia in 1995; Dance Africa '95 in Chicago; Africa '95 in the UK; First Harare Children's Festival in Zimbabwe (1995); France, Denmark, and Korea in 1996; African Choreographic Competition in Luanda (1998); MASA (Market for African Performing Arts Festival), Abidjan (1998); Expo 2000, Hanover, Germany (2002); and UK and Qatar in 2002.

6. Politics of Personality

1. Communist regimes, for example, largely have tended to equate unity with conformity/uniformity, limiting the rights or freedoms of individuals, while democratic states often emphasize the inalienable rights of individuals to express dissent. Nevertheless, in both cases states value unity, and individuals are goaded to abide by the cultural values, morals, and norms of the nation through the rule of law.

2. The memo can be found in the Ghana Dance Ensemble office files, Legon.

3. In 1975, Mawere Opoku was awarded the Grand Medal (Civil Division), which is the highest honor bestowed on a Ghanaian citizen. In 2000, Nii-Yartey received this same honor. Both received this award for their general contributions to the development of choreography in the country.

4. Abibigromma was established in 1983 by Dr. Ben Abdallah, Asare Newman (dance faculty at the University of Ghana, Legon), and William Adinku (founding GDE member, author, and dance faculty at the university). For further information on its history and mission, see http://www.ug.edu.gh/index1.php?linkid=995.

5. Jesse Weaver Shipley notes that Ghanaian hiplife musicians are particularly susceptible to jealousy due to their focus on the individual and their success (2013, 129).

6. See "Objectives of the Ghana Dance Ensemble" memo, no date, Ghana Dance Ensemble office files, Legon.

7. See, for instance, Chernoff 1979; Locke and Agbeli 1982; Nketia 1971.

8. Debra Klein similarly has noted that travel became a competition among *bàtá* drummers in Nigeria as they strove to access foreign markets and capital (2007, 83).

Conclusion

1. A trotro is a multiple-passenger van that serves as a form of public transportation throughout Ghana.

2. For further discussion of neoliberalism and the widening income gap in Ghana, see Obeng-Odoom 2012.

3. Referring to the Nigerian oil boom of the 1970s (see A. Apter 2005).

4. This phrase used by dance ensemble members is reminiscent of a highlife song by Kwame Ampadu, "Ebi Te Yie" (Some Are Favorably Positioned), which references the ways individuals cleverly negotiate their social status (cf. Yankah 2001).

References

INTERVIEWS WITH THE AUTHOR

All interviews were recorded, translated when necessary, and transcribed by the author.

Abdallah, Ben. 2007. Digital recording. April 25. Legon, Ghana.

Abdellah, Zachariah Zablong. 2005. Digital recording. July 28. Legon, Ghana.

———. 2006. August 3. Legon, Ghana.

Abdullahi, Shaibu. 2007. April 26. Accra, Ghana.

Abua, Augustana. 2007. Digital recording. May 9. Accra, Ghana.

Adadae, Foli. 2006. Digital recording. July 11. Accra, Ghana.

Addy, Mustapha Tettey. 2007. Digital recording. March 3. Kokrobite, Ghana.

Agbedanu, Wisdom. 2005. Digital recording. August 9. Legon, Ghana.

———. 2007. May 29. Legon, Ghana.

Agyari, Solomon Atagi. 2007. Digital recording. May 9. Accra, Ghana.

Agyette, Leslie. 2007. Digital recording. August 17. Legon, Ghana.

Akowian, Evelyn. 2006. Digital recording. July 25. Accra, Ghana.

Amenumey, Apetsi. 2006. Digital recording. July 30. Legon, Ghana.

———. 2007. March 20. Accra, Ghana.

Amenumey, Grace. 2006. Digital recording. July 16. Accra, Ghana.

Ametefe, Christopher. 2005. Digital recording. August 3. Legon, Ghana.

Amoo, David. 2006. Digital recording. July 22. Accra, Ghana.

Amoquandoh, Solomon. 2006. Digital recording. July 15. Accra, Ghana.

Amotonyo, Christopher. 2005. Digital recording. August 8. Legon, Ghana.

———. 2007. April 16. Legon, Ghana.

Asante, Kwame [pseud.]. 2005. Digital recording. June 5. Legon, Ghana.

Asari, Yaa [pseud.]. 2007. Digital recording. July 23. Legon, Ghana.

Atsikpa, Afadina. 2006a. July 19. Accra, Ghana.

———. 2006b. Digital recording. July 25. Accra, Ghana.

———. 2007. March 20. Accra, Ghana.

Ayettey, Benjamin. 2005. Digital recording. August 16. Legon, Ghana.

———. 2007a. April 25. Legon, Ghana.

———. 2007b. May 15. Legon, Ghana.

Ayettey, Mercy. 2007. Digital recording. May 14. Legon, Ghana.

Azadekor, Mawutor. 2007. Digital recording. May 10. Accra, Ghana.

Azandor, Kwame [pseud.]. 2007. May 10. Accra, Ghana.

Badu, Kwaku [pseud.]. 2007. Digital recording. July 21. Legon, Ghana.

———. 2012. July 16. Legon, Ghana.

Brown, Kwesi. 2009. April 19. Bloomington, IN.

Darko, Jennies. 2007. Digital recording.
May 2. Legon, Ghana.

Diku, William. 2005. Digital recording.
July 26. Legon, Ghana.

Djabatey, Grace. 2006. Digital recording.
July 25. Accra, Ghana.

Duodu, E. A. 2007. Digital recording. June
27. Legon, Ghana.

Gademeh, Kofi. 2005. Digital recording.
August 5. Legon, Ghana.

Imorro, Sulley. 2007. Digital recording.
August 1. Accra, Ghana.

Ketsri, Ephraim. 2012. November 14.
Nashville, TN.

Kofi, Samuel [pseud.]. 2006. Digital recording. June 4. Legon, Ghana.

Kwakwa, Patience. 2006. Digital recording. June 26. Legon, Ghana.

Kwei Sowah, Oh! Nii. 2006. Digital recording. August 3. Legon, Ghana.

Mensah, William Kwesi. 2007. Digital recording. May 9. Accra, Ghana.

Merigah, Salifu Abubakari. 2006. Digital
recording. July 26. Accra, Ghana.

Mihesu, Abraham Kodzo. 2007. April 10.
Accra, Ghana.

Nii-Yartey, Francis. 2006. Digital recording. August 6. Legon, Ghana.

———. 2012. May 20. Legon, Ghana.

Nketia, J. H. Kwabena. 2005. Digital recording. August 18. Legon, Ghana.

———. 2007a.. May 11. Legon, Ghana.

———. 2007b. June 26. Legon, Ghana.

Quaye, David "Baby." 2007a. March 15.
Legon, Ghana.

———. 2007b. Digital recording. June 27.
Legon, Ghana.

Seki, Emmanuel [pseud.]. 2006. Digital
recording. July 23. Legon, Ghana.

Tekpa, Abraham [pseud.]. 2005. Digital
recording. August 9. Legon, Ghana.

Woma, Bernard. 2013. April 20. Bloomington, IN.

Yeme, Caroline. 2006. Digital recording.
July 25. Accra, Ghana.

Zigah, Wisdom. 2007. April 12. Legon,
Ghana.

PRIMARY AND SECONDARY
REFERENCES

Abdulai, Baba. 1997. "Dance, Dance, and
More Dance." *Weekly Spectator.*

Abu-Lughod, Lila. 1990. "The Romance of
Resistance: Tracing Transformations
of Power through Bedouin Women."
American Ethnologist 17 (1): 41–55.

Abu-Saad, Ismael, and Duane Champagne. 2006. *Indigenous Education and
Empowerment: International Perspectives.* Lanham, MD: AltaMira Press.

Achimota College. 1932. *Report of the
[Achimota College] Committee.* London:
Government of the Gold Coast.

Acogny, Germaine. 1980. *Danse Africaine.*
Frankfurt: D. Fricke.

Addo, Ebenezer Obiri. 1997. *Kwame Nkrumah: A Case Study of Religion and Politics in Ghana.* Lanham, MD: University
Press of America.

Adedeji, J. L. 2001. "The Legacy of J. J. Rawlings in Ghanaian Politics." *African Studies Quarterly* 5 (2): 1. http://web.africa
.ufl.edu/asq/v5/v5i2a1.htm.

Adinku, William. 1994. *African Dance
Education in Ghana.* Accra: Ghana Universities Press.

———. 1996. "To Build Dancing Steps on a
Story." *African Quarterly on the Arts* 1
(3): 59–62.

———. 2000. "The Early Years of the Ghana
Dance Ensemble." In *Fontomfrom: Contemporary Ghanaian Literature, Theatre
and Film,* edited by Kofi Anyidoho and
James Givvs, 131–35. Atlanta: Rodopi.

Agawu, Kofi. 2003. *Representing African
Music: Postcolonial Notes, Queries, and
Positions.* New York: Routledge.

Agovi, Kofi. 1989. "Culture, the State, and the Artiste." *Uhuru,* March, 14–15.

Agyemang, Fred. 1988. *Amu the African.* Accra, Ghana: Asempa.

Ahlman, Jeffrey S. 2011. "Living with Nkrumahism: Nation, State, and Pan-Africanism in Ghana." PhD diss., University of Illinois.

———. 2012. "A New Type of Citizen: Youth, Gender, and Generation in the Ghanaian Builders Brigade." *Journal of African History* 53: 87–105.

Akyeampong, Emmanuel. 1996. *Drink, Power, and Cultural Change: A Social History of Alcohol in Ghana, c. 1800 to Recent Times.* Portsmouth, NH: Heinemann.

Allman, Jean. 1993. *The Quills of the Porcupine: Asante Nationalism in Emergent Ghana.* Madison: University of Wisconsin Press.

———. 1994. "Making Mothers: Missionaries, Medical Officers and Women's Work in Colonial Asante, 1924–1945." *History Workshop* 38: 23–47.

———. 1996. "Rounding Up Spinsters: Gender Chaos and Unmarried Women in Colonial Asante." *Journal of African History* 37 (2): 195–214.

———. 2004. "Fashioning Africa: Power and the Politics of Dress." In *Fashioning Africa: Power and the Politics of Dress,* edited by Jean Allman, 1–12. Bloomington: Indiana University Press.

Ametewee, Victor. 2007. "Ethnicity and Ethnic Relations in Ghana." In *Ethnicity, Conflicts and Consensus in Ghana,* edited by Steve Tonah, 25–41. Accra, Ghana: Woeli Publishing Services.

Anderson, Benedict. [1983] 1989. *Imagined Communities: Reflections on the Origin and Spread of Nationalism.* London: Verso.

Appadurai, Arjun. 1988. "How to Make a National Cuisine: Cookbooks in Contemporary India." *Comparative Studies in Society and History* 30 (1): 3–24.

Appiah, Kwame. 2006. *Cosmopolitanism: Ethics in a World of Strangers.* New York: W. W. Norton.

Apter, Andrew. 1992. *Black Critics and Kings: The Hermeneutics of Power in Yoruba Society.* Chicago: University of Chicago Press.

———. 1999. "The Subvention of Tradition: A Genealogy of the Nigerian Durbar." In *State/Culture: State Formation after the Cultural Turn,* edited by George Steinmetz, 213–52. Ithaca, NY: Cornell University Press.

———. 2005. *The Pan-African Nation: Oil and the Spectacle of Culture in Nigeria.* Chicago: University of Chicago Press.

Apter, David. 1963. *Ghana in Transition.* New York: Atheneum.

Ardener, Edwin. 1975. "The 'Problem' Revisited." In *Perceiving Women,* edited by Shirley Ardener, 271–314. London: Malaby Press.

Arkin, Lisa C., and Marian Smith. 1997. "National Dance in the Romantic Ballet." In *Rethinking the Sylph: The New Perspectives on the Romantic Ballet,* edited by Lynn Garafola, 11–68. Hanover, NH: Wesleyan University Press.

Asante, S. K. B. 2007. *Ghana and the Promotion of Pan-Africanism and Regionalism.* Accra: Ghana Academy of Arts and Sciences.

Asirifi-Danquah. 2007. *History of Ghana: Prez. Nkrumah to Prez. Kufuor.* Ghana: Asirifi-Danquah Books.

Askew, Kelly Michelle. 2002. *Performing the Nation: Swahili Music and Cultural Politics in Tanzania.* Chicago: University of Chicago Press.

———. 2003. "As Plato Duly Warned: Music, Politics, and Social Change in Coastal East Africa." *Anthropological Quarterly* 76 (4): 609–37.

Atkins, Keletso E. 1993. *The Moon Is Dead! Give Us Our Money! The Cultural Origins of an African Work Ethic, Natal, South Africa, 1843–1900.* Portsmouth, NH: Heinemann.

Austin, Dennis. 1964. *Politics in Ghana: 1946–1960.* London: Oxford University Press.

Basso, Keith. 1970. "To Give Up on Words: Silence in Western Apache Culture." *Southwestern Journal of Anthropology* 26 (3): 213–30.

Bates, Robert. 1974. "Ethnic Competition and Modernization in Contemporary Africa." *Comparative Political Studies* 6 (4): 457–84.

Baudrillard, Jean. 1994. *Simulacra and Simulation.* Translated by Sheila Faria Glaser. Ann Arbor: University of Michigan Press.

Bauman, Richard. [1977] 1984. *Verbal Art as Performance.* Prospect Heights, Ill.: Waveland Press.

———. 2001a. "Genre." In *Key Terms in Language and Culture,* edited by Alessandro Duranti, 79–82. Oxford: Blackwell.

———. 2001b. "Mediational Performance, Traditionalization, and Authorization of Discourse." In *Verbal Arts across Cultures: The Aesthetics of Communication,* edited by Helga Kofthoff and Hubert Knoblauch, 91–117. Tubingen, Germany: Gunfer Narr Verlag.

Bauman, Richard, and Pamela Ritch. 1994. "Informing Performance: Producing the Coloquio in Tierra Blanca." *Oral Traditions* 9 (2): 255–80.

Bayart, Jean-Francois. [1989] 2009. *The State in Africa: Politics of the Belly.* 2nd ed. Malden, MA: Polity.

Bendix, Regina. 1997. *In Search of Authenticity: The Formation of Folklore Studies.* Madison: University of Wisconsin Press.

Benjamin, Walter. 1973. *Charles Baudelaire: A Lyric Poet in the Era of High Cap-* *italism.* Translated by H. John. London: New Left Books.

Berger, Harris M. 1999. *Metal, Rock, Jazz: Perception and the Phenomenology of Musical Experience.* Hanover, NH: Wesleyan University Press.

Berger, Peter L., and Thomas Luckmann. 1966. *The Social Construction of Reality.* New York: Anchor.

Berman, Marshall. [1982] 1988. *All That Is Solid Melts into Air: The Experience of Modernity.* New York: Penguin.

Best, Curwen. 2005. *Cultural @ the Cutting Edge: Tracking Caribbean Popular Music.* Kingston: University Press of the West Indies.

Bhabha, Homi. 1994. *The Location of Culture.* New York: Routledge.

———. 1996. "Unsatisfied: Notes on Vernacular Cosmopolitanism." In *Text and Nation: Cross-Disciplinary Essays on Cultural and National Identities,* edited by Laura Gracia-Moreno and Peter Pfeiffer, 191–207. Columbia, SC: Camden House.

Blum, Odette. 1973. *Dance in Ghana.* New York: Dance Perspectives Foundation.

Boateng, Akosua Boatema. 2002. "African Culture in the Global Marketplace: The Case of Folklore and Intellectual Property in Ghana." PhD diss., University of Illinois.

Bohlman, Philip V. 2004. *Music, Nationalism, and the Making of the New Europe.* 2nd ed. New York: Routledge.

Borneman, John. 1993. "United the German Nation: Law, Narrative, and Historicity." *American Ethnologist* 20 (2): 288–311.

———. 1998. *Subversions of International Order: Studies in Political Anthropology of Culture.* Albany: State University of New York Press.

Bosman, Willem. [1705] 1967. *A New and Accurate Description of the Coast of Guinea.* London: Frank Cass.

Botchway, Karl. 2004. *Understanding "Development" Interventions in Northern Ghana: The Need to Consider Political and Social Forces Necessary for Transformation.* Lewiston, NY: Edwin Mellen Press.

Botchwey, Judith. 1993. "A Descriptive List of the General Records Relating to the Arts Council in the National Archives of Ghana, 1954–1982." Diploma, University of Ghana, Legon.

Bottomley, Gillian. 1987. "Folk Dance and Representation." Paper presented at the Conference of the International Organization of Folk Art on Folk Dance Today, Larissa, Greece, July 1–5.

Botwe-Asamoah, Kwame. 2005. *Kwame Nkrumah's Politico-Cultural Thought and Policies: An African-Centered Paradigm for the Second Phase of the African Revolution.* New York: Routledge.

Bourdieu, Pierre. 1977. *Outline of a Theory of Practice.* Cambridge: Cambridge University Press.

———. 1993. *The Field of Cultural Production.* Cambridge: Polity.

Branco, Salwa El-Shawan Castelo, and Jorge Freitas Branco, eds. 2003. *Vozes do Povo: Folklorizacao de Portugal.* Oeiras, Portugal: Celta Editora.

Brass, Paul R. 1979. "Elite Groups, Symbol Manipulation and Ethnic Identity among the Muslims of South Asia." In *Political Identity in South Asia,* edited by David Taylor and Malcolm Yapp, 35–43. London: Curzon Press.

Briggs, Charles. 1988. *Competence in Performance.* Philadelphia: University of Pennsylvania Press.

Brown, Garrett Wallace, and David Held. 2010. *The Cosmopolitanism Reader.* Cambridge: Polity.

Butler, Judith. 1999. *Gender Trouble: Feminism and the Subversion of Identity.* New York: Routledge.

Castaldi, Francesca. 2006. *Choreographies of African Identities: Negritude, Dance, and the National Ballet of Senegal.* Urbana: University of Illinois Press.

Chabal, Patrick, and Jean-Pascal Daloz. 1999. *Africa Works: Disorder as Political Instrument.* Bloomington: Indiana University Press.

Charry, Eric. 1996. "A Guide to the Jembe." *Percussive Notes* 34 (2): 66–72.

Chatterjee, Partha. 1986. *Nationalist Thought and the Colonial World: A Derivative Discourse?* Minneapolis: University of Minnesota Press.

———. 1993. *The Nation and Its Fragments: Colonial and Postcolonial Histories.* Princeton, NJ: Princeton University Press.

Cheah, Pheng, and Bruce Robbins. 1998. *Cosmopolitics: Thinking and Feeling Beyond the Nation.* Minneapolis: University of Minnesota Press.

Chernoff, John Miller. 1979. *African Rhythm and African Sensibility: Aesthetics and Social Action in African Musical Idioms.* Chicago: Chicago University Press.

———. 2003. *Hustling Is Not Stealing: Stories of an African Bar Girl.* Chicago: University of Chicago Press.

Clark, Gracia. 1994. *Onions Are My Husband: Survival and Accumulation by West African Market Women.* Chicago: University of Chicago Press.

Clifford, James. 1983. "On Ethnographic Authority." *Representations* 1: 118–46.

———. 1992. "Traveling Cultures." In *Cultural Studies,* edited by Lawrence Grossberg, Carry Nelson, and Paula A. Treicher, 96–111. New York: Routledge.

Clifford, James, and George E. Marcus, eds. 1986. *Writing Culture: The Poetics and Politics of Ethnography.* Berkeley: University of California Press.

Coe, Cati. 2005. *Dilemmas of Culture in African Schools: Youth, Nationalism, and the Transformation of Knowledge.* Chicago: University of Chicago Press.

Cohen, Anthony. 1996. "Personal Nationalism: A Scottish View of Some Rites, Rights, and Wrongs." *American Ethnologist* 23 (4): 802–15.

Cohen, Joshua. 2011. "Stages in Transition: Les Ballets Africains and Independence, 1959 to 1960." *Journal of Black Studies* 43 (1): 11–48.

Collins, John. 1987. "Jazz Feedback to Africa." *American Music* 5 (2): 176–93.

———. 1992. *West African Pop Roots.* Philadelphia: Temple University Press.

———. 1993. "The Problem of Oral Copyright: The Case of Ghana." In *Music and Copyright,* edited by Simon Firth, 146–58. Edinburgh: Edinburgh University Press.

———. 1996. *Highlife Time.* Accra, Ghana: Anansesem Publications.

Comaroff, Jean, and John Comaroff. 1991. *Of Revelation and Revolution: Christianity, Colonialism, and Consciousness in South Africa.* Chicago: University of Chicago Press.

———. 1992. *Ethnography and the Historical Imagination.* Boulder: Westview Press.

———. 2009. *Ethnicity, Inc.* Chicago: University of Chicago Press.

Connor, Walker. 1978. "A Nation Is a Nation, Is a State, Is an Ethnic Group, Is a . . ." *Ethnic and Racial Studies* 1 (4): 379–88.

Cooper, Frederick. 1992. "Colonizing Time: Work Rhythms and Labor Conflict in Colonial Mombasa." In *Colonialism and Culture,* edited by Nicholas B. Dirks, 209–46. Ann Arbor: University of Michigan Press.

———. 1996. *Decolonization and African Society: The Labor Question in French and British Africa.* Cambridge: Cambridge University Press.

———. 2002. *Africa since 1940: The Past of the Present.* Cambridge: Cambridge University Press.

———. 2005. *Colonialism in Question: Theory, Knowledge, History.* Berkeley: University of California Press.

Corrigan, Philip, and Derek Sayer. 1985. *The Great Arch: English Sate Formation as Cultural Revolution.* Oxford: Basil Blackwell.

Cowan, Jane K. 1990. *Dance and the Body Politic in Northern Greece.* Princeton, NJ: Princeton University Press.

Cruickshank, Brodie. [1853] 1966. *Eighteen Years on the Gold Coast of Africa.* Vol. 2. London: Frank Cass.

Csordas, Thomas. 1990. "Embodiment as a Paradigm for Anthropology." *Ethos* 18 (1): 5–47.

Cultural Division of the Ministry of Education and Culture. 1975. *Cultural Policy in Ghana.* Paris: UNESCO Press.

Damasio, Antonio. 1994. *Descartes' Error: Emotion, Reason, and the Human Brain.* New York: Penguin.

Daniel, Yvonne. 2005. *Dancing Wisdom: Embodied Knowledge in Haitian Vodou, Cuban Yoruba, and Bahian Candomble.* Urbana: University of Illinois Press.

Danso, Nii Kwei. 1995. "Dance Ensemble for Africa '95." *Weekly Spectator.*

Date-Baah, S. K. 1972. "The Law of Copyright in Ghana." *Okyeame.* November 5. 96–111.

Dave, Naomi. 2014. "The Politics of Silence: Music, Violence, and Protest in Guinea." *Ethnomusicology* 58 (1): 1–29.

Davidson, Basil. 1989. *Black Star: A View of the Life and Times of Kwame Nkrumah.* Boulder: Westview.

———. 1992. *The Black Man's Burden: Africa and the Curse of the Nation-State.* New York: Three Rivers Press.

Davidson, Jane W. 1993. "Visual Perception of Performance Manner in the

Movements of Solo Musicians." *Psychology of Music* 21 (2): 103–13.

Davis, Arthur L. 1994. "Midawo Gideon Foli Alorwoyie: The Life and Music of a West African Drummer." PhD diss., University of Illinois.

Debord, Guy. 1995. *The Society of the Spectacle.* New York: Zone Books.

de Certeau, Michel. 1984. *The Practice of Everyday Life.* Translated by Steven F. Rendall. Los Angeles: University of California Press.

Denzin, Norman K. 1985. "Emotions as Lived Experience." *Symbolic Interaction* 8: 223–40.

——. 2007. *On Understanding Emotion.* Piscataway, NJ: Transaction Publishers.

Diouf, Mamadou. 2000. "The Senegalese Murid Trade Diaspora and the Making of a Vernacular Cosmopolitanism." *Public Culture* 12 (3): 679–702.

Djedje, Jacqueline. 2008. *Fiddling in West Africa: Touching the Spirit of Fulbe, Hausa, and Dagbamba Cultures.* Bloomington: Indiana University Press.

Dor, George. 2004. "Communal Creativity and Song Ownership in Anlo Ewe Musical Practice: The Case of Havolu." *Ethnomusicology* 48 (1): 26–51.

——. 2014. *West African Drumming and Dance in North American Universities: An Ethnomusicological Perspective.* Jackson: University of Mississippi Press.

Drewal, Margaret. 1992. *Yoruba Ritual: Performers, Play, Agency.* Bloomington: Indiana University Press.

Dumont, Louis. 1970. "Religion, Politics, and Society in the Individualistic Universe." *Proceedings of the Royal Anthropological Institute of Great Britain and Ireland,* 31–45.

Ebron, Paulla. 2002. *Performing Africa.* Princeton NJ: Princeton University Press.

Edmondson, Laura. 2007. *Performance and Politics in Tanzania: The Nation on Stage.* Bloomington: Indiana University Press.

Ellis, Alfred B. 1887. *The Tshi-Speaking Peoples of the Gold Coast of West Africa.* London: Chapman and Hall.

Emerson, Rupert. 1969. *From Empire to Nation: The Rise to Self-Assertion of Asian and African Peoples.* Boston: Beacon Press.

Eriksen, Thomas. 2002. *Ethnicity and Nationalism.* London: Pluto Press.

Erlmann, Veit. 1996. "The Aesthetics of the Global Imagination: Reflections on World Music in the 1990s." *Public Culture* 8: 467–87.

Esedebe, P. Olisanwuche. 1982. *Pan-Africanism: The Idea and Movement, 1776–1963.* Washington, DC: Howard University Press.

Fabian, Johannes. 1990. *Power and Performance: Ethnographic Explorations through Proverbial Wisdom and Theatre in Shaba, Zaire.* Madison: University of Wisconsin Press.

Fabian, Krista N. 1996. "Professional Dance in Ghanaian Society: The Development and Direction of the Ghana Dance Ensemble." Diploma, University of Ghana.

Falola, Toyin. 2001. *Nationalism and African Intellectuals.* Rochester, NY: University of Rochester Press.

Feld, Steven. 1982. *Sound and Sentiment: Birds, Weeping, Poetics and Song in Kaluli Expressions.* Philadelphia: University of Pennsylvania Press.

——. 2012. *Jazz Cosmopolitanism in Accra: Five Musical Years in Ghana.* Durham, NC: Duke University Press.

Ferguson, James. 1999. *Expectations of Modernity: Myths and Meanings of Urban Life on the Zambian Copperbelt.* Berkeley: University of California Press.

——. 2006. *Global Shadows: Africa in the Neoliberal World Order.* Durham, NC: Duke University Press.

Foucault, Michel. [1975] 1995. *Discipline and Punish: The Birth of the Prison.* Translated by Alan Sheridan. New York: Vintage Books.

———. 1980. *Power/Knowledge: Selected Interviews and Other Writings, 1972–1977.* Edited by Colin Gordon. New York: Pantheon Press.

———. 1988. "Technologies of the Self." In *Technologies of the Self: A Seminar with Michel Foucault,* edited by Luther Martin, Huck Gutman, and Patrick H. Hutton, 16–49. Amherst: University of Massachusetts Press.

Fox, Richard G. 1990. "Introduction." In *Nationalist Ideologies and the Production of National Cultures,* edited by Richard G. Fox, 1–14. American Ethnological Society Monograph Series 2. Washington, DC: American Anthropological Association.

Fraleigh, Sondra Horton. 1987. *Dance and the Lived Body: A Descriptive Aesthetics.* Pittsburgh: University of Pittsburgh Press.

Freund, Bill. 1998. *The Making of Contemporary Africa: The Development of African Society since 1800.* Boulder: Lynne Rienner.

Friedrich, C. J. 1963. *Man and His Government: An Empirical Theory of Politics.* New York: McGraw-Hill.

Friedson, Steven M. 1996. *Dancing Prophets: Musical Experience in Tumbuka Healing.* Chicago: University of Chicago Press.

———. 2009. *Remains of Ritual: Northern Gods in a Southern Land.* Chicago: University of Chicago Press.

Gaard, G. 2001. "Tools for a Cross-Cultural Feminist Ethics: Exploring Ethical Contexts and Contents in the Makah Whale Hunt." *Hypatia* 16 (1): 1–26.

Gbeho, Phillip. 1951a. "African Music Deserves Generous Recognition." *West African Review* 22: 910–13.

———. 1951b. "Africa's Drums Are More Than Tom-Toms." *West African Review* 22: 1150–52.

———. 1951c. "Beat of the Master Drum." *West African Review* 22: 1263–65.

———. 1952. "Cross-Rhythm in African Music." *West African Review* 23: 11–13.

———. 1954. "Music in the Gold Coast." *African Music* 1 (1): 62–64.

Geertz, Clifford. 1986. "Making Experiences, Authoring Selves." In *The Anthropology of Experience,* edited by Victor Turner and Edward Bruner, 373–80. Urbana: University of Illinois Press.

Geiger, Susan. 1997. *TANU Women: Gender and Culture in the Making of Tanganyikan Nationalism, 1955–1965.* Portsmouth, NH: Heinemann.

Gellner, Ernest. 1964. "Nationalism." In *Thought and Change,* 158–69. London: Weidenfeld and Nicholson.

———. 1983. *Nations and Nationalism.* Ithaca, NY: Cornell University Press.

Geurts, Kathryn. 2002. *Culture and the Senses: Bodily Ways of Knowing in an African Community.* Berkeley: University of California Press.

Ghana Statistical Service. 1964. *1960 Population Census of Ghana.* Accra, Ghana: Census Office.

———. 2002. *2000 Population Housing Census: Summary Report of Final Results.* Accra, Ghana: Census Office.

Gil, B., A. F. Aryee, and D. K. Ghansah. 1964. *1960 Population Census of Ghana: Special Report E Tribes in Ghana.* Accra, Ghana: Census Office.

Gilman, Lisa. 2004. "The Traditionalization of Women's Dancing, Hegemony, and Politics in Malawi." *Journal of Folklore Research* 41 (1): 33–60.

———. 2009. *The Dance of Politics: Gender, Performance, and Democratization in Malawi.* Philadelphia: Temple University Press.

Glassie, Henry. 1995. "Tradition." *Journal of Folklore Research* 108 (430): 395–412.

Goffman, Erving. 1967. *Interaction Ritual: Essays on Face-to-Face Behavior.* New York: Anchor Books.

Gore, Georgiana, and Maria Koutsouba. 1992. "'Airport Art' in a Sociopolitical Perspective: The Case of the Greek Dance Groups of Plaka." Proceedings of the 17th Symposium of the Study Group on Ethnochoreology. Nafplio, Greece, July 2–10, pp. 29–34.

Guibernau, Montserrat, and John Rex, eds. 1997. *The Ethnicity Reader: Nationalism, Multiculturalism, and Migration.* Cambridge: Polity.

Gukhière, Delphine. 2007. "Coopération Culturelle et Danse Contemporaine: Une Alliance Durable?" *Africultures* 69: 129–35.

Guss, David. 2000. *The Festive State: Race, Ethnicity, and National Performance.* Berkeley: University of California Press.

Hagan, George. 1985. "Nkrumah's Cultural Policy." Paper presented at the Symposium on the Life and Work of Kwame Nkrumah, University of Ghana, Legon, May 27–June 1.

———. 1991. "Nkrumah's Cultural Policy." In *The Life and Work of Kwame Nkrumah,* edited by Kwame Arhin, 3–26. Accra, Ghana: SEDCO.

Hagedorn, Katherine. 2001. *Divine Utterances: The Performance of Afro-Cuban Santeria.* Washington, DC: Smithsonian Institution Press.

Haizel, E. A. 1991. "Education in Ghana, 1951–1966." In *The Life and Work of Kwame Nkrumah,* edited by Kwame Arhin, 53–81. Accra, Ghana: SEDCO.

Hall, Stuart. 1996. "Ethnicity: Identity and Difference." In *Becoming National: A Reader,* edited by Geoff Eley and Ronald Grigor Suny, 339–52. Oxford: Oxford University Press.

Handler, Richard. 1986. "Authenticity." *Anthropology Today* 2 (1): 2–4.

———. 1988. *Nationalism and the Politics of Culture in Quebec.* Madison: University of Wisconsin Press.

———. 2002. "Anthropology of Authenticity." In *International Encyclopedia of Social and Behavioral Sciences,* 963–67. Amsterdam: Elsevier.

Handler, Richard, and Jocelyn Linnekin. 1984. "Tradition, Genuine or Spurious?" *Journal of American Folklore* 97 (385): 273–90.

Hanna, Judith Lynne. 1979. *To Dance Is Human: A Theory of Nonverbal Communication.* Austin: University of Texas Press.

Hanna, Judith Lynne, and William John Hanna. 1968. "Heartbeat of Uganda." *African Arts* 1 (3): 42–45, 85.

Hart, Jennifer. 2013. "'One Man, No Chop': Licit Wealth, Good Citizens, and the Criminalization of Drivers in Postcolonial Ghana." *International Journal of African Historical Studies* 46 (3): 373–96.

Harvey, David. 1989. *The Condition of Postmodernity.* Oxford: Blackwell.

Hasty, Jennifer. 2005. "The Pleasures of Corruption: Desire and Discipline in Ghanaian Political Culture." *Cultural Anthropology* 20 (2): 271–301.

Heath, Deborah. 1994. "The Politics of Appropriateness and Appropriation: Recontextualizing Women's Dance in Senegal." *American Ethnologist* 21 (1): 88–103.

Hecht, David, and Maliqalim Simone. 1994. *Invisible Governance: The Art of Micro-Politics.* Brooklyn, NY: Automedia.

Heidegger, Martin. 1962. *Being and Time.* Translated by John Macquarrie and Edward Robinson. New York: Harper and Row.

Herder, Johann Gottfried. 1773. "Auszug aus einem Briefwechsel über Ossian und die Liederalten Völker." In *Von deutscher Art und Kunst: einiege fliegende Blätter,* edited by J. H. Herder, 1–70. Hamburg: bey Bode.

Herzfeld, Michael. 1982. *Ours Once More: Folklore, Ideology, and the Making of Modern Greece.* Austin: University of Texas Press.

———. 1987. *Anthropology through the Looking-Glass: Critical Ethnography in the Margins of Europe.* Cambridge: Cambridge University Press.

———. 1988. "Rhetoric and the Constitution of Social Relations." *Working Papers and Proceedings of the Center for Psychological Studies,* no. 22.

———. 1991a. *A Place in History: Social and Monumental Time in a Cretan Town.* Princeton, NJ: Princeton University Press.

———. 1991b. "Silence, Submission, and Subversion: Towards a Poetics of Womanhood." In *Contested Identities: Gender and Kinship in Modern Greece,* edited by Peter Loizos and Evthymios Papataxiarchis, 79–97. Princeton, NJ: Princeton University Press.

———. 1992. *The Social Production of Indifference: Exploring the Symbolic Roots of Western Bureaucracy.* London: Berg.

———. 1997. *Cultural Intimacy: Social Poetics in the Nation-State.* New York: Routledge.

Higgins, Dick. 1985. "A Taxonomy of Sound Poetry." In *Precisely Complete,* edited by Richard Kostelanetz and Stephen Scobie. New York: Archae Editions.

Hirt-Manheimer, Isaac. 2004. "Understanding 'Fast Agbekor': A History of Ghana's National Dance Company and an Analysis of Its Repertory." MA thesis, Wesleyan University.

Hobsbawm, Eric, and Terrance Ranger. 1983. *The Invention of Tradition.* Cambridge: Cambridge University Press.

Hochschild, Arlie R. 1983. *The Managed Heart.* Berkeley: University of California Press.

Hodgson, Dorothy. 2005. *The Church of Women: Gendered Encounters between Maasai and Missionaries.* Bloomington: Indiana University Press.

Humphrey, Doris. 1959. *The Art of Making Dances.* Edited by Barbara Pollack. New York: Rinehart and Company.

Hurley, E. Anthony, Renee Larrier, and Joseph McLaren, eds. 1999. *Migrating Worlds and Words: Pan-Africanism Updated.* Trenton, NJ: Africa World Press.

Husserl, Edmund. 1931. *Idea: General Introduction to Pure Phenomenology.* Translated by W. R. Boyce Gibson. New York: Macmillan.

———. 1964. *The Phenomenology of Internal Time Consciousness.* Translated by James Churchill. Bloomington: Indiana University Press.

Hutchinson, John. 1987. *The Dynamics of Cultural Nationalism.* London: Allen and Unwin.

Hutchinson, John, and Anthony Smith, eds. 1994. *Nationalism.* Oxford: Oxford University Press.

Hymes, Dell. 1964. *Language in Culture and Society.* New York: Harper and Row.

———. 1975. "Folklore's Nature and the Sun's Myth." *Journal of American Folklore* 88: 345–69.

Iddrisu, Habib Chester. 2011. "The Price of Adaptation: Hybridization of African Music and Dance from Village to International Stage." PhD diss., Northwestern University.

Idhe, Don. [1977] 1986. *Experimental Phenomenology: An Introduction.* Albany: State University of New York Press.

Jackson, Michael. 1982. *Allegories of the Wilderness: Ethics and Ambiguity in Kuranko Narratives*. Bloomington: Indiana University Press.

———. 1989. *Paths toward a Clearing: Radical Empiricism and Ethnographic Inquiry*. Bloomington: Indiana University Press.

———. 1996. "Introduction: Phenomenology, Radical Empiricism, and Anthropological Critique." In *Things as They Are: New Directions in Phenomenological Anthropology*, edited by Michael Jackson, 1–50. Bloomington: Indiana University Press.

James, William. [1890] 2007. *The Principles of Psychology*. Vol. 1. New York: Cosimo.

July, Robert. 1987. *An African Voice: The Role of the Humanities in African Independence*. Durham, NC: Duke University Press.

July, Robert, and Peter Benson, eds. 1982. *African Cultural and Intellectual Leaders and the Development of the New African Nations*. New York: Rockefeller Foundation.

Kaminski, Joseph S. 2012. *Asante Ntahera Trumpets in Ghana: Culture, Tradition, and Sound Barrage*. Surrey, England: Ashgate.

Kanneh, Kadiatu. 1998. *African Identities: Race, Nation, and Culture in Ethnography, Pan-Africanism, and Black Literatures*. New York: Routledge.

Kapferer, Bruce. 1988. *Legends of People, Myths of State: Violence, Intolerance, and Political Culture in Sri Lanka and Australia*. Washington: Smithsonian Institution Press.

Kaschl, Elke. 2003. *Dance and Authenticity in Israel and Palestine: Performing the Nation*. Leiden: Brill.

Kearny, M. 1995. "The Local and the Global: The Anthropology of Globalization and Transnationalism." *Annual Review of Anthropology* 24: 547–65.

Kedourie, Elie. 1960. *Nationalism*. London: Hutchinson.

Kirshenblatt-Gimblett, Barbara. 1988. "Authenticity and Authority in the Representation of Culture." In *Kulturkontakt – Kulturkonflikt*, edited by Ina-Maria Greverus et al., 28, 59–70. Frankfurt: Institut für Kulturanthropologie und Europäische Ethnologie.

Kirshenblatt-Gimblett, Barbara, and Edward Bruner. 1992. "Tourism." In *Folklore, Cultural Performances, and Popular Entertainments: A Communications-Centered Handbook*, edited by Richard Bauman, 300–307. New York: Oxford University Press.

Kirshenblatt-Gimblett, Barbara, et al. 1991. "Art and National Identity: A Critics' Symposium." *Art in America* (September): 80–83, 142–43.

Kisliuk, Michelle. 1998. *Seize the Dance: BaAka Musical Life and the Ethnography of Performance*. Oxford: Oxford University Press.

Klein, Debra L. 2007. *Yoruba Bata Goes Global: Artists, Culture Brokers, and Fans*. Chicago: University of Chicago Press.

Knowles, Mark. 2002. *Tap Roots: The Early History of Tap Dancing*. Jefferson, NC: McFarland.

Kreisberg, Seth. 1992. *Transforming Power: Domination, Empowerment, and Education*. Albany: State University of New York Press.

Kringelbach, Hélène Neveu. 2007. "Cool Play: Emotionality in Dance as a Resource in Senegalese Urban Women's Associations." In *The Emotion: A Cultural Reader*, edited by Helena Wulff, 251–72. Oxford: Berg.

———. 2013. *Dancing Circles: Movement, Morality, and Self-Fashioning in Urban Senegal*. Oxford: Berghahn.

Kubik, Gerhard. 1977. "Patterns of Body Movement in the Music of Boys' Initiation in South-east Angola." In *The Anthropology of the Body*, edited by John Blacking, 253–74. London: Academic Press.

Kwakwa, Patience Abenaa. 1994. "Dance and African Women." *SAGE* 8 (2): 10–15.

Landau, Paul Stuart. 1995. *The Realm of the Word: Language, Gender, and Christianity in a Southern African Kingdom*. Portsmouth, NH: Heinemann.

Largey, Michael. 2006. *Vodou Nation: Haitian Art Music and Cultural Nationalism*. Chicago: University of Chicago Press.

Lentz, Carola. 1995. "Tribalism and Ethnicity in Africa: A Review of Four Decades of Anglophone Research." *Cahiers des sciences humaines* 31 (2): 303–28.

——. 2006. *Ethnicity and the Making of History in Northern Ghana*. Edinburgh: Edinburgh University Press for the International African Institute, London.

——. 2008. "Travelling Emblems of Power: The Ghanaian 'Seat of State.'" Working Papers 94, Institut für Ethnologie und Afrikastudien, Johannes Gutenberg-Universität, Mainz, Germany.

Lentz, Carola, and Paul Nugent. 2000. *Ethnicity in Ghana: The Limits of Invention*. New York: St. Martin's Press.

Lindholm, Charles. 2002. "Authenticity, Anthropology and the Sacred." *Anthropological Quarterly* 75 (2): 331–39.

Linnekin, Jocelyn. 1991. "Cultural Invention and the Dilemma of Authenticity." *American Anthropologist*, n.s., 93 (2): 446–49.

Lock, M. 1993. "Cultivating the Body: Anthropology and Epistemologies of Bodily Practice and Knowledge." *Annual Review of Anthropology* 22: 133–55.

Locke, David. 1978. "The Music of Atsiabekor." PhD diss., Wesleyan University.

——. 1990. *Drum Damba: Talking Drum Lessons*. Crown Point, IN: White Cliffs Media Co.

——. 2004. "The African Ensemble in America: Contradictions and Possibilities." In *Performing Ethnomusicology*, edited by Ted Solis, 168–88. Los Angeles: University of California Press.

Locke, David, and Godwin Agbeli. 1982. "A Study of the Drum Language in Adzogbo." *African Music* 6 (1): 32–51.

Loots, Lliane, and Miranda Young-Jahangeer. 2004. "African Contemporary Dance? Questioning Issues of a Performance Aesthetic for a Developing and Independent Continent." Proceedings of the 7th Jomba Contemporary Dance Conference, University of KwaZulu-Natal, Durban, August 22–24.

Mahmood, Saba. 2005. *The Politics of Piety: Islamic Revival and the Feminist Subject*. Princeton, NJ: Princeton University Press.

Maillu, David. 2007. *Nkrumah: Passionate Pan-Africanist*. Nairobi: Sasa Sema.

Mayen, Gérard. 2006. *Danseurs Contemporains du Burkina Faso: Ecritures, Attitudes, Circulations de la Compagnie Salia nï Seydou au Temps de la Mondialisation*. Paris: L'Harmattan.

Mbembe, Achille. 1992. "Provisional Notes on the Postcolony." *Africa* 62 (1): 3–37.

——. 2001. *On the Postcolony*. Berkeley: University of California Press.

McCall, John C. 2000. *Dancing Histories: Heuristic Ethnography with the Ohafia Igbo*. Ann Arbor: University of Michigan Press.

Merleau-Ponty, Maurice. 1962. *Phenomenology of Perception*. New York: Routledge.

——. 1968. *Visible and Invisible*. Translated by A. Linguis. Evanston: Northwestern University Press.

Meyer, Birgit. 1999. *Translating the Devil: Religion and Modernity among the Ewe in Ghana*. Trenton, NJ: Africa World Press.

——. 2010. "Aesthetics of Persuasion: Global Christianity and Pentecostalism's Sensational Forms." *South Atlantic Quarterly* 109 (4): 741–63.

Miescher, Stephan F. 2005. *Making Men in Ghana*. Bloomington: Indiana University Press.

Mitchell, Timothy. 1988. *Colonizing Egypt*. Berkeley: University of California Press.

Moore, Robin. 1997. *Nationalizing Blackness: Afrocubanismo and Artistic Revolution in Havana, 1920–1940*. Pittsburgh: University of Pittsburgh Press.

Moorman, Marissa J. 2004. "Putting on a Pano and Dancing Like Our Grandparents: Nation and Dress in Late Colonial Luanda." In *Fashioning Africa: Power and the Politics of Dress*, edited by Jean Allman, 84–103. Bloomington: Indiana University Press.

——. 2008. *Intonations: A Social History of Music and Nation in Luanda, Angola, 1945 to Recent Times*. Athens: Ohio University Press.

Nairn, Tom. 1977. *The Break-up of Britain: Crisis and Neo-Nationalism*. 2nd edition. London: New Left Books.

National Commission on Culture. 2004. *The Cultural Policy of Ghana*. Accra, Ghana: Anttis Publishing.

Nicholls, Robert. 1996. "African Dance: Transition and Continuity." In *African Dance: An Historical and Philosophical Inquiry*, edited by Kariamu Welsh Asante, 41–62. Trenton, NJ: Africa World Press.

Nii-Yartey, Francis. 1991. "Alvin Ailey: A Revolutionary in Dance: A Historical and Biographical Sketch of His Choreographic Works." *Institute of African Studies Research Review* 7 (1–2): 87–92.

——. 2009. "Principles of African Choreography: Some Perspectives from Ghana." In *Contemporary Choreography: A Critical Reader*, edited by Jo Butterworth and Liesbeth Wildschut, 254–68. New York: Routledge.

Nketia, J. H. Kwabena. 1959. "The Creative Arts and the Community." Lecture, Symposium on Building an Intellectual Community in Ghana, University of Ghana, Legon, November 25, 1959.

——. 1962. *African Music in Ghana: A Survey of Traditional Forms*. Accra, Ghana: Longmans.

——. 1963. *Drumming in Akan Communities*. New York: Thomas Nelson and Sons.

——. 1964. "National Theatre Movements and the African Image." *Pan-Africanist Review* 1 (2): 88–93.

——. [1967] 1993. "A Bold Experiment." In *International Reviews of the Ghana Dance Ensemble*, edited by A. M. Opoku, 12–14. Legon: University of Ghana Press.

——. 1971. "Surrogate Languages of Africa." In *Current Trends in Linguistics: Linguistics in Sub-Saharan Africa*, edited by Thomas Sebeok, 699–732. The Hague: Mouton.

——. 1998. "The Scholarly Study of African Music: A Historical Review." In *The Garland Encyclopedia of World Music: Vol.1, Africa*, edited by Ruth M. Stone, 13–73. New York: Garland.

Nkrumah, Kwame. 1961. *I Speak of Freedom*. London: Heinemann.

——. 1962. *Towards Colonial Freedom*. London: African Publication Society.

——. [1963] 1992. *The African Genius*. Speech delivered at the Institute of African Studies, October 25, 1963. As cited in *Handbook of the 30th Anniversary Celebration of the Institute of African Studies and School of Performing Arts*. Accra: University of Ghana, 12–21.

——. 1963. *Africa Must Unite*. London: Panaf.

——. 1973. *Revolutionary Path*. New York: International Publishers.

Nugent, Paul. 1998. *Big Men, Small Boys, and Politics in Ghana: Power, Ideology and the Burden of History, 1982–1994*. New York: Pinter.

——. 2000. "'A Few Lesser Peoples': The Central Togo Minorities and their Ewe Neighbors." In *Ethnicity in Ghana: The Limits of Invention*, edited by Carola Lentz and Paul Nugent, 162–82. New York: St. Martin's Press.

Nyamnjoh, Francis B. 2002. "'A Child Is One Person's Only in the Womb: Domestication, Agency, and Subjectivity in the Cameroonian Grassfields." In *Postcolonial Subjectivities in Africa*, edited by Richard Werbner, 111–37. London: Zed Books.

Obeng, Samuel G. 2003. *Language in African Social Interaction: Indirectness in Akan Communication*. New York: Nova Science.

Obeng-Odoom, Franklin. 2012. "Neoliberalism and the Urban Economy in Ghana: Urban Employment, Inequality, and Poverty." *Growth and Change* 43 (1): 85–109.

Okyerema: A Bi-Annual Newsletter of the Centre for National Culture, Kumasi, Ghana. 1995. 1 (1).

Olaniyan, Tejumola. 2001. "The Cosmopolitan Nativist: Fela Anikulapo-Kuti and the Antimonies of Postcolonial Modernity." *Research in African Literatures* 32 (2): 76–89.

——. 2004. *Arrest the Music! Fela and His Rebel Art and Politics*. Bloomington: Indiana University Press.

Opoku, A. M. 1968. *The Ghana Dance Ensemble*. Accra, Ghana: Pierian Press.

——. 1976. "The Presentation of Traditional Music and Dance in the Theatre." *World of Music* 18 (4): 58–67.

——. 1978. "Choreography and the African Dance." *University of Ghana Institute of African Studies Research Review* 3 (1): 53–59.

Opoku, A. M., and Willis Bell. 1965. *African Dances: A Ghanaian Profile*. Legon: Institute of African Studies, University of Ghana.

Ortner, Sherry. 1995. "Resistance and the Problem of Ethnographic Refusal." *Comparative Studies in Society and History* 37 (1): 173–93.

Osei-Kwame, Peter. 1980. *A New Conceptual Model for the Study of Political Integration in Africa*. Washington, DC: University Press of America.

Packman, Jeff. 2011. "Musicians' Performances and Performances of 'Musician' in Salvador da Bahia, Brazil." *Ethnomusicology* 95 (3): 414–44.

Parker, John. 2000. *Making the Town: Ga State and Society in Early Colonial Accra*. Portsmouth, NH: Heinemann.

Peel, J. D. Y. 1989. "The Cultural Work of Yoruba Ethnogenesis." In *History and Ethnicity*, edited by Elizabeth Tonkin, Maryon McDonald, and Malcolm Chapman. London: Routledge.

——. 2000. *Religious Encounter and the Making of the Yoruba*. Bloomington: Indiana University Press.

Perullo, Alex. 2008. "Conceptions of Song: Ownership, Rights, and African Copyright Law." In *The Garland Handbook of African Music*, edited by Ruth M. Stone, 44–53. New York: Routledge.

——. 2011. *Live from Dar es Salaam: Popular Music and Tanzania's Music Economy*. Bloomington: Indiana University Press.

Peterson, Derek. 2004. *Creative Writing: Translation, Bookkeeping, and the Work of Imagination in Colonial Kenya*. Portsmouth, NH: Heinemann.

Piot, Charles. 2010. *Nostalgia for the Future*. Chicago: University of Chicago Press.

Plageman, Nate. 2012. *Highlife Saturday Night: Popular Music and Social Change in Urban Ghana*. Bloomington: Indiana University Press.

Ranger, Terrance O. 1975. *Dance and Society in Eastern Africa, 1890–1970: The Beni Ngoma*. Berkeley: University of California Press.

Rathbone, Richard. 2000. *Nkrumah and the Chiefs: The Politics of Chieftaincy in Ghana, 1951–1960*. Accra, Ghana: F. Reimmer.

Rawlings, J. J. 1982. *A Revolutionary Journey: Selected Speeches of J. J. Rawlings, December 31, 1981 – December 31, 1982*. Accra, Ghana: Information Services Department.

Reed, Daniel B. 1993. "The Innovator and the Primitives: George Herzog in Historical Perspective." *Folklore Forum* 26 (1–2): 69–92.

———. 2003. *Dan Ge Performance: Masks and Music in Contemporary Cote d'Ivoire*. Bloomington: Indiana University Press.

Reed, Susan A. 1998. "The Politics and Poetics of Dance." *Annual Review of Anthropology* 27: 503–32.

———. 2010. *Dance and the Nation: Performance, Ritual, and Politics in Sri Lanka*. Madison: University of Wisconsin Press.

Rice, Timothy. 1994. *May It Fill Your Soul*. Chicago: University of Chicago Press.

Richards, Paul. 2001. "A Pan-African Composer? Coleridge-Taylor and Africa." *Black Music Research Journal* 21 (Autumn): 235–60.

Riggan, Jennifer. 2013. "'It Seemed Like a Punishment': Teacher Transfers, Hollow Nationalism, and the Intimate State in Eritrea." *American Ethnologist* 40 (4): 749–63.

Robbins, Bruce. 1992. "Comparative Cosmopolitanism." *Social Text* 31 (2): 169–86.

Robinson, Bradford. 2002. "Scat Singing." *New Grove Dictionary of Jazz*, edited by Barry Kernfeld, 3: 515–16. London: Macmillan.

Robinson, Francis. 1977. "Nation Formation: The Brass Thesis and Muslim Separatism." *Journal of Commonwealth and Comparative Politics* 15 (3): 215–34.

Rosenthal, Judy. 1998. *Possession, Ecstasy, and Law in Ewe Voodoo*. Charlottesville: University Press of Virginia.

Royce, Anya Peterson. 1977. *The Anthropology of Dance*. Bloomington: Indiana University Press.

———. 2004. *Anthropology of the Performing Arts: Artistry, Virtuosity, and Interpretation in a Cross-Cultural Perspective*. Walnut Creek, CA: AltaMira Press.

Sapir, Edward. 1934. "Emergence of a Concept of Personality in a Study of Cultures." *Journal of Social Psychology* 5: 410–16.

Sartre, Jean-Paul. 1948. *The Emotions: Outline of a Theory*. Translated by Bernard Frechtman. New York: Philosophical Library.

———. 1969. *Being and Nothingness: An Essay on Phenomenological Ontology*. New York: Routledge.

Schauert, Paul. 2005. "Representing Ghanaian Music: A Critical History." MA thesis, Indiana University.

———. 2006. "Instituting National Culture: Kwame Nkrumah's African Personality and the Arts in Ghana." Unpublished paper.

———. 2007a. "Emotional Ethnomusicology: Phenomenological Possibilities for the Study of Music and Affect." In *Over the Edge: Pushing Boundaries of Folklore and Ethnomusicology*, edited by Rhonda Dass, Anthony Guest-Scott, J. Meryl Krieger, and Adam Zolkover, 147–61. Cambridge: Cambridge Scholars Press.

———. 2007b. "A Performing National Archive: Power and Preservation in the Ghana Dance Ensemble." *Transactions of the Historical Society of Ghana* 10: 171–81.

———. 2014. "Managing Culture: Discipline, Artistry, and Alternative Education in Ghana's State Dance Ensembles." *Africa Today* 60 (3): 2–33.

———. Forthcoming. "Nketia, Nationalism, and the Ghana Dance Ensemble." In *Festschrift for Kwabena Nketia*, edited by Kwasi Ampene. Ann Arbor: University of Michigan Press.

Schechner, Richard. 1977. *Essays on Performance Theory 1970–1976*. New York: Drama Book Specialists.

———. 1981. "Restoration of Behavior." *Studies in Verbal Communication* 7 (3): 2–45.

Scher, Philip W. 2003. *Carnival and the Formation of a Caribbean Transnation*. Gainesville: University Press of Florida.

Scherzinger, Martin. 2007. "Double Voices of Musical Censorship after 9/11." In *Music in the Post-9/11 World*, edited by Jonathan Ritter and J. Martin Daughtry, 91–122. London: Routledge.

Schieffelin, Edward L. 1998. "Problematizing Performance." In *Ritual, Performance, Media*, edited by Felicia Hughes-Freeland, 194–207. New York: Routledge.

Schramm, Katharina. 2000. *Dancing the Nation: Ghanaische Kulturpolitik im Spannungsfeld zwischen Nation und globaler Herausforderung*. Vol. 74 of *Spektrum*. Hamburg: Lit Verlag.

Schutz, Alfred. [1932] 1967. *The Phenomenology of the Social World*. Translated by George Walsh and Fredrick Lehnert. Evanston: Northwestern University Press.

———. [1964] 1971. *Collected Papers II: Studies in Social Theory*. Edited by Arvid Broderson. The Hague: Martinus Nijhoff.

Scott, James. 1990. *Domination and the Arts of Resistance: Hidden Transcripts*. New Haven, CT: Yale University Press.

Senghor, Léopold Sédar. 1964. *On African Socialism*. New York: Praeger.

Sharma, Aradhana, and Akhil Gupta, eds. 2006. *The Anthropology of the State: A Reader*. Oxford: Blackwell.

Shay, Anthony. 2002. *Choreographic Politics: State Folk Dance Companies, Representation, and Power*. Middletown, CT: Wesleyan University Press.

Sheets-Johnstone, Maxine. 1966. *The Phenomenology of Dance*. Madison: University of Wisconsin Press.

Shelemay, Kay Kaufman. 2009. "The Power of Silent Voices: Women in the Syrian Jewish Musical Tradition." In *Music and the Play of Power in the Middle East, North Africa, and Central Asia*, edited by Laudan Nooshin, 269–88. Farnham, UK: Ashgate.

Shillington, Kevin. 1989. *History of Africa*. London: Macmillan.

———. 1992. *Ghana and the Rawlings Factor*. London: Macmillan.

Shipley, Jesse Weaver. 2003. "National Audiences and Consuming Subjects: A Political Genealogy of Performance in Neoliberal Ghana." PhD diss., University of Chicago.

———. 2013. *Living the Hiplife: Celebrity and Entrepreneurship in Ghanaian Popular Music*. Durham, NC: Duke University Press.

Smith, Anthony. 1986. *The Ethnic Origins of Nations*. Malden, MA: Blackwell.

Sörgel, Sabine. 2007. *Dancing Postcolonialism: The National Dance Theatre Company of Jamaica*. Bielefeld, Germany: Transcript.

———. 2011. "Transnationalism and Contemporary African Dance: Faustin Linyekula." In *Emerging Bodies: The Per-*

formance of *Worldmaking in Dance and Choreography,* edited by Gabriele Klein and Sandra Noeth, 83–93. Bielefeld, Germany: Transcript Verlag.

Speer, Kathryn. 2008. "The Globalization of Contemporary Dance in Franco-phone Africa: Embodying Cultural Identity while Discovering the New." Unpublished manuscript.

Spivak, Gayatri Chakravorty. 1988. "Can the Subaltern Speak?" In *Marxism and the Interpretation of Culture,* edited by Cary Nelson and Lawrence Grossberg, 271–316. Urbana-Champaign: University of Illinois Press.

Steinmetz, George, ed. 1999. *State/Culture: State Formation after the Cultural Turn.* Ithaca, NY: Cornell University Press.

Stoeltje, Beverly J., and Richard Bauman. 1988. "The Semiotics of Folkloric Performance." In *The Semiotic Web,* edited by Thomas A. Sebeok and Jean Umiker-Sebeok, 585–99. Berlin: Mouton de Gruyter.

Stokes, Martin. 1994. "Introduction." In *Ethnicity, Identity, and Music: The Musical Construction of Place,* edited by Martin Stokes, 1–34. Oxford: Berg.

Stoller, Paul. 1989. *Fusion of the Worlds: An Ethnography of Possession among the Soghay of Nigeria.* Chicago: University of Chicago Press.

———. 1995. *Embodying Colonial Memories: Spirit Possession, Power, and the Hauka in West Africa.* New York: Routledge.

———. 1997. *Sensuous Scholarship.* Philadelphia: University of Pennsylvania Press.

Stone, Ruth M. 1982. *Let the Inside Be Sweet: The Interpretation of Music Event among the Kpelle of Liberia.* Bloomington: Indiana University Press.

———. 2007. "African Music in a Constellation of Arts." In *The Garland Handbook of African Music,* 2nd ed., edited

by Ruth M. Stone, 7–12. New York: Routledge.

Straker, Jay. 2009. *Youth, Nationalism, and the Guinean Revolution.* Bloomington: Indiana University Press.

Tarr, D. H. 1979. "Indirection and Ambiguity as a Mode of Communication in West Africa: A Descriptive Survey." PhD diss., University of Minnesota.

Taussig, Michael T. 1993. *Mimesis and Alterity: A Particular History of the Senses.* New York: Routledge.

Taylor, Diana. 2003. *The Archive and the Repertoire: Performing Cultural Memory in the Americas.* Durham, NC: Duke University Press.

Taylor, Samuel E. 1994. "Kwame Nkrumah: A Case Study in Intercultural Leadership." PhD diss., United States International University.

Thompson, E. P. 1967. "Time, Work Discipline, and Industrial Capitalism." *Past and Present* 38: 56–97.

Thompson, Nikko S. 2000. "Tradition and Innovation in African Choreography: A Case Study of Kpanlogo." M A thesis, University of Ghana.

Thompson, Robert Farris. 1966. "The Aesthetic of the Cool: West African Dance." *African Forum* 2 (2): 85–102.

Thram, Diane Janell. 1999. "Performance as Ritual – Performance as Art: Therapeutic Efficacy of Dandanda Song and Dance in Zimbabwe." PhD diss., Indiana University.

Titon, Jeff Todd. 1997. "Knowing Fieldwork." In *Shadows in the Field: New Perspectives for Fieldwork in Ethnomusicology,* edited by Gregory F. Barz and Timothy J. Cooley, 87–100. New York: Oxford University Press.

Todorov, Tzvetan. [1976] 2000. "The Origin of Genres." In *Modern Genre Theory,* edited by D. Duff, 193–209. Harlow, UK: Longman.

Tonah, Steve. 2007. *Ethnicity, Conflict, and Consensus in Ghana*. Accra, Ghana: Woeli Publishing Services.

Tonkin, Elizabeth. 1990. "West African Ethnographic Traditions." In *Localizing Strategies: Regional Traditions of Ethnographic Writing*, edited by Richard Fardon, 137–51. Edinburgh: Scottish Academic Press.

Trilling, Lionel. 1972. *Sincerity and Authenticity*. Cambridge, MA: Harvard University Press.

Trimillos, Ricardo D. 2004. "Subject, Object, and the Ethnomusicology Ensemble: The Ethnomusicological 'We' and 'Them.'" In *Performing Ethnomusicology*, edited by Ted Solis, 23–52. Los Angeles: University of California Press.

Tuohy, Sue. 2001. "The Sonic Dimensions of Nationalism in Modern China: Musical Representation and Transformation." *Ethnomusicology* 43 (2): 107–31.

Turino, Thomas. 1999. "Signs of Imagination, Identity, and Experience: A Peircian Semiotic Theory of Music." *Ethnomusicology* 43: 221–55.

———. 2000. *Nationalists, Cosmopolitans and Popular Music in Zimbabwe*. Chicago: University of Chicago Press.

Turner, Edith. 1992. *Experiencing Ritual: A New Interpretation of African Healing*. Philadelphia: University of Pennsylvania Press.

Turner, Victor. 1969. *The Ritual Process: Structure and Anti-structure*. Chicago: Aldine.

———. 1982. *From Ritual to Theatre: The Human Seriousness of Play*. New York: PAJ Publications.

Turner, Victor, and Edward Bruner. 1986. *The Anthropology of Experience*. Urbana: University of Illinois Press.

Tyler, Stephen A. 1986. "Post-modern Ethnography: From Document of the Occult to Occult Document." In *Writing Culture*, edited by James Clifford and George E. Marcus. Berkeley: University of California Press.

Urban, Greg. 2001. *Metaculture: How Culture Moves through the World*. Minneapolis: University of Minnesota Press.

Van de Port, Mattijs. 2004. "Registers of Incontestability: The Quest for Authenticity in Academia and Beyond." *Etnofoor* 17 (1–2): 7–22.

Van Ginkel, Rob. 2004. "The Makah Whale Hunt and Leviathan's Death: Reinventing Tradition and Disputing Authenticity in the Age of Modernity." *Etnofoor* 17 (1–2): 58–89.

Van Maanen, John. 1988. *Tales of the Field: On Writing Ethnography*. Chicago: University of Chicago Press.

Verdery, Katherine. 1991. *National Ideology under Socialism: Politics in Ceaușescu's Romania*. Berkeley: University of California Press.

Vieta, Kodjo T. 1992. "Personality of the Week: Prof. Albert Mawere Opoku." *Weekly Spectator*, April 16.

Vigh, Henrik. 2006. *Navigating Terrains of War: Youth and Soldiering in Guinea-Bissau*. New York: Berghahn Books.

Weber, Max. 1948. *From Max Weber: Essays in Sociology*. Translated and edited by H. H. Gerth and C. Wright-Mills. London: Routledge and Kegan Paul.

———. 1968. *Economy and Society: An Outline of Interpretive Sociology*. Edited by Guenther Roth and Claus Wittich. Translated by E. Fischoff et al. New York: Bedminster.

———. 1994. *Weber: Political Writings*. Edited by Peter Lassman. Translated by Ronald Spiers. Cambridge: Cambridge University Press.

Weiss, Brad. 2009. *Street Dreams and Hip Hop Barbershops: Global Fantasy in Urban Tanzania*. Bloomington: Indiana University Press.

Welsh Asante, Kariamu, ed. 1996. *African Dance: An Artistic, Historical and Philosophical Inquiry.* Trenton, NJ: Africa World Press.

White, Bob W. 2002. "Congolese Rumba and Other Cosmopolitanisms." *Cahiers d'Études Africaines* 42 (168): 663–86.

———. 2008. *Rumba Rules: The Politics of Dance Music in Mobutu's Zaire.* Durham, NC: Duke University Press.

Wilks, Ivor. 1993. *Forests of Gold: Essays on the Akan and the Kingdom of Asante.* Athens: Ohio University Press.

Williams, Brackette F. 1990. "Nationalism, Transnationalism, and the Problem of Cultural Inauthenticity." In *Nationalist Ideologies and the Production of National Cultures,* edited by Richard G. Fox, 112–29. American Ethnological Society Monograph Series 2. Washington, DC: American Anthropological Association.

———. 1991. *Stains on My Name, War in My Veins: Guyana and the Politics of Cultural Struggle.* Durham, NC: Duke University Press.

Williams, Drid. 1997a. "Traditional Danced Spaces: Concepts of *Deixis* and the Staging of Non-Western Dances." In *Tanzkunst, Ritual und Buehne: Begegnungen zwischen Kulturen,* edited by S. Schmiderer and M. Nürnberger, 255–63. Frankfurt am Main: IKO Verlag-fuer inter-kulturelle Kommunikation.

———. 1997b. *Anthropology and Human Movement: A Study of Dances.* Lanham MD: Scarecrow Press.

———. 2000. *Anthropology of Human Movement: Searching for Origins.* Lanham, MD: Scarecrow Press.

———. 2004. *Anthropology and the Dance: Ten Lectures.* Urbana: University of Illinois Press.

Yankah, Kwesi. 1993. "Mohammed Ben Abdallah: Is He Killing the Arts?" *Uhuru* 6: 21–25.

———. 1995. *Speaking for the Chief: Okyeame and the Politics of Akan Royal Oratory.* Bloomington: Indiana University Press.

———. 2001. "Nana Ampadu, the Sung-Tale Metaphor, and Protest Discourse in Contemporary Ghana." In *African Words, African Voices: Critical Practices in Oral History,* edited by Luise White, Stephan Meischer, and David William Cohen, 12–27. Bloomington: Indiana University Press.

Yankson, Paul W. K., and Monique Bertrand. 2012. "Challenges of Urbanization in Ghana." In *The Mobile City of Accra: Urban Families, Housing, and Residential Practices,* edited by Elizabeth Ardayfio-Schandorff, Paul W. K. Yankson, and Monique Bertrand, 25–46. Dakar: Council for the Development of Social Science Research in Africa.

Younge, Paschal Yao. 2011. *Music and Dance Traditions of Ghana: History, Performance, and Teaching.* Jefferson, NC: McFarland.

Index

PAUL SCHAUERT has been studying Ghanaian music and dance for more than fifteen years, working with a number of leading master drummers and dancers. After receiving a BA in music from the University of North Texas, he received an MA and PhD in ethnomusicology from Indiana University with a minor in African Studies. He is a lecturer in ethnomusicology at Oakland University (Michigan) and has been working with Ghana's state dance ensembles since 2004.